A HISTORY OF SLAVERY AND
EMANCIPATION IN IRAN, 1800–1929

A History of Slavery and Emancipation in Iran, 1800–1929

BEHNAZ A. MIRZAI

UNIVERSITY OF TEXAS PRESS ⟨⟩ *Austin*

Requests for permission to reproduce material from this work should be sent to:
Permissions
University of Texas Press
P.O. Box 7819
Austin, TX 78713-7819
http://utpress.utexas.edu/rp-form

♾ The paper used in this book meets the minimum requirements of ANSI/NISO
Z39.48-1992 (R1997) (Permanence of Paper).

LIBRARY OF CONGRESS CATALOGING-IN-PUBLICATION DATA

Names: Mirzai, Behnaz A., author.
Title: A history of slavery and emancipation in Iran, 1800/1929/ Behnaz A. Mirzai.
Description: First edition. | Austin : University of Texas Press, 2017. | Includes
bibliographical references and index.
Identifiers: LCCN 2016024726 | ISBN 9781477311752 (cloth : alk. paper) |
ISBN 9781477311868 (pbk. : alk. paper) | ISBN 9781477311875 (library e-book) |
ISBN 9781477311882 (non-library e-book)
Subjects: LCSH: Slavery—Iran—History. | Slave trade—Iran—History. | Blacks—
Iran—History. | Slaves—Emancipation—Iran—History. | Iran—History.
Classification: LCC HT1286 .M57 2017 | DDC 306.3/620955—dc23
LC record available at https://lccn.loc.gov/2016024726

doi:10.7560/311752

TO MY SONS BEHROUZ AND ROUZBEH
IN MEMORY OF MY FATHER, MAHMOUD

CONTENTS

A NOTE TO THE READER

IN THE HOPES OF explaining the transformations of the slavery system in Iran not only to academic specialists in Iranian history, but also of reaching an audience unfamiliar with the history of Iran and literature on slavery in the Middle East, I have avoided the use of specialized jargon.

My aim is to maintain the spellings of names exactly as they appear in archival sources in the endnotes unless there is a major discrepancy, in which case I employ the correct modern spelling.

TRANSLITERATION

In this book, I have used the transliteration system of the *International Journal of Middle East Studies* for Persian, Arabic, and Turkish words.

TRANSLATIONS

Translations of all foreign sources (Persian, Arabic, Turkish, and French) are mine.

DATES

Dates in this book are written in the Gregorian style. In endnotes, the dates of English sources are Gregorian, Persian documents of SAM and books are cited in *Hijri Shamsi* (modern Iranian or solar calendar), and Persian documents of VUK are *Hijri Qamari* (Islamic or lunar calendar) unless noted Sh. (*Hijri Shamsi*).

UNITS OF MEASURE

WEIGHTS

Man is an Iranian unit of weight equal to 3 kg.
Ray is an Iranian unit of weight equal to 11.87 kg.[1]

CURRENCY

It is impossible to determine the exact value of coins used in Iran. The most common coin in circulation was the toman. Some coins were minted in Iran while others were foreign. The exchange in every province and city differed considerably, and there was a constant fluctuation in the value of coins. The following rates have been determined based on information extracted from historical sources. In the book the value is given in the original currency converting into toman in parenthesis, but it should be noted that the rate of exchange is approximate.

1) The German crown (GC) was one of the most common coins circulating at Musqat, having been imported from Baghdad. In 1825, GC100 = Br 217.[2]

2) Bombay rupees (Br) were a currency imported from India in exchange for goods shipped from Bushehr. In 1842, £1 = Br 10.[3] In 1917, 100 Rupees = 183 *Qran*.[4]

3) The toman (T) was an Iranian gold coin used chiefly in circulation with a fluctuating value. One toman consisted of ten silver *qran*.[5] In the mid-nineteenth century, T1 = $5.[6] In the late nineteenth century, T1 = $1.6.[7]

4) The *mahomedee* (M) was a copper coin. In 1825, $1 = Ma20, or T1 = Ma100.[8]

5) The British pound (£). In 1883, £1 = T2.5.[9]

6) The Spanish dollar ($). In 1840, £1 = $2.5.[10] In 1853, £1 = $4.[11]

7) The pence (Pe). In 1883, T1 = Pe100.[12]

8) *Shamees* (Sh) was a currency used in Basra. In 1847, £1 = Sh13.3.[13]

9) *Piastres* (PI) were silver coins minted in the Ottoman Empire. In 1840, PI 15 = $1.[14]

10) *Manat* was a Russian currency. In 1910, 1 *manat* = 1.5 *qran*.[15]

ACKNOWLEDGMENTS

GIVEN MY ABIDING CERTAINTY of the importance of sharing the subject of this book with the wider academic community, this work has been a labor of perseverance. It is the culmination of many years of research as well as the support of those in archival organizations and research institutions in the Middle East, Africa, and Europe, and from descendants of diasporic enslaved people communities scattered throughout Iran and the Persian Gulf region. There is a considerable demand from scholars, teachers, and students for a book on the subject of slavery and emancipation in Iran. Teaching the course "Slavery in the Middle East" without recourse to a textbook on the subject inspired me to seriously consider reworking my dissertation, "Slavery, the Abolition of the Slave Trade, and the Emancipation of Slaves in Iran, 1828–1928," and preparing it for publication.

Although it began as a doctoral thesis, in 1999 my research was hindered by circumstances beyond my control: these included the relocation of many Iranian archives along with complications and changes associated with document release policies and catalogue systems. Notwithstanding, I was always able to count on the support of staff and other archivists at various institutions. At Brock University, the staff of the James A. Gibson Library deserve special appreciation. In Iran, these included Mahmoud Esmaeilnia, Ramin Seirafi Far, and Beheshte Daneshmand at the archive of the Ministry of Foreign Affairs; Farimah Baqeri, Kobra Moqimi, and Roqayeh Shokri at the Research and Document Information Division of the National Archive and Library; Parvin Sadr Seqat al-Islami, manager of the Gulestan Palace; Javad Hasti and Zahra Asadian at the Photo Collection Center of Gulestan Palace; Mr. Khalili and Mr. Moradi at the Library, Museum and Document Centre of Iran Parliament; Abdulkarim Mashayekhi at the Centre of Iranian Studies — the Bushehr Branch; as well as staff at the Ministry of Environment and the Central Library of the University of Tehran. I would also like to express my gratitude to the founder of the Juma' Al Majid Center for Culture and Heritage in Dubai for sharing his archives and assigning staff to assist me, including Shaikha Al Mutairi as well as the staff at the Zanzibar National Library in Tanzania, who were immensely helpful. In Europe, I am grateful to the staff at National Archives of United Kingdom and British Library in London and the French Ministry of Foreign Affairs in Paris.

At these institutions and elsewhere, I have been able to count on the assistance and suggestions of many scholars at various stages in the preparation of this book and related publications, including two documentary films. In that regard, I would like to express my appreciation to Mohamad Tavakoli-Targhi, Hichem Ben-El-Mechaiekh, Lawrence Potter, Barry Grant, Martin Mhando, and Gwyn Campbell. I specially thank Abdul Sheriff and Olivier Pétré-Grenouilleau for reading chapters of this book and for their helpful suggestions. Edward Alpers, Ehud Toledano, and Indrani Chatterjee deserve special acknowledgment for the critical reading of the entire manuscript and offering detailed comments. During my long journey from graduate school to this book, I learned enormously from intellectual discussions and guidance of my then classmate, Olatunji Ojo, now my colleague at Brock University, to whom I thank for his generosity and thoughtful comments. I particularly want to single out and thank Houchang Chehabi for his continuous support, assistance, and many useful suggestions. Also, I would like to thank Paul Lovejoy for supervising my dissertation that developed into the current book.

While working on this project, I was fortunate enough to share my research with many academics whose comments and insights nurtured my own ideas. Several organizers of academic forums and conferences deserve special thanks: Yann Richard, who invited me to deliver a talk on slavery in Iran at the Sorbonne University in Paris in 2000; Gwyn Campbell, who in 2000 organized the events: *Slave Systems in Asia and the Indian Ocean: Their Structure and Change in the 19th and 20th Century* and *Unfree Labour & Revolt in Asia and the Indian Ocean Region* in 2001 at Université d'Avignon; the *Intercultural relations in multicultural societies* event at the universities of Tehran and Soreh in 2008; the UNESCO Slave Route Project events: *The cultural interactions resulting from the slave trade and slavery in the Arab-Islamic world* in Morocco in 2007, and *Slave Trade and Slavery in the Arab Islamic World: Untold Tragedy and Shared Heritage* in Nigeria in 2012; and Mohamad Tavakoli-Targhi at the University of Toronto who organized the Iranian Studies Seminar Series in 2013.

At the grassroots level, I would also like to thank Mansureh Ettehadieh, the late Abdulhusayn Navai, and the late Ehsan Naragi, who shared their own personal and family memories of slavery in Iran. I am also thankful to the local people of various Iranian villages and cities—in particular, in Baluchistan—who assisted me during my fieldwork in southern Iran. Similarly, Reza Tabanda Gunabadi of the Gunabadi Ni'matullahi Sufi order, was an invaluable source of information about his family.

I would like to single out for thanks and gratitude several other colleagues and friends who have helped along the way: Femi Kolapo, the late Dennis D. Cordell, Mark Spencer, Yacine Daddi Addoun, Chouki El Hamel, and the late Homa Nateq. I am particularly indebted to the Social Sciences and Humanities Research Council of Canada and Brock University in St. Catharines,

Canada, for their financial support. I thank all my colleagues at Brock University in my department and beyond. Students in my "Slavery in the Middle East" seminars at Brock University have also offered thought-provoking questions and inspired me with their interest in the subject. Special thanks are also due to Sarah King Head and Kristin Roth, who provided incisive critiques and editorial assistance for the manuscript. In particular, I would like to thank Jim Burr, the senior editor of the Middle East studies for his help and advice. Also, I wish to thank Michael Izady for preparing the maps.

My final acknowledgment is to my parents. Last and most significant is my heartfelt appreciation that goes to my sons Behrouz and Rouzbeh. I dedicate this book to both of you.

A HISTORY OF SLAVERY AND
EMANCIPATION IN IRAN, 1800–1929

THIS BOOK TRACES the legacy of more than a century of enslaved individuals who journeyed from enslavement to ultimate freedom. The mapping of their path and echoing enslaved people's voices (enslaved Iranians/non-Iranians and enslaved Muslims/non-Muslims), thus, brings together a vast picture and many stories of the societies that sponsored, perpetuated, and banned slavery, extending to Africa in the west and India in the east, to Russia and Central Asia in the north and northeast and the Arab states in the south. The convergence of these stories in Iran[1] transformed the nation and helped forge its unique culture and identity.

This study examines various factors that affected the institution of slavery in Iran in the period from the early nineteenth century to the mid-twentieth century. It explores a period during which the ancient practice of slavery was altered in terms of patterns of enslavement as well as the ethnicity of the enslaved people themselves. These changes emerged in the context of a period of great social, political, and economic change. The study also focuses on the impact of foreign military incursion, frontier insecurity, political instability, and economic crisis insofar as these forces exacerbated traditional slave-trading networks and infrastructures in the enslavement of people. What is most apparent is that the trade in enslaved people was inexorably linked to the authority of the state. Thus, just as slave trading increased during periods of greater decentralization, periods of greater governmental autonomy saw more freedom and peace.

The book's examination of the institution of slavery in Iran reveals that the ethnocultural heterogeneity combined with peculiar features of local social fabric and historical, economic, and political circumstances resulted in a unique expression both before and after abolition in the early twentieth century. Furthermore, it analyses issues of gender within the Iranian society—for both men and women—their differing occupational experiences and challenges.

SOURCES

There is a significant scholarly literature covering the diverse aspects of Iran's history, culture, politics, and traditions. However, no single monograph in Persian, English, or any other language has been written to examine the history of slavery in modern Iran. Although the subject has received some attention in recent years, most international scholarship has tended to focus on slavery in Africa and the Americas. It is within this context that this historical work intends to make an important contribution. The book builds on more than a decade's worth of archival research in Iran, Tanzania, England, and France along with fieldwork studies and interviews throughout Iran. As the title suggests, the book provides an interdisciplinary synthesis in its attempt to understand the complex issues surrounding the history of slavery in modern Iran.

This analysis of slavery in modern Iran considers the full social, political, and economic spectrum. It also serves as a counterpoint to studies of slavery in the Indian Ocean and the Ottoman Empire. Indeed, although these may be considered analogous (especially since Iran's Qajar dynasty [1785–1925] shared a belief system and language with its neighbor to the northwest), it is important to avoid generalizations; that is, it is important to view each country's achievement of political and intellectual reforms underpinning abolition through the lens of its own culture and history. As such, this work intends to complement the work of Ottoman historians such as Ehud Toledano,[2] Hakan Erdem,[3] and Madeline Zilfi.[4]

In reconstructing the past, we must use interpretative approaches that situate events within the social, economic, and even psychological context of that time—and not in accordance with the needs of the present. As the historian of the modern Middle East Roger Owen points out, there exists a lack of specialist studies on many aspects of Middle Eastern economic life as well as a scarcity of statistical and reliable census material.[5] With the exception of some data reported by British officials about the suppression of slave trading, there are few available figures regarding enslaved people of all ethnic groups in nineteenth-century Iranian sources. As such, traditional historiography has tended to focus on the details of those about whose lives we know more: rulers and other sociopolitical elites. This is similar for foreign policy and political developments. It is my intention therefore to give voice not only to ordinary Iranians, but also to a social group that has never been studied: the enslaved. As such, this work attempts to provide a fully comprehensive study of slavery in modern Iran and place it within the context of global slavery.

Although the ideology supporting abolitionism is considered to have worldwide relevance, the focus of this study has been the local conditions in the Indian Ocean and Persian Gulf, the Caspian Sea, and Central Asia. Thus, while foreign diplomatic correspondence has been examined, the principal sources on which I have relied are scattered data from archival materials and other primary and secondary sources written in Persian and various European languages. These include a range of slave narratives, travel accounts, histories and geographical studies, personal memoirs, chronicles, newspapers, letters of freedom, religious injunctions and decrees, and so on. In all, they can be divided into two groups: those addressing the banning of the slave trade and those considering liberation. Political correspondence between the British and Iranian governments largely comprises information on the former, while the other archival sources relate to the latter, providing rich descriptions of the internal changes and the socioreligious circumstances during the period. Indeed, they relay the kind of detail found nowhere else: poignant descriptions about the lives of enslaved individuals.

Terence Walz and Kenneth Cuno explain that until recently slavery was not a major area of study for historians of the modern Middle East for various reasons. One reason was the absence of anything resembling the traumatic American experience of slavery: indeed, that more than one tenth of the US population descends from enslaved Africans helps explain how slavery divided the nation and led to civil war. Postemancipation racial oppression and segregation has further driven scholarly research on the subject. By comparison, Walz and Cuno note that although slavery was integral to Middle Eastern societies, its history and notions of race were constructed differently. Moreover, minority and marginal populations have largely been ignored because of absent or inaccessible historical materials and archives.[6]

Given the exigencies described above, it has not been possible to rely on one single model to write this book. It has thus been necessary to collate and disaggregate the scattered, published and unpublished information that exists on the slave trade and the process of emancipation in Iran from the early nineteenth century from political, commercial, cultural, and social sources to vignettes, anecdotes, and even cinematic documentaries.[7] These together have been used to characterize the emergence of culture and identity in modern Iran and its transformation from a slave-owning society to one embracing full emancipation.

PRIMARY SOURCES

Just as it is problematic to suggest that the Iranian consciousness was uniquely disposed to racial inclusivity, it is noticeable that Persian documents generally do not contain reference to the racial provenance of enslaved people. By contrast, European travelers and officials appear to have gone out of their way to refer to race and racial classifications in Iran in their writings. It is not clear whether these attitudes or inclinations were the result of their own perceived Orientalist notions and ideas—or whether they were, in some way or another, seeking to fill a gap in Iranian documentation. Either way, this contrast does tend to suggest attitudinal differences and approaches between indigenous and colonizing peoples, which in turn appear to have influenced scholarship on the subject over the last decades.

Almost half of this study considers the reign of Nasir al-Din Shah (1848–1896), the Qajar king, given his role in passing several pieces of legislation banning the trade in enslaved Africans. As such, the study relies heavily on sources pertaining to this period. In both Persian and English, these come from courtiers, reformers, intellectuals, court physicians, the royal family, government officials, and travelers. Of these, the most common source was the travelogue, a highly popular genre in nineteenth-century Europe. These offered perhaps the best and most objective insights into the lives of enslaved people in Iran at the time. One of the best examples is that of Jakob Polak (1818–1891), Nasir al-Din Shah's private physician. His two-volume memoir recounted his time in Iran from 1851 to 1860.[8] In addition to providing general information on culture, social mores, and medical attitudes and practices in the country, a short section of his work focused on several enslaved people and eunuchs of various races, noting their purchase prices and social status. Other similar examples are those of the official courtiers, like that of Abdulghaffar Najm al-Daula[9] (1843–1908)—known as Najm al-Daula—a notable Iranian mathematician. When in the 1880s, he was sent as a consultant to oversee the construction of dams and roads in Khuzistan, he paid special attention to the inhabitants' economic and social conditions of the settlements he visited.

It was not uncommon in the nineteenth century to refer to the lives of enslaved people as part of lengthy descriptive passages about geography, people, social life, and economic conditions. Firuz Mirza Farman Farma[10] (1817–1885), the son of 'Abbas Mirza (1798–1833), wrote such an account describing the economy, geography, and the lives of people in Kerman and adjacent Baluchistan when he was appointed governor of the former in an attempt to stabilize political unrests there.[11] His son, Abdulhussain Mirza Farman Farma[12] (1858–1900), who later became the governor of both provinces, carried on the tradition begun by his father and wrote an extensively detailed account of the communities and inhabitants. The *Geography of Baluchistan*[13] was written in 1871 by a member of the Qajar royal family, Ahmad 'Ali Khan Vaziri (d. 1878). Amidst extensive descriptions of the region's geography, he made sporadic—but important—references to the slave trade. Another author of this caliber was Muhammad 'Ali Sadid al-Saltana Kababi[14] (1874–1902), a senior governmental official in Iranian port cities and on islands of the Persian Gulf. His works provide richly detailed information about customs, culture, economy, and communities.

Perhaps the best-known works of this nature are the writings of John

Gordon Lorimer (1870–1914), an official of the British Indian Civil Service. In 1903, he was assigned to compile the *Gazetteer of the Persian Gulf, Oman and Central Arabia*,[15] based on British government archives and fieldwork. Published twelve years later, the work ranges from factual data and historical analysis to descriptive geographical information including significant references to enslaved Africans in the Persian Gulf region.

Even if subjective and personal, memoirs have also been used as an invaluable source of information for this study. During a campaign to suppress the Turcoman raids into Iran in 1853, the high-ranking general Esma'il Khan Mirpanjeh[16] was enslaved. Escaping a decade later, he was ordered by Nasir al-Din Shah to produce a memoir of his years in captivity, providing details of the Turcoman people and their culture. His observations offer a fascinating firsthand account of the sociopolitical insecurity of the northern and eastern frontiers as well as the extent to which Turcomans enslaved Iranians. At the other end of the spectrum, the shah's grandson, Dust 'Ali Khan Mu'ayyir al-Mamalek (1819–1873),[17] takes us into the royal harem, where he himself grew up. The memoir details the personal lives, behavior, and duties of enslaved individuals.

Chronicles have similarly played an important role in this study. One example is *Nasekh al-tawarikh tarikh-i Qajariya* (*Effacement of the chronicles of the history of Qajar*)[18] by the prominent historian Muhammad Taqi Lesan al-Mulk Sepehr (1801–1879). In 1842, Muhammad Shah (1808–1848) ordered him to write a history of the Qajar dynasty, and the result is an insightful overview of the country's social conditions on the cusp of great sociopolitical transition.

The works of political leaders, intellectuals, and reformers of the Qajar period can also help us understand more fully the society in which the suppression of slavery was viewed as necessary. *Tarikh-i bidari-yi Iranian* (*History of the awakening of Iranians*) is a three-volume work written by Nazem al-Islam Kermani (1863–1918), a leader in the Constitutional Revolution movement of the latter part of the nineteenth century.[19] In addition to describing political and social changes at this time, Kermani offered a glimpse into Iranian attitudes as they gradually coalesced in opposition to the institution of slavery. In this regard, he was able to demonstrate the extent to which the protestations of ordinary people against the enslavement of their fellow citizens and relatives were influential in prompting the 'ulama' to urge the shah that justice and the country's security depended on full emancipation.

Autobiographies written by members of the elite provide information about the slave trade and slavery within the context of social change. *Under Five Shahs* by General Hassan Arfa (d. 1984)[20] is one such example. Born in

Tiflis in 1895, Arfa was an army officer for thirty-three years before producing memoirs based on his political and diplomatic career. In describing the effects of Reza Shah's attempts to bring all provincial governors under centralized control, he described the enslavement of many Iranians by Turcomans before military campaigns pushed them back to the Russian hinterland. Sources such as these offer us the opportunity to gain useful historical insights into the lot of the enslaved Iranians.

A final primary source is political and diplomatic correspondence between the British and Iranian government officials that focused on aspects of the suppression of the trade in enslaved Africans. Source materials examined include the extensive holdings of the National Archives and British Library in London, Zanzibar National Library, and various provincial and state archives in Iran.

SECONDARY SOURCES

The study of slavery in Middle Eastern and North African societies has elicited considerable scholarly attention over the last several decades, and especially since the turn of the millennium. There have, however, been important limitations within this scholarly output. First, a disproportionate number have focused on the Ottoman Empire. Second, many of these studies have overemphasized the relationship between Islam and slavery (within various contexts and from different perspectives) and, as such, have failed to appreciate fully the subtle nuances of Islamic law as expressed in varying local, historical, socioeconomic, and cultural circumstances. Finally, a meaningful assessment of the evolving nature of the western imperialist mandate in the development of and implementation of abolitionist legislation in the Indian Ocean and Persian Gulf is absent from the literature.

It is important to note that there have been several important contributions to the study of slavery in Iran by Persian scholars over this same period. Fereydun Adamiyat's 1983 book *Amir Kabir va Iran* (Amir Kabir and Iran), for instance, considers the abolition of the trade in enslaved Africans in the Persian Gulf within the context of diplomatic and political relations of Iran and Britain. Limited to a subsection of one chapter, his theories rely on correspondence and treaties between the two nations as found in British archives.[21] Asserting that while the British Slave Trade Act of 1807 was inspired by the liberal idealism of the French abolition of slavery in 1794, he suggests that the legislation became a political tool wielded by the British government to enforce its economic and political interests in other countries including Iran. Similarly considering abolition within the context of British imperialism by recourse with Adamiyat's work and Persian archives, Esma'il Ra'in argues that the British expanded the sphere of their political, military, and commercial influences in Asian and African countries under the guise of humanitarianism and abolitionism.[22]

Afsaneh Najmabadi adopts a different perspective by writing a tale about the enslavement of Iranian females by the Turcomans.[23] Based on primary and secondary Persian sources dating from the Constitutional period (1905–1911), she illustrates how poverty and insecurity in the Khorasan province forced peasants to sell their daughters into slavery. The author skillfully situates these events within a political context, showing Parliament's reaction to slavery. She also considers issues of gender and the vulnerability of women under slavery.

Mohammed Ennaji makes an important contribution to the study of slavery in relation to Islam by exploring notions of state and slavery in pre-Islamic and Islamic Arabian societies through the lens of terminological analysis.[24] He reviews slavery, power relationships, social construction of servitude and hierarchy in the Arab world through the examination of Arabic texts during the advent of Islam, and the dynasties of Umayyad (661–750) and Abbasid (749–1258). Importantly, he argues that only through an examination of those Arab societies that have not embraced democracy and freedom can one fully appreciate the power mechanisms of the past. He believes "that slavery was a determining aspect of social relationships in the Arab-Muslim world."[25]

In contrast to Ennaji's nuanced assessment of the relationship between slavery and religious protocols, the approach of many Western scholars has been to link slavery specifically to Islam. In detailing the history of abolitionism between Persian Gulf countries and Britain, J. B. Kelly, for instance, views the institution of slavery as forming an inherent part of the Islamic teachings and as such being entrenched in the social structure of the "Islamic world"—from the period of Muslim expansion to the jihadi enslavement of "infidels."[26] Two chapters of his book are devoted to the study of slavery in the Indian Ocean: first, "The Arab Slave Trade, 1800–1842" provides a narrative in which principally Omani Arabs are identified as being responsible for developing sophisticated trafficking trade networks from the East African coast to the Persian Gulf; and second, "The Attack on the Slave Trade, 1842–1873" evaluates the "humanitarian" roots of the British policies that resulted in the conclusion of agreements with local rulers to bring an end to slavery in the region. Kelly, thus, sees abolition as a single, ineluctable process.

Recognizing the complexity of the situation, the scholar of African history Frederick Cooper has insisted on the importance of cultural sensitivity in the analysis of slavery vis-à-vis religion: "The role of Islam among the peoples of the Indian Ocean must be approached as cautiously as that of Christianity in Atlantic societies. Profit could undermine piety, and laws could be ignored."[27] By comparison with plantation slavery in the Americas, he identifies profound differences in the experience of slavery in Middle Eastern and African societies: from the fact that the Indian Ocean commercial system was composed of a heterogeneous assemblage slave holders to the importance of kinship and the master-slave relationships.[28]

William Gervase Clarence-Smith's work claims to study the concept of slavery and abolition through recourse to Islamic jurisprudence and various schools of thought.[29] Although his book commendably collates Western scholarship on the subject of slavery in Muslim societies, he fails to organize the material in a way meaningful of the varied social and political circumstances in which slavery was practiced and abolished in these countries. Moreover, he does not link the proclamations of Muslim jurists and political leaders to the Qur'anic texts on which they were based.

In spite of systemic differences, scholarship on slavery in the Ottoman Empire and elsewhere in the Middle East can provide a useful comparative framework for the study of slavery in Iran. For example, Toledano examines the complex nature of Ottoman slavery and "the variety of modes of servility" including "*kul/harem*" and "agricultural slavery" practiced by Circassian refugees. He contends that abolitionism first emerged when the semi-independent Ottoman province of Tunis established direct links with the British in 1841.[30] Emboldened by this success, the British exerted more pressure on the Ottoman government with a resultant series of negotiations and treaties to suppress the trade in enslaved Africans that were strikingly similar to that later found in Iran. Similarly, the abolitionist discourses on liberty and equality as expressed by writers and intellectuals during the Tanzimat period of the mid-nineteenth century are not dissimilar to those expressed during Iran's Constitutional Revolution in the early twentieth century.[31]

Erdem's examination of the Ottoman Empire's gradual transformation from a slave-holding to a free society considers employment opportunities for enslaved people as well as the government's stance on slavery and abolition. As later seen also in Iran, he demonstrates both that "official British policy was directed against the slave trade rather than the institution itself in foreign countries"[32] and that the government's antislavery policies were closely linked to constitutional reform and the efforts of reformists.[33]

For her part, Zilfi focuses on gender and social representations and vulnerabilities of women and enslaved females in the final days of the Ottoman Empire. She argues that the racialized notions of "blackness" and "Africanness" seen in the Atlantic cannot be fit into a Middle Eastern and North African context. By examining historical complexities and social values, she demonstrates that all women, regardless of skin color, shared common difficulties and entitlements.[34]

The focus of El Hamel's work on slavery, race, and gender in Morocco are the three groups: the Berbers, Arabs, and Africans. He explores the development of racial stereotypes from the sixteenth century to the beginning of the twentieth century, arguing that although Morocco was a Muslim society, the status (enslavement, freedom, and integration) of enslaved people was informed by deeply entrenched cultural practices and Maliki interpretations of Islamic law. The slave-holders' denial of the fundamental prohibition against Muslims enslaving other Muslims helped justify the enslavement of the Muslim Haratin (free blacks or ex-enslaved people). Not only did this support the overt division of society based on skin color, but it also helped articulate a racial ideology of enslavement based on color and culture.[35] Parallels in this dichotomy of Islamic ideals and historical realities can be found in arguments used by Iranian slave holders.

In recent years, two Western scholars examined the twentieth-century slave trade in the Persian Gulf. While both Jerzy Zdanowski[36] and Suzanne Miers[37] have compiled useful information, their works are limited by reliance on British sources. As such, they fail to appreciate regional and local subtleties along with the impact of social, economic, and historical developments. By referencing slave narratives, Zdanowski examines the involvement of the British in suppressing the slave trade in the Red Sea and the Persian Gulf. Miers examines the British-led antislavery movement and considers the growth of various forms of slavery in the twentieth century. She also examines the extent to which philanthropy or national interests ended slavery, noting that international abolitionist treaties have not yet succeeded: "At the outset of the twenty-first century, it is fair to say that while more is known of these evils, and much effort has been spent in describing and analyzing them, the goal of eradication seems as distant as ever."[38]

ORGANIZATION OF THE BOOK

The scope of this study spans the years 1800 to 1929. The starting period represents the importance of the global slave trade in the context of foreign influence in Iran. The terminus marks the legal emancipation of enslaved people in Iran, when the country faced dynamic and complex pressures about the slave trade and after it embarked on a series of agreements and reforms regarding its abolition. Importantly, this book seeks to provide an analysis of the way slavery transformed culture and identity in Iran within each specific geographical division from a historical perspective.

The book is organized into three interrelated sections. First, the initial two chapters provide some historical background by focusing on the commercial and geostrategic importance of Iran. Because the slave trade occurred predominantly on the fringes of the country, the two chapters examine Iran's commercial contacts, diplomatic relations, and military encounters with foreign powers with a particular emphasis on the transformations on Iranian frontiers. The first chapter begins with an overview of the commercial activities including the slave trade on Iran's borders during which slavery was globally legal. Chapter 2 describes how complex patterns of war and peace treaties handling captives and their liberation extended over many frontiers of land and sea for nearly one hundred years. This will demonstrate the extent to which foreign diplomatic relations and territorial encroachment changed the pattern of the slave trade in Iran and impacted its ultimate suppression.

Chapters 3, 4, and 5 consider the ongoing social, political, military, and economic processes that shaped issues of ethnicity as regards slave-trading patterns during the Qajar period. Aspects of the trade are explored with reference to war, poverty, and industry both internally and externally. Of particular note, chapter 5 describes the lives of enslaved people in nineteenth-century Iran in the context of their social and political functions. The objective throughout is not to present a comprehensive historical overview but rather to depict the ethnography of and ongoing transformations within the institution of slavery in Iran.

A third area of consideration addresses issues central to understanding the process of emancipation and the postliberation era in Iran. Chapter 6 examines diplomatic and political correspondence between British and Iranian governments and with various religious leaders about the suppression of the trade in enslaved Africans. It also discusses royal decrees and treatises. The chapter considers strategies and responses by the Iranian state in terms of enforcement in jurisdictions where its authority was weakest. It also explores the foreign and domestic reactions to an escalation of the enslavement of indigenous Iranians after the ban in 1848 on the trade in Africans. The perception that abolition was necessary in the context of internal religious, cultural, secular, and national reform movements is treated in chapter 7. The final chapter narrates stories of enslaved people—black and white, male and female—and echoes their voices and examines various methods (Islamic and governmental) through which enslaved people were liberated before Iran proclaimed emancipation. Special attention is paid to the process of identity formation in the postemancipation era.

PURPOSE

The main objective of this study is to provide an account of the development and ultimate decline of the institution of slavery in modern Iran in order to enhance our appreciation of the link between the slave trade and emancipation within the context of culture and identity transformation. In so doing, it has been essential to interpret the role foreign nations played on the development, perpetuation, and eradication of the slave trade. Once identifying their impact, it has then been necessary to disaggregate what—for the purposes of this study—I have termed the "internal" and "external" factors that influenced these processes.

While the Middle East and North Africa share many inherently similar ethnocultural characteristics, many of their differences emerged as a result of historical processes driven by foreign influences. In the nineteenth century, Iran was governed by rulers whose authority was effectively restricted to their capital cities and environs, thus leaving outlying regions to the suzerainty of autonomous chiefs and princes. It was during this period that European powers were partitioning Africa and extending their spheres of influence into the Arab regions of the Persian Gulf. As such, by the end of World War I, Britain and France had begun to establish an imperialist momentum throughout the region.

But, since British traders were the single most important traffickers of enslaved Africans to the New World before 1807, the process of dismantling the slave trade not only occurred in areas under British imperial domination but was subject to its prodding during the nineteenth century.[39] For this reason, Britain was able to exert geostrategic domination in the Persian Gulf region. This situation has not escaped the attention of many scholars of British, African, and Middle Eastern history. Seymour Drescher, for instance, argues that "the six-decade British campaign for the suppression of the slave trade entailed 'imperialist' methods by mixtures of coercion and intimidation, stretching and breaching international law."[40] Similarly, Robin Law writes,

> the British suppression of the slave trade was in practice carried out, in part, by "imperialist" methods, that is, by coercion and intimidation of other states—albeit normally by techniques of "informal imperialism," rather than actual annexation.[41]

While Middle Eastern and North African religion, mores, and values shaped society and politics even when its constituent nations were at their weakest and most passive, Charles Issawi notes that they were never able to shake off the impact of foreign economic intervention: "The Middle East was the 'periphery' and subjected to impulses emanating from the 'center.'"[42] First drawn by the rich natural resources available in the Persian Gulf and the Indian Ocean during the sixteenth century, European powers initiated commercial contacts with Iran. Local economies were damaged internally by lawlessness, insecurity, and political instability and were continually weakened by the incursions of neighboring countries through open conflict and territorial losses. Nobel Prize–winning economist Amartya Sen has observed that local peace, order, human freedoms, and economic development are all closely interconnected.[43] Without these guarantees, the descent into chaos is inevitable—as it was for Iran, a country that increasingly embraced the institution of slavery at a time when it was declining elsewhere in the world.

Although the oil industry in the early twentieth century relied to some extent on the persistence of the slave trade in the Middle East (especially in the Arab states of the Persian Gulf),[44] it also came to provide the kind of wealth that allowed Iran to break free of these ties. Exportation of oil that started just before World War I began to yield large revenues to the governments in the late 1930s.[45] To this day, the world's dependency on Middle Eastern oil and natural gas, as reflected in the geostrategic importance of the Persian Gulf, began with the signing of the first oil concession between Muzaffar al-Din Shah (1853–1907) and the British businessman William Knox D'Arcy in 1901.[46]

We cannot understand slavery in Iran unless we are sensitive to the nuances of the country's complex social character in terms of its transformation of traditional, social, political, and economic institutions as per communal structures, reform movements, foreign influences, and employment patterns over this period. Indeed, notions of family, community, government, religion, and culture all developed within these contexts. It would be perhaps more accurate to avoid conceptualizing slave systems in terms of "Islamic," "African," "Indian Ocean," and "Atlantic Ocean" and instead discuss the particular roles enslaved people played in the society and the place slavery played in the economy. As Cooper aptly notes, the study of a slave system "involves analyzing the ways in which the various influences on slavery—economic, institutional, social, political, and ideological—reinforced, contradicted, or transformed one another."[47] Toledano also asserts that a differentiated approach to the complex realities of slavery is required: "Here is a *continuum* of various degrees of bondage rather than a *dichotomy* between slave and free."[48] As elsewhere, so too in Iran: slavery found expression in the restricted spheres of domestic and agricultural servitude, but also more casually in the bureaucratic apparatus of government. As such, this analysis of the institution of slavery and the emancipation process has closely referenced the complex economic needs, values, norms, religious beliefs, and social settings that have shaped historical processes at all levels of society.

HISTORICAL CONTEXT

Without a doubt, foreign influences impacted the growth, development, and suppression of a market-driven slave trade in Iran. Because it stands in a unique geographic position—bridging the rest of the Middle East to the south and west, the Asian subcontinent to the east, Central Asia, the Caucasus Mountains, and the waters of the Caspian Sea to the north, and the Persian Gulf, the Gulf of Oman, and the Indian Ocean[49] to the south—Iran has always been a multiethnic and heterogeneous country, with inhabitants having come voluntarily (and involuntarily) from as far away as China. For centuries, foreign invasions have remapped the country's borders and have caused therein the relocation, captivity, and enslavement of people of various ethnic groups. Comparing the economic development of Japan and the Middle East, the historian Issawi has pointed to Japan's geographical isolation as being one of the most important reasons for "the aggressive imperialism of the nineteenth-century—British, French, and Russian—could reach Japan only at the end of a very long line of communications, where their impact was greatly attenuated."[50] He argues that countries situated at important crossroads were especially vulnerable to foreign intervention, thus affecting economic freedom and political independence.

Issawi's theory bears scrutiny. Indeed, in the seventh century CE, Iran was occupied by invading Arabs, who replaced the official Zoroastrian religion with Islam and relegated the indigenous Persians to second-class citizens or clients (*mawali*) especially during the Umayyad Caliphate. A central feature of the expanding Islamic Arab Empire of the Abbasids was the policy of enslavement. While they were often the spoils of war from as near as Africa and as far away as Spain, enslaved people were also used as forms of payment for taxation, used in pawnship (in lieu of debts), purchased, and given as gifts. Many were also born into slavery. In addition to their labor in agriculture, industry, and domestic contexts, there emerged an institution of military slavery as seen, for instance, with the Turks from Central Asia who were enslaved as imperial soldiers from the eighth century.[51] The Abbasid Empire came to a catastrophic end in the thirteenth century at the hands of invading Mongols.

Three centuries later, the Safavids took power (1501–1722) and helped forge modern Iranian cultural identity through the declaration of Shi'i Islam as the official religion. To counterbalance military threats and internal conflict, this dynasty recruited enslaved people from the Caucasus region and formed a new army to respond to foreign incursions and internal threats.[52] Until the early twentieth century, slavery remained a social, political, economic, and military phenomenon. Although enslaved people were involved in a range of economic activities in Iran, the workforce relied heavily on rural or peasant labor.[53]

SLAVERY IN THE MODERN ERA

The trade in indigenous Iranians did, however, experience growth after the *firmān* in 1848 brought an end to the importation of enslaved Africans into Iran from the Persian Gulf. The weakening centralized authority in Iran was also responsible for this growth. This in turn allowed some provincial governors and chiefs to exploit the trade in indigenous populations on the peripheral provinces and frontiers of Iran in order to enhance their economic advantages. But other factors were also responsible for exacerbating the situation and encouraging the perpetuation of slavery: that is, political instability, social disruption and ethnic displacement, economic fragmentation, and military encroachment combined with disease, natural disaster, and famine from the mid-nineteenth century to the first decade of the twentieth century.

There is no denying that internal mismanagements, foreign territorial occupations and diplomatic pressures affected the traditional social, political, and economic order. One of the impacts was the rendering of otherwise free peasants equivalent to indentured feudal servants. Not only did the Qajar rulers replace indigenous modes of local production with a dependency on European commercial goods, but they also severely undermined export networks, repossessed lands, and gave concessions to foreign powers. Internal political rivalries and exploitative acts of local rulers led to the imposition of self-determined judicial and taxation laws on local people. It was in this atmosphere of deteriorating economic, political, and social realities that the internal slave trade began its ascendancy in Iran.

It is not surprising, therefore, to find that the slave trade became prevalent in regions most directly under the influence of the governors or occupiers where the Iranian government had least authority. From the mid-eighteenth century, for instance, much of the southern part of Iran was under the influence of the British, the Qawasem and Omani Arabs—the former through political and commercial bureaucratic infrastructures and the latter through land lease and capture practices. At the same time, Russian incursions into the Caucasus region and Turcoman invasions from the northeast resulted in the occupation of large tracts of Iranian territory. The ramification of these encroachments was the acceleration of regional insecurity and the expansion of the slave trade.

Territorial occupations—especially by foreigners—had important impacts on indigenous populations both in terms of social structures and popular reactions. For example, when the British established their political residency and commercial enterprises in Baluchistan, their policies produced a more hierarchical society. Thus, there evolved more rigid social groups called the *ghulām* (slave class), the *hakim* (the ruler), Baluch, and the *hidmatkar* (the dependent) in order to exert greater control over the indigenous peoples.[54] Although the semifeudal populations relied on social differentiation, the new dividing lines became more obvious and social mobility more difficult to achieve. Moreover, they financed sardars to facilitate their bureaucratic management of the area; but in doing so, they further entrenched social divisions, created economic stagnation, and led to the exploitation of the seminomadic and peasant masses. As the Indian scholar Aijaz Ahmad has noted: "The serfs, the slaves, the rural wage-workers, the seminomadic cattle-breeders thus began to face a double oppression—practiced directly by the Sardars but with the assistance of the new law-and-order apparatus paid for by the British."[55]

The British policies of suppressing the transportation of and trade in enslaved Africans in the Indian Ocean and Persian Gulf regions, which began in the early nineteenth century, also had a great impact on indigenous populations. These impacted long-established networks for trafficking not just Africans but also Iranians and Indians that the Qawasem and the Omani traders had established from East Africa to the southern coast of Iran to southern India.[56] In response to market forces, they sought to continue the steady importation of enslaved people throughout the region in spite of increasingly restrictive abolitionism over the course of the century by mobilizing the trade in various ethnic groups in Iran—most notably, the Baluchis. Border insecurity and local rulers' conflicts and rivalries within Iran had also an impact on the expansion of internal regional networks responsible for the kidnapping and exchange of enslaved people.

NATIONALISM AND MODERNIZATION

The idea of the Iranian nation and land (*Iranzamin*) was not a nineteenth-century innovation. Indeed, classical and ancient Persian sources reveal that the notion of a political and cultural entity with a modern statelike territory and boundaries existed from pre-Islamic times.[57] Modern nationalism, however, emerged in response to several forces.[58] Responding to perceived imperialist ambitions, nineteenth-century activists sought to preserve national honor as well as to articulate culturally innovative political arguments that focused on notions of Iranian identity.[59] Crucial to these activists were those that reacted to the problem of indigenous enslavement and the institution of slavery itself. The nationalist discourse found expression in various ways: it synthesized either pre-Islamic and Iranian identities or Islamic and Iranian identities, or opted for a modern Iranian national identity. Islamic modernists such as Sayyid Jamal al-Din Asadabadi (known as al-Afghani; 1838–1897)[60] sought to interpret Islam to make it compatible with the modern world. Intellectuals such as Mirza Fath ʿAli Akhund Zadeh (1812–1878) and mass protest movements such as the Tobacco Protest (1891–1892) and the Constitutional Revolution (1905–1911) all stressed modernization within the context of Iranian integrity and autonomy against the influence of foreign powers and culture. Echoed throughout was the call for equality and the banning of slavery.

The Pahlavi monarchy (1925–1979), which replaced the Qajar dynasty, developed under the influence of European models of modernity. The aim of its leader Reza Shah (r. 1925–1941) was to reform traditional customs and institutions with reference to Iranian nationalist ideals according to Western European models. Thus, modernization was driven by a nationalist idiom that blended a pre-Islamic Iranian identity within the context of Westernization.[61] Thus, not only was the institution of slavery abolished in 1929, but the consolidation of centralized government authority realized the goals of this legislation—by sealing national frontiers and eliminating the traditional slave-trade infrastructure.

The postemancipation era was characterized by other social, political, and economic changes. Being the first country in the Middle East to exploit its oil reserves in 1903,[62] Iran was able to shift relatively seamlessly from an agricultural to a semi-industrial economy.[63] The country's transformation to a wage-labor economy facilitated the disabling of traditional linkages between landlord and peasant, master and enslaved person. The profound impact the oil industry has had on Iran's social structure and national economy can be seen throughout society, but especially in the participation of freed Africans as recorded by the scholar Khusraw Khusravi of the community on Kharg Island in 1962.[64]

VILLAGE AND ENSLAVED PEOPLES' LIVES

The diversity of cultural identity, ethnic composition, and population distribution seen today in Iranian villages and cities, both coastal and inland, has been influenced by a myriad of political, social, and economic conditions. Nearly 85 percent of Iran's population was rural in the nineteenth century, being comprised of agricultural laborers, peasants, enslaved people, and gypsies. Village communities engaged principally in land cultivation and animal husbandry, while nomadic people tended to forage off the land.[65] Even though many of these communities were largely self-sufficient and not dependent on enslaved labor (thus distinguishing them from the large-scale slave-driven plantations that existed in Africa or the Americas), most of the rural population was economically dependent on landowners and masters for shelter and food.[66]

Iranian society was arranged along hierarchical lines with the king (*hakim*) at the pinnacle and the masses, literally known as "servants" (*ghulāmān* and *kanīzān*), at the bottom. This unequal and essentially exploitative feudal categorization meant that most Iranians had no rights over their lives and property. Similarly, the social system within villages was divided between the master, landlord or landholder (*arbāb*), and the subject, landless cultivator, peasant, or enslaved (*raʿyat*). Sharecropping was the most common tenancy system, in which disadvantaged peasants often received no more than one-fifth of their labors. Landowners were not the only exploiters; indeed, the government rented state lands and sold tax-collecting rights to various elites and the Arab *shaykhs* of the Persian and Oman Gulfs. Predominantly, local governors appointed a feudal landlord (*khan*)—often with noble ties—to be a superintendent and oversee the estates and collect taxes completely at their leisure and usually with the use of physical force. Under the *khan* was a village headman (*kadkhudā*) who administered village activities. Because the agricultural subjects had little or no control over their property or lives, their lot was harsh and cruel.

Kinship networks lay at the root of communal and collective identities, whether through family, clan, and community or the village itself. Each network was hierarchically structured and governed by a specific leader (*shaykh*) who administered customary law. Communal and household lives were also strongly patriarchal and based on seniority.[67] As per religious mores, men and women were subject to special rules that separated them in private and public spaces. This public-private dichotomy that dictated occupational specialization in labor, however, was more prevalent in urban settings, as the contingencies of rural life meant that women and men (including enslaved people) often had to work side by side in the fields. Economic and occupational organization could also serve as the basis for ethnic identity and unity. Thus, some tasks and activities fell under the purview of a particular ethnic or religious group—for example, the African specialization and involvement in music, dancing, and entertainment. Similar situations also existed in Egypt where the enslaved Sudanese regiments of the Egyptian army known for their musical performances formed musical bands.[68] An explanation may be that an occupation such as music and dance was considered unsuitable for Muslims and thus not only became associated with foreign communities but necessarily also became a hereditary ethnic occupation.

SOUTHERN COASTAL CITIES AND
THE LIFE OF ENSLAVED PEOPLE

Coastal cities in Iran such as Bandar ʿAbbas and Bushehr differed from those in the interior: not only were they situated along important economic maritime trade routes, but also they usually showcased a wider range of ethnic and cultural diversity. People of African descent largely concentrated in these areas and engaged in a range of occupations from the most menial to skilled. As a rule, enslaved male Africans were employed in labor-intensive outdoor activities, while the women worked in the marketing of produce and domestic activities. Labor conditions in these areas tended to be harsher and more exploitative.

The work and lifestyle of enslaved people living in cities contrasted strikingly with the work and lifestyle of those living in rural or coastal areas. Industrial, commercial, and administrative roles constituted the main activities in towns and cities. Urban enslaved people tended to be put to work in households (as domestic servants) and were subject to the rules of the harem. (As such, gender-based occupations were based on notions of private and public space.) But unlike their cohorts in the country, the lot for urban harem enslaved people was better overall—indeed they could realize opportunities for upward mobility by becoming liberated members of society. Notwithstanding, it was easier for liberated enslaved males to join the ranks of salaried laborers than for liberated enslaved females; indeed, various social and economic pressures made it all but impossible for them to maintain their own households or to live alone—accordingly, they tended to remain within more domesticated settings.

As with other Middle Eastern cities, those in Iran have traditionally been organized into quarters. These neighborhoods were occupied by people who shared occupations, ethnicity, or religion. Kinship, blood relations, or religious affiliations also tended to define the collective identity of these communities. For instance, nineteenth-century literature often refers to "black" or African quarters. This was the case for other religious and ethnic groups in Iran, such as various Jewish and Arab precincts[69] or the places such as the Turks' Mosque in Tehran. Importantly, these quarters were not ghettos, as the inhabitants were not segregated but rather willingly gathered in such locations to meet and enjoy the company of others with common bonds and identities.

Whether they hailed from urban, coastal, or rural settings, the economic impact of the burgeoning oil industry and the rapid urbanization it brought in the twentieth century had a profound impact on all liberated enslaved populations.

MASTER-SLAVE RELATIONSHIPS

The fundamental characteristic of slavery was its endorsement of the ownership of individual human beings by those in a superior socioeconomic position. In Iran, social status and prestige were equated with conspicuous consumption—owning enslaved people being one of the most obvious symbols of that wealth. Most enslaved people living in an urban household lived in or near the master's residence. Labor conditions for enslaved people were affected by differing social and cultural environments, but as a rule enslaved people could expect to be subject to the vagaries of their master's expectations. However, it is evident that, in rural regions, large peasant and enslaved groups created their communities, given their distant relationships with their masters.[70] As such, they tended to form distinct ethnic and social entities. By contrast, urban enslaved people had much closer relationships with their masters; as a result, they formed primary ties and found a degree of economic security and social protection in this environment. To some extent the social process of inclusion of enslaved people within the household reflected the master's need to control and dominate. In this case, enslaved people who lived far from their master enjoyed more freedom than their counterparts in urban areas. While enslaved persons' owners' control and their cultural hegemony are undeniable, enslaved people also possessed a degree of mobility.

SLAVERY, RACE, AND ISLAM

Considerable attention has been paid to a perception that there was a penchant for slavery in Islam, as scholars like Clarence-Smith have suggested. The notion that "Islamic slavery" is a unique category is something this study seeks to disprove through recourse to the evidence.

Iran has long been a pluralistic society and a heterogeneous nation: thus while the majority of Iranians follow the Athna 'Ashri school of Shi'a Islam,[71] there are many other branches of Islam and non-Islamic religions represented in Iran, including Christianity, Judaism, and Zoroastrianism. It is worth noting that Iran was a Sunni nation until the sixteenth century when the ruling Safavids converted to Shi'i Islam in order to distinguish themselves from the Turks against whom they were at war. Due to the country's geographical location and political boundaries, those populations living in frontier provinces tended to adopt the faith and culture of their neighbors—such as the Sunni Baluchis in the southeast, Aimaq and Persians in the northeast, Turcomans and Uzbeks in the north and northeast, and Persians and Arabs in the south along the coast. The enslaved people, thus, adopted the prevailing schools of thought practiced in their respective regions. For example, while the Sunni Hanafi school is predominant in Baluchistan, many descendants of enslaved Africans are followers of the Zikri sect of the Hanfi school prevalent in the Makran region. And yet, even though this extensive ethnocultural diversity shaped many aspects of regional, social, and economic interactions among the varying populations, both branches of Islam adopted laws regarding slavery within the context of specific local ethnocultural mores and customs. As such, the nature and practice of slavery in Qajar Iran of the nineteenth century needs to be studied through the lens of local and regional contexts.

Although Islam provided protocols for the legitimation of slavery, there was as much divergence in opinion among religious scholars as there was violation of the religion's basic tenets.[72] Ignorance of the Qur'an meant that many texts were open to interpretation by jurists and were defined within specific contexts and practices. As such, some religious scholars, ruling elites, and slave owners enforced a legal system that justified and maintained the perpetuation of slavery. It is a fact that while religion could be used to justify the slave trade, the reality is that it was motivated, formulated, and perpetuated by factors including customary attitudes and economic need. Indeed, people practiced slavery within their own cultural, economic, political, and social milieux. In the same way, the process of the integration, assimilation, or marginalization of freed enslaved people was determined by local socioeconomic factors. As such, given the complexities inherent in religion and society, an interpretation of slavery via the general term "Islamic slavery" can be highly misleading and distort the realities of slavery in the Middle East. This is apparent when Clarence-Smith asserts: "A preliminary and tentative stab at quantification further shows that slavery in Islam was on a grand scale. Conjectures as to how abolition came about are mixed, and the central suggestion made here is that Islam played a neglected role in the process."[73] In a review of this work, Toledano states that this interpretation of slavery ignores the impact of local practices and cultures in societies as distant and different as Morocco and Indonesia.[74] Chouki El Hamel maintains a similar position: "Islam and Islamic law was surely a powerful social dynamic, but other cultural and ethnic factors figure prominently into how Islam was engendered in particular historical social settings."[75] In noting that racial distinctions and tribal prejudices were no more rooted in Islam than a charac-

teristic therein that encouraged the sponsorship of slavery, he suggests that
"the othering of blacks goes back to the biblical Ham, son of Noah, and the
Hamitic curse and discourse."[76] Moreover, nowhere in the Middle East was
legalized or customary racial segregation found as it was in the Americas,
states Ronald Segal; instead, Islam "confronted the emergence of racism as
a form of institutionalized discrimination, because the Koran expressly condemned racism along with tribalism and nationalism."[77] The study of slavery
in Middle Eastern societies therefore requires the consideration of specifics,
variations, and differences rather than an abstract view of "Islamic" slavery. Its
practice within an Islamic context, therefore, requires an interpretation of the
various relationships: between the owners of enslaved persons and enslaved
persons; their occupations, rights, and personal circumstances; and the economic and social conditions of the communities into which enslaved persons
were brought.[78]

Bernard Lewis is one Western scholar who reinforces historical misinter-
pretation of the relationship between Islam and racial prejudice. Notably, his
assumptions have been challenged by scholars such as Frederick Cooper, who
suggests that Lewis "confuses religion with the societies in which that religion is practiced." He observes that the British-American historian cannot
"go beyond a *tu quo que* argument: Muslims, like everyone else, could be
prejudiced. A religion, however, cannot have attitudes; people living in societies develop them."[79] Moreover, his inability "to explain the significance of
race and colour to social structure"[80] has perpetuated a stereotype that Islam
could justify slavery because it does not recognize the fundamental equality of
all human beings. For this reason, Cooper suggests that the focus should be on
the historical processes that caused people within a single society to use and
reshape Islam to rationalize domination. Further, in order to study slavery
where Islam is important or dominant, one not only should refute the notion
of a unified Islamic society but also look beyond the idea of Islamic societies.
Eve Troutt Powell also challenges Lewis's conceptualizations of race in the
Islamic world (which defined the geographic separation of slavery in the West
and the East), when he was suggesting that "slavery in the 'one' is the obverse
of slavery in the 'other', so what African slavery really meant is described only
in the negative."[81] Noting that his "black" and "white" distinction in Middle
Eastern societies was influenced by the race debates in Afro-American studies,
she adds that "although cited by many scholars, [Lewis's] *Race and Slavery in
the Middle East* remains part of the tradition created by the British 'men on
the spot,' whose descriptions of African slavery in the Muslim world left much
to the imagination of their readers."[82] And, of course, it has been shown that

race and color were by no means the only factors influencing slave trading and owning patterns, for the simple fact that there were nonblack enslaved people in Iran too.

Again, it must be reiterated that the relationship between Islam and the institution of slavery is complicated. Indeed, Qur'anic teachings and concepts acknowledged the reality of slavery and, in offering advice for its regulation, guidelines were provided for the treatment of enslaved people, including where they could be sourced, aspects of their personal lives (including marriage), and so forth. Not surprisingly, theory and practice were often discordant.[83] One important example regarded the liberation of enslaved people, which was considered a sign of piety. Although "the Shi'i legal school recommended that the Muslim slave should be set free after seven years of service,"[84] documents demonstrated this was rarely put into practice.[85] In the same way, it is possible to compare slavery with polygamy and concubinage. Although legal and practiced by some, they were frowned upon by the great majority of Iranians.

As a rule, the Shi'i 'ulama' were divided on the issue of slavery in Iran. Even acknowledging the absence of any explicit provision in Islamic law banning slavery, some of them tended to voice disquiet about the practice of buying and selling human beings throughout the mid-nineteenth-century abolitionist debate. But rather than issuing edicts or proclamations to this effect, they tended to focus on the social and religious ramifications of full emancipation, particularly as it pertained to the liberation of enslaved females. What emerged at this time was a distinct antireformist movement that tended to view abolition as both a conspiracy of colonialists and a betrayal of Muslim values: it was perceived as cultural imperialism.

Abolitionism inspired a debate that remains current to this day: that of the view among the more patriarchal societies in the Middle East about the protection and support of women by men. Not only is it viewed as a symbol of sexual morality, but also it is seen as an affirmation of Islamic tenets and cultural traditions. The whole debate about controlling female sexuality within the context of a value system that preserves group identity is closely related to the complex concept of honor—or a man's pride and his own sense of value. As such, abolition and liberation were to have significant implications on the position of women in Iranian society. It is not surprising that from the moment the abolitionist discourse began in 1847 until the *firmān* banning the importation of enslaved Africans was passed a year later, Muhammad Shah focused on the social destabilization and moral disorder the process would engender. And it was to remain the topic of intense discussion and the subject of many royal, governmental, and religious decrees up until the institution of slavery was finally abolished in 1929. Notably, it was the liberation of enslaved female Africans that attracted the most attention, since as a result of being displaced and uprooted from their homelands, they required special social and economic protection. By contrast, indigenous enslaved females elicited less concern because it was understood that they could return to their families for protection.

SLAVERY AND ETHNICITY

Ethnic identity in parts of the Middle East tends not to be associated with phenotypic race or biological variations, as the region is home to so many different and overlapping populations. As such, identity has generally been expressed in terms of cultural expression, tradition, and so forth, rather than according to specific racial characteristics. In Iran enslaved people came from all racial and ethnic groups: "white" enslaved Circassians and Georgians were often war booty, and Iranians were enslaved in lieu of paying tax and tribute gifts or served as wageless laborers, while "black" Africans usually came into Iranian ports as commodities and were distributed through well-organized trade networks. Attempts to establish interpretative models to determine the features governing the choices of the enslavement of one group of people over another have led scholars, like Zilfi, to emphasize the role of religious affiliation and geographic origin: "Islamic regimes like the Ottoman Empire," she observes, "defined liability to enslavement not in terms of race, color, or ethnicity but in accordance with the conjoined attributes of geography and religion." [86] Although this is evident in Iran as well, the Iranian paradigm also suggested an emphasis on society, culture, and class (translating into power or wealth). It is important to realize therefore that the exigencies characterizing the slave trade in the Atlantic were quite different than those in Iran: indeed, where the divide between slave holder and enslaved for the former was always racial, for the latter it was tended to be more subtle and to rely on a range of cultural, social, and geographical considerations. As such, it is important not to overemphasize the fact that enslaved people from certain racial backgrounds tended to be found in certain positions. Instead, one must look at the socioeconomic factors that found them in these roles. For instance, it was common for African eunuchs, who were highly prized because of their functions, to be chosen for the harems.

Many indigenous Iranians were also taken into slavery as the result of political instability, especially along the Iranian frontiers. Sectarian rivalry, military weakness, and famine were responsible for the enslavement of Iranians by Turcomans and their sale at the bazaars of Khiva, Ashgabat, and Bukhara. Economic depression also led to the voluntary enslavement of Iranians in

Khorasan. In the south and southeast, many Iranians were kidnapped and sold as enslaved people in Arab countries. In this region, Baluchis were particularly vulnerable. A combination of factors, including systemic socioeconomic poverty and political instability, almost guaranteed a worsening of the situation after 1848. Indeed, while there was a decline in the sale of other ethnic groups hereafter, the trade in Iranians actually accelerated.

Historical processes affect the development of identity and ethnic expression for individuals and groups in many ways—just as it did for enslaved people. Their ethnic identity was often reinvented in the host society according to new norms but also relied on the experiences of shared kinship history, culture, and language. What is notable about the status of former enslaved Iranians in the postemancipation period after 1929 is that many lost their distinct ethnocultural identities through a process of integration and collective social liberation. First, demographic patterns were forever altered with the wide-scale migration of populations from rural areas to the cities. In turn, the emergence of semi-industrial economy transformed the social and cultural aspects of rural life. Second, liberation meant that not only did they become guaranteed wage laborers, but many former enslaved people partnered with free peasants in rural areas and established communities.

TERMINOLOGY

An examination of the use of various expressions and terms in the Persian literature provides a fascinating picture of societal attitudes about enslaved people. The translation of the word "enslaved" in Persian is *bardeh*, and it referred to enslaved people from all geographic regions, although *asīr* ("war captive"; plural *usarā* or *asīrān*) and *zarkharīd* ("purchased with gold") were also used. The most commonly used words were the gendered terms *ghulām*[87] (plural *ghulāmān, ghulāmhā*) for a man and *kanīz*[88] (plural *kanīzān, kanīzhā*) for a woman—both meaning "servant" as distinct from "enslaved" and referred to domestic servitude. Notably, references in nineteenth-century Persian literature to the *ghulāmān* and *kanīzān* of the king were understood to include free Iranians, too. According to ʿAbdullah Mustaufi, a Qajar courtier, black *kanīzān* and *ghulāmān* were specifically identified as *ḥājī* (a male) and *ḥajīa* (a female)[89] because many came to Iran from Mecca.[90] A eunuch was called a *khauja* (plural *khaujagān*)—or an *āghā*, as a title before their names— while a liberated enslaved person was designated an *āzād*. *Sīyāh* ("black") was the most commonly used term by which enslaved Africans were designated in nineteenth-century manuscripts. Within the context of kinship, *kākā* ("brother" or "home-grown enslaved man") was respectful and familiar ways of referring to black enslaved people; in fact, *dādā* and *dada* ("sister" or "home-grown enslaved woman") were common terms used to describe an enslaved female, who served the master since childhood and looked after children. *Sayfeh* and *jāriyah* ("concubine") were terms used to designate the relationship of an enslaved female to her master. Terms like Āfrīqā'ī, Sudanī, Ḥabashī, Zangī, Nubī, and Sīdī all referenced geographical origin of enslaved Africans.[91] The fluidity of these terms not only indicates that the identity of enslaved people could be transformed, but that they were not confined to a static position within the system and could, in fact, elevate their statuses.

In conclusion, the study of slavery in nineteenth-century Iran presents a model both for understanding internal political, economic, and social structures and international relations in the Middle East, as well as for enhancing our knowledge of culture and identity transformation in modern Iran. It is therefore of interest to those who desire to learn not only about the history of Iran but also to understand the root cause of societal transformations in this region. Centuries of old institutions and traditional customs were altered as a consequence of global interactions and internal changes. Policy makers and intellectuals influenced by new Western ideologies implemented reforms and centralized the government to secure the borders and protect the motherland. Within this context, we may say that the question of national identity became symbolic to both free and enslaved Iranians in the struggle for nationhood, a struggle that found expression in the universal concepts of freedom, equality, and brotherhood.

CHAPTER 1

COMMERCE AND SLAVERY ON IRAN'S FRONTIERS, 1600–1800: AN OVERVIEW

IRAN BECAME THE FOCUS of European powers from the late fifteenth century for its strategic location, bridging east and west, when various countries—both near and far—pursued ambitious policies of commercial and territorial expansion in the Persian Gulf region. Among the first were the European countries—led by Portugal before Holland and then England—that exploited their technological and naval supremacy and established bases not only for commercial benefit but also to secure their positions and counterbalance the ambitions of their rivals. Although attempts to access sea trade routes to India from Africa had begun in the late fifteenth century, it was, however, not until the early seventeenth century that Europe's great trio of maritime nations began competing in earnest to utilize Iran's geostrategic position. At that time, the country also began to face challenges from its northern neighbor, Russia, and closer to home from various countries and ethnic groups, such as the Omani Arabs, who sought to realize commercial and territorial expansion for wealth and power.

This chapter examines the global slave trade in the context of foreign commercial activities, political penetration, and military expeditions in Iran, with an eye to understanding the forces that underpinned the emergence of an attitude seeking its suppression at the beginning of the nineteenth century. This chapter provides a brief overview of the circumstances that led to the captivity of peoples across multiple frontiers, on the one hand, and responses to it, on the other.

SOUTHERN COASTS

THE PORTUGUESE

The sixteenth-century arrival of the Portuguese in the Persian Gulf began with the capture of Hormuz Island in 1507. Its strategic significance was great[1] because, as Rudolph Matthee explains, it was an

> entrepôt in the trade between south and southwest Asia. The north–south [Caspian Sea–Persian Gulf] trade route expanded accordingly, with silk, raw as well as manufactured, being among the goods transported to Hurmuz.[2]

From here goods were exported to India. Indeed, according to João Teles e Cunha, the Portuguese chose Hormuz because it was "at the intersection of three major trade routes: to India, to Basra, and to the Iranian market."[3] A foothold in the Strait of Hormuz meant that the Portuguese could realize their goal of expanding their trade and influence from the African coast and the Indian Ocean to various ports and islands in the Persian Gulf. On the island, they built a fortress and, in doing so, transformed it into their administrative headquarters, a maritime post, and a stronghold from which they could control trading activities in the Persian Gulf and the Gulf of Oman.[4] As the dominant maritime power in the region, they were able to control existing trading networks through fortified stations at Masqat and Bahrain. They restricted local commercial activities by extracting tribute payments and issuing passes to native trading vessels. In the same way, the Portuguese set their eyes on the largest island in the Persian Gulf: Qeshm, which they captured in 1514. They controlled both islands for nearly a century, until their expulsion in 1622.[5]

In addition to maritime activities, the Portuguese were involved in many industries inland including those associated with copper mines at Bandar Kong in southern Iran, the exportation of salt, red oxide mud, and horses from Hormuz to Europe.[6] But, their most lucrative activity was that of slave trading: capturing, purchasing, and reselling Africans and supplying markets in Portugal and their colonial settlements, such as Goa in India.[7] The Portuguese exploits are reflected in the early twentieth-century British chronicler John Gordon Lorimer's work recounting of a recovery expedition at Hormuz in 1515 where a fleet of fifteen hundred Portuguese, six hundred Malabaris, and three hundred enslaved Oromos[8] (Gallas) were involved.[9] Enslaved Africans from the Swahili Coast tended to be used to transport goods, work in mines, perform administrative duties, or work as soldiers, sailors, and servants.[10] The Portuguese, as pioneers of the colonial slave trade, expanded the

African trade into the Persian Gulf and controlled this region until rival Europeans challenged their position at the end of the sixteenth century. The historian Mohammad Bagher Vosoughi assesses the Portuguese impact over the century that:

> [T]he native economy of Hormuz was heavily damaged. By applying their overwhelmingly militaristic policies the Portuguese disrupted the trade of the region and created conditions under which the merchants and traders of Hormuz were not able to continue their activities and, as a result, gradually left the region's economic scene.[11]

Cunha similarly notes overall negative impacts over this period: "Hormuz declined thanks to the oppression and violence exercised by Portuguese captains and officials."[12] Gregory L. Bondarevsky goes as far as to characterize this episode as "the first colonial empire in the modern time," emphasizing that it "began with the consolidation of the Portuguese positions on the northeastern coast of Africa, in the Gulf of Aden, and, especially, in the Persian Gulf."[13]

THE BRITISH

Competition on the seas by European powers in the sixteenth century brought the Portuguese influence in the Persian Gulf to an end and paved the way for English commercial monopoly and political influence in the region.[14] Together with the Omani Arabs, their challenge of the Portuguese presence in the Persian Gulf began energetically in the early seventeenth century.[15] Like their Iberian rivals, England sought unchallenged naval supremacy and hegemony over the waters and coasts of the Persian Gulf, the Red Sea, and the Indian Ocean as well as a penetration of the hinterlands. Their informal influence began with commercial treaties concluded with local governments, which ultimately legitimized their further formal military presence in the region.

In 1608, the first ship of the East India Company arrived in Surat, India; here, the company set up a trade agreement with the Mughal emperor and established a trading factory in 1612.[16] From there, the Company expanded its influence by moving into the Persian Gulf, establishing a factory at Jask in 1619, and then moving inland and setting up factories in Isfahan and Shiraz. The priority was to safeguard English interests and most importantly to protect trading activities in India.[17] Trade agreements granted by Shah 'Abbas I (r. 1588–1629), as well as free navigation in the Persian Gulf, opened up Iran's frontiers to English political and commercial influence. By the end of the eighteenth century, the East India Company dominated trade in the Persian Gulf and operated from established political residencies and agencies from Basra in the northwest to Masqat in the Gulf of Oman.

British expansion into the Persian Gulf and Indian Ocean in the mid-eighteenth century was of some concern to the Iranian government, and especially their access from the south. In 1763, the East India Company settled at Bushehr not only for its suitable strategic position but also because its natural and built fortifications made it easy to defend against attack. The depth of the surrounding waterways also provided sufficient anchorage for shipbuilding. The port for Shiraz, Bushehr, became the principal route through which Iranian goods—including wine, carpets, rosewater, and so forth—were then exported to the Ottoman Empire, Europe, and Arab countries.[18] This commercial penetration meant that Iran's economic activities were directly affected by and dependent upon global market fluctuations by the nineteenth century.[19] Not only did this development effectively destroy the indigenous textile industry, for instance, but also it profoundly altered traditional socioeconomic networks through the introduction of new modes of production.

The slave-trading activities of the British in the Americas and West Indies are well documented:[20] it is estimated that European and American traders purchased about eleven million enslaved people in Africa between the fifteenth and nineteenth centuries to work on plantations and other colonial settlements, with four-fifths of them being exported from 1700 to 1850 alone.[21] It is important to note, however, that the use of enslaved persons for labor and as soldiers was not only crucial for the protection and development of the British economy in the Americas and West Indies, but it was also essential for their political and military advancement in the Persian Gulf.[22] For example, in 1741, the British provided Nadir Shah Afshar (r. 1736–1747) with a detachment of African soldiers to suppress a rebellion, which broke out in the Iranian naval service.[23] Enslaved people were little more than commodities, the chattels of agreements as is seen in the agreement of 1759 that followed the capture of a British factory at Bandar 'Abbas by the French: here, it was stipulated that the latter were to be transferred all contents, including "the Artillery, Arms, Ammunition, Provisions, Money, Merchandize and Slaves."[24] Another example can be found in one of the privileges granted to the British in 1763 by the founder of the Zand dynasty in Iran, Karim Khan (r. 1750–1779), that "British deserters, whether soldiers, sailors or slaves, should be delivered up by the Persian authorities, on condition of their not being punished for a first or second offence."[25] It has been estimated that in 1790 British merchants owned nearly half of the seventy-four thousand enslaved persons exported from Africa to British colonies or to foreign countries.[26] Recognizing the economic bene-

1.1. An African nanny of the British official's child in Iran. Courtesy of the Centre of Iranian Studies—Bushehr Branch.

fits to be accrued through slave-trading practices in the area, the British were eager to suppress all competition.

THE DUTCH

The Dutch, who had helped the English and Iranians defeat the Portuguese, engaged in commercial activities at Bandar 'Abbas in the 1620s.[27] Although attention of the United or Dutch East India Company had traditionally been focused on the Indonesian Spice Islands, the Dutch were eager to prevent the English from monopolizing the Persian Gulf region[28]—something they themselves had enjoyed throughout much of the seventeenth century.[29] Thus, as English interests in and control of the region increased, tensions and rivalries intensified. Their eruption in the 1650s resulted in four naval wars that were played out until the end of the eighteenth century. In 1753, the Dutch seized Kharg Island and converted it into their commercial and military settlement, where—we are told—they employed sixty Dutch soldiers and one hundred enslaved Africans armed with swords and shields.[30] Their sojourn was short-lived, however, and Mir Muhanna, the chief of Bandar Rig, expelled them in 1765.[31] At this time, the activities of the British East India Company increasingly shifted from commercial to political.[32]

THE OMANI ARABS

As with the British and Dutch, the Omani Arabs were also eager to exert their influence in the region in the eighteenth century.[33] The only difference was that while the Europeans were newcomers and outsiders, people such as the Omanis were indigenous to the Persian Gulf.[34] Initial forays to secure their influence in southern Iran were achieved through commercial treaties and military expeditions. Threatening the British commercial presence, they were known for making Zanzibar the center of the Indian Ocean slave trade—and much of this activity extended into the Persian Gulf.[35] Indeed, in about 1705, a group attacked a British vessel, capturing and enslaving all on board.[36]

Raw materials, a suitable climate, and proximity to the Iranian shores were sufficient reasons to convince the Omanis to advance toward the Persian coasts—and many came to settle in the region.[37] Moreover, political fragmentation—including wars, raids, and internal rivalries among chiefs and khans—had made the Iranian southern coast vulnerable to constant attack.[38] The island of Qeshm exemplifies this: the Omanis first seized it in 1720,[39] and again in 1735 by the Ya'ariba Imam of Oman. In 1743, it was recovered by Nadir Shah, who granted it along with Bandar 'Abbas and Hormuz to the Bani Ma'in Arab tribe, asking instead for an annual tribute.[40] Following the shah's death in 1747, the Qawasem occupied Qeshm and the port of Lengeh.[41] Meanwhile, in

1765, Karim Khan expelled the Qawasem from the port of Lengeh and Qeshm Island, but they reclaimed Lengeh with his death in 1779.[42] In the same way, Bushehr was ruled by various individuals including the Matarish Arabs, Rig by the Za'ab Omani Arabs, and Kuhistak by the Bani Ma'in Arabs.[43]

In the mid-eighteenth century, the Imam of Oman Ahmad ibn Sa'id (r. June 10, 1749–December 14, 1783) used his own vessels to import ivory and enslaved people from Zanzibar and Kilwa. He is described as forming a bodyguard of enslaved Africans and a mounted contingent of free Arabs for the defense of Rustaq in Oman.[44] In fact, he and his successors' use of enslaved Baluchis and Africans in their armies[45] exemplified the extent to which military relied on enslaved labor in the Persian Gulf at this time.[46]

The monetary gains from conquered or leased lands could be great, as the Al-bu Sa'id dynasty discovered when they leased Bandar 'Abbas in 1784 and collected an annual revenue of 8,600–10,000 Maria Theresa dollars (1,720–2,000 tomans).[47] The year 1784 was pivotal for the unsuccessful pretender to the sovereignty of Oman, Sayyid Sultan ibn Ahmad (r. 1792–1804). Taking refuge at Makran, he maneuvered himself into power in 1792 and then took Gwadar with the help of his commander Seif ibn 'Ali. Later that year, Seif also captured Chabahar in the name of Sayyid Sultan.[48] The sultan also ousted the Bani Ma'in Arabs (originally from Al-Hasa and Riyadh) from Qeshm and Hormuz Islands in 1794.[49] Bandar 'Abbas and its dependencies (including Minab, Shamil, Tazian, and Khamir), which had been leased to the Bani Ma'in by Nadir Shah, fell to the sultan that year too. The ruler of Iran, Lutf 'Ali Khan Zand (r. 1789–1794) leased these lands to the sultan for about four thousand tomans annually; but Sayyid paid nothing for the islands of Qeshm, Hengam, Hormuz, Kharg, and Larak, which were occupied by him or his troops until as late as 1798.[50] (A year later, however, Shaykh Nasir—under order of the governor of Shiraz—recovered Kharg.[51])

Increasing economic profits and advantages in trade, agriculture, and taxation were the main motives behind the Omanis' expansion into southern and northern Iran. They imported enslaved Africans as laborers for agricultural and maritime purposes.[52] Qeshm salt, Khamir sulfur, and plentiful fruits and raw materials from other regions were also exported to Masqat and as far as Aden, Zanzibar, and India. Indeed, we read that the Banyan Indians paid five thousand dollars (one thousand tomans) to the Sultan of Masqat annually to be allowed to export salt from Hormuz, Qeshm, Larak, and Bandar 'Abbas.[53] These great natural resources meant high revenues for the sultans—as much as one hundred thousand rupees (ten thousand tomans) annually.[54] The wealth they generated from the leased and captured Iranian territories was used for the growth of the Omani Arabs' economy.[55]

NORTHERN AND EASTERN FRONTIERS

THE RUSSIANS

In the north of the country, the situation was different. Heavy taxes and extortion by local governors in areas far from the Iranian capital were manifested in economic crises, political uprisings, and religious dissatisfaction—so much so that the Armenians and Christian Georgians in the Caucasus region responded by looking north, believing that the Russian Empire would offer political stability, economic progress, and security.

Iran and Russia had concluded the first official trade agreement in the seventeenth century, but by the turn of the century, their relations became increasingly political.[56] The attack on Iran's eastern frontiers by the Afghans in 1720 not only resulted in a seven-year occupation but also the termination of the Safavid dynasty (1501–1722). The breakdown of government was an important factor in the area's decline, but Charles Issawi claims that the main reason was economic. With a reduction in the amount of cultivatable land available and competition from the influx of cheaper European goods, villages were abandoned and the population shrank.[57] The Russians took advantage of this political instability by moving in ostensibly to help the Iranian government protect indigenous Christian populations against Afghan incursions.

In 1715, Artemii Volynskii was commissioned by Peter the Great to strengthen commercial contact with Iran. After reporting that Iran's weak position provided an ideal opportunity for Russia to attack, Russian forces captured Rasht in 1722.[58] By 1723, they had taken control of the Caucasus regions, Darband, Shirvan, Baku, and the northern provinces. There is no doubt that these regions—especially the silk-producing areas west and south of the Caspian Sea—were economically and strategically important.[59] Indeed, not only did this move offer access to natural resources, agricultural lands, and provide new trade routes and markets, but the acquisition of Crimea and Central Asia paved the way for Russia to gain access to India.[60]

CONCLUSION

The commercial and geopolitical importance of Iran had drawn the attention of foreign powers since the sixteenth century and inspired them to seize control over important geographic and strategic positions. For Iran, these encounters resulted in the conclusion of commercial and political treaties as well as military operations. The Portuguese, English/British, Dutch, and Omani Arabs expanded trade networks and influence from the African coast and the Indian Ocean to the Persian Gulf, while the Russians seized upon political insecurity in the north and began annexing territory. For all, commerce was the primary concern and military force was used in its realization. During this period, the global slave trade operated unregulated with those enslaved being used as commodities for trade and military purposes. Indigenous Iranians were also often enslaved, especially along the frontiers and in neighboring countries. By the mid-eighteen century, the slave trade was accelerating in Iran both as a result of Afghani incursions and occupation of the eastern territories and through intensified trade competition from Russia in the north challenging British activities in the Gulf.

CHAPTER 2

SLAVERY AND FORGING NEW IRANIAN FRONTIERS, 1800–1900

THE ENTIRE NINETEENTH CENTURY saw Iran's highly fragmented and perennially ineffective Qajar dynasty facing challenges to its sovereignty from sea and land.[1] A triangle of imperialist nations—Britain, Russia, and Oman—sought to dominate the three major sea routes (the Caspian Sea, the Persian Gulf, and the Gulf of Oman) and realize ambitions in the region. Even though Britain's focus remained India and that for Russia and Oman was increasingly Iran, all three realized that positioning themselves in Iran would help strengthen and maintain their interests in the Persian Gulf. In so doing, they imposed free navigation rights, devised commercial treaties and political agreements, and drew new maps that had the effect of undermining Iranian sovereignty. Challenges also came from economic and militaristic encroachments to the country's frontiers, with territorial incursions from its neighbors to the west, north, and east: the Ottoman Empire, Russia, and the Turcomans. This chapter will demonstrate an important consequence of this insecurity, which was population displacement and slavery on the borderlands and an escalation of slave trading.

THE NORTHERN AND NORTHEASTERN FRONTIERS

THE RUSSIANS

Iran's frontiers today are the result of centuries' worth of interactions with neighbors through war or political and economic conditions. Its boundary with Russia is case in point, gradually shifting south through the Caucasus region from the sixteenth to the nineteenth centuries.[2]

Following the decline of the Safavid dynasty, Nadir Shah was able to reassert Iranian hegemony in the Caucasus and push back the Russian Empire's annexation of territories as it had moved south along the Caspian Sea toward

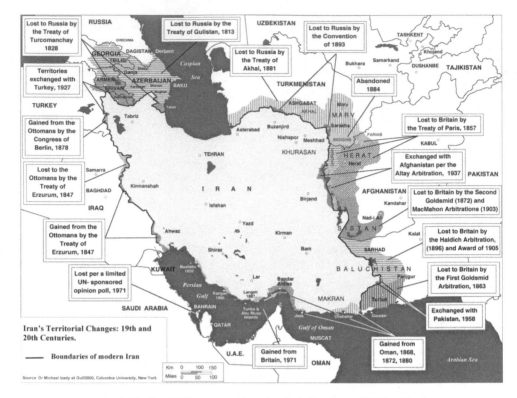

MAP 2.1. Iran's Territorial Changes: 19th and 20th C. Courtesy of Michael Izady.

the warm waters of the Persian Gulf.[3] Notably, the Ganjeh treaty of 1735 with Russia restored the lucrative Georgian territories to Iran and established the Sulagh River as the border.[4] But, this was short-lived. Following the revolt of Georgia in 1783, Russia defeated Iran and again pushed its boundary south.[5]

The reign of Fath 'Ali Shah Qajar (r. 1797–1834) was marked by two major wars in response to Russian territorial encroachments and resulted in the Treaty of Turkamanchay in 1828. Alexander I's annexation of Georgia in 1800 was not met with much resistance; but when they occupied Ganja in 1803, Fath 'Ali Shah demanded their withdrawal. Building on this tension, war broke out in 1804, with Prince 'Abbas Mirza, governor of Azerbaijan, the commander-in-chief of the army. The almost constant state of war with Russia in which Iran found itself over the next years prompted the shah in 1808 to obtain a fatwa of jihad[6] *fī sabīl Allāh* (holy war for the cause of God) against the Russians from several prominent 'ulama' including Mulla Ahmad Naraqi Kashani, Aqa Sayyid 'Ali, and Mirza Abulqasim.[7] But the Russians were victorious and ended the war in 1813 with the Treaty of Gulestan in which Iran's borders were again redrawn. Thus, not only did the treaty allow Russia to establish sovereignty over Iran's northern regions—including Georgia, Qarabagh, and many other important territories, such as Ganja, Shirvan, Darband, and Talesh[8]—but Russia was also given free military navigation in the Caspian Sea.[9] Their merchants were also exempted from taxes.

The Treaty of Gulestan of 1813 paved the way for greater Russian economic and political hegemony in Iran, so much so, in fact, that the British increasingly regarded Russia's military expansion as a potential threat to their commercial interests in India. Thus, taking advantage of prevailing anti-Russia sentiments, the British subsequently imposed a treaty in 1814 obliging Iranians to restrict Russian access to overland territory leading to India.[10]

Seeking to supply a steady demand for enslaved people, various merchants from the Caucasus region—including Georgians, Circassians, and Kurds—capitalized on the political instability along Iran's borders by kidnapping or purchasing local people and exporting them for sale to the Ottoman Empire, Egypt, Oman, and East Africa.[11] Many enslaved people were also brought into Iran since local governors had relaxed policies about foreign merchants traveling and trading within the country.[12] Young girls tended to fetch a higher price: in 1810, for instance, a young Georgian girl could be purchased for about eighty pounds (sixty-four tomans).[13] Enslaved Circassians could also command a high price as Richard Francis Burton, the explorer, scholar, soldier and writer observed in 1853.[14]

A notable feature of documents such as the Treaty of Gulestan was their reference to the trade in prisoners of war, enslaved, or free people. For instance, the sixth article stipulated that all captives and enslaved Georgians had to be returned to their homeland.[15] As such, in 1819, the ambassador Alexander Griboyedov was successfully able to negotiate the return of 158 Russian captives.[16] The economic crisis and political insecurity resulting from these wars had a great impact on people as is seen in the emigration of ten thousand Iranian families, including Persians and Armenians, to Georgia in 1820.[17]

In 1825, Fath 'Ali Shah embarked on another war with Russia over the disputed district of Gokcheh. Here, the concern about the discontent among and mistreatment of Muslims by Russians in these occupied lands[18] was the trigger of the second major war and Iran's attempt to recover lost Caucasus regions. The campaign led by Fath 'Ali Shah's son 'Abbas Mirza to reach Gokcheh and Tiflis got no further than Ganja, where his army was defeated in 1826 and a treaty was signed at the village of Turkamanchay in early 1828. With a new boundary at the Aras River, Georgia, Erivan, Nakhjavan, Armenia, and North Azerbaijan were lost to Russia. Moreover, in addition to having to pay twenty million rubles (five million tomans) in compensation,[19] the treaty effectively

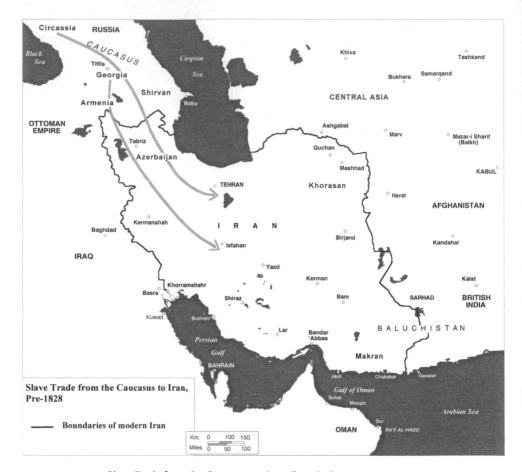

Slave Trade from the Caucasus to Iran,
Pre-1828

——— Boundaries of modern Iran

MAP 2.2. Slave Trade from the Caucasus to Iran, Pre-1828

ended trade in enslaved Georgians and Circassians.[20] Indeed, the thirteenth article granted freedom to former and to new captives of both countries.[21] The Russians' maltreatment and encroachment on inhabitants led many families to leave the Caucasus and migrate to Iran after 1828[22]; one family worth noting was that of Taj al-Mulk, who was the daughter of Taymur Khan and later wife of Reza Shah.[23] The descendants of thousands of these Caucasian refugees (whose surnames indicate their origin) live in today's Iran.[24]

The attempted repatriation of other enslaved Armenians, Georgians, and Circassians hereafter illustrates not only the complexity involved in—and often tragic outcomes associated with—such a process, but also reveals the extent to which enslaved people could be used as pawns.[25] Indeed, it is clear that purportedly humanitarian injunctions were often very much secondary to the efforts by the victors to humiliate the vanquished—or extend their influence. Thus, in 1828, when Griboyedov traveled to Tehran and demanded the release of the enslaved people from these regions, it was inevitable that the situation would not easily be resolved.

Repatriation also caused logistical problems. For instance, Agha Ya'qub Markanian—an Armenian eunuch of the royal court who had been employed in the royal army for about fifteen years—requested Griboyedov to return him to his hometown, Yerevan and provided a list of enslaved Georgians and Circassians, who resided in Iran. But the attempted repatriation of two Georgian women of Allah Yar Khan Asef al-Daula provoked outrage.[26] A group of people led by Mirza Masih, the mujtahid of Tehran, gathered and surrounded the Russian legation, demanding the women's release, but resulted in the deaths of eighty Iranians, Griboyedov, and all thirty-seven embassy staff.[27] In order to preserve diplomatic relations, the Iranian government sent an apology through Khusru Mirza, the son of 'Abbas Mirza, to the court of Russia, executed Reza Quli Baig Talesh, who was involved in the riot, and exiled the culpable mujtahid to Iraq.[28] Other examples of the often vocal requests of enslaved people to remain in their host country reveals the systemic flaws in the Treaty of Turkamanchay.[29] This was demonstrated especially by the well-documented case of enslaved female Georgians who had married and converted to Islam[30]—and were not keen to become repatriated.[31] In the end, since most enslaved Armenians, Georgians, and Circassians[32] had been absorbed into Iranian society—through conversion to Islam or marriage—Russian attempts to liberate them failed.

While the first half of the nineteenth century marked the consolidation of Russian control over the western reaches of the Caspian Sea, the latter half witnessed its advancement eastward. Seeking to secure greater political and commercial gains, it moved into Central Asia as well. Russia's pretext for attacking Khiva, Bukhara, and Kokand was to establish security and prevent the enslavement of its peoples by the Uzbeks and Turcomans.[33] But, after its unsuccessful invasion of Khiva in 1839, British diplomacy intervened to prevent any further advancement by Russia into Central Asia. At the time, the British Captain Richmond Shakespeare successfully negotiated with the khan of Khiva for the release of four hundred enslaved Russians.[34] Importantly, Russian advances through the century had profound impact on the supply infrastructure of enslaved people: not only did it cause price inflation, but it also encouraged many traders to look northeast and to southern Iran, where they could purchase enslaved Iranians and Africans at more affordable prices.

THE TURCOMANS

Taking advantage of the Qajars' preoccupation with the Caucasus region, the Turcomans expanded their raids into Iran, enslaving many people—including Russians—in the process.[35] Ill-advisedly, Muhammad Shah sought further assistance from the Russians, who, on pretext of suppressing the Turcoman raids and helping disable the slave trade, occupied the Caspian Sea island of Ashuradeh in 1840. Here, they established a military naval base at the port of Anzali.[36] The Russians justified this move by claiming that in extending their control along the Caspian Sea, they would prevent further attacks from armed vessels. But, from this position, the Russians were able to better carry out their colonial expansion further into Central Asia and slow the British advancement into Afghanistan.

By the 1850s, both the Russians and the British argued that their continued presence in the region was designed to help bring about the end of the slave trade—even though it was universally acknowledged that this was all part of the two empires' political and strategic policies.[37] Thus, in 1851, the British imposed a slave-trade agreement on Iran,[38] while the Russians justified their right to search Turcoman vessels for arms and enslaved people.[39] At the Tsar's request, Qizil-Su was occupied in 1864, Tashkent in 1865, and Kokand in 1866.[40] They also occupied Samarqand and Bukhara in 1868, and by 1873 had concluded a treaty with the ruler of Bukhara, Amir Sa'id Muzaffar, which resulted in banning the enslavement of Russians and securing their liberation.[41] Further, they carried out significant military action against Khiva, occupying it in 1881. In 1884, Russia made its way toward the frontiers of Afghanistan and occupied Marv in 1886.[42] These new Russian frontiers were considered a major threat to Iranian sovereignty.[43] As was their continued military expansion into Central Asia perceived as threatening to Khorasan and India, so it was viewed with consternation by Iran and Britain.[44]

Albeit expansionistic in design, these Russian incursions along the northern and northeastern frontiers of Iran helped undermine the slave trade. But they also brought considerable political instability and economic crisis, which resulted in the displacement of populations and mass starvation.[45] By 1900, about one million Iranians were living abroad; and in 1905 alone, sixty-two thousand Iranians left Azerbaijan for Russia.[46] Russia's encroachment on Iranian territory and continued displacement of populations culminated in the Anglo-Russian agreement of 1907 at which time the country was divided into three spheres of influence—Russian, British, and neutral.

SOUTHERN COASTS AND THE EASTERN FRONTIER

THE OMANI ARABS

Distracted and overstretched by Russian penetration in the north and Tur-coman incursions in the northeast, the Iranian government was able to do little in response to a strengthening Omani presence in most of the southern territories. Indeed, throughout much of the nineteenth century, this region was under the control of the Omani sultanate. Acting autonomously, Oman imposed heavy taxes and engaged in the slave trade.[47] So extensive was the trade along the Iranian coasts of the Persian Gulf and Gulf of Oman that the ethnocultural and racial character of the region was profoundly impacted, a factor noted in 1933 by the Pahlavi commander Hassan Arfa when he was easily able to identify Afro-Iranians as descendants of those enslaved people who had been brought over by the Omanis from Zanzibar.[48]

Operating from Masqat, the Omanis battled for control of or leased many strategic regions in southern Iran. For instance, Bandar ʿAbbas and its depen-dencies were leased[49] annually for about four thousand dollars (eight hundred tomans) from Iran to the Sultan of Oman, Sayyid Sultan ibn Ahmad (r. 1792–1804); but a year after his death, the Qawasem captured the region with the help of their kinsmen from Lengeh and the Bani Maʾin, an Arab tribe from Qeshm and Hormuz.[50] A political and trade center, Lengeh was regarded as one of the most important port cities on the Iranian coast.[51] The trade at Bandar ʿAbbas was mainly in the hands of British Indians, and they did not want the sultanate to lose its control on the Iranian coast.[52] Captain David Seton, the British resident in Masqat, assisted Sayyid Sultan's successor and nephew Sayyid Badr (r. 1804–1806)[53] in recovering the leased Iranian territo-ries, including Bandar ʿAbbas, Minab, and Qeshm from the Bani Maʾin. Thus, in 1805, Badr, with the support of the British, landed his troops in Bandar ʿAbbas and Minab. Badr then ordered that Mulla Husayn, the head of the Bani Maʾin, be kidnapped and held hostage until Qeshm and Hormuz were delivered as the ransom for his release.[54] The Sultan of Masqat established a garrison in Hormuz Island, which was guarded by 120 enslaved Africans and eighty Arabs against the Qawasems.[55]

After the assassination of Badr, Sayyid Saʿid (r. 1806–1856), Sayyid Sultan's son, became the new ruler of Masqat. In 1823, he appointed a governor to control Qeshm, and exercised full sovereignty with no tribute to the shah. Saʿid claimed that the island was a dependency of the Oman sultanate and a place suitable for carrying out any expedition against Raʾs al Khaymah, which was a haven for pirates. He arrived at Bandar ʿAbbas with two warships and maintained his fief for two years.[56] In further exercising his authority over

Iran's territories, the sultan of Oman captured three vessels near Qeshm,[57] capturing Shaykh ʿAbdul al-Rasul, the governor of Bushehr, in the process; but the sultan liberated him in 1827 after obtaining a ransom of eighty thousand German crowns (sixteen thousand tomans).[58] So profitable was the slave trade that one quarter of Sayyid Saʿid's yearly revenue was derived from it.[59]

BANDAR ʿABBAS

After his death in 1856, Sayyid Saʿid's realm was divided between two of his sons: to Thuwaini (r. 1856–1866), the offspring of a Georgian concubine, he gave Oman; and to Majid,[60] he gave his domain of Zanzibar in East Africa, where he himself resided from 1852 to 1854.[61] Before Saʿid left Zanzibar in 1854, Iran expelled his deputy Seyf ibn Nabhan,[62] thus terminating Oman's lease and occupation of Bandar ʿAbbas and its dependencies.[63] Thuwaini's attempt to retake the port town failed that year, and did not return to Omani hands until Saʿid was able to negotiate a new lease with Iran in 1856.[64] Saʿid appointed Seyf ibn Nabhan as the governor of Bandar ʿAbbas; his younger brother as the governor of Hormuz; and Shaykh ʿAbdul Rahman as the governor of Qeshm.[65] In these regions, Iranians were forced to pay heavy taxes imposed on them by the Arab rulers.[66]

The Omani sultanate's lease with Iran over Bandar ʿAbbas and its dependencies legally terminating in 1866 following the death of Thuwaini ibn Saʿid that year and with the accession of Salem ibn Thuwaini (1866–1868), a grandson but not son of Saʿid. Since the lease agreement between Iran and Oman was made with only Saʿid and his sons and declared terminable at the will of Iran after twenty years or a change in Omani rulership. For this reason, the new governor of Bandar ʿAbbas, Shaykh Saʿid, had to renegotiate terms for a new lease agreement with Iran—a 25 percent annual rate increase (i.e., twenty thousand tomans). Unable to pay this amount, he was forcibly removed from by the governor general of Fars in 1868. Only with the help of the British resident in the Persian Gulf was Salem able successfully to obtain a new lease for the port and its dependencies.[67] In response to these challenges and to secure their authority on Iranian territory, the Omani rulers built a fortification around Bandar ʿAbbas.[68] The lease treaties of 1856 and 1868 between Iran and Oman placed Bandar ʿAbbas and its dependencies firmly within the realm of the Fars province of Iran, challenging any claims to sovereignty made by Salem;[69] indeed, Oman was considered a fief holder under the Iranian government. But, this fiefdom was not to last long: with Salem's deposition from the sultanate of Oman at Masqat by Azzan ibn Qais (r. 1868–1871), Iran annulled the lease of Bandar ʿAbbas.[70]

BALUCHISTAN

Iran was also plagued by incursions into Baluchistan and Khorasan on its southern and eastern frontiers by those seeking to exploit the region's economic profitability, with slave trading along with other forms of commercial and agricultural enterprise being important sources of revenue. From the mid-eighteenth century onward, the Omanis focused their attention on Iran's southern islands and ports. The Makran coast was in particular valued for its plentiful resources, both human and natural.[71]

In addition to the highly lucrative pearl fisheries along the coast, agricultural production focused on the cultivation of dates, grains, and cotton. Labor was provided by enslaved persons as well as by free people in exchange (usually) for one-fifth of their gross cultivated produce.[72] Many, however, were expected to pay tribute to their Omani overlords as well, even if they were living in poverty.[73] This extensive use of enslaved labor by the Omanis guaranteed that they were able to both participate in and influence the nineteenth-century global economy.[74] They also relied on enslaved labor in their standing armies. Sayyid Sultan, for instance, could count on three hundred armed enslaved people and seventeen hundred Sindhi, Baluchi, and Arab mercenaries.[75] (Lorimer tells us that this number swelled to seven thousand men, twenty-five hundred of whom were Persians, in an expedition against Bahrain in 1802.[76])

When Sayyid Sultan's son Saʿid assumed the mantel of leadership in 1806, Omani territories extended from Makran to Kutch in Sind, and from Qeshm, Larak, and Hormuz Islands in the Persian Gulf to Zanzibar in the Indian Ocean,[77] an area that was at the heart of the European and Arab slave trade.[78] It is reported that Saʿid derived seventy-five thousand dollars (fifteen thousand tomans) revenue from the slave trade annually.[79] So extensive was this trade in the mid-nineteenth century that an estimated thirty-five hundred enslaved people were imported annually into the Oman sultanate (including Iran's southern regions under the Omanis' control), Qatar, and Hasa.[80] Three thousand enslaved Africans and Baluchis alone were used as soldiers and mercenaries.[81] Contemporary reports also identify enslaved Iranians from Makran and Africans from Mozambique and Zanzibar in the Arab merchant navy.[82]

The port towns of Chabahar and Gwadar on the Makran coast were administered by representatives of the Omani sultanate for nearly one hundred years from the second half of the eighteenth century—although its sovereignty was not ironclad.[83] Thus, while in 1861, much of the land between Bandar ʿAbbas and Gwadar came under the control of Sayyid Thuwaini (granted to him according to a treaty of 1856), minor Baluchi chiefs maintained authority over the areas east of Gwadar, under the protection of the khan of Kalat and other local overlords.[84] It was not until 1864 that the Iranian government gained control over the entire area including Baluchistan, considering Makran to be an integral part of the province of Kerman and of Iranian territory in general. Once it was able to reassert its authority, the Iranian government made broad moves to bring this region under direct economic and political control.[85]

Lost revenues[86] were a major factor in efforts by ʿAbdul ʿAziz ibn Saʿid to attempt to reassert sovereignty over Chabahar in 1871,[87] but the governor of Bampur, Sartip Ebrahim Khan, wrote to remind him that the region belonged to Iran. To support ʿAziz's position, Captain Samuel Barrett Miles, British assistant political agent in Gwadar, referred that the Indian government had always regarded Chabahar as belonging to the Omani rulers.[88] But Ebrahim Khan disregarded this British imposition and, in 1872, led troops under the command of Husayn Khan of Nikshahr to Chabahar. After ʿAbdul ʿAziz was forced to evacuate the town,[89] most of the British subjects took refuge at the telegraph station and demanded the Iranians leave. The request was denied and Ebrahim Khan appointed Husayn Khan as Chabahar's governor.[90] By the 1880s, Bampur and Makran became part of the province of Kerman under the governorship of Nusrat al-Daula (also known as Farman Farma), who tried to bring the local chiefs under his control.[91] After the Omani government lost Chabahar, its influence was limited to Gwadar in Makran.[92]

In spite of nominal Iranian control of the region, the area remained largely unregulated with considerable influence of the British and Omanis. Thus, it was difficult to enforce the various nineteenth-century treaties that sought to suppress slavery, including the royal *firmān* of 1848. Indeed, the Omanis' continued supplying of enslaved labor[93] did not stop the British from assisting them as, for instance, in providing military training for Sultan Turki's (r. 1871–1888) enslaved Baluchis and Africans in 1883.[94]

It is well documented that the Omanis continued to be heavily involved in the trade of enslaved Africans and Baluchis in territories under their control from East Africa to the Persian Gulf until the early twentieth century.[95] Lorimer provides ample evidence of the slave trade among the Omanis. For instance, he describes how Baluchis were used in their armies in districts under their influence.[96] We also read of riots that took place at Matrah in Oman between the enslaved Baluchis and Africans of the Khojah in June 1894.[97] Again, following a rebellion in 1895, Sultan Faysal strengthened his defenses by re-enlisting forty African guards who had served his father, and arming his palace retainers with rifles.[98] Likewise, he describes a group of enslaved Baluchis who were brought from Wudam and sold in Dubai in 1896.[99]

In 1902, the Portuguese governor of Mozambique ordered an investigation into the Omanis' involvement in the slave trade in Samuco Bay, about
one hundred miles north of Mozambique Island. This investigation was followed by the search of a large camp that housed 725 enslaved people who had
been sold to the Omanis for about three pounds each (7.5 tomans). The investigation revealed that complicity of Nampuita Muno, the shaykh of Samuco.
Upon this discovery, the Portuguese armed forces captured 114 Omanis and
twelve vessels, as well as several other vessels belonging to the Arabs of Bani
Bu 'Ali and the Janabah of Sur.[100] The documents in Arabic and Swahili found
on board proved that there had been a long-established slave-trade connection between the Arabs and the inhabitants of Samuco. These actions resulted
in the arrest of many Omani slave traders in East Africa and enabled the Portuguese authorities to sever the slave-trade connection between the two regions. Notwithstanding, the trade continued. For instance, neither the British
political agent of Oman nor the Sultan did anything when, in 1904, they were
advised that the military commander of the sultan of Oman had bought enslaved Iranians—from Makran at Sohar. Rather than repatriating them, the
Sultan accepted two for himself.[101]

BRITAIN AND RUSSIA: BALUCHISTAN

Frontiers as zones of contact between two socially and politically independent
entities have existed between Iran and its neighbors for millennia, but political
boundaries as territorial delineations between autonomous states are modern
phenomena. Pirouz Mojtahed-Zadeh, a scholar of political geography and
geopolitics, writes that it was the development of imperialism and the emergence of a global economy in the nineteenth century (with attendant trade and
communication systems) that necessitated the definition of precise points of
contacts between states and demanded the creation of boundaries.[102] The ge-
ographer Mohammad Hassan Ganji adds that delimitation, demarcation of
international boundaries, and the sense of frontier consciousness grew out of
Iran's nineteenth-century relationship with Europe.[103]

These observations can also be said to concur with the realities faced by
Iran's eastern frontiers a century earlier. With no clear geographical limits,
they had easily been subjected to political meddling by foreign nations. The
assassination of Nadir Shah in 1747 not only represents a weakening of Iranian
sovereignty, but it coincided with both the ascendancy of Britain's imperial
ambitions in the Indian subcontinent and Russia's territorial expansion into
Central Asia.[104] The situation in the province of Baluchistan exemplifies the
challenge faced by Iran for more than a century: local chiefs, the Omani sultanate, the Russians and British all struggled to dominate this economically

and strategically important region. The latter two were particularly interested in the region's access to Afghanistan and India, with the Russians seeking to establish naval bases in the Persian Gulf and the Indian Ocean and the British eager to safeguard their interests in India by blocking Russia's expansion.[105]

In an attempt to extend their influence further throughout the Middle East and South Asia, the British embarked on a program of developing the communication infrastructure in southern Iran from their base in Kalat (after 1854) through the construction of railroads, roads, and telegraph stations and by securing free navigation at the point of confluence of the Euphrates and Tigris on the Arvandrud River in the west of the country.[106] Such development projects were typical for nineteenth-century European colonialists: the exploitation of local natural and industrial resources and markets in order to realize political and military goals. And, indeed, the laying of telegraph lines tacitly revealed Britain's perception that a foothold along the Makran coast played a crucial role in securing its Indian interests.[107] Part of the process of establishing this infrastructure involved resolving boundary disputes between Iran and Kalat as well as gaining the confidence of local chieftains—something that was observed by Colonel Frederic Goldsmid, the director of telegraphs in Iran, during a surveying visit in 1862. At this time, he focused on convincing these local leaders that supporting British interests was preferable to paying Iranian taxes. In so doing, they helped protect the telegraph lines.[108]

When, in 1868, the Iranian government claimed its sovereignty over the Makran area west of Sind from Chabahar to Gwadar, the British insisted on its direct influence over Kalat through an 1854 treaty. Iran requested that its eastern border be adjusted so that it aligned with Afghanistan, but the British rejected this. Goldsmid proposed, instead, that Iran's border extend from Gwater Bay to Kuhak,[109] and he instructed a staff member to collect topographical data and map the eastern border from north to south. The Sistan frontier between Iran and Kalat (now in Pakistan) was determined by a joint Iran/Britain boundary commission in 1871. Even though this border included Chabahar, which the Sultan of Oman possessed but Iran claimed to own, it notably did not include Gwadar.[110] Although the Iranian Commissioner Mir Ma'sum Khan believed the British intended to create disorder in Iran's frontier districts, later that year the shah accepted Goldsmid's proposal and an agreement was reached in 1872.[111] Between 1895 and 1896, British officials from India adjusted borders in the region once more, delimiting the three hundred-mile Baluchi frontier between Afghanistan and Iran (from Gwater to Kuhak, and from Sistan to Kuh Malek Siah).[112]

HERAT

Russia and Britain both recognized the strategic importance of Afghanistan and the access it offered to overland routes to Central Asia, the Caspian Sea, and India.[113] In the mid-nineteenth century, Herat province was located in Afghanistan but was governed independently by the Sadozai family, who had paid tribute to the Iranian government since the Safavids. In the summer of 1837, Kamran of Herat invaded Sistan and enslaved about twelve thousand Iranians[114]—a move Russia hoped might enhance its own chances of expanding its sphere of influence toward the Indian border. Muhammad Shah answered the Afghan incursion with a military expedition to liberate the enslaved Iranians[115] and to consolidate Iran's sovereignty. In particular, he wished to end the governor of Herat's interference in Iran's internal affairs, its support of the khans of Khorasan, and its claim of sovereignty over Sistan. He was also eager to support the area from incessant Turcoman invasions.[116] Regarding the siege of Herat as a threat to Kabul and Qandahar,[117] Britain dispatched troops from India and occupied Kharg Island,[118] and by September 1838, Iran began withdrawing its troops.[119] But it was not until the Treaty of Commerce in 1842 that the British withdrew their troops completely.[120]

The threat of an Afghan takeover of Sistan and Khorasan, as well as their alliance with the Turcomans, pushed Iran to occupy Herat again in 1852 and 1856.[121] Justifying its political response by relying on its abolitionist mandate and its need to protect its Indian interests, Britain sent warships to Qeshm and Kharg Islands and Bushehr.[122] In early December 1856, forty-five British military steamships landed eighty-five hundred British soldiers in Bushehr. After Bushehr, Khorramshahr was also annexed.[123] The London *Morning Post* reported that the British "did not send this troop for the sake of the shah of Persia; rather the Russian government wants to send troops to Herat and proceed to India."[124] And, one of the first things Sardar Saheb Bahadur, the British commander, did while establishing a new order in Bushehr was to prohibit "buying female and male slaves." He also proclaimed that "all *ghulāmān* and *kanīzān* are free."[125]

Following the occupation of Bushehr, the Iranian government asked Farrukh Khan Ghaffari Amin al-Mulk, the ambassador of Iran in Paris, to begin negotiations with Britain, which led to the signing of the Treaty of Paris on March 4, 1857.[126] The terms of the treaty stipulated that Britain had to withdraw its forces from Bushehr and Khorramshahr[127] and liberate all prisoners of war. It also renewed the slave-trade agreement of August 1851.[128] Within three months of its ratification, Iranian forces were required to withdraw from the city of Herat and other parts of Afghanistan. The shah had to relinquish any claim of sovereignty over these areas and recognize their independence, which included the cessation of the use of any marks of subordination (such as claim of coinage and tribute payments).[129] Iran evacuated Herat, and the British withdrew their forces from Bushehr in October 1857. Notwithstanding, a second Herat war lasted from 1878 to 1879 and was followed by a third war in 1880 when, through negotiations, the British gained control of Herat from Iran.[130]

Throughout this period, Britain competed to acquire commercial and political agreements with the Iranian government in order to strengthen its geopolitical and strategic position in the region almost entirely in order to secure its interests in India. Establishing this foothold, the British set about to secure important communication conduits by signing treaties with local chieftains in Afghanistan, Baluchistan, and along the Makran coast. Iran's inability to hold on to these valuable territories was, as Mojtahed-Zadeh notes, largely due to "the incompetence and ignorance of those who ruled the country at the time the borders were delimited."[131]

THE PERSIAN GULF

Nineteenth-century British policies concentrated on controlling piracy and slave trading in the Persian Gulf and the Indian Ocean.[132] It was under the guise of fighting the Qawasem pirates[133] who had settled on the coast of Iran that provided the pretext for the British occupation of the islands of Kharg and Qeshm in 1809 and the establishment of military bases there in 1820. Edward Alpers succinctly observes that "many indigenous rivals to the European powers were characterized as pirates, but however one thinks of them, the cumulative effect of their activities was to render control of the sea-lanes precarious at best."[134]

Emerging as the dominant maritime power in the Persian Gulf, Britain's ostensible motive for defeating the strong naval force of the Qawasem was to protect its subjects and property and to control the main trading activities of the Arabs and their rivals.[135] In 1820, they obtained permission from Sayyid Sa'id to establish a naval and military garrison on Qeshm Island.[136] Pointing out that Sa'id was only a vassal and had no authority to permit foreign troops to land in Qeshm, Fath 'Ali Shah argued that not only did this set a dangerous precedent, but that Iran was capable of fighting piracy on its own.[137] Notwithstanding, the British struck an agreement with the Qawasem and concluded a peace treaty that year in which the Arab signatories were required to stop piracy.[138] Two years later, the sultan agreed to the banning of the sale of enslaved Christians.

The shift from the suppression of piracy and to that of the trade in enslaved

Africans seems to suggest Britain's intention of exercising authority over local government as well as maintaining its military presence in the Persian Gulf. This goal was achieved through the implementation of the British political resident that was established in Bushehr.[139] Although its location shifted to the western end of Qeshm Island at Bas'idu in 1823 despite protests from the Iranian government, the plan failed due to the unfavorable climatic conditions.[140] For the remainder of the century, Bas'idu served as a coal depot for the Indian navy as well as the British headquarters in the Persian Gulf, but more importantly from the 1850s it served as a place of refuge for liberated enslaved people.[141] Indeed, from 1863 to 1868, Iran often demanded the surrender of fugitive enslaved people who had taken refuge under the British at Bas'idu.[142] Even after the British left in 1883, the settlement continued to serve as an asylum for enslaved people refugees until the early twentieth century.[143]

Britain was not the only European country trying to make Iran into a marketplace for its own products and gain commercial concessions. Specifically, it competed with Russia through infrastructure development—in order to influence local governments and to maintain control over the regions. It was for this reason that the British established a mail system in the Persian Gulf in 1862, with the first post office opening in Bushehr in 1864, well before Iran established its own postal system in 1877.[144] They also established a mining rights corporation in 1890, but unsuccessful attempts at oil exploitation initially caused them to close their operations at Qeshm Island and Dalaki in 1894.[145] In the same way, an outbreak of the bubonic plague in India in 1896 gave Russia an opportunity to extend its reach by establishing a health service network first in southern Iran with headquarters in Bandar 'Abbas and Bushehr, with Cossacks being used to form a plague cordon. Their influence was expanded into eastern Iran when they established a quarantine area and settled troops in Khorasan in 1897 under the pretext of preventing the plague from spreading there too. The British also established quarantines at Bandar 'Abbas, Lengeh, Khorramshahr, and Bushehr.[146]

By the beginning of the twentieth century, Britain's economic interests in the Gulf region gradually shifted to oil exploration. By 1901, the Iranian government granted permission to exploit oil reserves in the country, and in 1905, the British Oil Company concluded agreements with the Bakhtiyari khans to extract oil from their oilfields in northern Khuzistan.[147] Economic successes like this inspired widespread anti-British sentiments, especially in the south. In 1905, a serious demonstration took place against the British agency in Lengeh.[148] Further anti-imperialistic attitudes intensified with the direct intervention of Russia and Britain in Iranian domestic affairs following a 1907 agreement that divided Iran between the two powers.[149]

This backlash reveals the extent to which the Iranian population resented the influence foreign countries had over local economies by the early twentieth century. But with the waning of Russian influence by the end of the nineteenth century, these negative attitudes were fixed on the British economic ascendancy in the country—especially in the Persian Gulf, where it enjoyed generous and lucrative oil concessions. The revenue from oil lost to the British, along with the importation of low-priced commodities, ruined the Iranian economy in the areas of agriculture, traditional industry, and handicrafts. Iran, which had been a main exporter of gums, asafetida, pearls, horses, wine, copper, medicinal drugs, rosewater, dried fruits, raw silk, raw cotton, sulfur, and rock salt, was now a major energy supplier for foreign powers and an importer of their products.[150] The vibrant life of Iran's islands and port cities was greatly affected by the search for oil, and the geographical expansion of the oil industry posed limitations for the agricultural and fishing industries and even affected people's movement. Many left their occupations to join the newly established oil industry, but the impact of modernization destroyed many traditional occupations, wreaking havoc on socioeconomic networks.

THE WESTERN FRONTIER

The relationship between Iran and the Ottoman Empire throughout the nineteenth century was characterized by almost constant border disputes, but Iran was not often strong enough to defend itself since the bulk of its forces were occupied with the Russians to the north.[151] The result was the enslavement of border populations and population displacement. It also provided another opportunity for foreign interference.

Iran was, however, provoked into declaring war in 1821 in response to escalating border disputes, reports of the ill-treatment of Iranian pilgrims, the Ottoman claim of sovereignty over Sulaymaniyeh, and the Ottoman support for Iranian fugitives. 'Abbas Mirza easily took Kurdistan, Armenia, Kirkuk, and Baghdad, but the conflict ended in stalemate two years later: while the Ottomans agreed to respect Iranian pilgrims, the western frontier remained unspecified.

Economic competition between the two ports of Iranian Khorramshahr and Ottoman Basra on the Arvandrud and indeterminacy of the border between the two countries resulted in war again in 1837. This time, the governor of Basra exploited Muhammad Shah's preoccupation with the invasion of Sistan by Kamran of Herat in the east to invade Khorramshahr. Without a settlement in sight after nearly a decade, the British took the opportunity to show their goodwill and mediate between Iran and the Ottoman Empire.

The resulting Treaty of Erzurum confirmed Iran's sovereignty over Khorram-shahr and recognized Sulaymaniyeh as part of the Ottoman Empire. Not-withstanding, Iran's western border remained undefined. Central to the terms of this agreement was access to the Arvandrud, being the only navi-gable waterway into the Persian Gulf from the north. Khorramshahr was an important port for both local and foreign trade.[152] Britain's insistence on en-suring the terms of the peace treaty gave Iran the right to free navigation in the Arvandrud as well as sovereignty over the eastern bank of the river, there-fore, was designed to help safeguard the interests of their Euphrates and Tigris Steam Navigation Company.[153]

Border disputes around Khorramshahr and Basra and the slave trade re-mained a pretext for future foreign intervention in the region.[154] In a letter to Foreign Secretary Lord Palmerston, the British diplomat Justin Sheil wrote,

> I took advantage of the conclusion of the treaty at Erzeroom to address a letter of congratulation to the Shah, and I availed myself of the same occa-sion to point out to His Majesty the injustice of rendering Mohemmera [Khorramshahr], which had been owned to Persia through the mediation of England, a mart for slaves, and thereby preventing in the Shahul-Arab [Shatt al Arab (Arvandrud)] the beneficial results which would otherwise follow from the arrangement entered into by Great Britain and Turkey.[155]

Increasingly Khorramshahr was becoming a significant port for the slave trade, especially after the 1847 suppression of the slave trade by the Ottoman Empire closed the port of Basra for this purpose. Anxious about the situation, the British appealed to international law, and pressured the Iranians to issue a *firmān* to close the port of Khorramshahr to traders.[156] With both ports closed, the major slave-trade route between Iran and the Ottoman Empire was blocked.[157]

CONCLUSION

Iran in the nineteenth century can only be described as a vulnerable state. Ineffective leadership from the Qajar dynasty and encroachment by foreign nations along the frontiers brought insecurity and economic crisis, culmi-nating in population displacement, slavery on the borderlands, and an esca-lation of trading in enslaved people. In assessing changing jurisdictions and evaluating shifts in the provenance of enslaved peoples, we can see how the patterns and directions of the slave trade were directly linked to foreign pres-sures—especially those from Russian to the north and British in the Persian

Gulf and along the southern coasts. Indeed, their military campaigns and political competitions not only resulted in the shift of Iran's borders, but also unsettled indigenous populations. Furthermore, the Omani sultanate, which had, throughout much of the nineteenth century, southern Iran under their control and a long history of slave trading, turned their attention from the Africans to the Baluchis in Iran.

CHAPTER 3

THE TRADE IN ENSLAVED PEOPLE
FROM AFRICA TO IRAN, 1800–1900

THE DEMAND FOR enslaved peoples increased in Iran during the nineteenth century for two main reasons: declining population growth and economic stagnation, largely due to the impacts of disease and famine along with the harsh climate and bureaucratic mismanagement at the local level. But this was not all: while some Iranians may have opted to resettle in India or Oman, many were actually forced into slavery in Iran and brought to Central Asia, present-day United Arab Emirates, and Oman as a result of political instability and war.[1] Manpower was subsequently sought from abroad to meet demand. With the closing of Iran's northern frontier following Russia's occupation in 1828 the focus of the slave trade shifted southward. And, although the Arabs of the Persian and Oman Gulfs generally dominated the market, many local people recognized that profits could be made due to the volume of and low prices associated with enslaved people being brought into the country. This chapter offers an account of the acquisition of enslaved Africans in nineteenth century Iran by exploring the dynamic patterns of enslavement, slave marketing, and the long-distance trade that developed from sources in Africa and extended to owners in the Indian Ocean and the Persian Gulf.

SLAVE-TRADING PORTS

The Persian Gulf has traditionally been important not only for commerce, political control, and military maneuvering, but also for providing an infrastructure for allowing communities to connect throughout the region, such as Iran, various Arab states, India, and eastern Africa. And, it was by means of these networks that the trade in enslaved Africans was made possible.[2] From the northeastern and eastern coasts of Africa, most were conveyed along the Swahili coast to the port towns on the Horn of Africa in the Indian Ocean to be taken to the strategic ports of Masqat and Sur in the Gulf of Oman. Their final destination would then have been the slave markets and transfer points at ports along the coastal areas in the Persian Gulf.[3]

NORTHEAST AND EAST AFRICA

Located in Somalia on the south side of the Gulf of Aden, beyond the straits of Bab el Mandeb, Berbera was one of the most significant slave-trading ports. Annually, merchants of various nationalities traveled considerable distances to trade everything from agricultural produce and coffee to copperleaf and cotton goods in exchange for enslaved persons. For each enslaved person sold at Berbera, the governor of Zeila received a duty of three-quarters of a dollar (0.68 tomans), while the sultan of Tadjoura received the remaining one-quarter (0.28 tomans).[4] Ethiopian[5] Christians were among the most popular enslaved people traded by Somali traffickers; they were brought by the Harari and Afar (Danakil) people in caravans from Shewa to Harar and Tadjoura and then to Berbera.[6] No fewer than half of the enslaved people were taken to Mocha, Al Hudaydah, and Jidda, while the rest were taken to ports on the southern and southeastern coasts of present-day Yemen, such as Shuqra, Bir Ahmed, Burum, Al Mukalla, al-Shihr, and Kishin. From there, they were transported onto ports in the Persian and Oman Gulfs and, perhaps, ultimately to the Kathiawar coast of India.

Those distributed to the Persian Gulf region were categorized into three groups based on profession: the majority were men destined for labor as iron-workers, carpenters, weavers, basket and rope-makers, gardeners, body-guards or domestic servants; women served as wives or concubines in harems or domestic servants; and the smallest group were castrated boys intended for service as their owners' personal servants, household managers, or security guards. Many from this latter group were sent to Mecca to guard the holy ground around the *ka'ba* and the tomb of the Prophet. Castrated between the ages of nine and fifteen by their parents or a village sorcerer,[7] eunuchs or *to-washi* could fetch double the price (between eight hundred to two thousand dollars) of an average enslaved male.[8]

Not all traders bought enslaved people at Berbera; many also proceeded down the Swahili coast to Zanzibar, where enslaved people were cheaper. One report makes a point of indicating that out of the ten thousand enslaved people exported from East Africa to the Persian Gulf at least one-half were shipped from Zanzibar.[9] Huge profits are recorded for some of these enslaved persons: indeed, some were resold for as much as six to ten times their buying price in Masqat.[10] (There were also profits to be made by the middlemen who coordinated the sales.[11]) Notwithstanding, traders tended to favor the more established markets in Berbera and in Massawa and Suakin on the Red Sea.

Similarly, the Yemeni port of Al Mukalla emerged as a principal market not only for the sale of enslaved Africans but also as a haven during monsoon season, after which cargoes were shipped to the Persian Gulf.[12] Further east and along the Batinah coast,[13] the Omani ports of Masqat, Sur,[14] and Sohar tended to serve as the crossroads for trading routes throughout the region,[15] with some enslaved people being transported to Iranian and Ottoman ports via canoe.[16] Enslaved Africans also came from Karachi, having been purchased in Baluchistan from Arab merchants usually at the ports of Chabahar and Konarak.[17]

MASQAT

In the early nineteenth century, Malcolm described the beach of Masqat as being crowded with enslaved people, recalling one particular instance where a dealer called out prices as he auctioned rows of enslaved people.[18] In 1819, Captain William Heude, an employee of the East India Company, also commented on the slave market in Masqat:

> I passed through the slave bazaar, where three times a week slaves are exposed for sale, and disposed of by auction or private contract. The sale had just commenced as I stopped to view a scene that had at least the interest of novelty. Twenty or thirty young Africans, brought across the desert and chiefly from the coast of Zanguebar [Zanzibar] were ranged in rows on either side of the bazaar and according to their sex. . . . A tall lusty Arab, who might evidently have claimed relationship with those whom he exposed was parading a boy of ten or twelve and crying out his price.[19]

In 1821, the population of Masqat was reported to be between ten thousand and twelve thousand people, the majority of whom were Arabs and enslaved Africans—but there were also a number of Baluchis, Persians, Indians, and Jews. During the 1820s, it was estimated that about four thousand enslaved people were sold at this port every year.[20] James Baillie Fraser, the travel writer and representative of the Foreign Office under Lord Palmerston, described that while these enslaved people were stout and well-formed, the men were sparsely clad in ragged trousers or waistcloths (and equally scanty turbans) and the women were covered head to toe in a coarse cotton and trousers.[21]

By 1831, about three-quarters of the enslaved people imported into Masqat had come by sea from the Swahili coast, with the remaining quarter hailing from Ethiopia via Yemen. One report suggested that no enslaved persons were "brought to Muscat through the interior of Arabia, on account of the badness of the roads."[22] The ultimate destination for these enslaved people ranged from Bahrain to the Ottoman Empire and western India. Those entering Iran came through the ports of Bandar 'Abbas, Lengeh, Bushehr, Qeshm, and Bandar Kangan as well as from Basra.[23]

BASRA

Various British Residents in the Persian Gulf observed the procession of enslaved people through the Persian Gulf in the mid-nineteenth century and into what is now Iraq. For instance, the British officer Arnold Burrowes Kemball described that enslaved people conveyed from the east coast of present-day Saudi Arabia and up through the Persian Gulf[24] were often taken to the island of Kharg, where fresh pilots were hired to sail on into Basra. Here they were sold.[25] From Basra, it was estimated that half of these enslaved people were

> usually sent to the Muntifiq town, on the Euphrates named Suk al-Shuyukh from whence they are spread over all of southern Mesopotamia and Eastern Syria. A quarter are exported directly to Baghdad and the remainder are disposed of at the Busoorah [Basra] market.[26]

The journey from Kharg to Basra usually took six to twelve days, but with a good wind, as few as two to three days.[27] Lengeh ships flying the Iranian flag often entered this port, where some enslaved people were sold before continuing on to Basra. Samuel Hennell[28] described the lot of enslaved Africans who were brought from Jidda to Khorramshahr and then on to Kuwait.[29] Those not purchased were reshipped to Basra. Situated on the Arvandrud at the junction of the Euphrates and Tigris and opposite Basra, the town of Khorramshahr played a pivotal role as a slave depot.[30] Because the area traditionally belonged to both the Ottoman Empire and Iran, the exchange of enslaved people between both states was easily facilitated, usually along an important inland tributary of the Arvandrud, the Karun River.[31]

It was not only slave traders who were responsible for supplying markets in Iran and in other Asian countries with enslaved Africans; indeed, pilgrims also played a significant role.[32] There was an almost continuous stream of enslaved people between both western and southwestern Iran and present-day Iraq and Saudi Arabian cities of Baghdad, Karbalā', Mecca, and Medina. Pilgrims were the usual stimulus for this trade, often purchasing one or two enslaved persons for their own use.[33] The journey from Baghdad to Tehran could take up to eighteen days by caravan.[34] The account by Richard Francis Burton of a slave market in Medina gives us useful information about slave traders as well as the enslaved people themselves:

The Bazar at Al-Madinah is poor and as almost all the slaves are brought from Meccah by the Jallabs or drivers after exporting the best to Egypt the town receives only the refuse. . . . Some of these slaves come from Abyssinia: the greater part are driven from the Galla country and exported at the harbours of the Somali coast, Berberah, Tajoura and Zayla. As many as 2000 slaves from the former place, and 4000 from the latter, are annually shipped off to Mocha, Jeddah, Suez, and Maskat.[35]

He also provided a vivid description of the crowded slave market in Mecca:

It is a large street roofed with matting and full of coffee-houses. The merchandise sat in rows parallel with the walls. The prettiest girls occupied the highest benches. Below were the plainer sort and lowest of all the boys. They were all gaily dressed in pink and other light-colored muslins with transparent veils over their heads; and whether from the effect of such unusual splendor or from the re-action succeeding to their terrible land-journey and sea-voyage, they appeared perfectly happy, laughing loudly, talking unknown tongues, and quizzing purchasers even during the delicate operation of purchasing. There were some pretty Gallas, douce-looking Abyssinians, and Africans of various degrees of hideousness, from the half-Arab Somal to the baboon like Sawahili.[36]

These pilgrims continued to import enslaved people until the practice was finally abolished in 1929 in Iran.[37]

SLAVE TRADERS

The slave trade in the Persian Gulf relied most heavily on the efforts of Arab merchants throughout the Indian Ocean and the Persian Gulf.[38] Ports like Sur and Masqat along the eastern coast of Oman traditionally played a significant role in the slave trade, serving as a hub between East Africa and destinations throughout the region.[39] For Iran, Arab merchants operated as middlemen by renting Iranian ships, purchasing enslaved people at African ports and then shipping them to ports where they were sold.[40] In September 1872, we read of the British capture of a ship owned by the sultan of Oman and of the 169 women and children found on board.[41] Another vessel was captured in Ra's al Hadd: this dhow carried six Arab slave dealers and 154 enslaved people (128 men and 26 women) on their way from Dar es Salaam to Oman and al-Khudra.[42] One report indicates that merchants sold anywhere from one to as many as sixty enslaved people per day.[43]

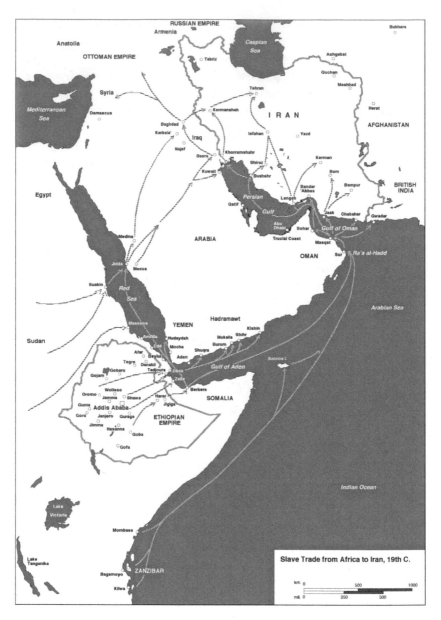

MAP 3.1. Slave Trade from Africa to Iran, 19th C.

It was the British opinion that maritime Arab chiefs were, in fact, princi-pally responsible for perpetuating the centuries-long slave trade.[44] Indeed, Arabs from the Persian and Oman Gulfs region continued to supply enslaved people to Iran even after the suppression of the seaborne trade was imposed in 1848, largely because until the end of the century, Omani sultans retained a foothold along the southern coast of Iran.[45] In addition to this simple access to the mainland, traders devised various strategies for evading British atten-tion on the seas, including the hiring of Iranian vessels or sailing under the protection of other nations.[46] Indeed, from the 1860s until the 1890s, subjects of the Omani sultan flew Spanish and French flags when transporting en-slaved people from Africa into the Persian Gulf.[47]

International attempts to control the slave trade were strengthened with the issuance of the 1848 *firmān* in Iran and subsequent agreements suppressing the seaborne slave trade. Although efforts were not always successful, slave trading in the Persian Gulf region gradually weakened. Indeed, in 1886 alone, about two hundred Arab vessels were stopped and searched in the Persian Gulf.[48] Moreover, in 1902, the anti-slave-trade operations of the Portuguese in East Africa also undermined the Omanis' slave-trading activities.[49]

Although, the law prohibiting slavery in 1929 finally ended the practice, it is well acknowledged that—by then—the economic benefits of slavery had declined considerably. Indeed, the Persian Gulf states' economy depended on revenues garnered from the employment of enslaved peoples in industries like pearling only until their collapse in the 1930s.[50] After the second half of the twentieth century, oil exploration and the resulting oil industry responded to the demand for fossil fuels; not only did these make slavery-based industries obsolete, but they forever transformed the Persian Gulf economies.

THE TRANSPORTATION OF ENSLAVED PEOPLE

Trafficking between Africa and the Persian Gulf was a seasonal activity that could only occur when wind directions were favorable.[51] The voyage from Zanzibar to Sur—a distance of about twenty-five miles—took between six-teen and twenty-five days. Vessels left the Persian Gulf during the northeastern monsoon (between November and February) and returned before or after the southwestern monsoon (in April, May, and June or in September and October).[52]

Kemball reported that during the voyage enslaved Africans were left un-restrained and treated in the same manner as the free passengers. Their diet consisted of sufficient amounts of rice, dates, and fish. The enslaved females were lodged in cabins, but they were not bound or manacled. He states that

the only differentiation between these enslaved people was that those identified as "African" were clothed with a coarse cloth around the middle, while
the "Ethiopians" were fully clothed.[53]

Many enslaved people succumbed to various diseases, such as smallpox,
and died during the voyages from East Africa to the Persian Gulf. If a contagious disease was found on board, the following was often the course of
action:

> At the first discovery of smallpox amongst them by the Arabs, all the infected
> slaves were at once thrown overboard, and this was continued day by day,
> until, they said, forty had perished in this manner. When they found the dis-
> ease could not be checked, they simply left them to take their chance, and
> to die. Many of the children were of the tenderest years, scarcely more than
> three years old, and most of them bearing marks of the brutality of the Arabs
> in half-healed scars, and bruises inflicted from the lash and stick.[54]

Reports from the 1860s indicate that between one and two hundred enslaved
people were packed in a single vessel; the resulting high mortality rates meant
that only one half arrived at the destination alive.[55]

MARITIME TRANSPORTATION OF ENSLAVED PEOPLE

The vessels carrying enslaved people ranged from small boats (called dhows
and *baghalahā*[56]) to steamships that could carry 350 tons. Even though the
latter were more common in the Persian Gulf by the 1830s, smaller sailing
ships continued to be used for trading activities.[57] Enslaved people tended
to be conveyed in boats belonging to the places to which they were being
taken: thus, those enslaved people destined for the present-day Saudi Arabian
coast traveled in vessels belonging to Al Mukalla and Shahr. Those travelling
within the Persian Gulf used boats from Basra, Bushehr, or Bahrain, many of
which sailed from ports under the authority of the imam of Masqat. Indeed,
trading vessels belonging to Masqat merchants consisted of ships, dhows,
brigs, dinghies, and square-rigged vessels and imported enslaved people along
with ivory and gold dust.[58]

Little information remains extant about the number of boats engaged in
the slave trade. Kemball reported in 1847 that the total number of vessels belonging to independent Arab chiefs in the Persian Gulf visiting Zanzibar and
the present Yemen coast did not exceed eight—a number that could carry
barely one-seventh of the enslaved people annually disembarked at the different ports of the Persian Gulf.[59] By contrast, the number of vessels that
carried enslaved people from Africa to Sur was reported in 1842 to be about

one hundred.[60] The British consul J. G. Taylor observed that enslaved people were imported principally in rented Swahili and Suri vessels to the smaller ports on the Arabian coast in the Persian Gulf, such as Kuwait, Qatif, and Abu Dhabi.[61] For instance, in 1850 Shaykh Husayn ibn 'Abdullah of Charak was reported to have hired a Suri vessel to bring forty enslaved people from Zanzibar to Charak and the island of Qeshm.[62]

Most enslaved Africans were brought into the Gulf on boats belonging to Arabs from the eastern and western coasts of the Persian Gulf and the Ottoman Empire as well as those living in the port of Lengeh.[63] Since only a few vessels brought enslaved people directly from Zanzibar, merchants were encouraged to hire Iranian vessels. Thus, it was not uncommon for Arab merchants from Ra's al Khaymah to hire Iranian vessels from Lengeh, Bandar Kangan, Charak, and Moghu to convey enslaved Africans.[64] According to Kemball, the only Iranian port equipped to send seaworthy vessels directly to Zanzibar was Lengeh, from which three or four boats were dispatched annually, each returning with about seventy enslaved people.[65] One Iranian agent reported that from 1847 to 1850, 380 enslaved people were disembarked at Lengeh.[66] The number of enslaved people carried on a single boat varied, although the general consensus is that they did not exceed fifty people.[67] A report by the British envoy Francis Farrant confirms that the Persian Gulf vessels importing enslaved people tended to be small, carrying between one and fifty enslaved people. He also noted that very few boats were fit for long voyages.[68]

From August to October 1841, it was reported that 117 boats docked at Kuwait, carrying a total of 1,217 enslaved people. Of these, 47 percent were men and 53 percent were women. Table 3.1 shows that most of the vessels belonged to merchants from Sur (nearly 31 percent of the vessels) while, of the nearly 21 percent that were Iranian (twenty-four vessels), most came from Lingah. These Iranian vessels transported 221 enslaved people, of whom 36 percent were men (79) and 64 percent women (142).

According to the East India Company General Henry Creswicke Rawlinson several years later (in 1847), independent Arab chiefs from the Persian Gulf supplied the Basra market with enslaved Africans: between fifty and one hundred vessels entered the Arvandrud annually.[69]

EVADING DETECTION

Other than bringing enslaved people into Iran via small vessels traveling at night in order to avoid detection by British cruisers,[70] it was common for Arab slave traders to hire Iranian boats to escape British naval attention. During the abolitionist period this was especially the case since Iranian vessels were granted partial immunity from the random searches to which other nations were subjected.[71]

Table 3.1. Number of Boats Arriving in Kuwait Transporting Enslaved People, August–October 1841

No. of vessels originating from each port	Highest no. of slaves per boat	Fewest no. of slaves per boat	No. of slaves			Average no. of slaves per vessel
			Males	Females	Total	
36 – Soorr [Sur]	28	2	212	143	355	10
20 – Lingah	27	1	72	122	194	9¾
16 – Muscat [Musqat]	42	1	92	74	166	10½
15 – Ras-el-Khymah	26	1	62	81	143	9½
6 – Sohar	44	4	33	54	87	14½
6 – Koweit [Kuwait]	40	5	38	65	103	17
2 – Khaboory [Khaburi]	5	2	6	1	7	3½
2 – Moghoo [Moghu]	1	1	1	1	2	1
1 – Island of Humra [Hamra]	12	12	2	10	12	12
1 – Muharaj	40	40	20	20	40	40
1 – Charrack [Charrak]	23	23	6	17	23	23
1 – Amulgavine [Umm al-Qaywayn]	2	2	2	—	2	2
1 – Aboothabee [Abu Dhabi]	1	1	—	1	1	1
1 – Bahrein [Bahrain]	1	1	—	1	1	1
1 – Yemen	11	11	6	5	11	11
1 – Kishm [Qishm]	2	2	—	2	2	2
111 boats			552	597	1151 [1149]	22½
6 other			26	42	68	
TOTAL: 117 boats	44	1	578	639	1217	10½

Source: Robertson to Willoughby, March 4, 1842, FO 84/426; Kemball, Report on the Persian Gulf, 1847, FO 84/692.

When, however, the British and Iranian governments agreed to cooperate in ship searches in the 1850s, the use of French flags became a frequent ploy to disguise slave vessels. France granted this privilege to maritime Arabs in order to counter Britain's hegemony in the Persian and Oman Gulfs.[72] Indeed, during this period, many slave-trading vessels used the French flag to proceed to Zanzibar and East Africa.[73] For instance, the use of French flag by Arab and Comorian slave traders was also common in the Mozambique Channel in the second half of the nineteenth century.[74] Reports of the 1870s, that acknowledged a reduction in the importation, did note that it was smaller vessels under French—as well as British—flags that continued to perpetuate the trade.[75] Restrictions imposed by the Brussels Conference Act of 1890 on France for allowing the use of their flag on Omani and Aden vessels were largely ignored. Thus, there are reports from 1892 onward describing vessels belonging to Sur still using the French flag to hide the importation of enslaved Africans into Basra and the Iranian ports of Lengeh and Bushehr.[76] It was not until 1900 that British pressure persuaded the French to investigate the illegal use of its country's papers and flag by Suri boats involved in the slave trade.[77]

THE NUMBER OF ENSLAVED PEOPLE IMPORTED INTO IRAN

The sheer number of enslaved Africans imported into Iran can only be truly appreciated when one is apprised of details associated with the principal markets—those from which the enslaved people came and at which they were sold. Alpers has pointed to the absence of reliable figures for the number of enslaved people during the nineteenth century and the tendency of contemporary observers to inflate the numbers.[78]

In the 1840s, the annual number of enslaved people sold in the Persian Gulf was estimated to be four to five thousand.[79] By the 1850s, the wife of the British Army officer and diplomat Justin Sheil, Lady Mary Sheil, observed that calculating the actual number of imported enslaved people accurately was impossible owing to the involvement of petty chiefs in the Persian Gulf, who routinely used their own vessels to dock at any number of small harbors along the length of the coast. That said, she estimated that, until the middle of the decade, the number of enslaved people coming into the Persian Gulf did not exceed two thousand to three thousand annually—of whom many had died en route.[80] By contrast, a contemporary estimate suggested a much higher number: that of the total 31,150 enslaved people exported from Zanzibar, fifteen thousand came to Masqat annually before travelling into the Persian Gulf and on to the ports of Bushehr and Basra.[81] A more conservative estimate by the British consul and agent Colonel C. P. Rigby put this number around five

Table 3.2. Number of Enslaved Africans and Habashis Sold at Iranian
Ports in 1842

Port	No. of African slaves [from the east coast] sold in 1842	No. of Habashi [Ethiopians] slaves sold in 1842
Bushehr	250	25
Lingah	350	15
Bandar ʻAbbas (Gambroon)	300	20
Bandar Kangan	150	10
Asaluyah	100–150	10
TOTAL	1,150–1,200	80

Source: Data from Kemball to Robertson and Sheil, July 8, 1842, NAUK, FO 84/426.

thousand per year in 1861.[82] From 1826 to 1850 the total number of 1,770,978 enslaved people was exported from Africa to the Atlantic world.[83]

Paul Lovejoy has estimated that about 718,000 enslaved people were exported from East Africa throughout the nineteenth century. Of these, 347,000 went to present-day Saudi Arabia, Iran, or India with a peak annual average of 6,500 achieved between 1850 and 1873 for these three Asian markets. Assuming that one-third of these enslaved people disembarked at Iranian ports[84] during the same period and extrapolating this ratio to the whole century, one may infer that of the 718,000 enslaved people exported from East Africa during the nineteenth century, approximately 16 percent disembarked in Iran.[85]

There are various circumstances that must be considered in order to appreciate the increase in slave-trading activities in this region after the early nineteenth century. Importantly, the abolition of transatlantic slavery combined with British control of Africa's Atlantic coast meant that slave traders of various provenances were forced to look elsewhere both for enslaved people and the markets at which they could be bought and sold in order to feed a seemingly insatiable appetite for enslaved labor.[86]

Although many of these enslaved East Africans found their way to the other side of the world, Table 3.2 provides a glimpse into the trading activity in the Persian Gulf by identifying the most popular Iranian ports and the number of enslaved people sold therein.

The central location between the eastern African coast and ports in the Indian Ocean and Persian Gulf meant that the Omani port of Masqat became a central hub for the distribution of enslaved people; indeed, there was a direct correlation between the number of enslaved people who docked there and those who ultimately found their way into the Ottoman Empire and Iran:

> The average import of slaves into Bussorah is 2000 heads. In some years the numbers have reached 3000, but for the year 1836, owing it is supposed, to the discouragement, which the traffic has sustained from the Imam of Muscat, no more than 1000 slaves were imported.[87]

The British government's attempt to block the entry of enslaved people into this port was largely unsuccessful. Records indicate that in 1846 about 1,150 Africans (of whom eighty were Ethiopians) were sold at Iranian ports, having come through Masqat.[88] Similarly, Suri vessels in 1849 brought about fifteen hundred enslaved Ethiopians to Bandar 'Abbas, Qeshm, and the Batinah coast to be sold via the same route.[89]

In September 1847, Hennell reported that two hundred enslaved people imported from Sur and Masqat had been sold at Bushehr.[90] Robert Binning, the linguist and traveler, reported that in this time period, the population of Bushehr was about eleven thousand.[91] That same year, it was estimated that a total of 3,488 enslaved people had been brought into the Persian Gulf, about one-third of whom were sent directly to Bushehr (see Table 3.3). It seems, however, Bushehr served as a transit route from where slaves were transported to other regions.

Table 3.3. Numbers of Enslaved People Imported into the Persian Gulf in 1847

Region	No. of slaves
Bushehr	1,230
Kuwait, Basra, and Muhammara [Khorramshahr]	1,828
Bahrain	300
Ras al-Khaimah	30
Dubai, Umm al Qaywayn, Ajman, and Abu Dhabi	100
TOTAL	3,488

Source: Farrant's Despatch Slave Trade, enclosing a report from Kemball, assistant resident of the East India Company at Bushire, on slave trade in the Persian Gulf to Palmerston, May 12, 1847, NAUK, FO 84/692, 149–152; Kemball, Report on the Persian Gulf, 1847, NAUK, FO 84/692.

The gender ratio of imported enslaved people varied based on their origin. Kemball suggested that of the enslaved Africans imported, "the number of males bears somewhat a greater proportion to the females, six to five. Of Hubushees, by far the greater number are females, two to one."[92] An 1847 British registry report found that of the fifty-six enslaved people bound for Basra who were captured near Bushehr, forty-seven were female and only nine were male. Because of the constant traffic in enslaved people between the Iranian ports and Basra, this figure might also indicate similar gender ratios in Bushehr.[93]

PRICES OF ENSLAVED PEOPLE

The price that could be charged for an enslaved person depended on various factors, including age, gender, geography, and local-market demands. Over the course of the nineteenth century, it is possible to observe how costs associated with these factors changed and therefore to draw conclusions about their relative importance. A disaggregation of available data derived from contemporary European sources reveals the extent to which an enslaved person's place of origin played a role.[94] Notably, the already lower price of enslaved people coming from eastern Africa tended to depreciate over the course of the century, while that for those from northern Africa or the Nile River delta held firm. It is important to consider the role disrupted trade networks and infrastructures as well as socioeconomic factors like famine and drought played in order to appreciate this change.[95]

ENSLAVED EAST AFRICANS' PRICES AT ORIGIN

Over the course of the century, it is possible to see that those enslaved people from East Africa who mostly worked as common laborers depreciated in value. In 1831, for instance, the price of enslaved Mombasans sold in Bahrain ranged from thirty to forty German crowns (five to six tomans),[96] while in 1842, it had fallen to twenty German crowns (3.3 tomans) for men and twenty-five German crowns (four tomans) for women—six years before the abolitionist legislation.[97] Around the same time, the price in Zanzibar of an African boy from seven to ten years of age was between seven to fifteen dollars (1.4–3 tomans). Those considered to be at their "peak"—between the age of ten and twenty years of age—ranged in price from fifteen to thirty dollars (three to six tomans), while those over the age of twenty commanded between only seventeen and twenty dollars (3.4–4 tomans).[98] Notably, enslaved males from the Swahili coast were cheaper than enslaved females sold in Masqat, costing between twenty to thirty-five German crowns (3.3–5.8 tomans) to the women's twenty-five to forty five German crowns (4.1–7.5 tomans).[99] More than fifty years later, it is possible to see how much some of these prices had depreciated for laborers: an extract from letters found in a slave dhow shows that the price of enslaved people in Dar es Salaam ranged only from five to thirty dollars (3.12–18.75 tomans).[100]

ENSLAVED NORTH AND NORTHEASTERN AFRICANS' PRICES

Enslaved people from north and northeastern Africa were among the most prized by traders throughout the nineteenth century. Indeed, this was especially the case for Ethiopian women. Notorious for their beauty and symmetrical figures, slave traders could command relatively high amounts of money for them.[101] One report from 1884, for instance, noted the differentiation in price between enslaved males and females from north and northeastern Africa (being sold in in Masqat), where the latter cost between thirty-five and 150 German crowns (17.5–75 tomans) and the former ranged between thirty-five to one hundred German crowns (17.5–50 tomans).[102] In spite of the higher cost of enslaved females over males, both genders depreciated in value after the age of twenty. Notably, eunuchs from all parts of Africa were the most expensive enslaved people; in one report costing between eighty and three hundred German crowns (40–150 tomans).[103]

There are specific data from the mid-nineteenth century that indicates enslaved female Ethiopians being sold in Iran for about seventy-five German crowns (12.5 tomans), while their male counterparts being valued at seventy German crowns (11.6 tomans).[104] Pretty enslaved female Ethiopians, mostly Oromos, rarely sold for less than twenty pounds (16.6 tomans) and often fetched as much as sixty pounds (fifty tomans).[105] These women were greatly prized in Iran and were often used as concubines. One report, from 1842, for instance, suggests that their price could be between fifty and two hundred dollars each (10–40 tomans).[106] Indeed, in 1847, two Ethiopians (*ghulām* and *kanīz*) were bought as dowry gifts for thirty tomans each in Tehran.[107]

SLAVE PRICES IN IRAN

That they were known as *zarkharīd* (purchased with gold) in Iran tends to support the claim that enslaved people were viewed primarily as commodities and that racial attributes ranked second to their market value as units of labor. And, yet, it is important to emphasize the reason certain Africans were sold higher in price: indeed, enslaved people purveyors were conscious of race as a social ideology and divided enslaved people based on race. Notably, however, these criteria directing the selection process from Africa and along the transit routes to the Persian Gulf tended not to rank as highly once the enslaved people arrived in Iran—except in southern regions where racially motivated practices may have existed.

Notwithstanding, it is worth noting that overall the difference in the price attached to an enslaved person such as an Ethiopian or a Mombasan was more a feature of market forces than ideological considerations. Indeed, the price of enslaved people in Iran was influenced mostly by the volume, the location, and the time at which they were purchased, although it is clear that they were cheaper upon their arrival in the coastal areas and increased in value as they moved further north or into the interior. The profit on the sale of enslaved people at Masqat was about 20 percent, and at Basra and Bushehr, it was never less than 50 percent.[108]

Several factors led to the inflation of the price of enslaved people in Iran from mid-century, including the suppression *firmāns*, British efforts to stifle the importation of enslaved Africans into the Persian Gulf, and the closure of the Russian frontier that brought an end to the trade in Georgians and Circassians.[109] The result was that, in some cases, the prices of enslaved people actually doubled.[110] We can trace the pattern of inflation with the following examples: in 1850, the average price of an enslaved person in the interior was between twenty to one hundred tomans, while the cost of a eunuch was higher.[111] At the same time, the price of a child in Tehran was between twelve to eighteen tomans and a beautiful Ethiopian *kanīz* might cost seventy tomans.[112] By 1872, the value of one enslaved person included in a dowry amounted to fifty tomans.[113] In 1875, the price of a young boy in Shiraz was thirty-five tomans.[114] In 1883, the price of an enslaved Ethiopian girl aged twelve to fourteen years of age in Shiraz was forty pounds (one hundred tomans), a similarly aged Somali twenty pounds (fifty tomans) and a Mombasan fourteen pounds (thirty-five tomans).[115] In 1880, the price of one *kanīz* and one *ghulām* of eight or nine years of age was 120 tomans in Shiraz.[116] According to C. J. Wills in the 1880s, the price of a Mombasan boy was twelve pounds (thirty tomans), while a girl sold for one-third more. An Ethiopian girl cost as much as eighty to one hundred pounds (200–250 tomans).[117] As such, it would seem that while the price of enslaved people did increase after 1848, the rate of inflation was not significant.

SUPPRESSION LEGISLATION

The *firmān* of 1848 prohibited the importation of enslaved people into Iran by sea, shifting slave-trading routes from the Swahili coasts to Ethiopia and from there overland to Iran.[118] As a result it was increasingly conducted by pilgrims and minor traders along routes from Arabia[119]—what is present-day Saudi Arabia—to Iran. One of the most important consequences of the mandate after 1848 was a general decrease in availability of enslaved people within the country itself and the concomitant inflation in their cost.[120] Although little data exists, it is possible to compare the lower prices of enslaved people sold in nineteenth-century Saudi Arabia (where the trade was not outlawed) and the more inflated prices in Iran by the end of the century. In the 1850s, the cost of a young African girl in Medina was between forty to fifty dollars (eight to ten tomans). The price of a middle-aged enslaved person was slightly less, but a skilled adult woman could fetch as much as one hundred dollars (twenty tomans). A young African boy cost about one thousand piastres (13.3 tomans).[121] By 1886, enslaved people had become much cheaper in Mecca than in Tehran, with an African woman selling for between thirty and two hundred tomans (and an African man cheaper still). A young eunuch was about two hundred tomans.[122]

Faced with restrictions to trade, smugglers ignored the prohibition of the slave trade and brought very few numbers of enslaved people into the southern ports of Iran. They could also be bought along the coast of Oman well into the twentieth century, when a young African boy in Masqat could sell for 120 dollars (75 tomans), an adult man for 150 dollars (93.75 tomans), and a young African girl for between 200 and 300 dollars (125–187.5 tomans) in Masqat. In 1901, a young enslaved male might bring 130 to 175 dollars (81.25–106.25 tomans) and an enslaved girl 150 to 200 dollars (93.75–125 tomans).[123]

DISEASES

Iran's population—especially in the southern coastal regions of Makran and Khuzistan—suffered frequently from the impact of disease, pestilence, and famine during much of the nineteenth century.[124] Although widespread outbreaks of bubonic plague and cholera took their toll, it was smallpox that was especially devastating and especially on enslaved African populations.

The transience of the enslaved African population made it more vulnerable to infectious diseases—indeed, many died before the age of thirty of smallpox, tuberculosis, and scrofula. African women were especially vulnerable to these diseases, often dying during childbirth,[125] as well as suffering from mental illnesses.[126] While disease came into the country via slave ships, it spread inland usually from pilgrimage centers.[127]

IRANIAN TRADE ROUTES

Most of the enslaved Africans sold at southern ports—including Lengeh, Bushehr, Moghu, Khorramshahr, Bandar Kangan, Kalat, Bandar 'Abbas, and Qeshm Island[128]—remained close to the coast, as Sheil observed in 1850:

They certainly are not numerous [enslaved Africans] judging by the few to be seen in the streets of the large towns in the north of Persia. In the south they are doubtless in greater numbers and particularly in the low level tract bordering the coast of which Bushire and Benderabbas [Bandar 'Abbas] are near the extremities.[129]

Those conveyed to Iran's cities—including Kazerun, Shiraz, Isfahan, Kerman, and Kermanshah—were normally transported via mule along the Bushehr–Shiraz–Isfahan–Tehran route.[130] The trek from Bushehr to Shiraz—about five hundred miles or half the distance to Tehran—cost about one-and-a-half tomans in 1850 and took about two weeks.[131] A loaded mule took between thirty and thirty-five days to travel from Bushehr to Isfahan and another twelve to sixteen days to travel from Isfahan to Tehran.[132] Meanwhile, the trip from Bandar 'Abbas to Kerman took between twenty-five and thirty days. By the late nineteenth century, transportation by mule or camel cost nine pence (0.09 tomans) per ton and mile and took between fifteen and twenty days from Baghdad to Kermanshah; from there, it took about another eight days to reach Tehran and cost a further six pence (0.06 tomans).[133]

The letter of Jamila Habashi, who resided at Bushehr and Shiraz for at least nine years, illustrates the fact that enslaved people rarely stayed in one location after their capture.

My name is Jamila Habashi, my father is Lula'ddin from Saho,[134] my mother Loshabeh, and from the Omranieh[135] tribe. I was enslaved when I was a child then was brought to Mecca where I was sold to a broker; the broker took me to Basra from the Jabal, and sold me to an Iranian broker named Mulla 'Ali, who shipped me from Basra to Muhammara and from there he took me to the Bushehr port and there he sold me to a merchant called Hajji Mirza Ahmad Kazeruni who is in Shiraz now, I was his concubine for four years in Bushehr then Hajji took me to Shiraz and kept me there for five years; in total, I was with him for nine years and then he sold me to Naser Nezam the son of 'Ataullah. After one year, Naser sold me to Hajji Muhammad 'Ali Khan. Now it has been five years that I have been with him.[136]

Following the suppression *firmān* that prohibited the seaborne trade of enslaved Africans in 1848, traders had to establish illicit and circuitous systems to transport enslaved people into the country. The geographic position of Iran's ports enabled many slave traders to escape the watchful eye of officials. Of the enslaved people sold in Bushehr, no less than one-third were purchased by local inhabitants[137]; after 1848, however, others proceeding into the interior were dressed as women so as to conceal their identities.[138] The majority of Africans had come through either the ports of Masqat or various Iranian ports, but following the *firmān*, overland routes from Baghdad or through present-day Saudi Arabia became more common.[139]

TAXATION

Iranian governors enjoyed the proceeds of the slave trade in the form of tax revenues. Indeed, arrival at the various ports first involved a visit to the customs house, where duties were paid and distributed between the collectors and government.[140] Between Bushehr and Shiraz, there were nine customs houses. At Shiraz, goods were examined and valued before a duty of 2 percent was levied.[141] The tax due on each enslaved person varied: government tax tended to be about one dollar (0.2 tomans) at the ports of Bushehr, Lengeh, Bandar ʿAbbas, and Masqat, while it was about thirteen dollars (2.6 tomans) in Bandar Kangan.[142] At Bushehr, sellers were charged an additional tax of two Muhammad Shah rupees (0.16 tomans) for every enslaved person sold. At Bandar ʿAbbas, Masqat, and the ports of the Red Sea, the tax was half German crown (0.08 tomans).[143] These charges were reimbursed to the broker when the enslaved person was sold.

THE SELLING OF ENSLAVED PEOPLE

Specialized slave markets or specific market days did not tend to exist[144]; instead, vendors would take their cargo to a rented dwelling from which the enslaved people were sold privately or sell the enslaved people publicly on an ad hoc basis. Indeed, some reports indicate that enslaved people imported from Africa to Bandar Kangan, Qeshm, and Lengeh were openly sold in the bazaars, and those remaining were dispersed throughout the Garmsir.[145] If the markets were overstocked, the enslaved people were then shipped to places such as Basra, Khorramshahr, or Baghdad, where demand was always strong.[146]

Upon their arrival in the interior of Iran, the enslaved people were kept in private homes where they were scrutinized by prospective purchasers.[147] After negotiating a price, the seller produced a deed that transferred ownership of the enslaved person to the new master. The transaction was legalized and stamped at an Islamic (sharʿ) court by a religious scholar.[148] The bill of slave purchase—the same as commodities and assets, for example, house— included a description of the enslaved person, the price, the place of sale, the date, and any other conditions.[149] Not only did this give the new master legal proof of ownership, but also it codified the relationship between him or her and the enslaved person. In many cases, traders signed a legal contract guaranteeing the enslaved person's honesty and loyalty and committing (for a specific period of time) to compensate the buyer if the enslaved person's character was proven otherwise. Contracts also protected against desertion and robbery, both of which were prevalent.[150]

SLAVE DEALERS IN IRAN

Although slave traders in Iran were characteristically entrepreneurial merchants who came from a variety of social classes and ethnic backgrounds, most can be traced to the Persian Gulf ports, including Khorramshahr, Bushehr, Bandar Kangan, ʿAsaluyeh, and Lengeh.[151] As per their profession and in the absence of a structured slave market infrastructure in Iran,[152] they tended to travel extensively between the principal cities, buying or exchanging enslaved people. Principal slave merchants were known in their communities.[153]

Renting enslaved people was a common practice that could earn handsome profits for the dealers. Signed by witnesses, contracts to this effect required the authorization of religious scholars. They also stipulated each party's commitments and penalties for breach of contract; as for instance, that which concerned the twenty-year rental by the slave dealer Mirza Aqa of the *kanīz* Firuze to Muhamad Baqir Sadr al-Ashraf in 1911. A portion of the one toman she received annually was paid to the dealer.[154]

Regional governors also played a role in the slave trade, buying *kanīzān* and *ghulāmān* and periodically using them as gifts to the court or employing them in their own large harems.[155] After 1848, some governmental agents even took a percentage of the enslaved person's price, allowing middlemen to continue the illegal trade.[156] A good deal of trading activities occurred privately among the elite; for instance, we are told that the governor of Shiraz occasionally bought enslaved people and sent them as presents to the shah's court or to other high officials.[157] For instance, over nearly sixty years, Shaykh Haji Jaber Khan (1819–1881) monopolized imports into and exports from Khorramshahr and its dependencies.[158] Management of the slave trade appears to have been left to his wife, Fatemeh bint Haji Saʿd.[159]

When the trade of enslaved Africans was reduced significantly after the 1870s, enslaved Iranians came increasingly to supply market demand, as in the frontier provinces of Khorasan and Sistan va Baluchistan. Here, Arab slave traders would travel to obtain enslaved people. For example, in 1906, Ebrahim, an inhabitant of Bandar ʿAbbas, sent his *kanīz* to Hengam to be sold to an Arab slave dealer. An Iranian government agent at the telegraph station intervened in the matter and prevented her sale. However, Ebrahim's forcible return of her clearly indicated the government's weakness in controlling and implementing legislation in its peripheral regions.[160] During this period, enslaved people were also resold or transferred to other households individually or within a group.[161] In some cases, free Iranian women, who were married and lived in regions far from the central government's control, were kidnapped, sold, and transferred to several households.[162]

CONCLUSION

Since well before the mid-nineteenth century, the trade in enslaved Africans coming into Iran had relied on a highly organized trading infrastructures and networks. Characteristics of the trade changed, however, throughout the century for various reasons and in response to changes in the global character of slave trading. Thus, while enslaved people continued to come from east, northeast, and northern Africa via well-established networks, there were increased demands on their supply. A decline in Iranian population brought labor demands from within the country itself and elsewhere in the Middle East.[163] A surge in the sale of African and indigenous peoples along with increased trading activities in the country eventually brought the passage of suppression policies beginning with the *firmān* of 1848. Although this may have helped stem the number of enslaved people coming into Iran from the sea, it caused inflation in the price of enslaved people that further drove up demand that saw increased enslavement of indigenous populations. This in turn fueled market speculation associated with the trafficking of enslaved people over great distances.

CHAPTER 4

PATTERNS OF ENSLAVEMENT

SLAVE-TRADING PATTERNS in Iran were altered over the nineteenth century for various reasons. First, the mid-nineteenth-century suppression campaigns helped reduce the volume of the seaborne trade in enslaved Africans. Second, a blockade of the Caucasus region by the Russians around the same time resulted in a reduction in the flow of slave labor that had traditionally supplied markets in Iran, the Ottoman Empire, Oman, and Arab states. Supply therefore was met from sources within the country: notably from Baluchistan in the south (by Arabs who had grown wealthy from the trade in enslaved Africans) and along the northern and eastern frontiers (by Turcomans as the result of warfare and slave raiding). But, importantly, wars, taxation, natural disasters, poverty, and interethnic conflict were also responsible for enslaving many free Iranians. This chapter examines various ways new enslaved people were acquired for both the internal and external slave markets.

NORTHERN AND EASTERN FRONTIERS

WAR CAPTIVES

Prisoners of war and conflict had traditionally provided an important source of enslaved people for markets, both domestic and international. Notably, internal conflict played as much a role in providing enslaved labor as did invasion. This is seen during the tumultuous transfer of power from the Zand to Qajar dynasty in the late eighteenth century, when many of those faithful to the previous dynasty were enslaved. For instance, while seeking Lutf 'Ali Khan Zand in Kerman in 1794, the first Qajar king, Aqa Muhammad (r. 1785–1797), took revenge on the inhabitants of the city, killing all the men and capturing about twenty thousand children and women. These war captives were sold into slavery or used directly by his soldiers.[1] That same year, en route from Tehran to the Qebchaq desert, he attacked and enslaved many Guklan

Turks who had supported his own brother Ja'far Quli Khan in a battle for power.[2]

After establishing his rule within the country, Aqa Muhammad Khan decided to reassert Iranian sovereignty over the Caucasus region by proclaiming jihad—a strategy that was commonly used by rulers to protect their economic interests and political and territorial autonomy when threatened by outside powers. The wars with Georgia were notable for the number of prisoners that Iran took: many were either sold as enslaved people or kept as wives.[3] In 1795, after invading Georgia (whose ruler had placed himself under the protection of Catherine the Great of Russia in 1788), capturing Tiflis and defeating the army, it is claimed that Aqa Muhammad Khan enslaved about fifteen thousand Georgians and Armenians.[4] Even if this high number of captives may be exaggerated, it demonstrates the success of his military campaign in Iran's northern frontiers.[5] Subsequent military incursions in the early nineteenth century into Georgia by the Shi'a government of Iran and the Sunni government of the Ottoman Empire resulted in the enslavement of many Georgians and Circassians.[6] Moreover, state officials came to monopolize the dispersal and sale of large numbers of prisoners of war.

TURCOMAN SLAVE RAIDING

Slave raiding attacks by Turcomans were notorious for decimating communities living along the eastern and northeastern frontiers of Iran from the mid-eighteenth century onward.[7] The region of present-day Turkmenistan—situated between the eastern shores of the Caspian Sea and the Murghab and Amu Rivers—was controlled by amirs and local governors,[8] and was characterized by sociopolitical strife. Iranians were brought into slavery in various ways: some were kidnapped by the Turcomans, who trafficked in the Caspian Sea and came to Astarabad and Ashuradeh to sell oil and salt;[9] others were enslaved in the province of Khorasan, making the pilgrimage[10] to Mashhad and then taken through Marv and Sarakhs to Bukhara and Khiva (Khwarazm), in present-day Uzbekistan, to be sold.[11]

The Turcoman appetite for enslaved Iranians inspired many slave raiding expeditions,[12] but these would not have been possible were it not for weak governmental control from Tehran of the northeastern and eastern parts of the country. The pattern of the raids was fairly standard: usually between forty to fifty nomadic Turcomans and Uzbeks would plunder villages, killing the men and carrying off the women and children as enslaved people.[13] Moreover, these incursions were a source of perpetual disruption to Iran's commerce in the northeast and east—particularly in Khorasan. After attacking commercial caravans and plundering villages, the Turcomans would enslave viable laborers

4.1. An enslaved Iranian in Central Asia. Reprinted from Bayard Taylor, *Central Asia: Travels in Cashmere, Little Tibet, and Central Asia* (New York, 1889).

and kill the weak and old. Not only were Iran's northeastern provinces depopulated,[14] but many villages—like ʿAbbasabad—were completely razed.[15] Political upheaval, governmental ineptitude, and religious discord can thus be seen as the major factors contributing to the perpetuation of the slave trade in these areas.

In 1863, Arminius Vambéry, the Hungarian traveler, philologist, and professor observed the involvement of the inhabitants of Gomushtepe (near the Caspian Sea) in the slave trade. Remarking on the systematic nature of the Turcoman slave-raiding practice, he commented on how every night, seaborne slave traders would announce their arrival with gunshots. Ropes would be placed around the necks of captured Iranians and attached to horses' tails before the vessels disembarked. There were reports of Turcoman women killing captive women as well as those of replacing their captives' clothes with old garments or scanty rags, chaining their limbs and placing iron collars around their necks before setting them to work or selling them at the slave markets at Khiva or Bukhara.[16] Physical punishment, mutilations, and murder by slave owners were common practices; sometimes, enslaved people took their own lives. When the plan of Fatema, a Kurdish concubine, to commit suicide was revealed, her owner, Saʿid, resold her at a Khiva slave market.[17]

The case of the enslavement of two Gunabadi Neʿmatullahi Sufis provides further insight into slave-trading patterns in the early nineteenth century. On

October 25, 1824, Haji Mulla 'Ali (the uncle of Haj Mulla 'Ali Nur 'Ali Shah Sani) and Mulla Haydar Muhammad, who were followers of the order of the Gunabadi Ne'matullahi Sufi order and students of Nur 'Ali Shah Avval Isfahani and Mulla Muhammad, the congregational imam (*imām jum'a*), were taken captive by the Yamut Turcomans. They were sold into slavery in Central Asia (modern-day Turkmenistan) where they worked collecting wood and picking thorns for fire.[18] The sufferings of the followers of the Sufi order in the hands of the Turcomans may have contributed to their forbidding of slavery in the early twentieth century.

Turcomans of all social classes possessed enslaved Iranians, known as *gizil bāsh* (red heads).[19] Notably, although custom emphasized endogamous marriage in order to guarantee racial purity, Iranian women were occasionally employed as concubines and their offspring (known as *kul* or enslaved people) were granted equal rights as freeborn citizens. By contrast, children from the union of enslaved females and males were known as *dogmah*, and remained enslaved persons.[20] Nikolay Murav'yov, a Russian military officer met a religious cleric in Khiva, whose father had been an enslaved Russian who had converted to Islam and his mother an enslaved Iranian. And, yet, in spite of being an enslaved child, he studied, became socially prominent, and was ultimately able to purchase his family's freedom.[21]

Commercial considerations also played a big part in the Turcoman raids. Indeed, enslaved Iranians were regarded as valuable assets who could be relied upon to perform hard labor and agricultural work. Uzbeks bought enslaved Iranians from the Turcomans in Khiva and Bukhara mostly for this kind of work.[22] In Ashgabat, the enslaved people were forced to work naked and chained as they collected branches of thorn bushes for fire and looked after grazing sheep.[23] Those enslaved people brought from Iran were normally handled by a group of private merchants who were ranked according to their wealth and involvement in the slave trade. Vambéry described how the enslaved Iranians, three to sixty years of age, were sold by the Turcoman robbers to wealthy Turcoman slave dealers, who—in turn—would sell them in Bukhara. The remaining enslaved people were sold on to wholesale slave dealers.[24] Many Iranian girls, who were taken to Marv were sold at the markets in Badakhshan and Afghanistan.[25]

This kind of piracy continued well into the 1900s, such as an attack by the Turcomans, allied with the Iranian officer Salar Mufakham Bujnurdi, on the border town of Quchan in November 1905.[26] Salar was opposed to Ghulamreza Khan Asef al-Daula's governance of the area and, with more than eight hundred cavalrymen, supported the Turcomans in advancing on Quchan along the road from Bujnurd. Emboldened by their success, Salar persuaded the Turcomans of Yamut to attack Khorasan as well. The attack resulted in the death of about sixty people and the enslavement of sixty-two women.[27]

RELIGIOUS JUSTIFICATION FOR SLAVERY

Sectarian bigotry was a major reason Sunni Turcomans justified enslaving Shi'a Iranians.[28] Indeed, hostilities between the two branches of Islam were often greater than between Muslims and Christians. To wit, Turcomans invested considerable effort in obtaining ideological justification for their slave raids and had their Sunni religious leaders issue decrees permitting the enslavement and even death of those guilty of what they deemed apostasy.[29] For instance, in 1837 the governor of Herat, Kamran Mirza, obtained a fatwa of jihad from Yar Muhammad Khan Mulla 'Abdulhaq (one of the Sunni Afghan 'ulama' of Herat) against the Shi'a Iranians:

> If this [Iranian] troop comes to this city [Herat], your property and life will perish. It is obligatory to protect property and life; and the fight with this people [Iranians] is a *jihād fī sabīl allāh* [holy war for the sake of God]. If you get killed, you will go to heaven, and if you kill them, you will go to heaven too.[30]

They then allied with the Afghans to fight the Iranian government.[31] Therefore, not only was the Sunni Turcomans' right to sell Shi'a Iranians considered an agreeable act before God, but their enslavement of Khorasanis and the plundering of their city was also considered legitimate.[32] In the same vein, a description from 1876 extolls:

> They [i.e., the Shi'as] are not only relentless marauders, but [also], when their enemies are not of the Sonnee Mahomedan faith, inveterate men stealers and slave dealers, treating their captives, when too old for the market, or too young to be anything but an encumbrance, with the greatest brutality.[33]

Notably, while enslaved Iranians were forced to abandon their Shi'i practices and adopt Sunni Islam, the Turcomans were not concerned with non-Muslims; thus, in Khiva, enslaved Russians were permitted to practice Christianity.[34]

APPEAL OF SLAVE TRADING

There was a relationship between increasing poverty, political and military weakness in Iran, and the reduction in the price of enslaved Iranians.[35] Thus, in the spring after Asef al-Daula was appointed governor of Khorasan in 1904, a plague of locusts impoverished the country. Combined with high taxes, the people in Quchan were forced to sell their daughters into slavery, three hundred of whom were sold by the governor to Turcoman rulers—as described in a contemporary account:[36] "They [the officials] would count each girl for thirty-six kilograms of wheat, then sell them at a handsome profit to the Turkomans who engaged in trade across the Russo-Iranian border."[37] The self-sale and sale of family members to pay off debts was fairly common among borderland people.[38] Poverty caused Kurdish families of Kurdistan and Khorasan to sell their daughters to the Turcomans and Iranians as domestic enslaved people, although this sort of transaction was said to be a form of marriage.[39] As late as the early twentieth century, peasants were known for selling their young daughters during bad harvest years for fifteen to forty tomans to the Turcomans and Armenians, who then resold them at the slave market in Ashgabat or sent them to Russia.[40] In order to sell for a higher price, some travelled into Russia and sold their wife and children, known as the *zīnat* (ornament), to the Turcomans for between one to five hundred tomans.[41] In one day alone, fifteen enslaved girls from Quchan were sent to Russia, without being questioned by Iranian border guards; indeed, the chief of the Customs Bureau at Muhammad-abad stated at the time: "It is not our business."[42] Similarly, Muhammad Khan Qara'i, a chief in Khorasan sold the inhabitants of entire villages near Turshiz to Turcoman slave dealers, who exported and sold them in Bukhara.[43] Russians newspapers reported that between ten thousand to fifteen thousand Iranians were sold into slavery from 1900 to 1902.[44]

The Turcoman economy was highly dependent on revenues generated from the slave trade, ransom payments and agricultural slavery. The labor-intensive system of crop production and cattle herding demanded high volumes of enslaved people. Thus, Turcoman raids often occurred just before harvest, when local people were taken to slave markets and sold.[45] Slave prices varied in the Bukhara and Khiva markets; for instance, while a fit, strong man could usually be purchased for between twenty to thirty tomans in the middle of the century, by the last decades of the nineteenth century his price was between two (5 tomans) and three pounds (7.5 tomans).[46] But, while enslaved Iranians were cheaper than Russians, Kurds were the least expensive.[47] Forever speculating, merchants at Khiva and Bukhara were known to buy enslaved people, hoping they would be ransomed back by friends or relatives.[48] Vambéry wrote about an Iranian youth who begged him to "write his parents a letter, beseeching them, for the love of God, to sell their house and sheep, and ransom him."[49] Occasionally, enslaved Iranians could save up for their ransoms through the sale of allowances such as meals, but this process could take more than twenty years. The chance of re-enslavement was high—as the case of an enslaved girl, who managed to escape, was recaptured and sold for

250 tomans in 1905 illustrates.[50] In the same year, the Iranian government's agent in Ashgabat reported that the increased slave-trade activities were not only caused by poverty, but rather due to the demand of Russian Turcomans and the large sums of money that could be earned for Iranian women.[51]

REPATRIATION

Throughout this period, there were efforts by Iran's rulers to reclaim and free various enslaved populations. For instance, in 1788, when Aqa Muhammad Khan left for Khorasan to punish the Turcomans, he went to Bukhara and demanded the freedom of all the Iranians who had been enslaved by the Uzbeks.[52] Following his attack on the Guklan Turks in 1796, the Turcomans retaliated by invading Khorasan, killing and enslaving its women and children.[53]

By 1813, the authority of Iran in the province of Khorasan extended over Mashhad, Nayshapur, Turshiz, and Tabas. Further south, including Herat, was controlled by Pathans, Yamuts, and Afghans, while Uzbek Tatars and Turcomans controlled the east and north of the province. Because of frequent incursions by competing groups, the inhabitants of these regions were vulnerable to enslavement.[54] A European visitor to Khiva in 1819 estimated the number of enslaved Russians and Iranians there to be thirty thousand, the majority of whom had been sold into slavery by the Turcomans.[55] According to the poet and writer Lesan al-Mulk (d. 1880), there were about eighty thousand enslaved Iranians in Bukhara at this time.[56] Another report indicates that about thirty thousand enslaved Shi'a Iranians—mostly women and children—were in Khiva.[57] Some of the enslaved Iranians of the Khorasan province were resold many times before being brought to Russia and the Caucasus region. Indeed, their numbers reached thousands of people, high enough to create Iranian communities in various villages.[58]

Responding to the weakness of previous administrations, the Qajar dynasty deliberately began a process of centralizing government and repatriating Iranians captured by the Turcomans.[59] Indeed, in 1829, while studying in Russia, a group of Iranian officials, including Mirza Saleh Shirazi and Mirza Taqi Khan, had been shocked to see how many enslaved Iranians were sold in the markets of Khiva and Bukhara.[60] In the 1830s, therefore, 'Abbas Mirza captured the Turcoman town of Sarakhs and freed the many enslaved Iranians he found.[61] In response, the former enslaved people took their revenge and killed about four hundred and fifty Turcomans.[62] In the same way, Shah 'Abbas I had safeguarded the vulnerable road to Mashhad by establishing a caravansary and a village every five farsangs[63] (equivalent to fifteen miles), and had settled 143 Georgian and Christian families. By 1846, only thirty-two of these families remained, as the rest had been enslaved.[64]

The defense of the eastern and northeastern frontiers subsequently became the priority of the Iranian government, and in 1855, Sultan Murad Mirza (Muhammad Shah's brother) and governor of Khorasan, responded to the Turcoman attacks in the region by dispatching General Esma'il Khan Mirpanjeh to Marv. But the army was defeated and the general was enslaved in Khiva.[65] After the defeat of the Iranian army in 1858, the Iranian government replaced Murad Mirza with Hamzeh Mirza, making the latter governor of Khorasan. He successfully attacked Marv in 1860, but the Iranian army was later defeated again.[66] Since the army could not secure stability in the region, not only were many Iranians enslaved but the price of enslaved people was lowered.[67] In 1862, when Sultan Murad Mirza was assigned as Governor-General to Qalandar-abad between Mashhad and Herat, he employed several thousand soldiers to control the Turcoman incursions.[68]

In some cases, enslaved people could purchase their freedom and elevate their status by converting to Sunni Islam. For example, after Allah Verdi, an enslaved Iranian, denounced Shi'i Islam and converted to the Sunni faith in Khiva, he was able to marry. His son, Khauja Margam, was employed by Mahmud Ragim, the khan of Khiva, and was liberated after proving his bravery and loyalty. Granted land, Margam became a customs director and later paid ransom to free his father and have him employed in the khan's service.[69] Similarly, Khajesh Muharram, who was an enslaved Iranian government official, pretended to adhere to Sunni Islam so that he could be appointed as the khan of Khiva's servant.[70]

Following the annexation of Turcoman territories to Russia in the mid-nineteenth century, Iran was required to send an official request to the Russian government to acquire legal permission for the return of enslaved Iranians.[71] To facilitate the repatriation process, the Iranian government commissioned its consulate agent in Ashgabat to identify enslaved Iranians, shelter the refugee enslaved people and then appoint a lawyer to defend their freedom at the Russian court.[72] Securing financial assistance to support the return of the enslaved Iranians was a difficult matter, to the extent that occasionally Iranian agents themselves provided cash for what it was considered to be preserving the honor of the country.[73]

With the trade in enslaved Africans in the Persian Gulf limited by the suppression policies of the British and the enslaved Georgians and Circassians trade hindered by Russians in the early nineteenth century, other slave-trading infrastructures developed to meet the needs of external and internal slave markets. Among these, endemic border insecurity and the weakness of the central government meant that opportunistic cross-border incursions and slave raiding became both viable and profitable in a way hitherto unseen. Turcoman

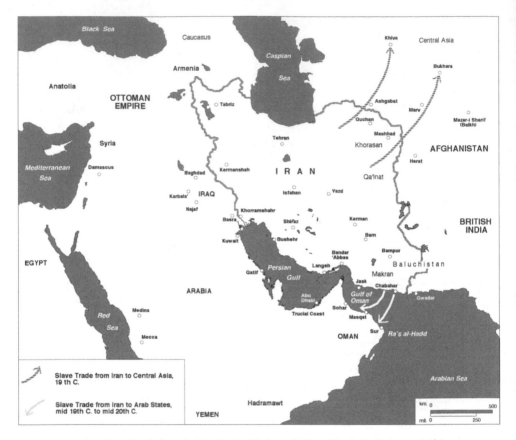

MAP 4.1. Slave Trade from Iran to Central Asia, 19th C. and to Arab States and Africa, mid-19th to mid-20th C.

raids were particularly frequent and intense until the Russian annexation of the khanate of Central Asia in the second half of the nineteenth century; hereafter, the trade in enslaved Iranians shifted in focus to the south and Baluchi populations.

THE SOUTHERN FRONTIER

THE MARKET FOR BALUCHIS

Commercial contact between the ports of southern Iran and those throughout the Indian Ocean had been established since antiquity. However, the expansion of the Omanis' orbit from the late eighteenth until the mid-twentieth centuries helped make the 450-kilometer shared frontier renowned for its role in the slave trade. Since it only took a day[74] to sail from Makran to Oman,[75] it was possible for huge profits to be earned and for an empire founded on slavery to be built. Business was conducted by means of piracy, with armed raids disrupting legitimate trade and intensifying the poverty of the indigenous Baluchi communities.

By the mid-nineteenth century, opposition to African slave-trading activities in the south and the blockade of the Caucasus region by the Russians in the north had reduced the importation of laborers into Iran, Arab states, the Ottoman Empire, Oman, and the Persian Gulf countries. Without access to enslaved Africans, Arab merchants—who had traditionally monopolized the slave trade in the south—began investing in the trade of Baluchis with the wealth they had accumulated.[76] Subjected to ongoing border instability, poverty, and interethnic conflict, these populations became easy targets for slavery and helped supply the demands of the external slave market.

The hierarchical nature of the Baluchi communities[77] meant that those enslaved generally came from the lower social and economic groups.[78] As for enslaved people captured along the northern frontiers, most enslaved people in the south were acquired by kidnapping. But since there were no specialized slave markets available inland (as it was contrary to established religious attitudes and social mores), trading was managed primarily by private or indigenous middlemen who took the enslaved people to the Makran coast where they were sold directly to the Arab slave merchants.[79] Petitions from relatives reveal the extent to which kidnapping was used; for example, in the early twentieth century, inhabitants from the Iranian ports of Minab and Bandar 'Abbas had been kidnapped by Bashagerdis and sold to the Baluchis, who then resold them to the Arab slave dealers along the coast of present-day United Arab Emirates, in Qatar and to other Arab states.[80] Similarly, slave dealers from the Jask district and Jadgals from Bahu and Dashtyari kidnapped or purchased enslaved Africans and low-class Baluchis in Bahu Kalat in Dasht, then sold them to the Omani merchants who had traveled there.[81]

Enslaved Baluchis taken from inland districts such as Bampur, Rudbar,[82] and Bashagerd were smuggled into Iranian ports, including Khor Galag and Sadaich, before being shipped to the Arab countries of Qatar, Dubai, Sharjah, and Oman via two main routes:[83] the northern route from Bungi and Sirik (in Iran) to Qatar, Abu Dhabi, Khor Fakkan, and Dibba; and the southern route from the Makran ports of Parak, Ra's Puzim, and Kunarak to the ports of Suwaiq, Qalhat, and Gohurt on the Batinah coast of Masqat.[84] The importance of the slave port of Wudam in Oman for the trade in enslaved Baluchis mirrored that of the port of Sur for enslaved Africans.[85]

By monopolizing the slave trade, the Omanis were able to keep prices low. For instance, in the early twentieth century, an enslaved diver was valued at more than 1,000 rupees[86] (183 tomans).[87] Prices of enslaved males and females varied: in 1907, the price of a strong, young enslaved male in Sistan averaged fifty to eighty tomans.[88] In 1921, an enslaved female Baluchi in Kalba, on the Gulf of Oman, could be bought for between 500 and 1060 rupees (91.5–193 tomans), while an enslaved male could be purchased for twenty rupees (366 tomans).[89] By 1929, an enslaved male Baluchi cost about four hundred dollars (457 tomans).[90]

SHIFTING APPEAL IN THE TRADE OF ENSLAVED BALUCHIS

Various elements favored the enslavement of free Baluchis. Among the most important external factors were the suppression legislation in the 1840s combined with Russian military actions in the north and market forces that stimulated demand for enslaved people within Iran and their exportation to other parts of the world. Military campaigns and political pressures in the north and south directed commercial activities inland from the Persian Gulf. Indeed, the ban on the importation of enslaved Africans by sea shifted the trade to overland infrastructures in Iran and also drove prices upward. Consequently, slave dealers crossed the Iranian frontier to obtain enslaved people in Baluchistan and its neighboring districts, where there was less of a risk of arrest.

Market forces were an integral factor in stimulating the trade in enslaved Baluchis, especially as the supply of enslaved Africans gradually diminished.[91] Focusing on the lucrative pearl fisheries, many Arab slave traders therefore turned to proximally located populations in Baluchistan as a source of enslaved labor.[92] In this particular case, a consequence of the shift in the source of enslaved labor was the formation of a class of professional pearl divers known as *ghasah* from a range of ethnic backgrounds: Persians, Baluchis, and poor Arabs, along with liberated and enslaved Africans.[93] In 1875, Arthur Arnold suggested that the industry's earning of 400,000 pounds (333,333 tomans) per year owed much to the enslaved people who fished for pearls along the Persian Gulf shores.[94]

As we have seen, internal factors contributing to the growth of the trade in enslaved Baluchis included persistent political insecurity[95] and legislative inconsistency regarding the government's attitude to slavery.[96] For example, in 1840s, the Iranian government sent Habibullah Khan Shahsavan, a military commander, to suppress the revolt of Aqa Khan Mahallati in Baluchistan. In so doing, he enslaved many local women, giving them to the soldiers as booty and distributing them throughout Iran.[97] In the same way, local rivalries, heavy taxation, and famine—especially at the end of the nineteenth century—depopulated Baluchistan and intensified the mercenary activities of slave traders.[98] Indeed, some traders were local or community officials who enjoyed a great deal of autonomy and state protection. Monopolizing the slave trade in their respective regions, they traded privately with middlemen and competed with their rivals to extend their commercial prosperity and military power. The result was that Baluchistan became a free "fair" for slave traders from surrounding countries and even within the country.

By the early 1900s, the enslavement of Baluchis was far-reaching: from Makran to Nikshahr (formerly Geh), Bent, Bashagerd, and surrounding regions.[99] We can read of the arrest in Batinah by the sultan of Oman of six dealers who belonged to a slave gang involved in kidnapping and purchasing Baluchis in 1896 to get an idea of the extent of the problem.[100] Or, in 1903, when Sa'id Khan was appointed as the chief of Nikshahr, he not only plundered and destroyed his rival Muhem Khan's properties but he extorted money from and sold local Baluchis as enslaved people.[101] Likewise, it is reported that Sha'ban, a slave dealer located in Jask, exported about 450 enslaved Baluchis to Arab ports from 1901 to 1904; of these, forty-nine were sold at an average of 150 dollars (171 tomans) each. In 1904, another gang of nine slave dealers was active in Gabrik.[102] In the same year, 'Alireza Khan, the chief of Bashagerd, raided Jagin, northeast of Jask. With the assistance of his sons Muhammad Khan and Alak, he captured many women and children and exported them as enslaved people to Sohar in Oman, where the military commander purchased some.[103]

Internal turmoil not only led to the enslavement of local inhabitants, but it also forced them to emigrate to neighboring cities and other countries, such as Oman, India, and Afghanistan.[104] Many from communities in Sistan immigrated to the Khorasan province to escape social, political, natural, and economic problems.[105] But their security was not guaranteed in these regions. In 1900s, the Iranian government was alerted to the kidnapping of many Iranian women in Baluchistan, Sistan, and Khorasan, who then were sold in India, Afghanistan, and as far as present-day Kazakhstan.[106] In 1921 Baluchis who were living between Chabahar and Jask were still being kidnapped[107] by Makrani local chiefs and by Baluchis from the Batinah coast and then exported to Oman, present-day United Arab Emirates and Qatar to be sold.[108]

Eventually, in 1924, the Minister of Foreign Affairs brought the situation of slavery in Baluchistan to the attention of the Ministry of the Interior, which in turn appealed to the Department of Defense to use military force to stop it.[109] That year, when its population was about four hundred thousand, Baluchistan was finally brought under the direct control of central government — thus ending the independent rule of Mir Dost Mohmmad Khan Baranzahi (Barakzai), who had ruled from 1919 to 1928 in Bampur and Saravan.[110]

FROM POVERTY TO SLAVERY

Poverty and the slave trade were directly connected. In the nineteenth century, specific administrative divisions within government authorized and empowered various individuals to rule autocratically within their territory. Divided into five provinces and thirty subprovinces, the country was known as the Protected Kingdoms of Iran (*mamālik-i maḥrusi-yi Īrān*).[111] Provincial governors, known as the *hokam*, were chosen from among the princes or those connected to the royal court. Although they acknowledged their submission to the shah, in practice, they acted independently, often being guided more by the interests of local merchants and the 'ulama'.[112] Slavery was a means to gain profit; indeed, there are many recorded incidents where peasants (*ra'yats*) were forced to sell family members in order to raise funds to pay extra taxes.[113] And, in spite of the efforts of Nadir Shah Afshar and Karim Khan Zand from the mid-eighteenth century, local administrators acted as they pleased, extorting from and imposing heavy taxes on peasants and the urban population.[114] The Qajars maintained the same social and political systems until the early twentieth century. Indeed, the term Qajar was used colloquially by the Baluchis to mean "ruthless people" in the context of a legacy of cruelty and distrust fostered by governors of this regime.[115] As such, the indifference of provincial governors to the needs of their people—both directly and indirectly—allowed the slave trade to thrive.[116]

Socioeconomically, Iranians were always slated as *ghulāmān* and *kanīzān* because they were considered to be property of the shah. Peasants faced with a more difficult situation than other social classes. For instance, in Sistan va Baluchistan, Kerman, Qarabagh, and Talesh, the people who dug canals—along with their wives, children, relatives, and possessions—were bought and sold with the land on which they worked. Although the same conditions may not have existed throughout the country, they nonetheless were considered bound to the land and, as such, were always viewed as properties. Landowners (*arbābān*) had absolute authority over all aspects of their geographic and human property, able to sell or punish their chattels at whim.[117] It was not uncommon for landowners to have thousands of peasants and enslaved people on a single estate; for instance, in the Rudbar district, the chief, Nur al-Din, alone controlled more than two thousand peasants and one thousand household enslaved persons.[118]

State officials and governors often used enslaved people and peasants as tribute payment.[119] Sometimes, as in the case of the governors of Kerman and Baluchistan,[120] enslaved people were the only means of monetary payment; thus, taxes were paid in enslaved Baluchis.[121] We read, for instance, of how in 1803, Ebrahim Khan Zahir al-Daula, the governor of Kerman, who was the cousin of the shah, appointed Abulqasem Garrusi to rule over Bam and Narmashir. Two years later, Abulqasem travelled to various villages, enslaved about sixty Baluchi children, and sent them as gifts to Zahir al-Daula.[122] In fact, Abulqasem's exploitation of local people became notorious.[123] In response, some Baluchis were forced to kill their wives and daughters rather than seeing them enslaved. Recognizing the gravity of the situation in 1841, Muhammad Shah sent 'Abbas Quli Khan Javanshir with 3,700 tomans to ransom those who were enslaved.[124]

Poverty was a major cause of voluntary enslavement in Iran, where the threat of starvation in various regions was great. In some famine-stricken regions, men sold their wives and children or enslaved persons they possessed.[125] Specific circumstances, such as economic depression and heavy taxation—which resulted from war and mismanagement by the local government—contributed to this situation.[126] For example, the governor of Bampur, Zayn al Abedin, was removed from office in 1897 because of his ineptitude and over-taxation.[127] The heavy involvement of Ebrahim Khan, the governor of Baluchistan, in the slave trade meant that the government was constantly asking for revenue and gifts.[128] The ill-fated tenure of Ghulamreza Khan Asef al-Daula as provincial governor illustrates how many Iranians were enslaved through mismanagement. For example, in 1897, while he was governor of Kerman and Baluchistan, people were obliged to sell their daughters to pay taxes.[129] Aqa Mirza Murteza Quli Khan, a parliamentary representative, claimed in the Parliament that tax-collecting officers seized not only the Baluchis' property but also their children.[130] Separated from their parents, these children were brought to Kerman and then to Tehran to be sold. In the Kerman province, peasants were not paid and suffered economic and social deprivation similar to that of enslaved people.[131]

As we have seen, there was a direct correlation between the slave trade and poverty; but, in the most extreme circumstances, parents were forced to sell their children at very low prices, thus making the business profitable for slave dealers. In particular, several serious famines in the late nineteenth and early twentieth centuries resulted in widespread starvation.[132] On December 31, 1921, A. P. Trevor, the Political Resident in the Persian Gulf, concluded that the increase in the trade of Baluchis on the Makran coast was due to drought.[133] He observed that "many of the poorer people [are driven] to sell their children and others to kidnap and sell children in order to provide themselves with funds";[134] adding that "it hardly seems suitable for us, after taking such effective steps to crush the trade in enslaved Africans in the Gulf, to take no active measures to nip in the bud the growing trade in enslaved Baluchis."[135] Voicing a similar sentiment, Denys de S. Bray, Foreign Secretary in India noted that a lack of governmental and local authority perpetuated the trade in Baluchis, and urged the khans to play a more active role in discouraging the trafficking.[136] Hugh Tothill, the East Indian commander-in-chief, asked the senior naval officer in the Persian Gulf, "Do you consider that the Slave Trade between the Mekran Coast and the Oman has recently materially increased?"[137] The response was that severe drought and famine in Makran in 1921 had indeed resulted in an increase in slave trafficking between these regions.[138]

ARMS TRAFFICKING AND THE SLAVE TRADE

One theme little addressed in the literature on nineteenth-century slave trade is that of the relationship between the trafficking of humans in exchange for arms. In Iran, this scenario was found most prominently along the southwestern frontier and southern coast. Thus, for instance, Barkat Khan was notorious for using the slave trade to build up his trade in rifles and ammunition in Makran.[139] Furthermore, war between Iran and Britain over Herat (1856–1857) accelerated the trade of modern arms and ammunition from Zanzibar to Herat. The rifles imported by slave dealers came mostly from Dubai and Sharjah and were sold in areas of Baluchistan, such as Rudbar and Bashagerd.[140] Governmental prohibition of the arms trade initially pinpointed individual governors (like those of Bandar 'Abbas, Yazd, Kerman, and Bampur) but ultimately culminated in a countrywide ban by the shah in 1881.[141] Notwithstanding, the illegal trade continued—even, as in the case of two firms in Bushehr, under British protection.[142]

In focusing on the global problem of slavery, the first article of the Brussels Conference's Act of 1890 referred specifically to the humanitarian implications of its relationship with: "[The] importation of fire-arms, at least of modern pattern, and of ammunition throughout the entire extent of the territories infected by the Slave Trade."[143]

Enforcement of the Act was uneven and not always successful. As such, while international pressure did help to persuade the sultan of Oman to ban the trade in arms and ammunition in Gwadar for a while (following similar legislation in East Africa in 1890),[144] the 1890s actually witnessed an increase in the exportation of European- and American-made arms from Zanzibar to Omani territories. Masqat and Gwadar remained key hubs in the dispersal of arms along the eastern African coast and throughout the Indian Ocean and Persian Gulf.[145] As part of his study of the arms trade in the region, the historian Emrys Chew has emphasized the transformation of Oman from a "raiding naval power into an expansionist commercial empire" in the eighteenth century as a result of exploiting the arms, slavery and ivory markets in the Indian Ocean.[146] Indeed, "Arab traders from the ports of Trucial Oman would actively reinvest the proceeds of piracy, pearling, and the date trade into the gun-slave traffic."[147] It is also possible to see that the eruption of social discord in Baluchistan in 1896 was a direct result of the arms trade, in addition to being a response to the death of Nasir al-Din Shah.[148] The sheer volume of arms and ammunition entering Iran in the late nineteenth century was staggering: indeed, Lorimer reports that about three-fifths of all British-made weapons were sent to Iran and, further, that in 1897 about thirty thousand rifles were imported to Bushehr alone.[149] One of the most notorious traders was Francis Thomas, a British citizen based in Bushehr, who earned more than 200,000 tomans from the importation of arms to the port.[150]

While efforts were made by the Iranian government—such as permitting British warships to search vessels for ammunition in 1898[151]—the means to respond to the problem were not possible before the Imperial Iranian Customs was established at the port of Bushehr in 1900. This legislation gave regional masters the mandate to exercise some authority over the situation—but it was no more able to control arms trading than was an agreement between the Governor General, Abdulhussain Mirza Farman Farma, and the British two years later.[152] Instead, in the early 1900s Sa'id Khan, the chief of Nik-shahr, invested profits obtained from enslaving and selling the Baluchis in rifles and ammunition. Even as late as 1924, there were reports of the chiefs, Din Muhammad Khan and Mahmud Khan, selling the Baluchis in Oman, Bahrain, and Kuwait in exchange for arms.[153]

Chew suggests that the persistence of France, Britain, and Russia to supply weapons to their allies in the Persian Gulf was part of a larger imperial game used by the great European powers of the nineteenth century to destabilize frontiers and in so doing to establish political and social hegemony over their peripheral satellites.[154] Extensive anecdotal and factual evidence confirms Chew's assessment, as is evident in an observation by Lieutenant Colonel Sir Armine Dew, agent to the governor general in Baluchistan in 1922, of the relationship between the slave trade and arms trafficking: "In order to be in a position to obtain arms, persons in Persian Mekran have, it is said, been selling slaves in greater numbers."[155]

CONCLUSION

Slavery in Iran before the middle of the twentieth century can be attributed principally to poverty and a lack of centralized governmental authority—both before and after abolitionist sentiments and suppression legislation began to emerge in the early nineteenth century. For a country like Iran—with its rich natural resources—labor shortages were endemic and were a major motivating factor in realizing the enslavement of large numbers of indigenous peoples. Thus, poverty, war, natural disasters, over-taxation, and political instability were crucial in determining patterns of development in the internal and external slave markets. And yet while the main criteria for enslavement tended to be political and economic in Iran, it becomes clear that the suppression legislations that helped bring an end to the seaborne trade in enslaved Africans actually accelerated the enslavement of indigenous Iranians, especially those of the southern coastal areas.

CHAPTER 5

SLAVES IN NINETEENTH-CENTURY IRAN

THE PRACTICE OF SLAVERY has existed throughout human history in every nation and religion and in every age. It was no different in Iran. In the nineteenth century, enslaved people were an important feature of the country's socioeconomic and political life and contributed to a range of industries—from the military and government to domestic service, agriculture, and harems. Moreover, they were owned by Iranians from various social, political, and religious backgrounds. However, it is important to note that specific markets for the sale or trade of enslaved people did not develop in Iran as they did elsewhere in the world at this time: indeed, the "slave market" as an official occupation and business did not exist in nineteenth century Iran.[1] Instead, those interested in purchasing enslaved people relied on sales in private homes. This chapter will explore the various functions enslaved people performed in this society, with special emphasis on the institution of the harem where their role was not only essential but peculiarly empowering. It will also explore the issue of racial differentiation, gender divide, and hierarchical social relationship.

RACIAL CONSIDERATIONS

ENSLAVED PEOPLE'S CATEGORIZATION IN IRAN

While socioeconomic and political conditions obviously exerted the greatest impact on the demand for enslaved people in various regions throughout Iran, racial, religious, and cultural considerations did also play a role in the selection process. However, it is crucial to appreciate that the heterogeneous nature of Iranian society tended to undermine a commitment to rigorous racial profiling. Thus, just as one might find an enslaved Mombasan working in a pearl fishery along the southern coast, it would not be entirely improbable to find one of his countrymen working as a eunuch in one of the royal households in Tehran. As such, racial considerations should not be used as the only measure to define the character of slavery in preemancipation Iran. Instead, it is more useful to appreciate other considerations like geography and socioeconomic realities in identifying patterns of access to and ultimate choice of enslaved people. It is possible to see a correlation between greater racial differentiation and stereotyping along the coasts, where most enslaved Africans were disembarked; this characteristic tended to become less pronounced the further inland enslaved people—of all racial backgrounds—were brought.

Notably, Persian documents and sources of the nineteenth century did not categorize enslaved people and their socioeconomic activities based on racial differences. What information, therefore, we have of the provenance of enslaved people imported into Iran at this time comes from the information contained in personal correspondence, memoirs, and data compiled by Europeans and other Orientalists. Other than an idiosyncratic tendency to dwell on racial considerations governing the selection process, these chronicles do provide some data—including that Africans from Zanzibar, Mombasa, and other towns along the Swahili coast were distributed more often and cheaper than their northeastern counterparts from Sudan and Ethiopia. This factor alone must be understood within the context of supply-and-demand chains based on maritime distribution networks that were better equipped to traffic human cargo via the Persian Gulf rather than overland through the desert. As such, a combination of greater availability (due to external forces like famine and drought[2]) and ease of transportation meant that enslaved people shipped through the Swahili coast could be sold cheaper at market than their counterparts from Ethiopia. In acknowledging that the Persian Gulf slave trade was almost always more about expediency than ideology helps explain the preponderance of enslaved people from the Swahili coast rather than northeast and the Horn of Africa in Iran.

The most commonly used terminologies in nineteenth-century Persian literature to describe enslaved people: *ghulām* (male servant), *kanīz* (female servant), and *jarīyah* (young woman) connoted both gender and status. By contrast, *bardih* and *bandih* simply meant "enslaved" and were most often used in literary works and poems. *Charkasī* or *gurjī* identified the enslaved people from the Caucasus region; while, those from Africa were described as *sīyāh* (black). In addition to these general terms, names such as Āfrīqā'ī, Sudanī, Ḥabashī, Zangī, Nubī, and Sīdī demonstrated aspects of geographical origin that were used to refer to enslaved Africans.

By comparison, nineteenth-century European sources tended to dwell on the geographical and racial origin of enslaved people and therein to look for patterns in labor distribution. This is abundantly obvious in the way that Mary Sheil, wife of the British official Justin Sheil, organized the three distinct groups of Africans living in Iran into specific modes of economic production. She noted that the "Bambassees [Mombasans], Nubees [Sudanese], and Habeshees [Ethiopians]"—who came from present-day Tanzania, Sudan, and Ethiopia respectively—were assigned specific tasks: the Mombasans were usually employed as field laborers, while the Sudanese and Ethiopians tended to be better respected and viewed as more faithful and intelligent and consequently became confidential servants in households and were never put to work in the fields.[3]

Another British diplomat, Kemball, referred to two types of enslaved Africans based on their geographical origin: the "Sowahilee or African from the coast of Zanzibar the territory principally of the Imam of Muscat; and Hubshee or Habasshi from the shores of the Red Sea, Judda, Howdeidah, Mocha."[4] Like Sheil, he described how the division of labor and duties was based on the origin and gender of enslaved people.[5] Enslaved persons from the Swahili coast were observed to be more often working outdoors and as field laborers, while the women often performed coarser household tasks.[6] They drew water, went to the market to purchase food, chopped wood, and performed other duties assigned to them as servants.[7] Enslaved female Swahilis and Mombasans, added Kemball, performed the most menial tasks in the household: "[They] cook the food, wash clothes, sweep the house, grind flour, take care of the children and other household work within their province."[8] He also noted that these women were rarely taken as concubines.[9] He was not able to see beyond racial considerations to fully appreciate that the demands of the labor-intensive activities in the coastal regions were being met by the supply of more easily obtainable numbers of enslaved people from the Swahili coast.

In the same way, C. J. Wills' travelogue *In the Land of the Lion and Sun* (published in 1891) considered the extent to which enslaved Africans were valued relative to their race in Iran. The medical officer attached to the British telegraph department from 1866 to 1881 noted that the fairer complexion of the Ethiopians was often seen to be more valuable than the darker-skinned Swahilis or Somalis. Darker yet, Mombasans[10] tended to be least valued and were usually forced to work as cooks or where physical strength was required.[11] For this reason, he concluded that enslaved people were incorporated into different socioeconomic sectors of Iranian society based on perceptions of physical suitability and supposed reputations. This type of stereotyping was not unique to the Africans; indeed the British applied the same notion toward other racial and ethnic groups such as the Baluchis.[12]

European archival and anecdotal evidence does tend to support these observations, especially that enslaved northeastern Africans (including the preferred Ethiopians) were often better cared for, clothed, and fed. They were often considered to be brave and intelligent; indeed, the men could expect to be sent to school early to learn how to read and write. Both men and women were often assigned to perform the lighter household (*andarūn*) duties as servants (*pishkhidmats*). If their competency was proven, they were placed in more important and confidential positions—such as stewards and superintendents—and were respected by the household. Both sexes were considered more attractive than other African ethnic groups, but enslaved Ethiopian females—in particular—were commonly retained as concubines.[13] Indeed, the most valued black harem servants were the Ethiopians; for instance, the children of these concubines had rights equal to those of the children of free women.[14] As young women, they attended to their mistresses, but as they grew older, they were treated by their masters as wives rather than as servants.[15]

ENSLAVED PEOPLE'S CATEGORIZATION
ALONG TRANSIT ROUTES

A mid-nineteenth-century report describing the importation of enslaved Africans on Zanzibar vessels distinguished between those destined to become either domestic enslaved people or agricultural laborers and artisans.[16] It also observed that the practice of categorizing these enslaved Africans was local. In fact, the Swahili language offered a range of terminological categorizations to indicate the social hierarchy of enslaved people along this coast. Even though the common term for enslaved people was *mtumwa* (pl. *watumwa*), there were important distinctions based on where the enslaved person had been born. As such a *mjinga* (pl. *wajinga*) was an older enslaved person, who had been born inland and was not assimilated into the coastal populations. He or she would have been considered to be of a lower social status than a *mzalia* (pl. *wazalia*), who would have been born into slavery on the coast. An important consideration in this system was the extent of an enslaved person's acculturation into the coastal Islamic culture of East Africa; non-Muslim enslaved people who did not belong to the Swahili culture were known as *mshenzi* (pl. *washenzi*) or "pagan."[17] The European slave traders used the term *cafre* ("unbeliever") to categorize Africans. The Portuguese, for instance, used it to describe all non-Swahili African peoples and later all Europeans in the region, with the Dutch and British extending the term to refer to those of south and southeast African descent.[18]

In practice, racial origins and religious backgrounds were noted on official documents and British passports. Anne Bang writes that the Omani Sultanate, for instance, had categorized people according to the categories of free/enslaved, Muslim/non-Muslim, and Ibadi-Omani/other Muslim denominations, but "the British administrators placed much emphasis on where people came from (literally, *where people arrived from*)."[19] These kinds of distinctions were known to have affected people's access to political representations, housing, employment, and education. There is no doubt that colonial ideas of racial origin can "convey glimpses" into the attitudes of European Orientalists, but they also can be seen to have affected decisions about the "supposed suitability of the various 'races' to schooling and later occupations," notes Bang. Thus, according to the British views and documents, "the 'Arabs' were envisioned as suitable for business, teaching and certain types of civil service, the 'Indians' purely for civil service, whereas the 'natives' were to have their natural place in industrial and agricultural courses."[20]

Notwithstanding some general trends, racial classifications tended to be applied arbitrarily among slave systems throughout the Middle East. In fact, differentiation among enslaved peoples was based on a combination of prejudice, reputation, and the enslaved people's functions. Socioeconomic and religious stereotypes may also have determined these patterns of preference. For example, the Oromo people did not constitute a desirable ethnic group among the nomads of Taima in Saudi Arabia. According to Charles Doughty, writing in the late nineteenth century, "this is because the first cost is more, and [the Oromos'] strength is less for any rude labor."[21] And, yet, these enslaved people were well regarded as faithful and kind by others. Thus, in Mecca, Medina, Ha'il, and Boraida, Oromo enslaved people were valued for their strength and height, and many were used as the bodyguards of the amirs. Indeed, Captain G. L. Sulivan found the enslaved Oromos more intelligent than other Africans.[22] Similarly, Sudanese and Ethiopians were not as commonly found in Ra's al Khaymah as they were in Iran or by the chiefs of Bahrain; indeed, the latter found them to be excellent soldiers.[23] Moreover, Rawlinson observed the classification of enslaved people and their price according to their origins at a market in Basra in 1847 in present-day Iraq (see Table 5.1).

Although British officials and other European observers tended to see nineteenth-century Iranian society as being differentiated strictly according to race, divisions influenced by geography, religion, socioeconomic, and cultural background were of greater importance. In reality, of course, the degree to which stereotypes and prejudice determined patterns of trading varied not only from one country and province to another and over time, but they were also based on the labor needs of communities. Moreover, it is critical to recognize that enslaved people were categorized at origin and along transit routes throughout the Middle East. As such, we must appreciate that those enslaved people categorizations used at market in Iran were to a great extent

Table 5.1. Slave Prices in Basra in 1847

Ethnicity	Sex	Price (shamees)	Price (£)
Abyssinians (Ethiopian)	M	120–200	9–15 [T7.5–12.5]
	F	160–300	12–22.5 [T10–18.75]
Nubians (Sudanese)	M	200–250	15–18.75 [T12.5–15.62]
	F	250–350	18.75–26 [T15.62–21.6]
Mombasans	M	60–180	4.5–13.5 [T3.75–11.25]
	F	60–180	4.5–13.5 [T3.75–11.25]

Source: Data from Rawlinson to Wellesley, April 28, 1847, BL, L/PS/5/450.

influenced by the ideologically based differentiation processes of the enslaved person purveyor.

SLAVE-MASTER RELATIONSHIPS

The complicated nature of slave-master relationships necessitates an examination of two issues: first, how laws governed the treatment and guaranteed the rights of enslaved people; and second, how these enslaved people were actually treated. The first can be assessed by reference to sources like religious texts and governmental legislation, while insights into the second can be uncovered through the study of archival material, including travelers' observations and slave narratives. The attitudes of foreign diplomats and visitors as well as many modern scholars have been largely comparative in approach—as for instance with reference to distinct economic systems and patterns of slavery worldwide. Because such an approach is often reductionist, it is my intention here to present the facts as they appear.

Most modern scholars have identified the differences between Middle Eastern and Atlantic slavery systems as resulting from either economic or socioreligious factors. Seymour Drescher asserts:

> In contrast with other slave systems, Atlantic slavery was a highly differentiated intercontinental system. Africa, the New World and Europe not only contributed separate components of labour, land and capital; they could remain relatively autonomous in their development for three centuries.[24]

Segal makes a similar claim, suggesting that a surplus of agricultural peas-antry in the Middle East meant that enslaved people tended to be employed in the service sectors. For this reason, twice as many African women were traded in the Middle East as men.[25] Issawi notes that, by comparison with Africa, the Middle East did not suffer from labor shortages. As a result, it was more common to see coercive measures being employed to increase the labor supply in Africa.[26] The American historian William Hardy McNeill compares the distinct roles enslaved people played in the Ottoman Empire (as personal servants, bodyguards, sultan's soldiers, concubines, and mothers of the ruling class) with the experiences of enslaved people in the Atlantic world: "The brutalized Negro field hands of the New World, who constitute the Western archetype of an enslaved population, were different indeed from the slaves who strutted the streets and staffed the palaces of Constantinople."[27] He adds,

> Turkish slavery did not in the least resemble the slavery Europeans were simultaneously imposing upon plantation field workers in the New World.
> . . . The comparatively mild character of Turkish slavery was due to the fact that slaves were not valued primarily for the economic usefulness of their labor. Slaves were used instead to satisfy the desire of upstart Ottoman notables (often slaves themselves) to accumulate a large household of atten-dants, thus attesting their own personal greatness.[28]

Zilfi describes the situation in the Middle East as "an open slave system" that "was not built on the kind of 'we-they dichotomy' that characterized the Western hemisphere's 'closed' system of racialized chattel bondage and social immobility from generation to generation."[29] In the same way, Robert Harms has argued that the practice and experience of slavery in the Indian Ocean re-gion varied considerably from that of those forced into New World chattel slavery.[30] Zilfi identifies two types of enslaved people in the Ottoman Em-pire: those pressed into military service (entitled to powers associated with their imperial attachment) and ordinary enslaved people who were owned by common people. She even questions whether those who worked in the royal courts were regarded as enslaved persons in the true sense or not.[31] This atti-tude can be found in early accounts by foreign travelers and diplomats who compared slavery in Iran with that seen in the Americas. Wills, for instance, wrote,

> The slaves in Persia have what Americans call a good time; well fed, well clothed, treated as spoiled children, given the lightest work, and often given

in marriage to a favorite son, or taken as a *"segah,"* or concubine, by her master himself.[32]

He further stated that the *ghulāmān* and *kanīzān* were not maltreated. In many cases, circumstances were dictated by the socioeconomic status of the owners. Thus, in a wealthy home, enslaved people might expect pilaf and mutton, while in poorer homes, the fare might consist only of dates and bread.[33] Some enslaved people enjoyed high status within their communities.[34] Enslaved females could even enjoy freedom in public, expressed in a preference for shiny and deeply colored clothing—but always deferring to conventional mores as, for instance, by wearing the *chādur* like other Iranian women.[35]

At the beginning of the nineteenth century, Iranian society was regulated by Islamic tenets. Among these, masters were required to treat their enslaved people humanely; indeed, the Prophet Muhammad enjoined masters to address their enslaved people as "my son" and "my daughter" and to treat them with kindness.[36] Islamic law regulated a pattern of domestic slavery in which enslaved people were protected and liberated by their masters. Abdul Sheriff, a historian of East Africa, observes that Islam neither encouraged nor discouraged slavery, but rather "had a built-in system of manumission that provided for gradual exit from servitude into freedom, and provided for the integration of slaves into society."[37] It acknowledged the existence of the institution as a progressive—rather than terminal—state; as such, Islam provided the means for enslaved people and their children to move beyond this status.

Islamic law regulated the way enslaved people were treated. An examination of the attitudes of varying Islamic sects can not only provide a better understanding of the range of experiences of slavery in Middle Eastern society, but it can offer insights into the way communities of enslaved people were structured and operated. For example, there are different approaches within Islamic jurisprudence as regards the marriage of enslaved people. Since an enslaved person could only enter into a marriage contract if he or she was free, a master's beneficence was key.[38] And, yet, while Shi'i Islam permitted a free woman to marry an enslaved person—or an Arab woman to marry a Persian man—Hanafi doctrine required both partners to be of equal lineage, ethnotribal ranking and social standing.[39] These kinds of differences affected social structures in areas where Shi'a was not dominant, as in Baluchistan where endogamous marriage was (and remains) prevalent and today's communities of Afro-Iranians are most heavily concentrated. By contrast, where exogamous marriages were more common it is possible to see the extent to which enslaved people's communities became integrated into the indigenous

5.1. Two children in the harem; the African boy is "Anis al-Daula's favorite." Courtesy of Gulestan Palace.

population. Furthermore, the Shiʿi school commended enslavement of people should be terminated after specific time period: "the Shiʿi legal school recommended that the Muslim slave should be set free after seven years of service."[40]

Rules governing inheritance in Islam also offer interesting glimpses into the status of enslaved people in these societies. While both Sunni and Shiʿi law recognize the right of inheritance based on the *valā* (or "friendship") relationship, the former gave greater proprietorial rights to former masters over their freed enslaved persons' effects than did the latter.[41] The circumstances governing and practical considerations affecting the disbursement of a master's or an emancipated enslaved person's effects varied within the various Islamic denominations and were dictated by religious leaders. In spite of widely divergent rules and conventions about aspects of inheritance, the laws regulating the relationship of a slave owner and his or her enslaved person as regarded ill-treatment were remarkably similar: that is, if the abuse was proven, an enslaved person was to be freed. For example, Nasir al-Din Shah's personal physician, the Austrian ethnographer Jakob Polak, observed that not only did enslaved people have the right to complain about maltreatment but that evidence thereof gave them sufficient grounds to request sale to another master. He was also interested in the vigilante solidarity that existed among enslaved people: for instance, groups of enslaved people were known to instigate court procedures against masters responsible for torture and injury by "swarming" the guilty party's residence.[42]

It is through an examination of various archival material including recorded narratives that we are given the best insight into slave-master relationships and the nature of slavery in Iran.[43] By its very nature, the basis of this relationship was a socioeconomic dependency that was regulated by law and religion. And yet while enslaved people had little choice but to comply with expected societal norms and mores, masters had more flexibility when it came to providing food, housing, health, marriage partners and, sometimes, education. Notwithstanding, it would appear that there was a degree of social pressure on masters to guarantee a certain standard of care for their enslaved people. Indeed, that a proportion of enslaved Iranians had become literate by the nineteenth century is evident in the many letters of request for liberation that remain extant. It was also not unknown for masters to cover the costs associated with sending their enslaved people on pilgrimage to sacred religious places in Iran and the Ottoman Empire (in particular, Mecca and Karbalā').[44] After his death, a master's enslaved persons were not cast aside; indeed, they were usually inherited.[45] Various religious conventions and laws regulated the ownership of an enslaved person's property (see above), but overall money and personal belongings were considered the master's property.[46]

Newly acquired young enslaved people tended to be renamed and were expected to convert to the religion and culture of their masters and adopted their faith, language, and customs.[47] For example, the uncle of the Bab,[48] Khal Akbar, bought a young boy, Masʿud, from Zanzibar who later became a leading proponent of the Bahaʾi faith. Masʿud in turn married an enslaved Ethiopian, who converted and raised their daughter in the Babi faith.[49] On her travels to Iran in 1849, Mary Sheil speculated that it was through conversion to Islam that many of the enslaved Caucasians in Tehran were able to take high governmental positions.[50] This was undoubtedly the case with Muhammad ʿAli Mirza to governor of Iranian Kurdistan, the eldest son of Fath ʿAli Shah, whose mother was a Georgian slave.[51] Similarly, ʿAli Asghar Amin al-Sultan, whose father came to Iran originally as an enslaved person, and who rose to the rank of prime minister in 1886.[52] The names given to enslaved females were generally associated with flowers such as Chaman Gul ("Lawn Flower"),

Gulchehra ("Flower Face"), Taza Gul ("New Flower"), Qadamshad ("Bringer of Joy"), Ziba ("Beautiful"), and Zivar ("Jewelry") while those for enslaved males with good fortune, precious stones and metals like Almas ("Diamond"), Firuz ("Victorious"), Mubarak ("Glorified"), and Bashir ("Bringer of Good Tidings").[53] There is little doubt that, as Troutt Powell has written, "the practices of naming and what the name a slave was given revealed about how his masters looked at him."[54] Surnames were usually associated with their place of origin: such as, "Gurji," "Swahili," "Zanzibari," "Sudani," and "Habashi." There is no evidence that slave names in Iran ever carried pejorative connotations.

The subordinate nature of their existence would have been reinforced in spite of any openness or relative freedoms that enslaved people might have enjoyed.[55] In addition to basic sustenance and shelter, masters controlled their enslaved people's sexual and reproductive functions; indeed, masters had the right to take enslaved females as concubines (*sīghahhā*) or include *ghulāmān* and *kanīzān* as part of a dowry.[56] Additionally, enslaved females could be given to favorite sons as wives. Dominance was usually expressed in terms of punishment—with the most common being banishment.[57] When an enslaved person was expelled from his or her master's house, the absence of a letter of freedom forever excluded him or her from society. Indeed, not only was it socially unacceptable for any free enslaved person to be without such a letter but, moreover, it was assumed he or she had committed a wrongful act.[58] Like banishment, repudiation was a form of liberation that cut an enslaved person adrift within Middle Eastern and African societies.[59] The lack of a defined position in society was not only debilitating but also often a more powerful inducement to stay than threats of violence.[60]

Discipline for violating behavioral norms and expectations was usually meted out by masters, as when Nasir al-Din Shah expelled from his harem several enslaved females who had beaten each other.[61] But, enslaved people were also subject to the law and could be prosecuted by the legal authorities, as were a group of enslaved Africans when they insulted the *imām jum'a* of Isfahan while his coach entered the gate of the city.[62]

It is difficult to generalize about the treatment of enslaved people. Zilfi notes that the term "slave"

> is not entirely appropriate to Ottoman realities. Everywhere in the world that slavery existed, slaves' liabilities and vulnerabilities varied according to the wealth and temper of individual masters, the role of religious and state institutions, and the nature of employment, among other things.[63]

Her argument is applicable to experience of enslaved people in Iran as well because of religious injunctions and similar social structure. For this reason, she responds to Toledano's denial of the "good-treatment thesis"[64] by pointing to an extensive body of historiographical literature (including primary source accounts by European observers) that attests to slavery's "mild" character in the Middle East. She adds that "Toledano has challenged the premises and standpoints of the benign school, but the nineteenth century's generalized verdict has been difficult to overturn with regard to the Ottoman Empire's central provinces."[65]

Although enslaved people served their masters, the overall picture of slave-master relationships highlights the fact that enslaved people generally enjoyed a degree of interaction within their masters' households. Some were even able to branch out into free society. Ultimately, kinship networks established by enslaved people with their masters and members of their communities facilitated their eventual transition from enslavement to freedom. It, however, should be noted that slave-master relationships were based on power inequity, and maltreatment was not uncommon, in which case could result in the slave's flight.

ENSLAVED PEOPLE IN THE HAREM

The most important sociopolitical institution of the Qajar dynasty was the royal court, comprised of the shah, queen, ministers, the harem, and the royal army headed by the shah. Here, the term "harem" refers specifically to the large private quarters attached to the royal family. Because of its hierarchical nature and the fact that various agents connected the household with the outside world and participated in imperial life, it is crucial to study links between the private and public spheres—the *bīrūn* and *andarūn*. Slavery in this multifunctional harem system was quite different than other iterations elsewhere in Iranian society.[66] As such, it is immediately obvious that those associated with harem life—enslaved people, eunuchs, servants, and women—were not voiceless, oppressed figures, but rather active individuals without whom the political system could not function.[67] Moreover, given the great operating expenses, the harem system served only elite members of society, including the shahs, khans, and other state officials.[68]

THE CHARACTERISTICS OF HAREMS

Harem slavery was distinguishable from domestic or agricultural slavery principally in that the enslaved people performed many of their duties indoors and were inexorably associated with domestic culture. Most Iranian houses were traditionally divided into two parts: the *bīrūnī* (exterior) apartment allocated to men and an inner sanctum, the *andarūnī* (interior) — or harem — which was the portion of the house devoted to women.[69] The royal *andarūn* comprised a large and beautiful garden and several buildings each allocated to one of the shah's wives. The bedroom was located in the middle of the building and was guarded by eunuchs.[70] The *andarūn* was a private space for the intimate social life of family members.

As per Islamic tradition, gender separation within the outer and inner domestic areas was determined by blood relationships; thus, women were not permitted to exit the *andarūnī* rooms until after the *quruq*,[71] when the shah or other master had sent out all men not related to the family.[72] *Quruq* was an announcement made by eunuchs that facilitated the separation of male and female spaces — in particular, ensuring that women were modestly covered or out of sight.[73] Only the shah and eunuchs could enter the *andarūn* unannounced.[74] A stranger could only enter following a eunuch's calling of the *quruq*. The duration women might be forced to wait could be considerable, and letters of complaint reveal the degree of frustration they felt.[75] Reliance on this social structure of separating spaces or domains maintained the integrity of the royal family: on the one hand, this system ensured that the royal family's purity and popularity with the public was safeguarded; while on the other, it secured the inside world from outside threat or contamination.

The world of the *andarūn* or harem was strictly regulated, with the service apparatus performing the crucial role of liaising and thus facilitating contact between the inside and outside domains on behalf of the women.[76] Importantly, it was a community of individuals whose tasks addressed the needs of the group. Residents of the royal harem were mainly wives, concubines, children, enslaved people, and free servants guarded by eunuchs.[77] The hierarchical nature of this system meant that the harmonious operation of the harem relied on the mutual loyalty and respect of its constituent members. As such, it was requisite that individuals subjugate themselves to the group and the royal system, observe strict control of conventional and customary relationships, and agree on the boundaries that directed interaction between harem members. At the pinnacle of this system was the shah, whose avowed authority was not to be contradicted.[78] Beneath him, strategies were devised as various individuals responded to the limitations and boundaries of their lives. Although their status was most lowly in the harem institution, the experiences of the many enslaved people are as vivid and evocative as any other member and are, as such, highly informative.

RACIAL DIVERSITY

Enslaved people in the harem were male and female, white and black, brought to the royal court from far and wide. Some were purchased by local governors and sent to the harem as gifts, and some were "booty" taken in war. Tribal chiefs even sent their daughters to the royal court to maintain political alliance with the government. The advantage of uprooting and detaching enslaved people from all social support groups and kinship networks was to guarantee their loyalty. Devotion and social detachment may seem paradoxical, but psychological and economic factors ensured that the slave-master relationship was maintained. Enslaved people's behaviors were formed within their master's institutions, where it was stressed that each enslaved person was a part of a single unit with shared objectives.

The centralized Qajar bureaucracy required a division of labor within the harem system. Enslaved people and eunuchs could be found in various positions: from manual labor and entertainment to protection as bodyguards and royal military slaves (*ghulām-i shāhīhā*) and nursing (males, *lalahā*, and females, *dadahā*).[79] Each, however, performed a specific duty under the supervision of older servants and eunuchs. Under administrative and bureaucratic arrangements, the functional patterns of the harem's occupants were coordinated and organized based on gender, status, and skills.

Enslaved people represented a variety of religious, racial, and ethnic backgrounds, including Africans, Turcomans, Kurds, Turks, Azeris, Shirazis, Qazvinis, Isfahanis, Georgians, Armenians, and Circassians.[80] Notwithstanding, preferences for certain enslaved people were articulated by individuals—as the specific reference of Nasir al-Din Shah's daughter Taj al-Saltana to a black *dada*[81]—or by tradition—as that a certain percentage of court enslaved people come from the ancient tribe of Alvar of Bakhtiyari.[82] Similarly, French traveler John Chardin noted, that from the sixteenth century, Georgians and Circassians were particularly desired for the position of eunuch and concubine: the women were valued for their beauty, while the eunuchs served overseers and bureaucrats.[83] Although it is undeniable that beauty was attached to fair or light complexions in the Middle East, Segal writes that "color prejudice, whatever its extent, did not preclude, in Iran as elsewhere in Islam, the humane treatment of black slaves, their frequent freeing and, for some at least, the relative ease of social assimilation."[84] Similarly, Zilfi asserts: "Color was undeniably important in Middle Eastern and North African slavery. . . . Still, it did not hold the same value as in the Atlantic context, nor did race play the structuring role that it did in the Americas."[85] She adds, notwithstanding, that while race and skin color did influence where an enslaved person was destined to work, racialized stereotypes did not dictate labor segmentation entirely.[86] Wills noted, "In Persia the colour of his skin brings no disfavor. The ordinary expression for an enslaved person is a 'black brother.'"[87]

We also read of the huge and racially diverse harems of several generations of the Qajar shahs. For instance, Fath 'Ali Shah had a costly entourage of between three hundred and one thousand African, Georgian, Turcoman, Armenian, Jewish, and Iranian enslaved people, eunuchs, and servants.[88] In addition to his four legal wives, it is reported that he had seven hundred women and six hundred children in the harem.[89] Indeed, his son, Muhammad 'Ali Mirza, the governor of Iranian Kurdistan, was born to one of his Georgian concubines.[90] In the next generation, Nasir al-Din Shah kept two thousand women, including *kanīzān*, female servants, 108 concubines,[91] and four legal wives.[92] These included Africans, Turcomans, Kurds, Turks, Azeris, Shirazis, Qazvinis, Isfahanis, and two Circassians, whom he had bought on one of his trips.

5.2. African eunuchs (from left: Kalbi, Salman, Sulayman, Hasan, Ghulam 'Ali, Balal), princes, and children in the harem. Courtesy of Gulestan Palace.

5.3a. "Insane Circassian" (right) and Shokat. Courtesy of Gulestan Palace.

Although the harem's occupants were racially and ethnically diverse, they asserted their individuality within the context of established behavioral patterns. Hierarchical ranking within the organized social system of each harem determined the responsibilities of each individual and shaped the relationships between the heterogeneous members of the harem. Within the framework of assigned tasks and activities, the members of the harem could maneuver, interact with royal members, and forge links with the outside world. The existing coherence and structured domestication of the harem allowed enslaved people and eunuchs to erect a framework that gave them opportunities to elevate their status and influence. Likewise, standardized patterns of employment paved the way for harem inhabitants to occupy sensitive offices in the palace working for the central government.

MEMBERS OF THE HAREM

Enslaved people, servants, and women formed a significant part of the royal court that centered on the shah; taken as a whole, they were vital to the existence, function, and development of the Qajar regime. Having an established and extensive harem was considered a mark of honor and dignity and was built upon the principles of advancement, wealth, and luxury. The harem system relied on free and enslaved servants being able to create alliances between the royal court and the outside world. Having access to both internal and external resources meant that they—even the lowest members—were exposed to a distinguished environment of arts, literature, fashion, politics, and entertainment. Moreover, as the domestic world of the harem was inexorably connected to the government and inseparable from its politics, membership could provide opportunities for social advancement and power.

The Qajars themselves inherited the tradition of employing enslaved people at court in a highly organized and bureaucratic fashion from the Safavids. Sharing the same court language, Turkish terms were used for administrative titles and to describe the harem system. For example, *qullar* was a term that referred to *ghulāmān* or enslaved people imported from the Caucasus region who were trained and employed in the court during the reign of Shah 'Abbas I[93] and later extended to Africans. These royal enslaved people enjoyed high status, honor, and prestige. The chief chamberlain or chief enslaved people (*qullar āqāsī*) and the chief of ceremonies (*īshīk āqāsī*)—or grand chief of ceremonies (*īshīk āqāsī bāshī*)—were regarded as part of the ruling elites, but the former was higher in rank. The chief enslaved person was in charge of the royal enslaved people and monitored their payments and finances, while the chief of ceremonies was in charge of governmental matters that took place outside the palace.[94]

THE GHULĀM-I SHĀHĪ AND MILITARY SLAVES

Both the Safavid and Qajar dynasties created armies comprised of enslaved people from various racial and ethnic backgrounds, including prisoners of war.[95] There were several special regiments created exclusively of one racial group. Shah 'Abbas, for instance, inaugurated a group of ten thousand white enslaved people.[96] As part of his military reform in the early seventeenth century, he created a contingent of personal bodyguards—called the shah's enslaved people (the *ghulām-i shāhī*)—who supplemented the standing army.[97] Traditionally consisting of enslaved Africans and members of communities like the Bakhtiyaris,[98] hereafter this group came to include young enslaved Georgians and Circassians as well.[99] One of the first steps in realizing this transition was having one hundred castrated Georgians and, after their military training, assigning a *yūzbāshī* (chief of one hundred personnel) to oversee them.[100]

After the defeat of Russia in 1803, Fath 'Ali Shah employed a group of captive Georgian merchants as his bodyguards.[101] Indeed, by the first quarter of the nineteenth century, the number of the shah's bodyguards approached ten thousand, 30 to 40 percent of whom were royal enslaved people.[102] Distributed throughout his residence, they were always present among his camp of attendants. A contemporary record describes them as being well trained and "armed with a matchlock or musket, a sword, and sometimes pistols; and they generally [carried] a shield over their shoulder."[103] Those who served honorably and loyally over a certain period of time were promoted to positions of authority, as was the enslaved Georgian Yusuf Khan Gurji who became a military commander in 1807.[104] By 1821, the *ghulām-i shāhī* numbered between three thousand and four thousand. In the late nineteenth century, 1,250 *ghulām-i shāhīhā* were granted specific governmental titles, and their sons could inherit the position of royal guard.[105] However, even if they were trained, they were not always well turned out, as the prince of Shiraz once discovered: "Crowds of cringing slaves and ragged troops were summoned from their peaceable occupations, to stand in mock array in the courts of the royal residence."[106]

Throughout the period, *ghulāmān* could earn between twenty and thirty tomans per year, along with a privileged position in the royal court.[107] "When the king receives anyone in state," wrote English politician Edward Scott Waring, Esq., of the Civil Establishment, "his sons, who are very numerous, stand in a line from the throne; his ministers and officers of state behind them; and in the avenues are perhaps more than two thousand Gholami Shahees."[108] Wills also noted that during special ceremonies at the palace, "a few of the royal body-guard, or 'gholams,' with their guns in red cloth cases, slung over their shoulders, stood about in motionless groups."[109] They were also used to suppress internal or external military threats; indeed, they were considered the backbone of the state's military and administrative organizations. In 1835, Muhammad Shah dispatched 'Ali Asghar, the chief eunuch, and two hundred *ghulāmān* to fight in a campaign against the Turcomans in Gurgan and Astarabad.[110] Notwithstanding their elevated position, they were still subject to state law, as two slave guards (the *ghulāmān* of *kishīk khāna*) discovered in 1907 during the Constitutional Revolution, when they were publicly punished for robbery and murder.[111] Indeed, enslaved people were routinely expelled from the harem if they acted against religious rules or ethical norms.[112]

Nasir al-Din Shah had between two thousand two hundred to two thousand three hundred *ghulām-i shāhī*.[113] Among these, the mounted slave guards (the *savār-i kishīk khāna*, or *ghulām-i kishīk khāna*) were assigned to protect the palace and were headed by the chief of royal bodyguards (the *kishīkchī bāshī*[114] or *qullar āqāsī bāshī*). For effective administration purposes, *yūzbāshīhā* were appointed to head cohorts of enslaved Africans and Georgians from among their own racial groups.[115]

5.3b. African soldiers, referred to as my *kākās* (my brothers) by the master in the photo, December 1904. Courtesy of Iranian Students' News Agency.

Similarly, Sultan Mas'ud Mirza—one of Nasir al-Din Shah's sons and the governor of Isfahan and later of Fars, Kurdistan, Lurestan, and Yazd—organized an army called the *qazāq*, comprised of one hundred enslaved Africans. Drilled by two German soldiers, they were dressed in red felt uniforms with white trousers, polished black boots, a white fur hat, a golden belt, and a sword.[116] In the same way, the shaykh of Khorramshahr formed an army of four hundred strong soldiers of the Makrani and Arab mercenaries; this army was known as the Baluch-i Shah and was responsible for guarding Khorramshahr, the customs houses, and the shaykh's residences at Fallahya (Shadegan). These soldiers received payments from a portion of the shaykh's share of the crops gathered by all the residents in Khorramshahr.[117]

By the time Muzaffar al-Din Shah succeeded his father in 1896, the number of bodyguards had shrunk; indeed, he possessed only 162 *ghulāmān* and eight hundred slave guards (*ghulām-i kishīk khānahā*).[118]

EUNUCHS

Eunuchs played a pivotal role in the bureaucracy of the Qajars. Purchased to serve kings, nobles, and wealthy people in their harems and to protect the *andarūn*,[119] eunuchs often acted as overseers and administrators. In fact, the

5.4. "Mehrab," a eunuch in Nasir al-Din Shah's harem. Courtesy of Gulestan Palace.

development of Qajar bureaucracy reflects as much as anything else the autonomy gained by eunuchs in the outside world as within the harem. Their activities and roles included some of the most important internal, domestic, and external state-related responsibilities. They were called *khaujahā* and bore the title *āghā* (great), a title that signified respect and status as did the honorific dress (*khal'at*) they were given by the shah.[120]

Eunuchs played a central role in bridging the divide between private and public spaces for their genderless status and had done so since the pre-Islamic period in the ancient societies of Iran, the Byzantine Empire, India, China, and North Africa; thereafter, they were theoretically only available for purchase in markets outside Muslim societies since the Qur'an banned the mutilation of enslaved people.[121]

Once in the harem system, a eunuch's life expectancy and opportunities for social advancement was high.[122] Since his position required total allegiance, he could establish lifelong relationships of mutual respect and honor with his master; and with a generous income, he could enjoy the authority and prestige associated with financial independence. All together, eunuchs are reported to have earned more than one hundred thousand tomans annually; an individual such as Nasir al-Din Shah's eunuch, Bashir Khan *āghā bāshī*, could earn as much as two thousand tomans annually.[123]

The principal role of the eunuchs was to guard and safeguard the women and children in the *andarūn*.[124] Chardin described how well the system was regulated during the Safavid dynasty in the 1670s: while the first and second gates of the royal harem were guarded by the shah's porters and the captain of the gate respectively, the third gate, nearest to the women's residences, was guarded by the eunuchs.[125] Eunuchs regulated sexual practices and facilitated the harem's functions, such as escorting guests and alerting the women of the arrival of strangers.[126] Whenever the women ventured outside, it was their responsibility—along with other *ghulāmān* and *kanīzān*—to protect the women by managing their horses, holding umbrellas when it rained, and so on.[127] Remarkably enough, some eunuchs married—as when the Ethiopian *āghā bāshī* Bashir Khan married one of Muhammad Shah's wives—but this was inevitably for strategic reasons.[128]

By the end of the century, eunuchs had become increasingly ubiquitous in the royal household. For example, Nasir al-Din Shah's personal physician, the French soldier Jean Baptiste Feuvrier, observed that between 1889 and 1895 the shah's harem increased from about forty black and white eunuchs to one hundred.[129] Three or four of these served each of the first-ranked wives of Nasir al-Din Shah. Second-ranked wives had one or two eunuchs each, while third-ranked wives had none. The shah himself had seven special eu-

5.5. Eunuchs, servants (from left top: Faraj, Sulayman; down: Muhamad, Bahram, unknown, Kashi "the old dad," Ebrahim, and Safar 'Ali), and women of the harem. Courtesy of Gulestan Palace.

nuchs, with two guarding his bedroom and one possessing the keys to the *andarūn*. Another served the shah's wife Anis al-Daula.[130] After his death, the only remaining eunuchs were *āghā bāshī*, who was sent to Tabriz to serve the prince, and 'Ali Khan and Ahmad Khan, who were freed and remained in the palace.[131]

Beyond the sphere of the *andarūn*, eunuchs were able to exert often-considerable influence over politics. The extent of this influence on state affairs is seen clearly in the description of the lengths to which one of the 'ulama' Sayyid Muhammad Tabataba'i went during the Constitutional Revolution to alert Muzaffar al-Din Shah to the chaos in the country; his letter was hand delivered to the shah by the harem's trustee, the eunuch Haji Ghaffar Khan.[132] Similarly, the military commander Hassan Arfa expressed amazement in 1915 at the knowledge of politics and world events possessed by the Ahmad Shah's chief eunuch, 'Aziz Khan.[133]

Eunuchs were recruited to serve all ranks of nobility as well as highly placed merchants, although it was more common for the wealthy to employ old men (*rīsh sifīdhā*, literally: "white beards").[134] At court, they offered protection for the *andarūn* by warding off threats from outsiders.[135] They had opportunities for social and political advancement in advisory, protective, and educational capacities as well. Their roles included: grand chief chamberlain (*īshīk āqāsī bāshī*), chief of *ghulāmān* (*qullar āqāsī bāshī*), chief of eunuchs (*āghā bāshī* or *khauja bāshī*), and standing eunuchs (*khauja sarāyān*).[136] Some households employed several eunuchs, as the American ambassador Spencer Pratt described when he met Zahir al-Daula and a few other officials in 1886.[137]

It is not uncommon to read of those who, excelling in administrative positions in the harems, moved on to become governors of territories and provinces. Polak observed that Circassian and Georgian eunuchs were war captives brought to Iran by Aqa Muhammad Khan during attacks to the Caucasus region, some of whom were appointed to governmental positions.[138] The Georgian eunuch Khusru Khan Gurji was one such example: he had been brought to Iran by Aqa Muhammad Khan and ultimately moved through the ranks of the royal court to become the governor of Yazd, Kurdistan, Isfahan, and Qazvin as well as a number of northern regions.[139] His ascendancy came abruptly to an end in 1825 when he was ousted in a popular revolt.[140] In 1839, Manuchehr Khan Muʿtamed al-Daula, a political talent and eunuch from Georgia, rose through the ranks to assume various elevated positions in the government—beginning as chief eunuch of the harem and culminating in appointment as governor of Isfahan, Lurestan, and Khuzistan.[141] For some time, he was also responsible for the collection of taxes from northern regions and led an army of one thousand *ghulāmān* toward Bakhtiyari to collect outstanding revenues.[142] In the same way, Muhammad Naserkhan's appointment as head of the chiefs of ceremonies in 1855 was the first step in a process that culminated in his appointment as governor of Khorasan five years later.[143] Or, there is Ahmadkhan Nava'i, the deputy chief of ceremonies, who was appointed as the governor of Bushehr, Dashti, and the Dashtestan in 1862.[144] Polak writes that by the mid-nineteenth century, white eunuchs were waning in number and influence in Nasir al-Din Shah's harem; indeed, the last Circassian eunuch died in Tehran in 1856.[145]

The practice of employing eunuchs in harems and within the bureaucracy was common throughout the Middle East, from the harems of the Ottoman sultans and Saudi shaykhs to the Iranian state apparatus. They were rare and valuable commodities principally because the process of creating a eunuch was dangerous and had a high fatality rate.[146] Not only was the price of a eunuch often three times that of another enslaved person,[147] but only few actually arrived in the country annually.[148] Indeed, as intermediaries between

5.6. Fathullah, the eunuch. Courtesy of Mohammad Hasan Semsar and Fatemeh Saraiyan, eds., *Kakh-i Gulestan (Albumkhana): fehrest-i 'aksha-yi barguzideh-yi 'asre-i Qajar* (Tehran: Vezarat-i Farhang va Ershad-i Eslami, 1382).

women and outsiders, eunuchs guarded the honor and prestige of the royal family. Omniscient, they existed outside time and space and often assumed almost mythic qualities. Without them, the royal harems could not have existed.

THE FEMININE WORLD

The world of the harem—and the lives of women in it—has been misrepresented due to its very isolation and exclusivity. Indeed, the idea that these women were voiceless victims in a misogynistic world is utterly a creation of European Orientalists.[149] Rather, these women established their own power structures within the gendered harem space, based on customary and traditional social norms that actually empowered them within a male-dominated world.

These observations of women's lives in the harem were almost all relayed by nineteenth-century Europeans and provide insights into their attitudes as much as they reveal the actual nature of the harem. For instance, when Wills chronicled his visit of 'Ayn al-Mulk in the mid-nineteenth century, he focused on aspects such as hospitality and racial differentiation. He described seeing children being watched by enslaved female Africans as a white eunuch guided him through the *andarūn*. After taking a seat on the ground, the eunuch and Wills were brought a water pipe and tea by other enslaved Africans.[150] European women were also offered glimpses into this private world, as was the English traveler, writer, and first female member of the Royal Geographical Society, Isabella Bishop, when she visited the khan of Qezel Uzun in a northern Iranian village. Her observations are as equally telling of the author's attitudes as they are of the realities of the circumstances; for example, after an old eunuch accompanied her to the *andarūn*,

> the principal wife received me in a fine lofty room with fretwork windows opening on a courtyard with a fountain in it and a few pomegranates, and a crowd of Persian, Kurdish, and Negro women, with all manner of babies.[151]

WOMEN IN ROYAL HAREM

It is useful to begin by considering the role of women in the nineteenth-century royal harem, including the shah's mother, legal wives, concubines, and servants. What is most apparent is that beauty and skin color was not always a determining factor in establishing status and superiority. Since kinship networks—through marriage or by blood—defined women's prestige and ranking,[152] queens were commonly chosen for having royal links or because they belonged to powerful tribal groups. The harem system relied on a hierarchical relationships managed by the women, with the shah's mother at the apex.[153] She enjoyed considerable status and prestige—such as Nasir al-Din Shah's mother, Mahd 'Ulya, who possessed four eunuchs and twenty servants.[154] A wife of royal origin whose son had the right to the throne was considered first in rank and possessed a separate residence, thus signifying her authority as first-ranked wife in relation to the other members of the harem. The senior legal wives of the shah were next in rank. The concubines or temporary wives (*ṣīghahhā*) were last in rank.[155] Nasir al-Din Shah's favorite concubine was an enslaved Kurd known as Amin Aqdas ("trusted of the Sovereign"), whose job was to care for the shah's favorite cat.[156] It was not uncommon for some to have had such infrequent contact with the shah that they wrote letters requesting his visit.[157] Some were later married to government officials or were passed on to other members of the royal family.

The shah's wives were given jewelry and lived independently in separate residences with their own servants in his various palaces.[158] They resided in the Ark Palace along with the Saheb Qerania and 'shrat Abad palaces, but the most important wives were housed at the Niavaran palace.[159] The independence enjoyed by his wives was due in large part to the income they received, which in turn was managed by the customs house through the office of the *E'temad al-ḥaram*.[160] For instance, Nasir al-Din Shah's favorite—the daughter of a Kurdish miller—Anis al-Daula, was first a concubine and when promoted to legal wife received thirty thousand tomans annually for her personal expenses.[161] The highest ranked wives received monthly stipends of 750 tomans, while those among the second tier received between two and five hundred, and the third tier ranked received between 100 and 150 tomans.[162] With their incomes, these women could enjoy considerable financial independence and exercise power in the harem.

However, when Nasir al-Din Shah was assassinated on April 30, 1896, he

5.7. Women, African and non-African female servants, and one boy (from left top: Bolande, Zaqhi, Zahra, and Ebrahim). Courtesy of Gulestan Palace.

5.8. The 'Eshratabad harem. Courtesy of Mohammad Hasan Semsar and Fatemeh
Saraiyan, eds., *Kakh-i Gulestan (Albumkhana): fehrest-i 'aksha-yi barguzideh-yi
'asre-i Qajar* (Tehran: Vezarat-i Farhang va Ershad-i Eslami, 1382).

left five hundred wives and concubines behind. Initially, those with children
were permitted to stay, while the others were expected to leave.[163] In June
1896, all of them were dismissed from the harem—many returning to their
relatives—and were replaced by those of his son, Muzaffar al-Din Shah, who
already had four wives and eight concubines.[164]

KANĪZĀN IN THE HAREM

Kanīzān were a category unto themselves. They were involved in household
reproductive and administrative activities within the palace as well as serving
as maids, domestic servants, and menial laborers. The enslaved females did
housework, served food, brought the water bowl of the hookah (*qalīān*) for
smoking, and cared for his children; as wet nurses (*dāyahā* or *dadahā*), they
were regarded as second mothers.[165]

They also served as female dignitaries who represented the interests of their
mistresses. Like the shah's wives and concubines, they had the opportunity to
rise to high positions; if they reached his ear, they changed residences, earned

higher stipends and were granted the use of servants. If they were taken as their master's concubine, the children born of this union were legally recognized as being equal to the children of freeborn women. After the death of the master, any *kanīz* who had borne him children was granted her freedom.[166]

In contrast to the shah's wives, enslaved females were less confined to the harem compound. Their mobility and independence outside the prescribed boundaries determined the limits of their freedom and provided them with access to the public domain. The harem was a complex social world encompassing everything from politics to the arts, where members could express their individuality and talents therein. Indeed, enslaved females recognized that they could elevate their status through special skills that demonstrated a respectful subordination and affection to others.

The close relationships that developed between enslaved people and freeborn members of the royal household reduced many of the prejudices and social boundaries that existed within the harem. Enslaved people were responsible for training and nurturing royal children along with their own—

5.9. Females in the harem, including one African and one Circassian (from left: Zivar, Circassian, a nanny holding Hasan Khan, Bashi). Courtesy of Gulestan Palace.

5.10. Children in the harem.
Courtesy of Gulestan Palace.

5.11. African and non-African females and children in the harem (from left: Gulchehra, Jujugh, Haji the brother of the Circassian, Mahdi Khan the Circassian, Amin Aqdas, Pari, Zynab Oshani). Courtesy of Gulestan Palace.

and often together.[167] Senior enslaved females trained the younger ones to take on various administrative duties within the *andarūn* and maintain relationships with the shah, the royal family, and others. Nasir al-Din Shah's brother-in-law Mirza Muhammad Khan Malijak had two sons. Since the shah paid greater attention to the younger one, Ghulam 'Ali, he was attended by several enslaved African nurses (among them one white nurse, Jujugh, and one black nurse, Gulchehra), who brought him thirty enslaved children as his playmates.[168] These same kinds of intergenerational relationships existed elsewhere too: 'Ayn al-Saltana, the courtier and the grandson of Muhammad Shah, grew up and studied with his *kanīz*, Taza Gul ("New Flower"). When he married, Taza Gul was given to his wife; when the latter died, she and her husband continued to work for 'Ayn al-Saltana. Feelings of belonging to the royal family motivated many enslaved people and domestic servants to work collectively. Indeed, the Qajar harem was represented as an extended family to its enslaved people and servants.[169]

ARTISTIC LIFE IN THE HAREM

Enslaved people performing as singers and dancers for the amusement of the rich in the harems were described by Waring. Although there is an element of idealized Orientalism, it does give some insight into the role artistic expression played in this world:

> When it becomes dark, the carpets are spread in the open air, and with either his friends or dependents he prepares to pass the night. The *kuleean* [hookah] supplies the intervals of silence; and, if he can afford it, a set of Georgian slaves exert themselves for his amusement.[170]

Theatrical entertainment and the artful manner of dance and musical performance have been seen to indicate the extent to which harem inhabitants were empowered. Whether or not the case, artistic pursuits along with more academic studies were traditionally integral to harem life.[171] Georgian boys often were kept to sing and play instruments at various ceremonies.[172] Other enslaved children (*ghulām bachahā*) also played musical instruments, including the *dāyere* and *dunbak* (two types of frame drums) and the *santur* (dulcimer).[173] For instance, the African Haji Qadamshad led a group of dancers in a wedding ceremony:[174] "This Qadamshad wore a man's coat and trousers, and put a black felt hat on her curly hair, and on the street with the same hat wore a black *chādur* without covering her face."[175] In harem culture, sports were also popular. Eunuchs, like Haj Mubarak, performed as wrestlers before the shah.[176]

As we have seen, the harem was an exclusive space where the inhabitants worked, congregated, exchanged information, and learned about society and politics. Whether it was members of the large Qajar family or the most humble village khan, the harem was a safe domestic sphere where prestige and power were maintained largely through the efforts of servants and enslaved people who served as agents of communication between the *andarūn* and the *bīrūn*. This section has attempted to dispel the stereotypical representation and imagery of the secluded harem by emphasizing its crucial role in palace operations and administration. Moreover, enslaved people and servants transformed and revitalized the traditional culture of the harem by facilitating the integration of the various social, religious, and ethnic backgrounds within the *andarūn* culture. Importantly, a unified harem culture signaled the smooth functioning of the external social structure. Indeed, the patterns of dependency and empowerment that underpinned Iran's unique iteration of the slave-master relationship were so inexorably linked in the harem institution that it would take much more than the first abolitionist *firmān* of 1848 to reform them. Political transformations and changes in regime directly affected the harem system. Indeed, the Pahlavi regime quickly dispersed the Qajar court when it came to power in 1925: thus, when Prince Muhammad Hasan Mirza fled to Baghdad, the chief eunuch and trustee of the harem and all the women were ordered to leave the royal court. Among these, the shah's wives Badr al-Muluk, Khanum Khanumha, and Lili Khanum returned to their parents.[177]

NON-ROYAL HAREMS

Some members of the upper social groups, ranging from provincial governors to village khans, formed harems because they were a necessary means of establishing status within the hierarchical society. For instance, the description of the harem of the governor of Khorramshahr, Nusrat al-Mulk, is revealing. He bestowed on the two Georgian *kanīzān* he owned in the 1880s considerable material wealth: to Gul Fada ("Flower Garnish") he gave a large house with one thousand tomans, eight hundred sheep and eighty cows, while to Gul Hayat ("Flower Spirit") he presented the same amount of cash as well as about three thousand tomans' worth of property.[178] (It is noteworthy to compare these monetary gifts with the amount of tax collected annually in the entire province of Khuzistan: that is, approximately seventy thousand tomans.[179]) The household of the governor of Bandar 'Abbas, Haji Ahmad Khan, included many Georgian *kanīzān* and an Egyptian *kanīz*.[180] In 1890, Isfandiyar Khan, the leader of Bakhtiyaris owned a harem with several enslaved Africans.[181] Even though it was made of mud, Fathullah Khan was still able to lay claim to owning a harem in the village of Du Pulan on the Karun River:

> Within is a rude courtyard with an uneven surface, on which servants and
> negro slaves were skinning sheep, winnowing wheat, clarifying butter,

carding wool, cooking, and making cheese. . . . Heaps of servants, negro slaves, old hags, and young girls crowded behind and around, all talking at once and at the top of their voices.[182]

So intertwined did their lives become as a result of harem life that some masters married their enslaved people. Indeed, the shah's courtier, Muhammad Hasan Khan Eʻtemad al-Saltana, described how much he admired his own Sudanese wife, whom he had married after she was brought to Tehran as an enslaved person.[183]

Notably, the people who owned harems and possessed enslaved people belonged to various religious backgrounds. The Bab, leader of the Babi faith and precursor to Bahaism, who preached equality himself, owned many enslaved Africans.[184] Indeed, slave trading continued among the Babis until 1873, as Abul-Qasim Afnan recalled: "The last slave purchased by my forefathers was a Swahili youth named Salmán. He was acquired in Shiraz around 1870, well before the revelation of the Kitáb-i-Aqdas in which Bahá'u'lláh forbids slavery."[185] Harems were also common among highly influential and prosperous 'ulama' such as Aqa Sayyid Muhammad Baqir, who possessed many enslaved people and concubines.[186]

RURAL SLAVERY

The proliferation of rural slavery in nineteenth-century Iran was due to various factors, including the country's vast territory and socioeconomic and political conditions. More than anything else, the country's semifeudal modes[187] of production and patterns of land ownership along with regional differentiation and geographic isolation not only determined the conditions of rural life but also established an ideal environment for the perpetuation of slavery. Until 1931, the administrative and political division of the country included the four large provinces (īyālāt) of Azerbaijan, Khorasan,[188] Fars, and Banader and Kerman,[189] along with various smaller districts that were later known as governances.[190]

VILLAGE STRUCTURE

Traditionally, a village or local community head (khan) owned at least one and often several villages within a province; and each province was ruled by a governor (hakim). Each village consisted of several families—both free peasants and enslaved people—living in mud houses or mat huts, keeping animals and working the fields with primitive farming methods.[191] By the mid-nineteenth century, free peasants—as those in Kerman province or Baluchistan—were only nominally different from enslaved people: that is, they were inexorably bound to the land and could, with their families, be bought and sold.[192] Notwithstanding, the two groups differed insofar as peasants had their own holdings while enslaved people had no autonomy, but in practical terms there was little to differentiate the two groups. Indeed, in terms of livelihood, since cultivated crops had to be paid out to as rent to superintendents assigned by the landowners, in effect, peasants — like enslaved people — worked for free.[193]

In addition to providing able-bodied men for armed service or the militia, each village had to pay taxes in cash or in kind. Since there was no single, standardized national system of taxation, variations in collection and assessment depended on the khan.[194] The authority of the local khan was great and often arbitrary: for instance, in the province of Kurdistan, peasants needed his permission to marry. In other areas, they were required to pay a "freedom" tax in order to receive a permission letter if they wanted to move to and reside in another area.[195]

By the mid-nineteenth century, land in Iran was used in five main ways: as large-scale farms, royal lands, government lands, endowment lands, and small-scale farms.[196] Various political allegiances over the preceding centuries meant that shahs, aristocrats, and provincial governors owned most of the country's land. Not until the Land Reform Law in 1962 would this situation change.[197]

Peasant life depended entirely upon the availability of work within the village and was susceptible to the vagaries of nature and the whim of government.[198] In consequence, those who were free to do so often sought livelihoods elsewhere, thus leaving landowners reliant on forced labor and immigration. In spite of these general points of similarity, regional variations meant that the experience for indentured labor was different throughout Iran.

SOUTHERN COASTAL REGIONS

In order to meet seasonal labor shortages along the southern coast of Iran, enslaved people became a viable way of responding to the needs of various domestic, maritime, and agricultural industries, including fishing, the pearl industry, date production,[199] shipping, and herding.

Without a doubt, most enslaved Africans were to be found close to the ports on the Persian Gulf where they disembarked, frequently becoming seamen, fishermen, or engaging in other related industries.[200] Indeed, it was observed in 1875, that the number of enslaved people from Shiraz to Bushehr increased as one approached the coast.[201] Similarly, in 1890, the total population of Lengeh was reported to be about ten thousand, a mixture of Arabs, Africans, and Persians.[202] The total population of Minab in the summer, when immigrants from Bandar 'Abbas and Hormuz arrived, was about ten thousand, and in the winter, it was about seven thousand, during which time the population consisted of Persians, Arabs, and enslaved Africans.[203]

One of the most lucrative industries to the region was pearl fishing, especially in the nineteenth century; Iran's "pearl banks" were located along the coast between the ports of Lengeh and Taheri and near Kharg Island and the port of Larak.[204] Trading was another important maritime industry, with goods being imported from ports in the Indian Ocean and as far away as East Africa.[205] In the middle of the century, the chief secretary to the British government in Bombay Arthur Malet observed the presence of enslaved Africans who were employed as sailors in Bandar 'Abbas on vessels that belonged to Arab families.[206] Over the century, enslaved people also played an important role in the shipbuilding industry as craftsmen. Maritime vessels including the *Baghalahā* and smaller *bagharahā*, were produced at the major shipbuilding ports of Bushehr and Lengeh. However, when the British India Steam Navigation Company relocated to Sharjah,[207] many inhabitants migrated to the Arab states or to India.[208]

Regional concentrations of enslaved people can thus be explained with regard to their participation in various industrial or economic activities. For instance, the 'Abbasis (the people of Bandar 'Abbas) were a mixture of several different ethnic groups: Persians, Baluchis, Arabs, and Africans.[209] Even as late as 1934, the composition of the region had not much changed as Hassan Arfa noted: "Most of the inhabitants were living in reed huts, about one-third of them being Negroes who had been imported by the Masqatis."[210]

The Jask district was a division of Makran region, just inland from the coast. It existed under the jurisdiction of the governor of the Gulf ports, who appointed local rulers. In the early 1900s, two joint chiefs—Mustafa Khan and Mir Hoti—were reported to have collected taxes for themselves annually, including land and poll taxes as well as taxes on fishing boats and camels. They also owned enslaved people, some of whom were a part of their own personal militia.[211] Thousands of enslaved people lived in Darabsar and Marz, near Bashagard, who worked the land and served as fighters.[212]

Many of these enslaved people were herdsmen, but they also were used as fishermen, net makers, and were involved in date-grove cultivation and other forms of agriculture. Other villages within the Jask district included Kuh Mubarak, a village seven miles west of Kangan. Governed by Shaykh Ra'is, there were one hundred huts where both Baluchis and Africans lived. They were involved in the cultivation of wheat, maize, arzan, and dates and were responsible for herding camels, sheep and goats.[213] The smaller village of Yekbuni was inhabited by Africans, Baluchis, and Maids.

Although the Baluchis had long been involved in the slave trade, their demand for enslaved labor arose in the early 1900s, due to needs associated with date and wheat cultivation as well as fishing and husbandry. Similar socioracial patterns of habitation were found elsewhere, such as Zawaru—located between the Jagin and Gabrig Rivers, six miles from the sea—where enslaved Africans lived and were involved in herding and the cultivation of dates.[214] For example, fifty families who lived in Angahran village, near Bashagard, and were the enslaved people of ʿAlireza Khan were exclusively involved in cultivating dates.[215]

In the early twentieth century, the port city of Jask was divided into two: the European station that was headed by a political representative of the British government; and the Iranian village, consisting of mud houses and date-leaf huts that were inhabited by Baluchis, Sayyids, Mulaʾis, Raʾisis, Maids, and Africans. The latter were predominantly laborers or domestic enslaved people.[216] Elsewhere in this region were found diverse communities that engaged principally in agricultural activities (the cultivation of dates, grains and cotton) or husbandry (the herding of cattle, goats, and camels).[217] Notably, many village chiefs—such as Nur Muhammad in the Gabrig district—traded in enslaved people. This practice was waning by the early twentieth century, but it still impacted the socioeconomic character of these small coastal communities.[218]

SISTAN VA BALUCHISTAN

Surrounded by date palm trees, each village in Sistan va Baluchistan comprised a cluster of huts around a fort where the khan lived.[219] As elsewhere along this coast, the principal industries were fishing and agriculture, with many of the local peoples—Maids and Lattis—being either fishermen or cultivators.[220] Inhabitants living on the southeastern coast of the Persian Gulf depended on surface rainwater (*birka*), since the water from wells was undrinkable due to the Hormuz salt series.[221] For this reason, near the coast of Makran, the date was a principal item of cultivation, while cotton,[222] wheat, barley, millet, and jowar were produced further north, where there was more arable soil.[223]

Enslaved Baluchis and Africans were used mostly as domestic workers, cultivators, laborers on date plantations, and divers and pearl fishermen.[224] Enslaved people were considered to be a significant form of capital investment that returned profits. Landowners kept enslaved people, who were passed down within their families from one generation to the next. Slaveholder families sold enslaved people during economic reversals and to finance purchases of land or to pay their debts.[225] Importantly, while enslaved people were a constant feature of life in these areas, their presence was not necessary solely for reasons of labor—as there was a ready supply of unemployed peasants eager to work for low wages.[226] In these cases, enslaved people were kept often as a sign of prestige by wealthy families.[227] Thus, enslaved Baluchis and Africans, free peasants and serfs were all laborers, more or less treated the same. They had no hope for the future and no control over the land on which they worked since the government overseer could take back the land at anytime. Given the harshness of this life, many emigrated to Afghanistan, the Arab states, and Khorasan.[228]

Most of the land in Sistan va Baluchistan was government-owned and rented to hereditary tenants and governors.[229] Middlemen like khans earned their livelihoods from the profits garnered from the peasants and enslaved people working the land that was then paid as taxes to the government.[230] Known as *pa gav* (literally: "cow-foot"), this system of sharecropping developed for two main reasons. First, those working the land were not able to provide their own equipment or seeds and found it more efficient to work in groups of five or six.[231] Second, this system gave landowners more control over the means of production. There was no standard method for sharing crops, but one of the most common methods was the allocation of one-third of the crops to the landowner, one-third to the peasants/enslaved people, and one-third for the payment of expenses.[232] The inherent inequity of this system meant that few peasants thrived, and poverty was widespread.[233] Because it benefitted the landowners most, few farmed under a fixed-rent system.[234]

Sistan va Baluchistan was unique throughout Iran for the emergence of a social class known as the Bandi. This group descended from *ghulāmān* and *kanīzān*, who had been purchased from slave dealers or captured during internal wars with other Baluchi communities. They were formally attached to local village or community chiefs.[235] Many of these enslaved people and their families had strong links with the indigenous populations further inland.[236] Thus, in Jebal Barez, a mountainous district situated south of Bam and bordering Jiruft, there was a high incidence of interracial marrying between enslaved Africans and the local populations.[237] The fortress of Zangian in the vicinity of Kerman referred to inhabitants who had emigrated from Zanzibar.[238]

Over the centuries, various chroniclers and travelers described the peoples of this region. For instance, we read of the journey through Khorasan in the early 1820s of the Scottish author James Baillie Fraser, who noted, "slaves are made use of here as throughout Arabia, in the labors of agriculture."[239] Half a century later, British explorer and the first station chief of the Indo-European

Telegraph at Jask, E. A. Floyer, had similar observations about the enslaved people living near the coast in Bent who worked as field laborers.[240] In 1880, Firuz Mirza Farman Farma, the governor of Kerman, visited Rigan in Bam and commented that the majority of the cultivators were a combination of newly purchased enslaved Baluchis and those who had been brought to the village years beforehand.[241]

KHUZISTAN

Khuzistan was a fertile and productive province, due to the Arvandrud and the Karun rivers. The centers of Khorramshahr and Failiya were important for the large-scale cultivation and exportation of dates to India, Europe, and America.[242] The high date harvests produced in the region owing to fertile soil and ample water for irrigation from nearby rivers employed the large populations of enslaved Africans and indigenous Arabs.[243] For example, in Khorramshahr, Arabs were the majority and Persians, Jews, Christians, Sabians, Hasawiyas, Sayyids, Baluchis, and enslaved Africans were the minority groups.[244]

URBAN ENSLAVED PEOPLE

Politically, urban areas were under the direct control of government officials, and economically they were dependent on the goods produced in rural areas. Enslaved people residing in urban areas worked mainly as domestic servants after being appropriately trained.[245] Although data are scarce, we do have some information about the numbers of enslaved people living in urban settings. For instance, when Tabriz was occupied by Russia in 1827, it was reported that there were many household enslaved people.[246] In 1852, the total population of Tehran was 155,736, of whom 756 were black *ghulāmān* and eunuchs and 2,525 were black *kanīzān* and concubines.[247] It demonstrates that enslaved people of African descent constituted more than 2 percent of the city's total population. In 1877, during the reign of Nasir al-Din Shah, Mirza Husayn Khan was appointed to write a book about the city of Isfahan. He reported that the total population of the city was about fifty thousand, many of whom were enslaved Africans from Zanzibar and Ethiopia; some were free, but most were house-born enslaved persons who had become members of their master's family. With his permission, many enslaved Africans married — some of them to the servants of the master and the others to the native locals, which resulted in biracial offspring.[248]

In Shiraz and Kashan, enslaved Africans performed domestic tasks and household duties.[249] When paying a visit to Kashan in 1875, Arthur Arnold

observed the enslaved people's duties at the home of the governor's representative. Describing the scene of two enslaved Africans in white tunics and turbans carrying presents he wrote,

> Each of [them] carried on his head a circular metal tray, about a yard in
> diameter, on one of which there were six plates piled high with fruit, apples,
> pears, pomegranates, dried apricots, figs, and oranges, and on the other
> sweetmeats on an equal number of plates. . . . The slaves laid the huge trays
> at my feet, and according to custom, all held out their hands for money. . . .
> Nothing less than ten krans will satisfy the servants.[250]

A report by a member of the Anti-Slavery Society in Tehran observed in 1898,
between thirty thousand and fifty thousand enslaved Africans, half of whom
were Oromo women, lived in Iran, and in 1902 that the total African population in Iran was thirty-eight thousand, about 0.38 percent of the country's
total population of nearly ten million.[251]

Household enslaved people were common well into the early twentieth
century, right up until the abolition of slavery was legally mandated in 1929.[252]

ENSLAVED PEOPLE IN PUBLIC SERVICE

Enslaved people in urban settings were often distinguished from their rural
counterparts by having special skills or an ability to adapt to the demands
of different socioeconomic circumstances; as such, they earned more money,
achieved higher social status, and had some level of independence. Gender and
age were important factors that impacted an enslaved person's opportunities
and expectations. Indeed, the most common public service positions available
to enslaved females were those that involved traditional service-based femi-
nine activities, such as aesthetician, cook, and nurse.[253] The work available to
enslaved males was considerably more diverse, such as a description of jewelry
making in Lengeh reveals.[254] As in many nineteenth-century urban settings,
there were many factotum itinerants eager for work, as was the beggar who
helped Henry Landor with his luggage into a hotel in Tehran in 1900:

> A strange figure appeared on the scene. A powerful, half-naked African, as
> black as coal, and no less than six foot two in height. . . . He hangs round
> the hotel, crying out "yahu! yahu!" when hungry—a cry quite pathetic and
> weird, especially in the stillness of night.[255]

Some enslaved people participated in governmental tasks, such as the one
eunuch and three *kanīzān* who accompanied Mu'tamed al-Sultan Nazem al-

Daula while he was on mission to investigate the safety of roads from Qom to Khurramabad in 1890.[256]

ENSLAVED PEOPLE AND CULTURAL PERFORMANCE

Many enslaved Africans were selected not only for their age, gender, and physical strength but also for their musicality and ability to perform.[257] Indeed, African dance and music were prevalent in Iranian society, and the former enslaved people were gradually formed into distinct and specialized artistic groups of dancers and singers. This can be traced back centuries, when the Arab author Abu Uthman Jahiz (776–869) described the involvement of Africans in dancing, singing, and playing the tambourine in Basra.[258] Enslaved African entertainers were integrated in various social sectors and performed in a wide array of contexts: from the royal court and weddings to street performances[259] and healing rituals. For example, the musical and dance performances (called "*makarih*") in the desert in Lengeh of liberated Africans attracted great crowds.[260] In 1923, the French Orientalist Henri Massé observed the Zar spirit possession ceremony in Jask.[261] It was also routine for Afro-Iranians to participate in the festivities associated with the third Esfand (February 22), the anniversary of the coup d'état of 1921, by performing group dances accompanied by rhythmic African music.[262] Similarly, the Haji Firuz character in the Iranian Norouz (New Year's) celebrations was traditionally represented as a black man wearing colorful clothing and a pointed red hat who beats a small round drum called *dāyereye zangī* ("drum of Zanzibar"), dances and sings[263] in the streets. He was a symbol of happiness and joy without whom the celebrations would not be complete. Today, although some entertainers blacken their faces[264] to emulate the true African Haji Firuz, the practice is not widespread; it is only limited to Tehran, the capital, and very few provinces, and entirely absent in others (e.g., Sistan va Baluchistan and Hormozgan). *Sīāh bāzī* ("black person's play") is a play with the main actor *kākā sīāh* ("black brother") or *sīāh zangī* ("black person from Zanzibar") performed during the Iranian New Year. These customs were prevalent in the royal court culture and have become so deeply integrated that most Iranians are not aware that they are not ancient—and indeed are relatively recent imports. Although the Islamic government discouraged many such traditions, they are still practiced by some performers or beggars as a source of revenue.

CONCLUSION

Enslaved people contributed to a myriad of different positions in Iran during the nineteenth century, from agricultural labor to the military. They came from different racial and ethnic backgrounds but their cultural and identity formation was largely influenced by their ultimate destination, work, and gender. As with any slave-master relationship, those that developed in Iran during the nineteenth century bore certain characteristics that reflected social convention, religious injunction, and legal precepts. Arguably the best known is that of the highly stratified harem system as it existed among the upper echelons of society. Other slavery systems coexisted with the harem. Because many of these were less rigid and formalized, a study of them provides an opportunity to analyze the experiences of enslaved people.

The experience of enslaved people of African descent differed in Iran as opposed to that of their kinsmen in the Americas and Europe. Key here is that while race could determine initial socioeconomic placements for enslaved people, this differentiation must not be seen as doctrinaire and invariable. Instead, the heterogeneous nature of Iranian society meant that many of these initial classifications were not fixed and remained fluid. As such, it was possible for enslaved people of all racial backgrounds to achieve varying degrees of social mobility—as seen in the postemancipation period.

CHAPTER 6

SLAVE-TRADE SUPPRESSION LEGISLATION

PREVIOUS CHAPTERS HAVE DESCRIBED the extent to which Iran relied on enslaved labor to fulfill various socioeconomic, administrative, military, and political functions before the twentieth century. These enslaved peoples were sourced both from within the country and externally via the northern frontier or by sea from eastern Africa. Patterns associated with this centuries-long trade, however, changed in the nineteenth century. First, the Russian Empire's occupation of Iran's northern territories and its expansion into Central Asia and the Caucasus region around the middle of the century stemmed the flow of enslaved people and forced traders to look south to communities along the east and southern coasts. And, second, Britain helped reduce the importation of enslaved Africans through policing maritime distribution networks. Along with the royal decree of 1848, these factors and successive agreements helped suppress slave-trading activities in latter nineteenth-century Iran.

The suppression of slave-trading activities in Iran can be linked to the international, state, and domestic challenges the country faced in the nineteenth century as well as to national, transnational, and regional reform movements, idealism, and politics. This chapter explores the extent to which British imperial ambitions in the Persian Gulf and ports along the Indian Ocean accelerated attempts to realize the abolitionist mandate throughout the century. In this regard, diplomatic initiatives of the 1840s and 1850s that culminated in the Brussels Conference Act of 1890 will be analyzed. Results of this campaign included a series of *fatwahā*, treaties and *farāmīn* that began with the 1848 royal *firmān* issued by Muhammad Shah. This decree along with the subsequent treaties in 1851, 1857, 1882, and 1890 were intended to eliminate the seaborne trade of enslaved Africans. And, although these measures did contribute to the decline and eventual termination of the trade in enslaved Africans throughout the Indian Ocean and Persian Gulf regions, demand pressured traders to enslave indigenous Iranians—causing outrage within the country. The resulting impact of these external and internal abolitionist pressures forced the Iranian state to take increasingly decisive action against slavery, which culminated in full abolition in 1929.

SUPPRESSION IN THE PERSIAN GULF

The suppression of the trade in enslaved Africans in Iran was not achieved through enslaved people, rebellions, or revolts; rather, as in the Ottoman Empire, it was the result of diplomacy—"government-to-government negations," as Toledano has described it.[1] The humanitarian concerns that drove the international discourse were not those that resonated in Iran, where discussions about the slave trade focused instead on religious and political concerns and issues of nationhood. But, because the British Resident had exerted significant influence in the Persian court since the mid-eighteenth century and had at his disposal the means to realize abolitionist goals, Iran was obliged to follow the lead of Britain.

Trade, new markets, and a desire to minimize competition from European rivals initially motivated Britain to enter the Persian Gulf after the East India Company was founded in 1600, but it was not until the 1763 establishment of an official subdivision residency that its sphere of influence was guaranteed.[2] From his headquarters at Bushehr,[3] the Resident was empowered not only to negotiate with the other Gulf States and oversee commercial activities, but— more importantly—to facilitate the foreign policy ambitions of the Company from its superior, the governor of Bombay and later viceroy of India:

> As Britain began to deepen its mastery of India in the eighteenth century, the Gulf emerged a peripheral concern of India, rather than as a strategic concern of London. As a consequence, British policy regarding the Gulf up to the Second World War was primarily formulated and conducted by the Government of India and not Whitehall.[4]

As such, Britain's presence in the Persian Gulf in the mid-nineteenth century pivoted on its commercial interests—and later political ambitions.[5] It was preoccupied with protecting its trade routes in the Indian Ocean and safeguarding its territorial suzerainty over the Indian subcontinent.

Scholars and historians agree that the abolitionist campaign in the Indian Ocean grew out of an antislavery discourse that had begun by European philosophers, social reformers, and political economists. Beginning in the mideighteenth century, the British abolitionist movement culminated in the Act of Abolition of 1833. Although there is debate, most scholars tend to concur that the roots of abolitionism lie in economic circumstances and imperial ambitions. Few, however, adopt the progressive view of the Muslim jurist and political leader in India, Ameer Ali (d. 1928) who observed that slavery "has died away with the progress of human thought and the growth of a sense of justice among mankind."[6]

Critiquing Eric Williams's interpretation of abolition based on economic forces,[7] Drescher states that: "The key to the timing of slavery's ultimate demise in the Western economy lies not in its economic functioning but in its social peculiarity."[8] Instead, he notes that the antislavery movement gained its greatest momentum at a time "when the economy was growing fastest, where real wages were rising, and where the local labor shortage was most acute during the last third of the eighteenth century."[9] In analyzing the root causes of the antislavery movement, Blackburn observes, "the European anti-slavery prejudice tended to be egotistical and ethnocentric."[10] He also demonstrates that aligning moral and political arguments with the increasingly apparent fact that the trade in enslaved Africans was economically unprofitable inspired the British parliament to call for reform.[11] At the other end of the spectrum, Robin Law sees in the abolitionist project an inherently European imperialist strategy, one that held within its purview an alternative course of development for Africa. Further, he argues, the British measures to suppress the slave trade were those that specifically relied on the techniques of informal imperialism, including the coercion, intimidation, and annexation of other states.[12]

Whatever the root causes, the abolitionist movement was one that relied on considerable popular support. Indeed, events like the slave revolt in St. Domingue in 1791 that piqued humanitarian outrage against the institution of slavery and galvanized public opinion were those that inspired countries such as Denmark and even some North American states to take measures to end the slave trade in the last decade of the eighteenth century. The British parliament for its part responded to popular pressure by passing a bill in 1792 for the gradual end of the slave trade by 1796.[13] Even though the legislation never came into effect, that it received serious political attention suggests that the Abolition Act of 1833 was an ex post facto piece of legislation—one that placed a stamp of approval on a movement that had begun decades before: including an Act of 1807 that made illegal the embarkation and disembarkation of enslaved Africans within British territories; and, in 1811, another law banned the slave trade.[14] The historian Robert Harms pointedly notes: "When the British Parliament passed the Act for the Abolition of the Slave Trade on March 25, 1807, it transformed Britain almost overnight from the world's leading slave-trading nation to the world's leading crusader against the slave trade."[15] But, as regards the history of slavery in nineteenth- and early twentieth-century Iran, this European initiative and its subsequent legislation, focused on the seaborne trade in enslaved Africans.

In the Persian Gulf region, antislavery policies were achieved through the signing of treaties with the local governments in the Persian Gulf—and in so doing, British authorities were given opportunities to exploit hitherto unrealized political and judicial powers. For instance, when the sale of Indians was banned in 1812,[16] local authorities were obliged to allow the British to search their commercial and private vessels both at sea and on land. The realization of suppression legislation, therefore, provoked considerable disquiet among local rulers, seeing in it British ambitions to expand their imperial hegemony throughout the region.[17] And, yet in spite of Persian Gulf governments misgivings about the ramifications of the role the British played in the implementation of these policies, endemic political instability meant that local rulers had little alternative but to sign agreements and rely on the British bureaucratic apparatus to provide peace and security.

This British authority was further extended in the signing of other maritime treaties with Arab rulers in a region extending from the Horn of Africa to Iran's southern coasts, where the Qawasems continued to retain sovereignty.[18] In 1820, the shaykhs of numerous Persian Gulf countries (Dubai, Sharjah, Bahrain, Ra's al Khaymah, 'Ajman, and Umm al Qaywayn) agreed to abstain from plundering, piracy, and slave trading.[19] The sultan of Masqat, Sayyid Sa'id, agreed to desist in the sale of enslaved people to Christian nations in 1822. Thus, under the pretext of regulating slave-trading activities, the British were able also to establish a base on Omani territory and as such establish a stronger foothold in the region.[20] Hereafter, it was a matter of gaining control of seafaring vessels. For instance, when following reports of the Qawasems' involvement in transport of enslaved people from East Africa into the Gulf, the British in 1838 obtained the right to search sea vessels and seize those carrying enslaved people.[21] At this time, they also enforced a treaty by which any vessels carrying enslaved people that crossed a boundary running between Cape Delgado on the Swahili coast to Ra's Puzim on the coast of Makran could be confiscated. As part of the agreement, it was stipulated that while slave dealers operating within the boundary could not take their trade into the Indian Ocean, they were free to do so between Africa and the Persian and Oman Gulfs.[22] It was not until the middle of the century that the treaties provided for the punishment of slave trading. Thus, in 1845, Sultan Sa'id agreed to prosecute those who were engaged in exporting enslaved people from his African territories into his Asian territories.[23] A further treaty in 1847 with the Trucial shaykhs, present-day United Arab Emirates, was meant to enforce a ban on the importation of enslaved Africans into their territories.[24] Overall, while the agreements did not pertain to those already enslaved, they did help curb the excesses associated with importing from the African coast.[25]

THE ABOLITIONIST DEBATE

There is no doubt that the only way the suppression of the seaborne trade in enslaved Africans could be enforced was through Britain's superior naval presence—but the means to achieve this presence relied on extensive diplomatic negotiations with the Iranian government.[26] In 1841, British Foreign Secretary Lord Palmerston instructed his ambassador in Iran, Sir John McNeil, to collect information about slavery and the slave trade in the areas under Iranian jurisdiction in order to identify the legal grounds for its termination.[27] Since the goal was the issuance of a royal edict or *firmān*, Palmerston counseled McNeil to "urge the Shah [Muhammad Shah] to extend his prohibition to the importation of slaves by sea as well as by land, and to the importation of slaves from Africa and India, as well as from the countries bordering upon Persia."[28] Although—in principle—the British sought to abolish the slave trade entirely, reality forced them to concentrate their attention on devising ways to block the transportation of Africans by sea rather than dealing with the institution of domestic slavery.[29]

Even though the two nations agreed to consider an abolitionist strategy, Palmerston predicted that Iranian religious and cultural customs and beliefs would present the most serious barrier. Specifically, he worried that slavery was more ingrained in Islamic than Christian cultures.[30] It is worth noting that, as Hakan Erdem has observed, "many British officials of all levels regarded slavery as an exclusively Muslim affair." In so doing they disregarded "the fact that Judaism and Christianity, before Islam, had also sanctioned slave-holding."[31]

Negotiations were delayed by Britain's role in occasioning the secession of Herat from Iran until 1846.[32] Facilitated by the efforts of Muhammad Shah's Prime Minister Haji Mirza Aqasi, McNeil's replacement Justin Sheil began to counsel the Iranian court to ban the slave trade in the Persian Gulf and prohibit the trade in enslaved Africans entirely.[33] In a letter of 1847, he wrote:

> Your Excellency, I respectfully write this correspondence to you following our discussion on the transactions in blacks. You are aware of the strong insistence of the British government to prohibit this obscene trade. As part of this process the British government solicits the support of the Iranian government in this praiseworthy act.[34]

Muhammad Shah would not consent:

> There is no necessity to press me so urgently on this subject. The Queen of
> England has ordered her ships of war to stop and seize all slaving vessels, and
> there is an end to the trade. No more slaves will be brought to Persia.[35]

Given the shah's intransigence on the matter, the British realized that
diplomatic pressure was not sufficient and thus adopted a moral position, emphasizing the negative humanitarian impacts of the slave trade on the African
population.[36] Since Muhammad Shah remained unmoved (claiming that
abolitionism contradicted Islamic faith and Iranian customs[37]), the British
focused on the impact banning the slave trade would have on Iran.[38] They
emphasized that Iranian slave dealers would incur heavy financial losses if enslaved Africans found on their vessels were liberated.[39] In response, the Iranian government complained that external interference like this would only
serve to undermine diplomatic relations between the two countries.[40]

Colonel Francis Farrant replaced Sheil after his recall to London in late
1847.[41] Negotiations between Farrant and Haji Mirza Aqasi were more successful, especially after the signing of the Treaty of Erzurum. Farrant wrote
confidently to Haji Mirza Aqasi:

> I have written and have had several communications with your Excellency on
> this subject, and your Excellency has given me assurances both verbally and
> in writing, that after the arrival of Meerza Jewad with the ratification of the
> Turco Persian Treaty from Constantinople that you would bring this subject
> [abolition] to a favorable termination.[42]

Throughout his commission in Tehran, Farrant urged his Iranian hosts to
adopt such a measure speedily.[43]

The turning point appears to have been the acknowledgment that if the
Ottoman Empire could ratify such a *firmān* in their dominion (as they did on
1 June 1847), then Iran could follow suit.[44] But before Iran was prepared to
do so, it needed to be assured that the legislation had been successful. This is
conveyed in a message relayed by Haji Mirza Aqasi from the shah:

> The Ottoman govt is equally a Mohamedan govt and the traffic in Negro men
> and women exceeds in that country all other places. Let them (the Britt govt)
> convey an intimation on this subject to the ports, and let them announce the
> answer to us. This exalted government will then give a suitable reply.[45]

Indeed, it was clear that slave trading would continue unless both countries adopted similar legislation.[46] (It was also understood that the effective implementation of abolitionist legislation relied on parity further abroad.[47]) But, for the time, the focus of attention was the Ottoman Empire: a country with which Iran shared both a common frontier and religious principles—albeit denominationally different.[48] Observing the actions of their Ottoman neighbors, the Iranians adopted a similar strategy: that is, a refusal to enact an outright ban on slavery as per Islamic conventions and instead to adopt "a policy of 'gradual abolition' by cutting off the supplies." The result was, as Erdem notes, designed to appease the British without challenging the religious scholars.[49]

Although the shah would not accept the European abolitionist model, he was prepared to adopt changes similar to those implemented by the Ottomans. His approach not only underlined the significance of religion as a reason for abolishing—as well as maintaining—the slave trade, but also demonstrated that it might be possible to observe the Sunni Turks' initiatives within the framework of the Shariʿa:

> Between the religions of Europe and our religion there is great distinction and difference, and we cannot observe or join in matters which are in accordance with their religion and in opposition to ours, why we wrote that the exalted English government should make enquiries of the Turkish government on this subject, was because that government being a Mahomedan state and in that country the traffic in slaves being much more extensive than any where else, we might observe what answer it will give, that then we may give a reply which should not be opposed to tenets of the Mahomedan faith.[50]

Following the Ottoman example would thus be its recourse: "The Iranian government should perform the promise it gave of imitating the example of the Ottoman Empire in this question."[51] Muhammad Shah was, however, not entirely convinced by the religious argument, suggesting that the institution of slavery was not necessarily a bad thing, since it actually increased the Islamic community, as Sheil explained:

> He affirmed that there was not the slightest doubt of the prohibition demanded from him being contrary to the Mohamedan faith, in as much as multitudes of people would be prevented from becoming Mussulmans, the penalties of which violation of the law equaled the rewards of those who obtained converts to Islamism.[52]

Perhaps unexpected, the response revealed the extent to which the example of the Ottoman Empire influenced Iran's decision to accept the abolitionist mandate.

Securing an agreement with Oman was not so successful in persuading Iran to follow suit. Traditionally a major supplier of black enslaved people from East Africa to southern Iran, legislation that curbed the seaborne slave trade would have far-reaching ramifications—especially given the range of Sultan Saʿid's political influence throughout the Indian Ocean and the Persian Gulf.[53] In 1847, Sheil wrote to Haji Mirza Aqasi explaining the agreement:

> The British government has lately concluded an agreement with the Imam of Muscat, which will come into effect on the 15 Muharram 1263 [January 3, 1847]. By the provisions of that convention, the trade in slaves and their exportation from the extensive African dominances of His Highness is prohibited under the severest penalties, and their importation into the territory he occupies in Asia is equally rendered illegal.

Continuing, he noted that British permission to establish military bases in Masqat to enforce the legislation would be of use to Iranian authorities too:

> And to give effect to these stipulations, British ships of war are authorized to seize and confiscate any vessels belonging to His Highness's subjects engaged in that trade. Her Majesty's Government considers it would have most beneficial influence that His Majesty the Shah should issue a ferman to come into operation simultaneously with the above convention, prohibiting the slave trade in the Persian ports of the Persian Gulf and authorizing Her Majesty's Government to enforce the commands of His Majesty the Shah, in the same way as has been done by the Imam of Muscat.[54]

Considering the implications of a blockade of Masqat and its possible economic consequences, the shah concluded that an abolition decree was no longer necessary: "Since no more slaves are to be brought, our merchants will not be able to purchase them, consequently there is no necessity to issue a prohibition to them."[55]

FATWAHĀ

Muhammad Shah's resistance is understandable when one appreciates the importance of Islamic institutions at this time in Iran. The mid-nineteenth century was characterized by an ideological conundrum in which materialistically based reform efforts challenged traditional cultural values and religious idealism. While the former were driven by the social and political mores of foreign powers such as Britain, the latter were safeguarded by the 'ulama' (or mujtahidin[56]). It was their duty to regulate daily routines in the lives of the common people through various *fatwahā* and decrees—the shari'a—derived from an interpretation of the Qur'an and the teachings of the Prophet and the twelve imams.[57]

The Shi'a 'ulama' also influenced political activities, including several occasions when they directed mass movements against the government and foreign intrusions into Iran. In addition to the foreign legations and consulates and the house of the shah's eunuchs and wives, any religious place—such as a mosque, shrine, or residence of the 'ulama'—was considered to be a sanctuary.[58] Challenges to the government often took the form of taking refuge at these places.[59] Not only did the 'ulama' have close ties with the people, but also they had a secure financial foundation through which their religious and political autonomy could be consolidated: by administering various Islamic almsgiving institutions such as the *waqf* and *zakat*,[60] and through endowments and donations made to the shrines in the holy cities of Najaf, Karbalā', Kazemain, and Samarra.[61]

Although the Qajar rulers theoretically possessed absolute power, in practice their authority was limited by the injunctions of the shari'a and by those who felt themselves to be custodians of Iran's religious heritage. It is for this reason that the abolitionist movement lacked momentum in Iran and the British efforts were resisted: indeed, the shah actually argued that in upholding the slave trade, he was adhering to Islamic law and articulated how its practice differed from that of other religions:

> If according to their religion [Christianity] this traffic is considered an abominable practice, in our religion it is lawful. Why should the things which our Prophet has made lawful to us be imputed detestable.[62]

He underlined the difference not only between Islam and Christianity, but also between Shi'i Islam and other denominations. In this regard, the examples set by other Islamic countries were neither necessarily relevant to Iran nor attractive to the shah. They were essentially divergent interpretations of the Islamic law: denominations could agree upon the Qur'an and the *sunna*[63] while differing slightly in belief and practice. Distinguishing between the various branches of Islam, he also wrote:

Turks are Sunni and they are in opposition to the Iranians. The Imam of Masqat is also from the Khawarej, and one level better than a *kāfar* [unbeliever]. Then, we, who are the leaders of Shi'i Islam will not follow them.[64]

Although Iran would later adopt the Ottoman Empire's policy vis-à-vis slavery, these socioreligious differences made it hard for the two countries to follow the same path.

Muhammad Shah also explained his prolonged opposition to abolitionism by suggesting that any interpretation of Islamic law was beyond his dominion. In a letter to Haji Mirza Aqasi, he explained:

> Buying women and men is based on the shari'a of the last Prophet.
> I cannot prohibit my people from something, which is lawful on the
> shari'a. It is clear that when the British ships prevent the importation
> of slaves, they will not be carried in, and Iranians will not buy, but when-
> ever they bring [enslaved people], then the people who are willing to buy
> will be able to do so. This issue is like that of the Georgians [enslaved white
> people]; now the slave traders do not bring them, and people do not buy.
> But I cannot issue a decree and sign an agreement which is against the
> shari'a.[65]

For this reason, he deferred to the mujtahidin on these technical issues of legal interpretation. This pragmatic approach was politically judicious in that no action would be taken until an authoritative religious decision sanctioned the end of slavery.

Supporting a belief that the consent of Iranian religious leaders was essential in the formation of a new law, Sheil asked Mirza Aqa to approach Mulla Mirza Mahmud, one of the 'ulama' of Tehran, for religious opinions on the issue of slavery.[66] The proposed question was this:

> What do the learned Doctors in Religion and the Law decree on the
> following point. If they should abolish the transport of black male and
> female slaves, and abstain from the traffic, is it any injury or not to the
> faith?[67]

A second question was designed to determine his general reaction to slave trafficking. In response to the decree, "Selling male and female slaves is an abomination according to the noble faith—'the worst of men is the seller of men'"[68] Aqa Mahmud replied: "No, it is no injury to the faith; moreover, this trade according to the law is one of baseness, to discontinue it is best."[69]

Other 'ulama', including Mulla Husayn Burujerdi and Aqa Muhammad Ja'far Tehrani agreed. Mulla 'Ali Kani's fatwa was less decisive:

> Trading in, and buying and selling male and female slaves is not unlawful, but it is an abomination, as is stated in the tradition "the worst of men is the seller of men." . . . If it is abandoned on this account, it is good, but if on account of its being unlawful it is wrong.[70]

The proposed question to Aqa Mahmud was the following:

> What do the learned Doctors in the Religion and Law of Islam decree on the following point: If a Mussulman should trade in, and buy and sell, Negro slaves, and should bring them by all sorts of deceits and contrivances from their own country; and they now desire to discontinue the trade and transport, is it an injury to the religion of that Mussulman?[71]

His reply was, "The act of selling men and trading in them is abominable, and it is certainly better not to do it."[72] Even though these 'ulama' generally encouraged abolition on the basis that the sellers of free men are sinful,[73] Muhammad Shah wavered and requested the conclusions of Ottoman and other Iranian Shi'a 'ulama'.

Sheil instructed Rawlinson, the British official in Baghdad, to search for a favorable fatwa by focusing on the mujtahidin of Karbalā' and Najaf.[74] He explained what he hoped to find:

> The decree should be very clear and concise, and the seal of the chief Priest should be vouched by other persons of repute, as otherwise its authenticity will be contested by the Shah. The argument to which I attach most weight is that a prohibition merely to transport by a given route is not illegal; although a prohibition to buy or sell might admit of that interpretation.[75]

One of the most prominent 'ulama' of Karbalā', Shaykh Muhammad Hasan, told Rawlinson that slavery was legal and "the temporal power cannot forbid a lawful act, consequently, such a prohibition would be illegal."[76] Shaykh Muhammad reiterated, saying,

> The transport of slaves is nowhere condemned or even reprobated in the Coran or the traditions. All acts are lawful except those which are thus condemned on revealed authority. The temporal power cannot forbid a lawful act. Consequently, the prohibition in question would be illegal.[77]

From the mujtahid of Najaf, he received this response:

> The possession of slaves is in accordance with the acknowledged, and long established customs of Islam. The practice is authorized by the example of the Prophet and his immediate followers, and is now recognized as praise worthy observance of religion. The tradition of the Imams' denouncing "the seller of men as the worst of men" refers exclusively to those who make a business of the slave trade, passing their whole lives in this particular traffic. As a mere abstract question of sale, there is no more harm in selling slaves than in any other species of commerce.[78]

More specifically, this religious leader indicated that "the prohibition of the transport of slaves from Africa to Iran by sea would not be illegal under the Mohammedan law."[79] In spite of Rawlinson's lack of success, Sheil was, however, able to obtain a fatwa stating that "a prohibition lending to impede the conversion of Pagans and infidels to the true faith is contrary to the precepts of Mohammedanism."[80]

Inconsistency in interpretations of Islamic law about the prohibition of the slave trade forced the British to propose the superiority of state law over religious injunction:

> Perhaps the best argument that could be held at Teheran would be to found upon the text [Qur'an] which enjoins obedience to the temporal power without specifying how that power is to be exercised, and which is always quoted in the East as authority for the divine right of kings. But this is a point particularly distasteful to the jurists [religious jurists] and which it would be fruitless to discuss with the chief Priest of Nejjef.[81]

Sheil thus wrote to the shah in the hopes he might implement limited laws:

> We are informed from religious educated people [the 'ulama'] that their buying and selling [of enslaved people], on the basis of shari'a, is lawful, but it does not mean that the prohibition of the slave trade is against the shari'a of Islam.[82]

He acknowledged that several 'ulama' of Tehran had decreed the traffic in enslaved people was not in opposition to Islam.[83]

In a much more powerfully worded message to Haji Mirza Aqasi, Sheil pressed for an immediate anti-slave-trade *firmān*:

According to the response of some of the Mullas and mujtahidin in Tehran, the importation of blacks is not against the Muhammad [Islamic] law. The Iranian government was uncertain about that one point concerning the mujtahidin's fatwa, which was eventually issued. Therefore your government's failure to issue the *firmān* will cause the British government to resort to other ways, which are not pleasant. Your cordial friend expects that the authorities of this government accept the request of the British government and issue the *firmān* without any delay.[84]

Muhammad Shah replied:

It is contrary to my religion and religious faith. He [Sheil] has written that Moollas have issued their decrees. Heaven defend us! One of the Moollas is Agha Mahmood, who the Minister says was one of those who had written (a decree) I showed the Minister his handwriting and signature the Minister did not write the question proposed to the Moollas properly, or ask it properly.[85]

His continued resistance led Sheil and other critics to conclude that political motives — rather than religious factors — underpinned the issue:

Moreover the decree obtained by His Majesty from Agha Mahmood had no bearing on the present question. That moolla merely declared that to prohibit religious war against infidels, or the capture in war of infidels by Mussulmans, was unlawful; but what connection is there between a religious war and the sale of pagan Negroes by other pagan Negroes. But I am combating a phantom under the name of religion, for assuredly it is not religion that deters the Shah from yielding this point. Some political motive must then be the impediment.[86]

Frustrated, the British could find no means to end the slave trade, as Rawlinson noted:

Slavery has been an integral part of Mahomedanism for the last 1200 years that it is hallowed by the example of the Prophet and all the Imams; that there are several passages of the Coran regulating the treatment of slaves that the plea of proselytism operates powerfully in its favour and above all that it is essential to the domestic comforts of Orientals, you will understand that a jurist of eminence will be naturally cautious in committing himself to written declarations of the law, which are obviously directed against it.[87]

Muhammad Shah held his position with two arguments. First, he maintained that a suppression of the trade in enslaved people would impede the conversion of unbelievers to Islam: "By prohibiting [the slave trade] I will prevent the conversion of five thousand persons into Islam; this will result in [both] my having a bad name and my perpetuating great religious sin."[88] Second, he emphasized the abolition as an act against Islam: "Those who do not believe in what God sent [Quran], are *kāfirun* [infidels], *munāfiqun* [hypocrites] and *fāsiqun* [profligates] . . . the three issues are in Quran."[89] Nevertheless, the British suspicion that politics—not religion—were key to the matter was confirmed by Haji Mirza Aqasi, as Sheil explained to Palmerston:

> Hajee Meerza Aghassee informed a person of my acquaintance that the opposition of the Shah was not really owing to religious scruples, but to the bitterness of his feelings towards the British government in consequence of the violation of its engagements with reference to Agha Khan Mehellatee,[90] the imprisonment of the Persian consul at Bombay, and the protracted negotiations with Turkey.[91]

Understanding that a fatwa was a necessary first step in the procurement of an abolitionist *firmān*, the British explored all the options; among these was the realization that the *fatwahā* issued by Iranian 'ulama' were more moderate about slavery than their colleagues' attitudes in the religious centers of Karbalā' and Najaf. And yet it is clear that British interference in Iran's internal affairs was key to Muhammad Shah's refusal to cooperate: indeed, it was strongly felt that such an agreement would bring Iran under more direct control of the British.

THE IMPERIAL *FIRMĀN* OF 1848

Because of the reticence of Muhammad Shah, the British delegation in Tehran shifted tactics: from implementing a policy of total abolition to one banning the importation of enslaved Africans within specific geographical boundaries.[92] Thus, when Taylour Thomson proposed the idea of only restricting the naval importation of enslaved people in June 1847, negotiations began to move forward. As a result, the agreement only altered seaborne trade routes—not those by land.

The royal response (as reported by Haji Mirza Aqasi) was later recalled by Sheil in a letter to Palmerston: "The Shah applauded this argument and promised he would give it reflection; and Hajee Meerza Aghassee said that now at length he had some tangible grounds for urging the Shah to agree to issue the ferman."[93] Indeed, two weeks earlier, on June 12, 1848, the shah issued a *firmān* in an autographed note addressed to his prime minister. It represented a limited transition from traditional practice to new law by following various religious and customary protocols:

> Your Excellency the Hajee let them not bring any Negroes by sea, let them be brought by land, purely for the sake of Farrant Sahib [Lieutenant Colonel Farrant], with whom I am much pleased; I have consented to this. On this subject write to the governor of Fars and Arabia/Persian Arabia [Khuzistan]. Surely on account of the goodness of Farrant I have consented otherwise some trifling discussions still exist between the English government and us.[94]

The following message was then sent to Lieutenant Colonel Farrant by Mirza Aqa[95] confirming the Iranian government's willingness to suppress slave trafficking by sea:

> With a view to the request made by you, my sincere and esteemed friend, and solely on account of the sincere friendship and good feelings I entertain towards you, I did not consider it proper to withhold or delay the fulfillment of your desire, and exerted my endeavors to pressure the existing friendship between the two exalted governments of Persia and England by laying your request in detail at a most fortunate time before His Majesty the Shah.[96]

The shah later summed up the legislation in a single sentence written to the British government: "We banned the importation of the blacks by sea."[97]

RESPONSES TO THE IMPERIAL *FIRMĀN*

In only prohibiting the importation of enslaved people from Africa into Iran by sea, it was understood that the shah did not intend to suppress the trade completely. It would be reduced, of course, because transportation by land alone was less profitable.[98] Interestingly, although the term "sea" in the context of the shah's *firmān* referred specifically to the Persian Gulf, it was understood to refer to all bodies of water. Thus, as Farrant observed, various regions such as Khorramshahr were included among those "sea" routes prohibited.[99] That said, the 1848 edict responded to the influence of external political pressures but had little impact on the institution of slavery for the next half-century. Not until 1929 was the trafficking of enslaved people completely blocked and legislation recognizing the equality of all Iranians authorized. Importantly, the 'ulama' did not contest the *firmān* and committed the country to fulfilling its pledge to end the slave trade. In reality, however, the mujtahidin had no grounds to oppose the law since it did not directly affect the internal socioreligious structure.

The shah issued two separate *farāmīn* to the governors of Fars and Isfahan and Khuzistan, southern provinces that were particularly susceptible to slave trading. The complementary nature of these orders undoubtedly helped to speed the process of undermining the trade in enslaved Africans in these regions. One *firmān* was addressed to Husayn Khan Nezam al-Daula, the governor of Fars: "From now on your Excellency should prohibit to merchants and voyagers the importation of Blacks by sea; except by land that will not be banned."[100] The governor complied by sending letters to his subordinates along the coast ordering them to terminate the importation of enslaved Africans at the ports and authorizing the British navy to search for enslaved people vessels. Notably, he did not refer to trafficking by land.[101] The British resident in Bushehr, Samuel Hennell, subsequently attempted to enforce the legislation by liaising directly with the leading shaykhs associated with this province.[102]

The other *firmān* was addressed to Mirza Nabi Khan, the governor of Isfahan and Khuzistan: "It should be forbidden to all people who were involved in buying and selling blacks imported by sea; and from now on, the importation of Blacks should be stopped by sea but not by desert."[103] The governor, in turn, sent letters to the chief of Khuzistan and the governor of Khorramshahr prohibiting the buying and selling of enslaved people imported by sea, explaining that this was wish of both the governments of England and Iran. He added that if Africans were to arrive by sea, they were not to be bought and sold.[104]

The problem of ascertaining who among the resident African population was an enslaved person—and if so, for how long—was a problem that the *farāmīn* sought to resolve through a process of ascertaining the individual's linguistic proficiency. If they had a reasonable mastery of either the Persian or Arabic languages, it was concluded they were longtime residents.[105] This strategy also facilitated the release of Africans on board maritime vessels.

In order to affect the ban, the British pushed for a policy of search and seizure involving Iranian vessels suspected of engaging in trafficking enslaved people. The strategy was first proposed by Hennell in September 1848[106]; and by 1849, it had become procedure that the British navy and the East India Company should be allowed to search suspicious Iranian vessels. Any enslaved people found on board were to be sent to India, where they would be freed, and the offending crews were to be punished by the Iranian government.[107] The British regarded naval patrols as an effective means of enforcing their abolitionist mandate not only in Iran, but also throughout the Persian Gulf. And, in so doing, they were able to extend their naval control of the area.

THE POLICY OF SEARCH AND SEIZURE

There is little evidence that the *firmān* was initially effective, given the number of enslaved people being smuggled into southern Iranian ports between 1848 and 1850. Indeed, the death of Muhammad Shah four months after the issuance of the royal edict meant that the validity of his decrees was questioned until they were confirmed by his successor, as dictated by custom.[108] Concluding thus that "the Shah's ferman is a dead letter, and that the trade is prosecuted without remorse,"[109] the British sought to conclude an agreement that would allow them both to detain slave dealers and free any enslaved people found on Iranian vessels. Although Sheil had resumed negotiations with the new Iranian Prime Minister, Amir Kabir, requesting the punishment of those who continued to import enslaved Africans, Nasir al-Din Shah did confirm the *firmān* in 1850.[110] The new shah articulated his belief that no further measures were necessary and appealed to the 'ulama' for their imprimatur.[111] This response provoked outrage from the British:

> There is no need to ask the opinion of the 'ulama'. This is a governmental matter not *mulla'i* [related to a religious scholar]. No doubt, the 'ulama' of Islam believe so many things are *harām* [illegal] and against the *shar'*, but, the execution of some people legal. They will keep quiet, when the [Iranian] government intervenes. They [the 'ulama'] should obey the sultan, the master of the country, in particular, in this case, the British government has requested the shah, and will only be convinced by his order [not the 'ulama'].[112]

The British felt that the 1848 *firmān* was insufficient unless it included provision for a mandatory inspection of vessels:

> I trust these examples will satisfy the Persian government that the ferman of the Shah, issued at the desire of the British government for the abolition of this traffic by sea, will prove null and useless, unless the Persian government consents to the request of Her Majesty's government that English cruisers should be allowed to detain Persian slaving vessels, and convey the slaves to a British colony devoted to this object, where slaves are freed and where they subsist by the voluntary labour of their own hands.[113]

The government believed that allowing British authorities the right to search Iran's vessels not only violated its sovereignty, but also established a dangerous precedent.[114] In fact, Prime Minister Amir Kabir articulated his concern that the Russian Empire might then also demand similar rights in order to end piracy and the slave trade conducted by the Turcomans on the shores of Astarabad and Mazandaran, thereby further expanding its sphere of influence in Iran's provinces bordering the Caspian Sea.[115] Protecting this area from Russian incursions concerned the Iranians as much as the British control over its southern regions.[116]

Considerable evidence of political intrigue can be found in Tehran during this period, revealing not only real threats to Iran's sovereignty, but also that matters of policy were being used as the forum for European countries to play out their rivalries.[117] For instance, British allegations about the passing of British and Iranian communications by the Armenian translator Jean David to Prince Nicolas Dolgorouki, the Russian minister at Tehran, provided concrete evidence of the two empires' efforts to undermine Iranian autonomy.[118] The British also remonstrated against the French, accusing them of fueling Iranian objections to abolitionism: "The late French mission at this court has I find filled the minds of the Persian Government with imaginary terrors on the subject of the 'Right of search.'"[119] Farrant elaborated on the circumstances in the following letter to Palmerston:

> I have lately been informed, my lord, that it is not on religious grounds that the Prime Minister founds his objection, but [that] he has been led to believe, I understand by the French party, that England is only anxious to obtain this farman to give her the "right of search" over all vessels belonging to Persia in the Gulf.[120]

For this reason, not only the Iranian government remained firm in its objections to the search-and-seizure policy, but also cited three other reasons. First, its merchants could incur financial loss if their vessels were stopped for inspection at sea.[121] In spite of assurances, there was serious concern about the impact of this policy on the lucrative commercial trade with India through the Persian Gulf.[122] Second, there were concerns about the violation of decorum, as Sheil explained in 1850: "Persian females returning from pilgrimage to Mecca might be exposed to rudeness by forcing them to raise their veils in order to ascertain their race."[123] Finally, Iranian officials feared a loss of their naval authority in the Persian Gulf if they accepted the policy, because it gave "the British government an inconvenient and preponderating influence and control over the maritime chiefs of the Persian Gulf."[124]

To justify the British position, Sheil obtained testimony from Bushehr merchants who supported the policy of ship searches at sea connecting piracy to the slave-trade debate:

> the movement of the British ships in the Persian Gulf led to the security of the Arab and Persian ports, and they have not caused any damage to anyone at sea. In contrast, they bring security and assurance to merchants who are suffering from the attacks of some of the Arab tribes, such as the Jawasim.[125]

Support like this was not enough. Instead, they increasingly turned their arguments to the issue of the adverse effects of slave trafficking in the Persian Gulf.[126]

The British believed that demonstrating evidence of violation of the 1848 *firmān* would influence the Iranian government to support the search-and-seizure policy.[127] They identified culprits, such as Haji Khan Dashti, the governor of Dashti, who had imported eighteen enslaved Africans into Bushehr. Even though Dashti was under the jurisdiction of the Fars province, it was rented to and ruled by an arbitrary and often a corrupt Arab khan.[128] Situations like this showed that unlimited power of local governors and their administrations in the remoter regions was probably the most significant impediment to implementing the state's law than anything else.[129] They also realized that while larger vessels were targeted, smaller boats that often evaded detection were also smuggling enslaved people.[130] Similarly, it became evident that enslaved people were being smuggled in on British ships.[131] The table below supports the claim that after an initial period of increased activity, the 1848 decree did have an important impact on the maritime importation of enslaved people into the region. However, the increase in the number in 1850 demonstrated the necessity for the implementation of the search-and-seizure policy. It is possible that the figures may have been deliberately adjusted to suggest that the policy was working.

THE 1851 CONVENTION

Amir Kabir conditionally agreed to the policy of searching Iranian vessels believed to be engaged in the trade in enslaved Africans — but on condition that an Iranian official accompany the British or East India Company naval inspectors. A slave commissioner based in Bushehr would manage this office. Most importantly, it was agreed that Iranian government vessels would not be searched.[132] Although this final concession was moot, consensus was achieved and the agreement was ratified in August 1851 for a period of eleven years.[133]

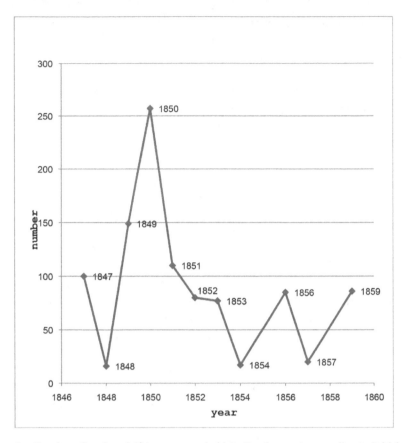

6.1. Number of enslaved Africans smuggled into Persian ports according to British reports (1847–1859)

It became effective on January 1, 1852. Any African *ghulām* or *kanīz* found aboard would be set free, and the Iranian government would be responsible for the punishment of culpable ship owners. This usually involved offenders losing their illegal bounty along with being punished and fined. Notably, all enslaved people already living in Iran were to be provided with passports from authorities at Bushehr if they were traveling by sea across the Gulf or to India so that their status would not be challenged.[134]

The onus was on British inspectors to ascertain whether the vessels they inspected belonged to countries that had signed a banning treaty. Detailed instructions were given regarding the detention of vessels. Once detained, the vessels and owners were to be taken immediately to a port of adjudication in Zanzibar, Aden, Bombay, or Masqat, and enslaved people were given letters of

Sources for Chart 6.1:

Samuel Hennell to A. Malet Secretary to the government, 1847, FO.84/692, NAUK.

Hennell to Malet, September 11, 1847, L/PS/5/452, BL, London.

James Tronson, November 19, 1847, L/PS/5/452, BL, London.

Gregor Grant to Malet, November 19, 1847, L/PS/5/452, BL, London.

Grant to Malet, November 19, 1847. L/PS/5/452, BL, London.

Mollah Hussein to Hennell, January 27, 1848, FO. 248/129, NAUK.

A. B. Kemball to Hennell, February 29, 1848, L/PS/5/456, BL, London.

Hennell to Malet, Bushir, October 9, 1849, L/PS/5/462, BL, London.

Alan Hyde Gardner to I. P. Porter, July 11, 1849, L/PS/5/463, BL, London.

Resident in the Persian Gulf to Farrant, October 8, 1849, FO. 248/138, NAUK.

Ameer-i Nizam to the Prince Governor of Fars, November 18, 1849, FO. 84/774, NAUK.

Hennell to Justin Sheil, August 14, 1850, L/PS/5/466, BL, London.

Moolla Ahmed to Jones I.N, July 15, 1850, FO.248/168, NAUK.

Draft to Sheil, February 9, 1850, FO. 84/815, NAUK.

Resident in the Persian Gulf, February 9, 1850, FO.248/138, NAUK.

Sheil to Ameer-i Nizam, February 10, 1850, FO. 84/815, NAUK.

Hennell to Sheil, June 20, 1850, FO. 84/815, NAUK.

Ahmed ben Hussein to Hennel, June 6, 1850, FO. 84/815, NAUK.

S. Hennell to Colonel Sheil, June 14, 1850, FO. 84/815, NAUK.

Hennell to Sheil, Bushire, August 14, 1850, FO. 84/815, NAUK.

Hennell to Sheil, Bushire, September 9, 1850, FO. 84/815, NAUK.

Hennell to Sheil, Bushire, September 10, 1850, FO. 84/815, NAUK.

Sheil to Ameer-i Nizam, October 16, 1850, FO. 84/815, NAUK.

Justin Sheil to Palmerston, Ispahan, August 8, 1851, FO. 248/144, NAUK.

Sheil to Mmeer Nizam, January 27, 1851, L/PS/5/469, BL, London.

Sheil to Palmerston, Ispahan, September 1, 1851, FO. 248/144, NAUK.

Hennell to Sheil, Bushire, July 9, 1851, FO. 84/857, NAUK.

Mullah Ahmed, British agent at Lingah, to Captain A. B. Kemball, July 5, 1852, L/PS/5/475, BL, London.

Draft to Taylour Thomson, Tehran, September 30, 1853, FO. 84/919, NAUK.

The British agent at Lingah to Kembell, June 6, 1853, FO. 84/919, NAUK.

Kamball to Thomson, September 14, 1853, FO. 84/919, NAUK.

Kamball to Robinson, November 7, 1853, FO. 84/949, NAUK.

Ahmed to Robinson, October 10, 1853, FO. 84/949, NAUK.

Ahmad to Robertson, October, 16, 1853, FO. 84/949, NAUK.

Thomson to Clarendon K.G, January 17, 1854, FO. 84/949, NAUK.

Statement of a boy named Meerjohn seized at Lingah, July 24, 1856, FO.248/168, NAUK.

Statement of a woman named Khyzran seized by the agent at Lingah, July 24, 1856, FO.248/168, NAUK.

R. Ethersey to Felix Jones, Bassadore, July 24, 1856, FO.248/168, NAUK.

Ahmed to Felix Jones, May 26, 1856, FO.248/168, NAUK.

Ahmed to Jones, June 26, 1856, FO.248/168, NAUK.

Abstract of collection accompanying Bombay Political Despatech, dated May 23, 1857, FO.84/1090, NAUK.

Mirza Abdul Kerim, slave commissioner, to Jones, October 30, 1858, FO.248/176, NAUK.

Jones to William Doria, Bushire, August 14, 1859, FO.248/183, NAUK.

Extract letter, No. 2, 6 July, 1859, FO.248/183, NAUK.

Extract letter, No. 4 to Resident, July 30, 1859, FO.248/183, NAUK.

From the Political Resident, November, 2, 1891, L/PS/20/C245, BL, London.

freedom. The vessel owners would subsequently be tried at one of these ports and would be punished, if proven guilty.[135] In 1851, the Iranian government appointed the son-in-law of the Minister of Foreign Affairs, Mirza Mahmud Khan, along with two servants and four associates, to oversee British activities, with the following instructions:[136]

> The first offence in the transport of slaves by sea is to be punished of 200 bastinado, and a fine double the value of the slaves; a repetition entails the same punishment with six months in jail, the third offence besides the above penalties, is to be accompanied by the confiscation of the vessel.[137]

From Britain's perspective, the 1851 convention was not only a great moral achievement for the abolitionist cause but also crucial in legitimizing Britain's presence in the Gulf. Indeed, the results were considered to be more significant and effective than those associated with the 1848 *firmān*, as Palmerston explained:

> The agreement concluded by Coll [Colonel] Sheil with the Persian Government in August 1851 authorizing the Detention of Persian Vessels carrying Slaves is more extensive and more important than the Firman of 1848 prohibiting the importation into Persia by Sea of African Slaves.[138]

Notably, the 1851 convention authorized them to enforce a more effective means of banning the trade in enslaved Africans and helping to ensure their liberation.

Still, there were sporadic reports of enslaved Africans being smuggled into Iranian ports—as for instance, of vessels coming into the port of Lengeh. In 1852, three prominent ship owners—Muhammad Khumes, Rajab al-Suri, and Haji Muhammad Saleh—were specifically identified as being guilty of perpetuating the trade in enslaved people in contravention of the legislation and were summarily charged.[139] Likewise, in 1854, 'Abdul Rahim, a slave dealer who had sold a girl and a boy in Lengeh was fined twenty tomans per enslaved person, and the enslaved people were given over to the British.[140] Persistence such as this sent a direct message that these activities were no longer tenable.

THE PEACE TREATY OF 1857

Recognizing their success half way into the eleven-year agreement of 1851, British and Iranian authorities agreed to extend the search-and-seizure policy for an additional decade: from August 1862 to August 1872. Article 13 of this treaty stated the following:

> The High Contracting Parties hereby renew the Agreement entered into by them in the month of August 1851 (Shawal 1267), for the suppression of the Slave Trade in the Persian Gulf, and engage further that the said Agreement shall continue in force after the date at which it expires, that is, after the month of August 1862, for the further space of ten years, and for so long afterwards as neither of the High Contracting Parties shall, by a formal declaration, annul it; such declaration not to take effect until one year after it is made.[141]

Prime Minister Mirza Aqa Khan Nuri accepted the treaty, and it was signed in Paris by Baron Cowley and Farrukh Khan on March 4, 1857—the same year that the Ottoman Empire enacted legislation to suppress the trade in enslaved Africans.[142] It is worth noting that negative reactions by the Ottoman 'ulama' to its government's legislation (which resulted in riots[143]) meant that the Hijaz region was exempted from the ban. This combined with the fact that there was no restriction on enslaved people being imported by land facilitated the legal importation of enslaved people by pilgrims from Africa into Arabia via Iran's western frontiers.

THE ERA OF "ILLEGAL" TRADE IN ENSLAVED AFRICANS

Although enslaved Africans continued to enter Iran, mid-nineteenth-century legislation focused attention only on those brought by sea. Along the southern coasts this was particularly problematic as they were usually conveyed by Qawasem and Omani traders, who remained a powerful naval presence in the Persian Gulf and Gulf of Oman.[144] Strategies for avoiding unwanted British interference and getting their bounty to market included disembarking the enslaved people in the Bay of Halileh, about ten miles south of Bushehr, bringing them to town, and boarding them onto new vessels headed to Basra. Another strategy involved transporting enslaved people in small boats by night to the Iranian ports, as explained by the Persian Gulf Resident, Felix Jones, in 1859:

> The Arabs of Oman have indeed discovered the deference we pay to Persia and the port of Lingah would appear to be gradually becoming the "entrepôt" for all Africans brought for sale from the great markets to the

south. Transferred by night in very small boats across the sea, they easily avoid our cruisers and agents.[145]

British reports detail these efforts.[146] Lorimer, for instance, estimated that there was a 2.5 percent (from approximately four thousand to nearly ten thousand) increase in the number of enslaved Africans brought into the present-day Saudi Arabia and the Persian Gulf between 1860 and 1861.[147]

Blatant violations of the new legislation caused the British to pressure the Iranian government into taking further steps to control the slave traffic more effectively. A first step by the Minister of Foreign Affairs was to replace in 1861 those charged with overseeing the implementation of the legislation, Mirza Mahmud Khan[148] and Ahmed Khan.[149] Their replacement was adroitly presented as the Slave Commissioner in Bushehr, the concession established as part of the 1851 convention. Mirza Sa'id Khan assumed this position until he was recalled to Tehran in 1876.[150] The extent to which the British Resident influenced the Iranian operation of government is evident in Taylour Thomson's description of this changeover:

> The reason assigned for the Persian Minister for Foreign Affairs for recalling the Persian slave commissioner from Bushihr was that as their services had not been required for a considerable length of time in the Gulf they had been instructed to return to Tehran with a view to financial economy.[151]

Importantly, the removal of Sa'id Khan from his office in Bushehr allowed the British to introduce a more assertive role in realizing its abolitionist mandate: one that obviated the need for an official Iranian presence aboard British ships as they patrolled in the Persian Gulf.

According to the 1857 peace treaty, Iran's commitment to a policy suppressing slave trading was only officially required until 1872, "after which it should continue to be in force until the expiration of one year after a formal declaration of annulment by Iran or Britain," explained Lorimer.[152] And, in 1873, the British authorities duly requested the Minister of Foreign Affairs propose a new slave-trade convention and bring the matter to the shah's attention.[153]

A near cessation in the importation of enslaved Africans into the Persian Gulf between 1873 and 1884 can be attributed to naval arrangements that more effectively enforced the mandate.[154] Indeed, the American ambassador to Iran, Samuel Greene Wheeler Benjamin (1883–1885), suggested that slavery, per se, no longer existed in the country, although the purchase of enslaved females for harems persisted.[155] In 1876, the British reported that the number of enslaved people imported into Iran had decreased considerably, even though the Iranian government had taken no new measures since the Treaty of Peace in 1857.[156]

The reality was that enslaved people were still being smuggled, but in much reduced numbers or under the French flag.[157] The latter practice began around 1875 and was usually by Omani traders coming with enslaved people from Africa to Sur.[158] The stubborn persistence of the trade in enslaved people demanded tougher measures, a treaty that would "put a stop once and for all to this traffic and place the whole question of the suppression of slave importation into Persian territory upon a new firm and satisfactory footing than it has hitherto been on."[159] The British required not only a permanent solution, but also one that guaranteed the right of search and seizure without requiring the presence of Iranian commissioners. The 1880 agreement between the Ottoman Empire and Britain about slavery was heralded as an example to Iran. Interested in the details of the agreement,[160] the Iranian government requested a copy for its perusal.

THE 1882 AGREEMENT

The treaty of 1857 was superseded by the 1882 Agreement, which dealt exclusively with the issue of the trade in enslaved Africans.[161] Although it had been the case since 1876, British authorities were now officially entitled to search all ships in the Persian Gulf without requiring the presence of Iranian supervisors.[162] They now dealt exclusively with enslaved people found onboard: those with governmental passports were released into the care of their masters while all others were declared free. Similarly, the provision that enslaved people be well treated meant that many enslaved people could claim maltreatment and take refuge at the British consulate. The matter of prosecuting the ship's owner and crew was left to the Iranian authorities.

And yet, neither treaties nor swift and harsh governmental penalties were able to bring a complete end to slave trading. A well-publicized example in 1882 illustrates the lengths to which some people were prepared to go to keep their enslaved people and the insistence of the authorities to prosecute malefactors: when the son of the customs agent at Shiraz, Haji 'Abbas, was foiled in his attempt to smuggle an African eunuch by covering him in a *chādur* (long veil or head-to-toe coverage), the enslaved person was freed and 'Abbas was indicted as an example for other state officials.[163] Indeed, Africans remained popular choices as enslaved people because they were cheap, especially when they came from famine-stricken regions. Records show that in 1884, the number of starving East Africans — mostly from the Zaramo and Nyika ethnic groups—imported as enslaved people had increased and were sold at the low price of about six shillings (8.3 tomans) each.[164] It was for this reason that, by the end of the decade, the need for an international mandate was felt keenly, and a conference was convened in Brussels to facilitate the successful abolition of slavery in the region.

THE BRUSSELS CONFERENCE OF 1890

The first international agreement prohibiting the trade in enslaved Africans on land and by sea was reached at the Brussels Conference in 1889–1890, with Nasir al-Din Shah's representative Nazar Aqa being one of the eighteen signatories.[165] The concluding Brussels Act of 1890 succeeded in mandating the suppression—if not complete abolition—of the trade in enslaved Africans in two ways: first, by cracking down on the seaborne slave trade wherever it still existed; and second by implementing various regulatory measures in Africa that included administrative, judicial, religious, and military services to prevent the inland movement of enslaved people and to liberate captured enslaved people therein.[166] The former included regulations about monitoring and boarding suspected vessels, the trial of seized vessel owners, and the protection of liberated enslaved people.[167]

The agreement included specific references to countries such as Iran that, while pledging to support measures suppressing slave trading, continued to perpetuate a system of domestic slavery.[168] Article 69 obliged these countries to adopt strict antislavery measures:

> His Majesty the Shah of Persia consents to organize an active supervision in the territorial waters and those off the coast of the Persian Gulf and Gulf of Oman which are under his sovereignty, and on the inland routes which serve for the transport of slaves. The Magistrates and other authorities shall, with this view, receive the necessary powers.[169]

Copies of the Act were sent to local authorities (the larger centers of Tehran, Isfahan, Shiraz, Khorramshahr, Lengeh, and Bandar 'Abbas) as well as to annexed regions in the south.[170]

And yet, in spite of this legislation, continued demand for enslaved labor meant that the trade in enslaved Baluchis along Iran's southern and eastern frontiers increased.[171] In the absence of effective regulations to combat slave trading,[172] the British repeatedly requested the Arab shaykhs desist—but took no measures to prosecute any guilty dealers. Instead, they deferred to the government, such as a letter from the British Resident in Bushehr to the shaykh of Abu Dhabi:

> I am surprised that you encourage men to act contrary to orders of Holy Koran by selling free born Muhamadans into slavery and allow such miscreants to sell them openly in your town. Since abovementioned correspondence I hear Nakhoda Seif ben Muhammad sold 3 Baluchis 1 man and 2 women in your town, and that when my agent representative reported matter to you took no action. I look to you to assist in suppressing this nefarious trade and shall be compelled to report matter to High Government and recommend drastic actions if you do not help.[173]

Although they had previously signed agreements to ban the trade in enslaved Africans, the shaykhs had been forced to look elsewhere to supply the demand. A statement by A. P. Trevor, the political resident in the Persian Gulf, acknowledges that the British understood the implications associated with the various agreements to suppress slave trading concerning enslaved Africans—not enslaved Baluchis:

> My object in writing this letter is to ascertain what line the Government of India desire me to take in regard to this Baluch slave traffic. I noticed that the slave trade engagement of 1847 signed by the Shaikhs on the Trucial Coast (No. XLI, page 178, Aitchison, Volume XII, part 2) is headed "Engagement for the abolition of the African Slave Trade" and though the words "and elsewhere" are inserted after the word "Africa" in the body of the engagement I think the latter is really meant to refer to African slaves. Further, while the engagement contemplates the seizure of vessels engaged in the traffic by H. M cruisers, the Shaikhs do not undertake any co-operation themselves. On the other hand, under article 3 of Agreement of 1839 (No. XL, page 177, Aitchison, Volume XII, part 2) the Shaikhs of the Trucial Coast agree to treat and punish as pirates any persons convicted of selling males, or females who are "hoor" or free, and this clause would naturally cover Baluchis and Mekranis who are "hoor" although it seems originally to have been inserted to meet the case of Somalis.[174]

Unable to force compliance, the Iranian government realized that it had to secure this region in order to prevent an escalation in the enslavement of its own subjects—something it achieved to a great extent with an outright abolition of slavery in 1929.

Notably, an increasingly strident desire to exploit Iran's rich oil reserves from the early twentieth century meant that the British position on enforcing abolitionist legislation shifted. Indeed, the Foreign Office's flippant remark that oil "is considered more important than slaves" illustrates the lengths to which they were prepared to cast a blind eye on slave-trading activities in order to secure oil concession rights from the various Arab rulers of the Persian Gulf and Aden Protectorate.[175] The League of Nations' slavery committees censured this behavior in the 1930s.[176] Although Reza Shah formally abolished it in 1929, slavery remained a feature in much of the Arab world until well after the Second World War. With Kuwait to impose abolition in 1949, three years later Qatar banned slavery, and in 1962 Saudi Arabia followed suit. However, slavery remained a feature of the area until the late 1960s. Indeed, the Omani Sultan Qaboos did not abolish slavery until he usurped his father in 1970.[177]

CONCLUSION

This chapter has provided an overview of Iran's attempt to accommodate the British mandate to suppress the trade in enslaved Africans for a half century— from the 1840s to the 1890s. Early voices for reform were inspired by a similar process that had begun in the Ottoman Empire and came to be reflected in agreements made by Iran, the Ottoman Empire, and Oman. Although the *firmān* of 1848 established a legal foundation for further prohibition legislation, the compromise that led to the selective banning of enslaved Africans trading by sea meant that other avenues for the importation of enslaved people were subsequently explored or intensified. As such, enslaved people increasingly were brought overland, notably by pilgrims returning from Baghdad, Karbalā', Mecca, and Medina. Similarly, with political developments along Iran's northern frontiers stemming the flow of available enslaved people and impacted trading routes in the Caucasus region, dealers began to enslave indigenous populations in greater numbers, especially in the south and east of the country. It was not until the ascendancy of the Pahlavi dynasty that abolition could be realized as part of modernization policies. Thus, when Reza Shah promulgated full abolition in 1929, the concept of an entirely free and fully self-autonomous population could be constitutionally etched on the Iranian consciousness. As Drescher notes, "Abolitionism did not halt imperialism, but it shaped even that procession of pride and power more profoundly than we realize. By the end of the nineteenth century antislavery had become the gold standard of 'civilization.'"[178]

CHAPTER 7

ANTISLAVERY DEBATES WITHIN IRAN

THIS CHAPTER EXAMINES the internal processes that encouraged the Iranian government to uphold a viable abolitionist mandate. Although attention will be paid to the process that led to full emancipation in 1929, much of the discussion will concern the political and judicial reforms that underscored its realization. In that regard, emphasis will be given to the relationship between Iran's response to slave-trading activities on its frontiers and the country's emerging sense of autonomous self-determination and national identity.

Political pressure and territorial occupations by both the Russians and British had undermined the operation of particular slave markets into and through Iran—by blocking the importation of enslaved Circassians and Georgians along the northern frontier and by hindering the entry of enslaved Africans through the Indian Ocean and the Persian Gulf from the south. The resultant decline in the supply of enslaved people meant that increasing numbers of indigenous people were enslaved to meet the continued demand of slave markets within and beyond Iranian borders. Although the situation worried many people, only a few individual religious leaders and intellectuals actually questioned the legitimacy of slavery; and it was through their efforts that political elites—inspired by a sense of national identity—were galvanized into taking decisive steps. As such, it will be shown that disparate reform voices— reacting to externally motivated events and situations—paved the way for the elimination of slavery in Iran. But, abolition could not become a reality until internal political developments could make institutional reforms possible within government and the judiciary.

ABOLITIONIST DEBATES IN ISLAM

While the implementation of legislation suppressing the trade in enslaved Africans was a British-led initiative in the nineteenth century, manumission—

the act of liberation by an individual master of his/her enslaved person—was a centuries-old practice based on Islamic law. Slavery is not forbidden in Islam; however, it is considered an abominable or disapproved act. An exegetical examination of the Qur'an allows El Hamel to conclude that "no single verse in the Qur'an calls for the acceptance of slavery as a normal social practice"[1]; in fact, not only does the scripture, "not support this practice, but actually places a high priority on manumitting slaves with the ultimate objective of abolishing slavery."[2] The reality was that the Islamic law was rarely put into practice.

Historically, the Qur'an abolished the pre-Islamic tradition of killing prisoners of war and only permitted them to remain in conditional bondage until they were ransomed. In the early years, the only legitimate way to acquire enslaved people, therefore, was through lawful war or self-defense against idolatrous enemies.[3] Slave trading was a later practice, first introduced into the Islamic world by Mu'awiyah, when he founded the Umayyad Caliphate in the seventh century.[4] It was he who also adopted the Byzantine custom of guarding his women with eunuchs.

THE BABIS AND SLAVERY

Muhammad Shah's 1848 *firmān* against the importation of enslaved Africans affected Iranians at many levels of society. Among these were followers of the Persian merchant Sayyid 'Ali Muhammad—known as the Bab—who founded a movement in 1844 that would ultimately become the Bahai faith.[5] Abolitionism was to become a powerful rallying cry of movements that, like this, emphasized the spiritual unity and equality of all humanity; indeed, in a statement from 1873, the half-brother of the Bab, Mirza Husayn 'Ali—known as Baha'ullah—was unequivocal: "Selling and buying female and male slaves is prohibited."[6] To Queen Victoria, he elaborated:

> We have been informed that thou hast forbidden the trading in slaves, both men and women. This, verily, is what God hath enjoined in this wondrous Revelation. God hath, truly, destined a reward for thee, because of this.[7]

His son and successor, 'Abbas Effendi (known as 'Abdulbaha'), reiterated these sentiments in a subsequent letter of 1911:

> We have known that you have prohibited the selling of slave boys and girls; this is what God has commanded in this unique epiphany (al-ẓuhūr al-badī').

. . . We have [also] heard that you have placed the supervision of consultation into the hands of the general public; well done![8]

The extent to which racial intolerance and discrimination were not characteristic of their milieu is apparent in the works of followers like Mírzá Mahmúd-i-Zarqání, who accompanied 'Abdulbaha' to America in 1912:

There exists among the whites in America a marked animosity for the blacks, who are held in such low esteem that the whites do not allow them to attend their public functions and think it beneath their dignity to mix with them in some of the public buildings and hotels.[9]

In the context of 'Abdulbaha''s message of equality and unity, Zarqání recalled the extreme examples of the racial intolerance. He described an incident when a fellow Bahai and resident of Chicago, Dr. Zia Baghdadi was evicted for inviting Louis Gregory, the son of an enslaved person from Georgia, into his home.[10] On another occasion, the negative reaction of a crowd to the announcement of the upcoming wedding of a white woman and an African American prompted him to write: "Incidents like these are little less than miracles; in fact, 'splitting the moon in half' would be an easier accomplishment in the eyes of the Americans."[11]

THE SUFI NIʿMATULLAHI AND SLAVERY

Traditional tensions between Sufis and the 'ulama' in Iran did not focus on the acceptance of the principles of Islam per se, but rather on its mystical doctrine that emphasized the goal of ecstatic union with the divine.[12] Thus, already at variance with mainstream religion, Sufism was well placed to challenge social attitudes and cultural mores, including those that supported slavery. By the nineteenth century, Sufis had become persuasive advocates for political and social action.

The penetration of Sufism into Iran—and especially of the Niʿmatullahi order[13]—began in the early years of the Qajar dynasty.[14] Indeed, already in 1819, the 'ulama' complained about its spread among the ruling elite in the northern Iranian city of Rasht. They demanded that Fath 'Ali Shah restrict the growth of the movement by observing that "now, because of this unrestrained group, nobody calls the *Jumʿa* and the *Jamāʿat* [congregational prayer on Fridays], and the verses of the shariʿa are destroyed."[15]

But, the movement did not gain a real foothold among intellectual elites and government officials[16] until Muhammad Shah was persuaded to follow Ni'matullahi Sufism by his prime minister, spiritual guide (*murshid*), and mentor, Haji Mirza Aqasi.[17] As Lesan al-Mulk observed, the shah believed Aqasi was "a pivot of shari'a and *ṭarīqa*" (the Sufi path to mystic knowledge).[18] Not only did Aqasi support modernization and Western education,[19] but he also secured the *firmān* for religious freedom in 1840.[20] In 1844, torture was prohibited.[21] Correspondence at this time with Lieutenant-Colonel Sheil illustrates the extent to which Aqasi advocated the banning of the trade in enslaved people[22]; indeed, both he and the shah congratulated the French ambassador, de Sartiges, following the 1848 Revolution on his government's reaffirmation of abolitionist legislation.[23]

Sufi doctrine, as expressed in the reformist practices of its policymakers, established the foundation for further antislavery measures, which was culminated in the 1848 *firmān*. But, it was not until the early twentieth century that spiritual and religious leaders began to speak of abolitionism in a more constitutionally binding way.[24] For instance, the Sufi fatwa prohibiting slavery that was issued in 1914 by Haj Mulla 'Ali Nur 'Ali Shah Sani, the spiritual leader of Gunabadi, a suborder of the Ni'matullahi order, states: "Nowadays, the buying and selling of human beings is contrary to the religion and civilization and all male and female slaves are free."[25]

POLITICAL AND JUDICIAL REFORMS

The government's first bold efforts to realize the banning of the slave trade began in 1848 when Amir Kabir was appointed as prime minister by Nasir al-Din Shah.[26] In the space of only three years, he implemented a series of radical political reforms that culminated in preliminary assertions of authority over the governors and the establishment of a more centralized government.[27] Among these was the creation of the government justice bureau (the *dīvān khāna-yi 'adālat*) in Tehran based on the Western approach to judicial due process and improved the treatment of suspects. He limited the power of the Islamic (*shar'*) court and extended the authority of the customary (*'urf*) court. Not only did he guarantee some rights to non-Muslim Iranians, but also he changed the direction of governmental policy toward the slave trade. It is important to note that Amir Kabir's actions were not entirely isolated. Indeed, they may be compared to Ahmad Bey's modernization programs in Tunisia in the 1840s, which included the abolition of sale of enslaved Africans.[28]

The policy of modernization was continued by Amir Kabir's successor, Mirza Aqa Khan Nuri,[29] but to such an extent that he was dismissed by the shah in 1858 and replaced by an accountable cabinet of six ministers, the

Council of Ministers (the *kābīna-yi shūrā-yi vuzarā*), headed by the British-educated Mirza Ja'far Khan Mushir al-Daula.[30] These first steps toward modernization and centralized authority not only gave Iran more autonomy and self-determination from the threat of foreign dominance, but also they paved the way for the reform in the provinces, where slave trading was particularly endemic.[31] In 1863, the nation's first supreme court (the *dīvān-i 'adlīya-yi a'zam*) was created.[32]

The political attitudes of Mirza Ja'far Khan's successor Mirza Husayn Khan Sepah Salar were forged while he served—like his predecessor[33]—as ambassador to the Ottoman Empire from 1858 to 1870, a period that coincided with social and political reforms associated with the middle phase of the Tanzimat period.[34] Upon his return to Iran and appointment as prime minister, he embarked on a series of reforms.[35] The first step was the establishment of a parliamentary system of government.[36] Thereafter, he set out to realize a mandate to improve the judicial system, chief of which were the creation of the supreme court (*darbār-i a'zam*) in 1873 and the so-called "Box of Justice" (*ṣandūq-i 'idālat*) in 1875. The latter was meant to regulate extrajudicial powers through the central government and to serve the needs of complainants, the police, jurors, and the court.[37]

Provincial reforms were necessary throughout the country, but were essential in bringing Iran's southern regions and northern frontiers under the direct control of the government. In addition to introducing a "Code of the Meritorious Reforms" (the *tanzīmāt-i ḥasana*) to help limit the authority of provincial governors and regulate their administrations,[38] Mirza Ja'far Khan established a ports administration in 1887 to govern activities in the Persian Gulf.[39] Like the "Box of Justice," these reforms brought Nasir al-Din Shah closer to his people and allowed him or his representatives to reinforce his authority—as did a manifesto published in 1888 that emphasized the rights and liberties of the people.[40]

A year after the assassination of Nasir al-Din Shah in 1896, another reformer Mirza 'Ali Khan Amin al-Daula was appointed as prime minister by Muzaffar al-Din Shah. He implemented the establishment of a governmental council (the *majlis-i a'yan*) to protect the people's rights during the reform process.[41] But, like his predecessor, his tenure was shortened by the 'ulama' and courtiers who forced his dismissal one year later. Unlike his predecessor, however, he was replaced—this time by Mirza 'Ali 'Asghar-khan Amin al-Sultan.[42]

Equality, freedom, and justice were the guiding tenets of the Constitutional Revolution. But, the movement was also inspired by events closer to home such as the 1905 revolution in Russia. In 1906, therefore, the demand of the reformists, 'ulama', merchants, and common people for the establishment of a House of Justice (*'adālat khāna*) was granted by the shah. Shortly thereafter, he further issued a constitutional decree laying the foundation for elected parliamentary government in Iran. The National Consultative Assembly (*majlis-i shurā-yi millī*) first met on October 6, 1906.[43] The impact of the formation of the constitutional parliament gave Iranians the confidence to expect justice and equality, including the emancipation of enslaved people. And, central to the Assembly's agenda for improving social and judicial conditions—including the abolition of slavery—was the establishment of an autonomous justice system that superseded the power exercised by the Islamic and customary courts.

Reza Shah[44] of the Pahlavi regime was the pivotal force in realizing the full modernization and centralization of Iran.[45] Indeed, modern civil codes were adopted by the first Minister of Justice, 'Ali Akbar Davar[46] (1927–1933) when he replaced Islamic courts with Western-style courts.[47] The social structure of Iran changed greatly under the first non-Qajar shah, as he accelerated the process of political reform and centralization that had begun decades earlier.

THE STATE AND THE SOUTHERN FRONTIERS

THE 1850S

Through their residency of the Persian Gulf, it has been shown that the British were central in facilitating the suppression of the trade in enslaved Africans into Iran.[48] But, it was the Iranian state that ensured the 1848 legislation was upheld. Not only were people encouraged to hand over suspect slave traders to the nearest British admiralty court,[49] but also the government enthusiastically prosecuted offenders who violated the law, relying on the testimony of local merchants and inhabitants and on the shari'a oaths of captains and crews of ships.[50] It also required governors of ports to restrict the slave trade within their jurisdictions,[51] going so far as to obtain written guarantees that any imported enslaved people would be confiscated and the importers fined.[52]

Thus, Prime Minister Amir Kabir ordered the governor of Fars, Firuz Mirza Nusrat al-Daula, impose a fine of three hundred tomans on the commander of Fath al-Khayr's ship, Muhammad Berdas, because he was accused of shipping eighteen enslaved people from Lengeh and Masqat to Bushehr in 1849.[53] So enthusiastically did Mirza Nusrat embrace his remit, that on one occasion he sent a rifleman with a letter to Mustafa Quli Khan, the governor of Bushehr, requesting the town cease its involvement in the slave trade.[54] Later, in 1852, when reports arrived of enslaved people being imported along the coast of Fars—in particular to Lengeh and Moghu[55]—Mirza Nusrat imposed a fine of 250 tomans on Shaykh Sa'id of the Qawasem Arab family, the late governor of Lengeh, which was paid by his son, Shaykh Khalifa.[56] In principle, the purpose was both to set an example for other governors and to show the superiority of Iranian state power over that of local chiefs.[57] Notwithstanding, the trafficking continued.[58]

Much of the problem in the Gulf region was the persistence of Omani shyakhs and the Qawasem of Ra's al Khaymah in slave-trading activities. Acknowledging the situation, Nasir al-Din Shah wrote to the British that Iran would be vigilant: "Of course, the dissolute Shaykhs should be fined and punished. Of course."[59] Thus, when, in 1850, enslaved Africans were reportedly being imported from Jidda into Khorramshahr by boats,[60] the shah sent orders to both Ardeshir Mirza, the governor of Khuzistan,[61] and other governors along the Persian Gulf, to import none of them.[62]

Nasir al-Din Shah attempted to prove Iran's commitment to prohibiting the slave trade by pointing to the country's loss of between 50,000 and 60,000 tomans in annual revenues.[63] The fact was that prohibiting the slave trade in the Persian Gulf required strength, financial investment, and technique—things that Iran did not have, but were the domain of the extensive and experienced British navy.[64] And, as part of its residency mandate, Britain had controlled these waters with the help of the British Indian navy for nearly a century.[65]

Especially after the middle of the century, the Iranian government actively attempted to establish an independent naval force—as much to fulfill its abolitionist mandate as to limit foreign influence and promote national security. Iran bought five vessels from France and brought them into Bushehr.[66] In July 1851, Amir Kabir instructed his agent Jean Davud Khan to purchase two powerful steamships from either Austria or Prussia for navigation in the Persian Gulf.[67] With its own navy, Iran could patrol the Persian Gulf waters and stop the illegal transportation of enslaved Africans into Iranian coasts without the intervention of the British.

THE 1860S UNTIL THE TURN OF THE CENTURY

A decade after legislation suppressing the trade in enslaved Africans, there were still reports of enslaved people being smuggled into Iranian ports.[68] Since the situation was particularly acute in the province of Fars, the government—in response—appointed Navvab Hesam al-Saltana Sultan Murad Mirza as the governor.[69] Immediately, Shaykh Khalifa, the Qawasem ruler of Lengeh was charged thirty tomans[70] for his negligence in permitting the importation of enslaved Africans to that port.[71]

With greater centralization, the government was increasingly able to establish its own sovereignty—and, thus, end the hegemony of Arab shaykhs—in these southern ports and islands. As such, the importation of enslaved Africans gradually diminished over this period. For instance, the suppression of slave trafficking in 1890 by Sa'd al-Mulk, the governor of Bushehr, was obeyed.[72] This he did by meeting with local people and merchants and notifying them to warn others of the negative consequences associated with slave trading—whether by land or sea.[73]

Establishing sovereignty was a lengthy process. Thus, when Haj Muhammad Mehdi Malek al-Tujjar was appointed governor of ports in 1886, he successfully negotiated with Abu Dhabi's ruler Za'ed Khalifa to have Lengeh defended against any invasions by the shaykhs of Sharjah and Ra's al Khaymah.[74] Just over a decade later, however, in 1898, Muhammad ibn Khalifa recaptured Lengeh. So well-received was this move that shaykhs like 'Abdullah ibn Faysal ibn Sa'ud, the ruler of what is now Saudi Arabia, sent gifts and expressed their opposition to the Iranian government. Even though Lengeh was recovered the following year, this political insecurity and instability had social ramifications on the local population.[75]

EARLY TWENTIETH CENTURY

In 1907, the head of the Customs Bureau for the South reported that although the establishment of offices in smaller centers along the coast was helping serve as a deterrent to the flow of enslaved Africans from via the Gulf of Oman into Iran, it had not completely stopped the traffic.[76] Even though an estimated two thousand enslaved people were still being exported annually, this was not enough to meet local and international demand.[77] For this reason, Iranians from Baluchistan (in the south) and Khorasan (in the north) were being enslaved to compensate for the reduced numbers.[78]

Although the situation caused considerable concern in Tehran, measures to suppress the enslavement of indigenous people by central government remained ineffective during the early part of the century. The shah's decree in 1904 that "Baluchis should not be sold and bought, [because] it is against the shari'a"[79] achieved little and provoked repeated outbursts like that of Nasir al-Daula, the Iranian government agent in Sistan, who vehemently complained in a letter to the Iranian Ministry of Foreign Affairs in 1917 that, "the trade in *kanīzān* [Baluchi women] is being continued in Iran, while blacks were liberated in Africa. Moreover, the buying and selling of people is against international law."[80] Refusing to acknowledge governmental incompetency, Mansur al-Mulk of the Ministry of Foreign Affairs replied with a surprise that the sale of girls was not reported to the central government.[81] Instead, the Iranian government claimed that the internal slave trade continued because little had been done to quell the demand for enslaved people in countries under

British control such as India and Afghanistan.[82] Six million enslaved Indians and Africans were estimated to live in territories governed by the East India Company in 1840. When, in 1843, the Company responded to pressure from Whitehall, it merely declared slave trading illegal, rather than enforcing its abolition.[83]

In Iran, the enslavement of indigenous peoples not only triggered controversy at a governmental level,[84] but also it provoked enmity among the religious communities—in particular, that of the enslavement of Iranians by Arabs. In 1921, Haj Sayyid Ja'far, the judge of the Islamic (*shar'*) court, wrote to Hesam al-Sadat, the governor of the port of Lengeh, asking for an end to the social disorder and insecurity that was facilitating the enslavement of southern Iranians.[85] Similarly, Shi'a 'ulama' suggested that the negligence of local chiefs and governors was responsible for creating a situation where Baluchis could be enslaved so easily.[86] Escalating sectarian tensions in the province of Baluchistan and other southern regions, therefore, was the final impetus for the government to resolve the situation decisively. Thus, in 1924, the ministries of Foreign Affairs, the Interior, and Defense worked together to bring the four hundred thousand inhabitants of Baluchistan under the control of the central government.[87] Henceforth, Iranian agents secured the southern ports and ensured that the trade in enslaved people ceased.[88]

THE STATE AND THE NORTHERN FRONTIERS

Developments in northern Iran regarding slavery were not substantially different from those in the south. In these regions, reforms also focused on suppressing local governors' autonomy as part of a larger process of national centralization; but here, they also had to address issues of foreign aggression. It has been shown that many Iranians were enslaved during Turcoman invasions because of the weakness and incompetence of the central government. Thus, the process of securing the northern frontiers led the Qajars frequently into battle with the Turcomans.[89]

In 1803, when Fath 'Ali Shah's troops defeated the Turcomans, not only were many enslaved Iranians freed,[90] but also land grants on the banks of the Caspian Sea in the village of Gurgan were given to loyal Turcomans if they moved away from the banks of the Atrek River.[91] Further Turcoman attacks in the 1830s led 'Abbas Mirza, the son of Fath 'Ali Shah, and Husayn 'Ali Mirza, the governor of Khorasan, to reclaim the border town of Sarakhs. A slave market, they found 450 Turcoman slave dealers and three thousand enslaved (mostly Shi'a) Iranians.[92] The many Turcomans captured in retaliation were later bought back by 'Allah Quli Tura, the khan of Khiva (Khwarazm), for five thousand tomans—with the proviso that slave trading in Khorasan was to be terminated.[93]

As in the south before centralized authority was exerted later in the century, the government relied on close cooperation with the powerful provincial governors of outlying territories.[94] Attempts to seed these positions with loyal retainers did not always work, as in the case of the appointment of Muhammad Shah's uncle 'Allah Yar Khan Asef al-Daula Qajar to the governorship of Khorasan in 1834.[95] Dissatisfied with what he considered a demotion, Asef al-Daula Qajar rebelled. Although he was exiled to Karbalā', his son and successor, Hasan Khan Salar, attempted to secede from Iran from 1847 until his execution in 1851.[96]

The Turcomans took advantage of this kind of political strife and insecurity to continue their border raids and enslavement of inhabitants. Indeed, throughout the 1840s and 1850s, they regularly invaded Khorasan and Turbat Haydariya. In an escalation of events after Salar's defeat in 1851, for instance, an army of four thousand Turcomans attacked and plundered several regions, but they were ultimately driven back by Hesam al-Saltana.[97]

The report of a conversation in 1851 between Reza Quli Khan of the Dar al-Funun school and Muhammad Amin, the khan of Khiva, illustrates the vulnerability of Iranians to enslavement in northern regions. Having met many enslaved Iranians requesting their freedom,[98] Reza Quli remarked:

> Although the people of Khawrazm [Khiva] are Muslim, they are hostile to other denominations. While in all territories believers and unbelievers coexist, in your city Muslims are taken into slavery.[99]

In response, the khan claimed, "Iranians insult Abu Bakr and 'Umar who are the caliphs of the Prophet; thus, our 'ulama' recognize Iranians as infidels and issued a fatwa for their enslavement and murder."[100] Although Reza Quli acknowledged that this insult had been a custom of the Safavid period, it was one that current Shi'a 'ulama' had banned. Notwithstanding, the khan said that he could not liberate the enslaved people because, having been purchased, their release would negatively impact the slave owners.[101] Thus, slave trafficking remained a feature of this area; indeed, in 1852, three hundred Iranians were enslaved in a single raid.[102]

By mid-century, the Iranian government attempted to impose greater control over this frontier and, at the same time, to rectify the situation of its enslaved indigenous people. The shah, therefore, issued a decree in 1907 stressing the suppression of the trade in Iranians.[103] Likewise, Prime Minister Mushir al-Daula sent an order to Mustufi al-Mamalek, the Minister of War, to discipline the soldiers found guilty of enslaving women and children in Sarakhs. He also demanded greater security in the borderlands.[104] Reports to the central government in Tehran from local agents in the provinces of Khorasan and Kurdistan about the excessive sale of Iranian women and children to Turcomans and Afghans by their relatives often suggested that this sort of transaction was considered to be a form of marriage.[105]

The situation became more complicated when, from the mid-nineteenth century onward, Turcoman territory became integrated into the Russian Empire. At this time, it was not uncommon for Iranian soldiers to be captured by Russian authorities while fighting Turcoman incursions.[106] As such, safeguarding cross-border activities, suppressing the slave trade and the repatriation of enslaved Iranians came to require the cooperation of the Russian government.[107] And, with the acknowledgment of the large-scale trafficking of Iranian women by the Turcomans, the Russian government did agree to commission its agents along the border to identify and repatriate enslaved Iranians.[108] Notwithstanding, circumstances often militated against better intentions to the point that, on several occasions, Iranians were forced to take sanctuary at the telegraph station on the Sarakhs border.[109]

Not until the 1880s was governmental control able to impose some degree of order to Iran's northern frontiers; indeed, well into the twentieth century, slave trafficking by the Turcomans continued. Efforts to respond to these incursions can be seen various military campaigns and attempts to secure villages with fortifications.[110] But, factors like poverty and insecurity forced many people into slavery.[111] As such, the slave trade benefitted more than just the slave dealers and was perpetuated regardless of governmental overtures.

CREATION OF THE MAJLIS AND THE END OF SLAVERY

CONSTITUTIONALISTS

The ideals of liberty and constitutionalism gained immense popularity at the end of the reign of Nasir al-Din Shah during the last decade of the nineteenth century. Although they were only marginal, the formation of secret societies following his assassination in 1896 reveals the extent to which Iranian society wanted change.[112] Within the mainstream, however, was the emergence of those seeking to establish constitutional democracy in Iran, as inspired by trends seen, most persuasively, in the Ottoman Empire from the mid-1870s onward.[113] The leading intellectuals in Iran—including Mirza Malkum Khan Nazem al-Daula, al-Afghani,[114] Mirza Saleh Shirazi,[115] and Mirza Fath 'Ali Akhund Zadeh—all unequivocally communicated their conviction that slavery, the slave trade, and castration not only violated basic human rights and freedoms but also should be prohibited.[116] They were also notable for their attempt to bridge the gap between the needs of society and their inherited cultural mores and doctrines. Thus, it was important for them to acknowledge that social revolution could make progress only if it was done so with reference to certain values and institutions.

Of these reformers, Akhund Zadeh is probably the most memorable today for addressing his fellow citizens in 1863 with the following lament: "Oh! Iranians! If you could realize the advantage of liberty and human rights, you would have never tolerated slavery and humiliation."[117] A vocal critic of Mustashar al-Daula's book *Yik Kalama (One Word)* (1875), he supported freedom of slaves, gender equality, and religious toleration.[118]

Malkum Khan was another highly influential constitutionalist: born a Christian Armenian, his conversion to Islam inspired him to develop a theory of constitutionalism for Iran.[119] He was deeply influenced by the Western constitutional thought he encountered during his time spent serving as the Iranian ambassador in London and Rome during the reigns of Nasir al-Din Shah and Muzaffar al-Din Shah. But it was the Tanzimat reforms he observed in Istanbul between 1863 and 1871 that were particularly influential, especially the calls for equality for all Ottoman subjects including enslaved people that underpinned the Constitution of 1876. As Erdem has noted: "The constitutional debate provided new impetus to the antislavery policy pursued in the [Ottoman] Empire."[120] In addition to his famous *Daftar-i Tanzimat (The Book of Reforms)*, Malkum Khan wrote more than two hundred other treatises on subjects including law, equality, the judiciary, freedom, and governmental reform.[121] He also founded the newspapers that advocated judicial reform including *Qānūn (Law)* in 1889 (published in London) as well as *Akhtar (Star)*.[122]

Articulating their complaints in works published in the Ottoman Empire,[123] writers such as Akhund Zadeh and Malkum Khan also criticized the government's failure to respond to the enslavement of their countrymen, especially those from the eastern provinces of Khorasan, Kerman, and Sistan.[124] These advocates of constitutional reform thus propounded the ideals of equality and antislavery, ensuring that they were inexorably bound in the tenets of any proposed legislation.

Over the course of the first decade of the twentieth century to the opening of the Constituent Assembly, the number of newspaper publications multiplied and Iranian reformers and intellectuals established more than ninety newspapers to voice these views on liberty, equality, and fraternity, including *'Adālat (Justice)*, *Mosāvāt (Equality)*, *Hoqoq (Rights)*, *Azādī (Liberty)*, *Akhavāt (Fraternity)*, and *Ādamiyat (Humanity)*.[125]

Of note, the Tehran-based *Irān-i No* (*New Iran*) published by the political activist Muhammad Amin Rasulzadeh (d. 1954), the theorist of the Demokrat Party, confronted the slave trade directly in stories like that entitled "Mr. Haji Mirza, The Slave Dealer" on October 20, 1909. Beginning with an attack on the "horrible act of the slave trade," the article then focused specifically on the case of an escaped *kanīz* named Ziba who had been given to Mirza by her master, ʿAlaʾ al-Saltana, to be sold. Outrage at her recapture was articulated in the following passage:

> Damn the life of whoever is the [slave] buyer! We would like to draw the government officials' attention to prevent the actions of such Hajis and ʿAlaʾ al-Saltanas. The government of Iran has signed the prohibition of the slave trade long ago and banned it.[126]

Three women responded the next day in the open letter "The Fervor of Iranian Women" by not only defending Ziba's right to escape because of mistreatment but also soliciting donations for her release. Rasulzadeh, for his part, praised the women for their contribution to Iran's future and suggested that the actions of ʿAlaʾ al-Saltana and Mirza damaged the image of a "free Iran."[127] Two days later, a subsequent article provided proof that Ziba had all along been free and lamented that:

> while in the twentieth century the rest of the world is struggling for political and economic rights [here] in the constitutional country [of Iran] we read news of a person who should not be sold like an animal.[128]

Another daily newspaper, *Nedā-yi Vatan* (*Voice of Homeland*), attempted to tackle similar problems through praising constitutionalism and criticizing Qajar despotism.[129] Published by the intellectual clergyman Majd al-Islam Kermani, it too focused on the problem of slavery, but with greater emphasis on the political ramifications. One such story described the sale of several thousand Iranians in the Kerman and Khorasan provinces to the Turcomans, Russians, and Armenians. Condemning governmental mismanagement through its inability to protect the frontiers, it levied blame at both the bureaucratic apparatus and high taxation for creating an environment that led inevitably to enslavement.[130] Deferring to one of the ʿulamaʾ Aqa Sayyid ʿAbdullah it requested people report cases of enslavement—and especially of girls from Quchan—for investigation by the parliament.[131]

RELIGIOUS CRITICISM

Support for abolitionism from Islamic religious leaders was also coupled with demands for constitutional reform and the creation of a parliament. Indeed, an Iranian official in the province of Khorasan wrote to the government: "Why does the trade in Muslims [Iranians] exist in the land of the King of Islam?"[132] It was notable that the religious establishment tended to ally with reformers from the lower social orders when protesting social insecurity, injustice, and the trafficking in Iranians. It was in this vein that the mujtahid, Sayyid Muhammad ibn Seddiq al-Husayni Tabataba'i, wrote to the shah requesting the establishment of a house of justice (ʻadālat khāna) in order to end slavery and poverty in the country:

> Last year they [government officials] took the daughters of Quchan in lieu of three rays [35.61 kilograms] of wheat tax that they [peasants] did not have to pay, then sold them for a high price to Turkomans and Armenians in Ashgabat. . . . [The establishment of a] majlis-i ʻadālat [parliament of justice] or a council comprised of [representatives of] all social groups of people where the shah and beggar are equal could bring justice for the people.[133]

He further explained the significance of establishing the Majlis and bringing justice to Iran insofar as it would end slavery.[134]

Chief among their demands was the creation of a constitution that would codify basic human rights and freedoms. Thus, one of the ʻulama', Haji Sayyid ʻAbdulʻazim ʻEmad al-ʻUlama Khalkhali, voiced his unequivocal support for political change, arguing that God created all human beings equally.[135] Similarly, Fakhr al-ʻUlama Shaykh Mahdi linked the creation of a constitution specifically with the abolition of slavery. Not only did he criticize a system that saw Iranian peasants selling their daughters in order to survive, but he also demanded the abolition of the trade in Habashi ghulāmān and kanīzān.[136] Mirza Hedayatullah ʻAllahabadi was aghast that the inhabitants of Quchan were forced to sell their children and wives to the Turcomans in order to pay their taxes.[137] He recalled having witnessed that injustice when a peasant family sold their three-year-old daughter to a Turcoman for seven tomans in order to pay state-imposed taxes.[138]

Religious leaders in Iran recognized that, like their Ottoman counterparts, the importance of allying national honor and public consciousness against slavery with an adherence to Islamic principles. As such, they tended to capitalize on opportunities when the two mandates could be seen to intersect, as when the Ottoman government decreed that the sale of Circassian immi-

grants to be illegal not only because they were Ottoman subjects but also because they were freeborn Muslims in 1867.[139]

SPECIFIC ACTIONS BY THE GOVERNMENT

Responding to calls by religious and political leaders to end slavery, the government's abolitionist ordinances became more frequent—even before the
formation of the Majlis in 1906. Thus, in 1904, following reports on the con-
tinuation of the trade in Iranian women and children by Turcomans along
the Khorasan province, Muzaffar al-Din Shah issued a decree requesting his
prime minister, 'Ayn al-Daula, "send necessary orders to the government of
Khorasan to ban these actions."[140] Stating that the honor of the nation was
at stake,[141] the Minister of Foreign Affairs, Mushir al-Daula, subsequently
ordered that Ghulamreza Asef al-Daula, the governor of Khorasan, enforce
the ban on trading Iranian women and girls.[142] One of the first casualties of
this legislation was the governor of Quchan.[143] The shah also allocated 35,000
tomans to the governments of Quchan and Bujnurd to facilitate the liberation
of enslaved people[144] and appointed Sardar Afkham as governor of Astarabad
to help release or ransom enslaved people.[145] He ordered the prime minister
to help redress the situation. For instance, in 1905, following a report that five
married Iranian women (one of whom was pregnant) had been sold to the
Russian Turcomans, the shah issued a decree:

> Your Excellency, the Grand Vizier, all wild nations have suppressed the
> slave trade. Why this obscene practice is prevalent on this frontier? Ban
> it completely; and work seriously to stop this action and report the result
> [to me].[146]

THE NATIONAL CONSULTATIVE ASSEMBLY

When the National Consultative Assembly—the Majlis—met for the first
time in October 1906, it is not surprising that the abolitionist discourse was
first and foremost. In fact, the new institution gave common people hope that
justice would be served when they petitioned for the prosecution of offenders
and slave traders, arguing that the slave trade was unconstitutional and in-
humane.[147] And, indeed, parliamentarians now had a forum from which to
redress this violation of human rights and, in so doing, bring Iran into the
modern world: "In Europe, the trade in *ghulām* and *kanīz* is abolished; [there-
fore] why does the trade in female Iranians still exist?"[148] Notably, while in
Europe the discourse revolved around guarantees of human rights and liberties, in Iran religious arguments still held sway,[149] as articulated by the parliamentary representative from Azerbaijan:

Till now, the issue of the liberation of slaves has been discussed [more than] ten times. How can we believe in Islam, [while] the Turcomans enslaved the women, whom we consider our sisters? If we are a true Muslim, we should not rest until the slaves are liberated.[150]

Aqa Shaykh Muhammad 'Ali and Aqa Sayyid Muhammad Ja'far were more direct about the subject of selling of Muslims: "Buyers and sellers [of enslaved people] are [like] beasts, even inferior than beasts, and something should be written that if from now on anyone does this act they will be punished."[151]

In addition to ratifying legislation, the Majlis dealt directly with the Ministries of the Interior and Cabinet in responding to reports of slave trading.[152] In particular, complaints from residents of frontier provinces prompted decisive responses by the Assembly. In February 1907, the Majlis received a telegram from the Iranian residents of Ashgabat that:

We 5,000 Iranians living in Ashgabat swear to honor religion and Islam and take God as a witness that we saw with our eyes that the Quchani children were being sold like sheep and other animals to Turcomans in Ashgabat.[153]

In response, the Majlis announced in May 1907:

To all compatriots and all of humankind, whether residents of Iran or elsewhere, the Holy National Consultative Majlis proclaims that anyone who knows anything about the situation of women and girls who anywhere along the Khurasan border-lands have been sold to the Turkomans or have been taken captive should write their information, specify their place of residence and send a signed copy of it through any possible means to the respected National Consultative Majlis, so that necessary actions for their release and retrieval could be taken with full knowledge.[154]

The subsequent inquiry headed by the new Minister of Justice, Abdulhussain Mirza Farman Farma, and seven other members of the parliament,[155] led to the dismissal of and fining of Asef al-Daula.[156] These frontier towns remained problematic until the 1920s. Indeed, the road between Mashhad and Semnan was notoriously unsafe, with caravans of traders and pilgrims subject to frequent attacks and potential enslavement.[157]

In addition to supporting the termination of institutional slavery, the Majlis and various political parties—including the Social Demokrats—attempted to reform the feudal (arbāb va ra'yat) system of agriculture that had helped perpetuate the enslavement of the rural poor. As part of their defense

of the rights of farmers, peasants, and serfs against the unjust and exploitative practices of landowners, in 1907 the parliament abolished the practice
of land grants (*tuyul*)[158]—especially the system of transferring government
lands to officials.[159] In spite of the practical good this legislation brought, it
fomented popular dissatisfaction to the extent that, in the same year, dem-
onstrations erupting in rural areas turned into revolts that spread across the
country. One particularly large uprising was comprised of enslaved people,
agricultural serfs, and peasants from Bam, Jiruft, and Narmashir, who rallied
under the banner of freedom and land reform from 1907 to 1908.[160]

In May 1908, the parliamentary representative from Kerman stated that
justice and equality must be implemented in all parts of the country and that
slavery should be abolished:

> Now, the constitution is established, and blacks and whites are the same
> before the constitutional law. I seriously request from all the respectful rep-
> resentatives [of the Majlis] to prohibit this abominable act [slavery and the
> slave trade].[161]

It was also at this time, however, that the democratic gains of the constitutional movement came under threat of the dictatorship of Muzaffar al-Din
Shah's successor Muhammad 'Ali Shah, who was supported by Russia. Not
only did he abolish the constitution, but he also bombarded the Majlis and,
after a failed assassination attempt in 1909, banned all political organizations.[162] His successor and son, Ahmad Shah (r. 1909–1925), reversed these
moves and implemented a far-reaching series of social reforms. Among these
was the allocation by the re-opened Majlis of 3318 Manat (497.7 tomans) for
the release of enslaved Iranians in Russia.[163]

The inauguration of Reza Shah Pahlavi's reign in 1925 brought the inten-
sification of the governmental policy of centralization.[164] This had a direct
impact on the frontier regions, with Turcoman communities being disarmed
and Iranian army pushing their forces back to the Russian frontier by January
1926.[165] Thus, after centuries, peace finally came to the province of Khorasan and northern Iran. In Gurgan, merchants bought land, employed semi-
settled and nomadic Turcomans to work the land and developed agricultural
activities.[166]

ENDING SLAVERY

Out of the spirit of international rapprochement that saw the creation of the
League of Nations after the First World War came renewed demands for the

termination of the trade in enslaved Africans as mandated in the Brussels Conference Act of 1890. Headed by the Temporary Slavery Commission, the resulting Convention to Suppress the Slave Trade and Slavery of 1926 established protocols for the suppression of all forms of slavery and slave trading worldwide.[167] Iran passed its own Abolition Act three years later signaling the Pahlavi dynasty's identification of abolition as a keystone of its sweeping national modernization policies. It also indicated the country's desire to pursue the policy independent of foreign intervention.

Iran's adoption of anti-slave-trade measures was gradual, taking nearly a century to implement—following various British diplomatic initiatives and internal reforms. But, ultimately, it was a desire to preserve national honor that accelerated the process of dismantling the slave trade and brought an end to slavery. The forces of modernization and burgeoning nationalism from the end of the nineteenth to the first decades of the twentieth century were part of "a global process that contributed to the hybridization of cultures and the invention of national selves."[168] These are seen, says the historian Mohamad Tavakoli-Targhi, in an emphasis on "Iran-centered proto-nationalist history" and "the emergence of a secular national identity." Together these forces helped popularize works such as the tenth century poet Ferdowsi's epic *Shahnameh* and those produced by Persian neo-Zoroastrian immigrants in India, who presented Iran's pre-Islamic past as a golden age.[169]

Abolition on a national scale, however, was achieved through diplomatic channels. Considered to be one of the first influential political figures of modern Iran, Reza Shah's Minister of the Court Abdulhussain Khan Teymurtash (1926–1932) began meeting with the British ambassador to Tehran, Robert Clive, in 1928 to discuss the situation and explore solutions. Because the division of Iran by the British and Russians in 1907 and the partitioning of the Ottoman Empire in the aftermath of the First World War had profoundly impacted the very character of the Middle East, Iranian politicians were acutely aware of the need to protect the country's political autonomy and national sovereignty.[170]

In his avowal of Iran's commitment to upholding international agreements banning the slave trade since the Brussels Act of 1890,[171] Teymurtash questioned whether more was needed.[172] Considerable resentment remained about the various Anglo-Persian treaties that had given the British increasingly broad maritime search-and-seizure powers in the enforcement of the 1882 Slavery Convention. In light of constitutional reform and the Pahlavi nationalist agenda, agreements such as these were now viewed as derogatory and outdated for a sovereign nation—and therefore deemed null and void.[173] As such, Teymurtash insisted on replacing or moderating the agreement before committing Iran to any further international agreements.[174] He insisted that Iran would be able to exercise the same authority as Britain in searching all suspicious vessels and detaining them if enslaved people were found on board.[175]

Opposed to the granting of reciprocal rights,[176] the British accused the Iranian government of excessively nationalistic ambitions.[177] In reality, however, their objection was premised on concerns that acquiescence would not only limit the British Navy's position in the Persian Gulf but also arouse the anger of those Arab traders whose vessels had flown the British ensign since February 1820.[178] In early 1929, Clive wrote:

> To give Persia the right to search on the high seas any vessel flying a British flag would be serious damage to our prestige, and almost certain to be abused as soon as Persia acquired the necessary vessels. Thus full reciprocity is manifestly undesirable.[179]

The British Resident also underlined the importance of holding firm: "If we give up at all, we shall by degrees lose our position altogether, and become on equality with her [Iran]."[180]

In early 1929, Teymurtash and Clive came to an understanding that if Britain was prepared to abandon its search-and-seizure policy, Iran would ensure that slave trading in the southern regions ceased.[181] To ensure compliance, the two countries would evaluate the success of the agreement's implementation in 1936.[182] Even though the British were satisfied with the agreement, the Iranian government insisted on more thoroughgoing reforms.

Reza Shah and his ministers realized that more binding legal categories would be necessary to ensure the success of the agreement because of the stubborn persistence of slave smuggling in parts of the country. The Minister of Justice noted in a speech to parliament (*majlis-i shurā-yi millī*) that:

> Although the slave trade has been abandoned in Iran, sometimes people bring enslaved people to the country. And since according to international agreements Iran does not recognize slave status, sometimes they [slave traders] delay the liberation of the slave until a special certificate is issued.[183]

Outright abolition would therefore obviate the need for certificates of manumission and presume the free status of all Iranians. Legislation terminating the institution of slavery was ratified and became law in February 1929. In communication with the Foreign Office, Clive observed that further agreements with Britain were not necessary: "In my discussions with the Minister of Court in regard to a new Slavery Convention he has twice referred to this Bill as showing the determination of the Persian Government to eradicate slavery from the Persian dominion."[184]

The Ministry of the Interior promulgated a general decree:[185]

> In the country of Iran, nobody is recognized as a slave. Each slave who enters Iranian territory, whether by land or by sea, will immediately be freed. Every person who sells or buys men or manifests rights over another person, or plays a role in trading or transporting in slaves, will be condemned to one to three years in jail.
>
> Note—as soon as the government officials are informed that a person has been traded or enslaved, it is their responsibility to free them, prosecute the offender, and inform the closest public prosecutor's office.[186]

Specific orders were sent to the governors of those areas more resistant to change, enjoining them to implement the new law and emphasizing that all offenders would be prosecuted.[187] Further, legislation was required to ensure that all inhabitants of these areas would be duly informed.[188] It is interesting to note that in contrast to the illegalization of slavery by the Iranian government, "slavery as a legal status and an institution was never abolished in the Ottoman Empire."[189]

Some scholars view the end of slavery as an inevitable historical process that grew out of Islamic law and the teachings of the Qur'an. And, indeed, the modern period has witnessed most Muslim states banning slavery on the grounds that its practice is a violation of Islamic precepts—as well as of basic human rights and international law.[190] For others, it was an inevitable consequence of the transition to a market economy, as seen in southwestern Morocco.[191] Importantly, the initial reluctance of Islamic societies to embrace the abolitionist mandate in the nineteenth century must not be seen as unique. In fact, it was not until the late nineteenth century that the Roman Catholic Church condemned slavery.[192] But, abolition was not a panacea to all social ills. Indeed, it was well understood that manumission would bring socioeconomic challenges and hardship to many freed enslaved people such as the 1936 report of the League of Nations.[193]

CONCLUSION

The process that culminated in the abolition of slavery in Iran began with the efforts to centralize governmental power and thus to reduce the influence of provincial governors, especially in the frontier regions and along the southern coast, where political instability and corruption fueled the slave trade. After the mid-nineteenth century the situation had worsened for the indigenous populations because of political instability, insecurity, the successful suppression of enslaved Africans trading infrastructures in the Indian Ocean and Persian Gulf regions, as well as the annexation by the Russians of much of the Caucasus. With the growth of internal slave markets, thus, it fell to social reformers—both secular and religious—to spearhead initiatives to terminate the trafficking of enslaved people in Iran.

"Despite some exceptional and brave voices," notes Toledano, "Islamic societies did not produce either an antislavery debate or abolitionist movement."[194] It was therefore within this context that social reformers like Babi and other Sufi and Shi'a religious leaders were influential in developing a language that could be used to condemn slavery. By contrast, the more secularizing or Western-oriented reformers voiced opinions that saw abolition as a matter of national honor and identity. Together with constitutional reform and the Pahlavi modernization of Iran after the First World War, these reformers were able to articulate persuasively the utter incompatibility of slavery in a civilized and devout society. Not only did their efforts help write Iran's first constitution and establish its parliament, the Majlis, but they also ensured that full emancipation could be achieved when the last remaining enslaved people were freed in 1929.

CHAPTER 8

EMANCIPATION

VARIOUS CONTEMPORARY SOURCES allow us to consider the circumstances of life before full emancipation was achieved in 1929. Cultural tradition and Islamic law justifying the liberation of individual enslaved persons had existed in Iran for centuries, long before the British inaugurated an abolitionist process that was not only limited and conditional, but also racially oriented in that it focused on Africans. In Iran, the liberation process that began with the freeing of the enslaved Africans in 1851 did not extend to include the status of other enslaved peoples. As has been shown, this racially based legislation actually made indigenous Iranians more vulnerable, given that demand for enslaved people throughout the region remained strong. For this reason, the circumstances that led to the enslavement of Iranians became a keenly felt national issue. This chapter explores the country's transformation from a society accommodating slavery to one that embraced full emancipation. It represents the voices of enslaved people who fought to escape enslavement, the difficult situations they encountered, and the various methods they employed to gain their freedom as well as the legal implications.

THE TREATMENT OF ENSLAVED PEOPLE

RELIGIOUS CONTEXT

The deep cultural and religious roots of domestic slavery in Iran not only justified enslavement of individual people but also provided for their liberation.[1] Thus, certain Iranian traditions, Islamic conventions, and tenets of the shariʻa made it customary to liberate enslaved people on auspicious occasions, such as weddings,[2] or as an act of atonement.[3] In 1885, princess Munavar al-Saltana's letter of freedom to liberate her enslaved person stated: "In honor of Fatema Zahra,[4] I liberated the black *ghulām* Jamal. May God keep you safe."[5] Indeed, the Qurʾan describes a system in which the payment of *zakat*, or alms, helped free enslaved people.[6] Islamic law also advanced legal rights to enslaved people, such as the right to marry or the right to request freedom, and supported the emancipation process in which enslaved people could become full citizens and achieve social prominence.[7] As such, an Islamic government could justify involvement in a campaign that would gradually lead to the emancipation of all enslaved people.[8] Until the early twentieth century, however, the implementation of emancipation was up to individual citizens and usually by reference to religious injunctions.[9]

Similar patterns of manumission based on religious and customary laws were also practiced elsewhere in Muslim societies. According to Gwyn Campbell, the paradigm found among many Indian Ocean societies (contrary to those found in the Atlantic Ocean) stressed the integration and assimilation of enslaved people into society through marriage and manumission and was enhanced by the absence of racial prejudice in Islamic law.[10] Esma Durugönül has found that African descendants in Turkey "have been assimilated into society and do not constitute a different social category as such."[11] Segal has also observed not only the widespread freeing of individual enslaved Africans by their owners but also their easy social assimilation.[12] Elisabeth McMahon, who specializes in East African history, argues that manumission—as in the voluntary release of enslaved people—existed in Africa long before abolition was imposed (often only reluctantly) by colonizers.[13]

The shariʿa regulated the master-slave code of conduct in various ways. For instance, it ensured that enslavement only occurred through captivity or by birth and prohibited parents from offering their children for sale. It was illegal under Iranian law for Europeans living in the country to own enslaved people, although this regulation was not always followed.[14] The legislation derived mainly from the fact that enslaved Muslims could not be employed by Christians; thus, enslaved people owned by Christians had the right to demand immediate freedom. Moreover, Islamic law advanced certain legal rights to enslaved people—such as the right to marry or the right to request freedom.[15] The practice of slavery is—at its core—an expression of a power relationship. The ideological, political, legal, and social manifestation of this relationship was complex and often contradictory in Middle Eastern and African societies.[16] In Iran, for instance, it is obvious that the absolutist Qajar monarchy turned to whatever ideological precedents and interpretations of Islamic laws it needed in order to legitimize the strictly hierarchical system of king–subjects–enslaved people.

MALTREATMENT AND SELF-DETERMINATION

The harsh realities of slavery existed in all societies. As they rely on power inequity, maltreatment was not an uncommon consequence of master-slave relationships—and one that could result in individual or group flight. Specific
religious, moral, and traditional teachings appear to have influenced social attitudes that disapproved of the mistreatment of the enslaved people. Christopher Rigby, who served as a secret service officer for two years in Iran following the Iran-Britain war and the occupation of Bushehr in 1856, observed
that Muslim societies recognize "the mild domestic slavery which we read of
in the Old Testament. The actual making a human being a slave in the market
is entirely illegal, and has always been carried on in spite of the treaties."[17]
Sheil also commented on the problem but noted that maltreatment of enslaved people by their masters did not seem to be prevalent in Iran:

> Ill-treatment must, of course, sometimes take place when there is unlimited
> power on the one hand and entire submission on the other. The fact is proved
> by the occasional instances in which slaves have taken refuge in the Mission
> to escape from punishment by their masters. Still it is believed that, in gen-
> eral, cruelty, or even harshness, is rarely practiced towards slaves in Persia.[18]

According to Islamic law, a master could be penalized for punishing his enslaved people: "The slave must be freed if a master beats him/her."[19]

This is seen in the case of the forty-five-year-old enslaved Zanzibari, Firuz
ibn Almas, who in 1927 described his maltreatment, but notably also articu-
lates how a growing awareness of other options to indenture developed:

> I was born in Zanzibar. When I was a child, I was kidnapped by Badus.
> He took me to Sur and then to Batinah and sold me to Haji Musa. After
> one year, I was sold to 'Abdullah ibn Chiran, one of the inhabitants of Qis
> [Kish Island]. I worked for him until he died. Then, I worked [for another
> person] and paid the wife [of the late master] half of my salary for four years.
> After that, I became free. My wife, Sa'ida, and I started working for Shaykh
> Ahmad but he deducted 40 Rupees [from my salary] each year. Last year, all
> the blacks [enslaved Africans] of Shaykh Ahmad 'Abdeli were divided among
> his creditors. My wife, my son and I were also given to Ahmad Uha. Two
> months ago, he took us to Lengeh and then to Kong. We worked for him,
> but he ill-treated us. We escaped and decided to come to the [British] con-
> sulate to be freed. At night, we lost our way. The people of Rudbar found us
> and brought us to the government office and then to the British consulate.[20]

This testimony shows that the concept of freedom did not crystallize in Firuz's mind until after he was maltreated. From his point of view, being an enslaved person was equal to being a laborer; it was only when he was abused by a new master that he was inspired to seek his freedom. Therefore, escaping or seeking refuge with higher authorities was a practice that was more common among enslaved people who were maltreated.[21]

This is seen again in the story of Khyzaran, a twenty-two-year-old enslaved female imported into Lengeh. She explained the great lengths to which she was prepared to go to gain her freedom:

> I gave myself up to the agent at Linga, and claimed protection, I was born at Marima [Mrima][22] near Zanzibar, and was taken quite young to Zanzibar, when I was sold to an Indian man who belonged to Swrat [Surat], I remained at Zanzibar until I was about thirteen years old, when my master died, and I obtained my liberty, and remained at Zanzibar free, until a few months ago, when I went to a dance and, on returning, I was met by Ferooze bin Sewed who had other three men with him, and as soon as my sister and myself had passed these men, they turned and caught us and dragged us to their Buteel, into which they put us and brought us to Rus-ul-Khyma, there was about twenty other slaves in this Boat, all were landed at Rus-ul-Khyma, I remained at Rus-ul-Khyma six days, when Ferooze brought three of us over to Linga and sold me to Kumal, a Busra man. He told me not to show myself outside the house because the English agent would see me, I met a slave girl in Linga, who told me not to go to Busra but to go to Ahmed, the agent, who would save me, which I did, and sent me to Bassidore.[23]

Although Islamic law justified the liberation of mistreated enslaved people,[24] slave narratives and governmental correspondence show that it was not uncommon for masters to discharge their enslaved people without granting them an official freedom letter in these circumstances. Aware of the need to document their new status, the Ministry of Foreign Affairs could issue official letters of freedom to facilitate the future employment of former enslaved people.[25] For instance, in 1905, the *kanīz* and wife of the late Haji 'Ali Khan, Chaman Faze, complained that she and her twelve-year-old daughter had been unjustly discharged and expelled from her master's house. When the government learned of this, a letter of freedom was issued.[26]

Enslaved people's decisions to remain with their owners thus depended on their treatment; if they enjoyed a measure of assimilation and beneficence, they were less likely to consider other options. It is important to note that the relationship between a freed enslaved person and former master did not necessarily become one of equals, but instead usually evolved into a personal relationship of clientage or one of voluntary subordination without fixed remuneration for services.[27] As such, emancipation for some enslaved people was a choice for freedom rather than an escape from servitude. In spite of these guarantees, Rigby observed that enslaved people in Iran often did not seek freedom:

> During the whole time that I was magistrate at Bushire and Karrack,
> I scarcely remember an instance of any slave coming to claim his freedom.
> We proclaimed that all slaves brought there were entitled to claim their
> freedom . . . but there was not one single instance of any slave coming
> before me as magistrate to ask that he might have his liberty.[28]

Even as late as 1927, the twenty-year-old enslaved African person, Zivar ibn Mabruk, made it clear upon his arrival at the British consulate that his reason for seeking freedom was not a result of maltreatment:

> Ibrahim ibn Yusuf bought me for 1,000 Rupees and brought me to Lengeh
> where he arranged my marriage with one of his *kanīzān*. I have been in
> Lengeh for 3 months; Ibrahim ibn Yusuf does not ill-treat me. . . . When I
> see that my father is free, I also want to be free. This is why I came here.[29]

ENSLAVED IRANIANS

The Iranian government first articulated its concern about the status of the many Iranians living abroad—enslaved by Turcomans and Arabs—during discussions with the British about the suppression of the trade in enslaved Africans. In 1847, Muhammad Shah directly challenged Britain's ambivalence on the subject of enslaved Iranians in Bukhara and Khiva:

> There are from two hundred thousand to three hundred thousand [enslaved
> Iranians] slaves in Bukhara and Khiva; why did they [the English govern-
> ment] prohibit me? If the enslavement is wrong why is not so in those places?
> And besides, the day I saw the English minister, I told him this. He admitted
> that I was right.[30]

Notably, the British acknowledged that while the enslavement of Iranians by Turcomans was heinous, the abolition of the trade in enslaved Africans was more important: "Whatever obscene actions the Turcomans commit, they are less [offensive] than [the actions of] those who buy and sell the blacks."[31] Even though they were not inclined to view this problem as seriously as that of the enslavement of Africans, their desire to secure Iranian cooperation meant that they did broach the subject in various diplomatic communications. In the following statement to Haji Mirza Aqasi, Justin Sheil acknowledged the problem:

> Beyond all other sovereigns, the King of Iran (so many of whose subjects languish in the slavery of the Toorkomans) ought to seek the extinction of slavery and shun all connection with man stealing and man selling, for such the traffic in Negroes is.[32]

In contrast to the legislated liberation of enslaved Africans, no legal mechanism was established to free enslaved Iranians either inside or outside the country. Ransom payments were one of the only ways out for these enslaved people; even though working to ultimately purchase liberty was another—but this could take between ten and twenty years, if ever.[33] Without financial means, many remained enslaved.[34] Worse yet, those who were able to purchase their freedom or whose freedom had been purchased risked being reenslaved on their way home.[35]

Running away was another way of gaining freedom, although it was an option rarely embraced.[36] The historian Edward Granville Browne recalled the story of an Iranian whom he met in the central Iranian town of Yazd. Enslaved near the border town of Kalat Naderi in 1848, the enslaved person had been sold at a Turcoman slave market, where he was "stripped almost naked, inspected and examined by interested buyers, and finally knocked down by the broker to the highest bidder."[37] After thirteen months, he managed to escape and returned to Iran. Before the abolitionist mandate acquired momentum after the mid-nineteenth century, the only destination for runaway enslaved people was religious shrines and sacred centers;[38] thereafter, as resistance against institutionalized slavery became popular they often took shelter in government buildings, consulates, and telegraph stations.

SUPPRESSION LEGISLATION AND LIBERATION

Despite a lack of international concern about the fate of its enslaved Iranian people in foreign lands, Iran nonetheless agreed to sign successive agreements affecting the importation of enslaved Africans into Iran from the Persian Gulf. This culminated in the royal *firmān* of 1848. While the consequences of this edict were only felt gradually in society, the legislation did encourage some domestic enslaved people to seek self-emancipation. Indeed, various governmental reports about runaway enslaved people after this period reveal the awakening attitudes of the public and authorities to the general idea of manumission.[39] They also show the extent to which local custom, cultural practice and societal expectation were changed.

IMPLEMENTATION OF THE ROYAL *FIRMĀN* OF 1848

Realization of the legislation was initially haphazard. The case in 1849 of a runaway enslaved person belonging to the Bushehr resident ʿAbbas Bazzazi illustrates British reluctance to interfere. In a letter to Samuel Hennell, Shaykh Nasir, the governor of Bushehr, notified British officials about the man after he had sought refuge on a steamer owned by Sir Charles Forbes:[40]

> A shopkeeper of Bushire, belonging to Brazgoon, has a slave, who has been with his master for a long time. Within the last three or four days he has gone on board the steamer. Although often sent for, he did not return. Mirza Ismail, the custom master, spoke to the captain from me (upon the subject) but he would not consent to give up the slave. The owner has come to me, and wants his slave. As I did not know what answer to give him, I considered it necessary to bring the circumstance to your notice, in order that I may reply to the owner of the slave, and also for the future, when more slaves follow this example, I may be aware of what ought to be done. Please let me know your opinion.[41]

In the end, the British deferred to Iranian authorities to make the final decision:

> As slavery is permitted [in Iran], a commander of an English vessel cannot detain a slave on board against the consent of the owner, and on refusal to deliver up the slave, the police authorities of the place could enforce it.[42]

It is important to note that the principal emphasis of the 1848 *firmān* was to prohibit the importation of African slaves by sea, while subsequent agreements in 1851 and 1857 concerned the punishment of slave dealers and focused on freeing enslaved people found on ships. Although these conditions guaranteed the rights of every new enslaved African brought into Iran, various factors limited the implementation of these policies. Thus, since the agreements only covered the seaborne trade and not internal slavery, enslaved Africans already in the country could not claim their freedom. This is evident in remarks made by Amir Kabir:

> From Bushire to Mashhad, and throughout Persia there are numbers of slaves to be found but no one has any right to make any remonstrance about one of them or to make any enquiry as to when they came from the sea. The convention has reference solely to the sea.[43]

Enslaved people's owners, therefore, rested assured that many of these edicts would not affect them. For example, the British demanded the liberation of one female and one male African who had been bought by Najaf 'Ali Tajer in 1862 as per article 13 of the 1857 Convention. The Iranian government responded by claiming that the agreement did not apply, since it was only the traffic in enslaved people by sea that had been prohibited: as such, the British had no right to intervene in the act of selling and buying enslaved people within Iran's provinces.[44] A similar case occurred in 1872, when two enslaved people aboard the *Magpie* that anchored near Bushehr requested their liberation from Colonel Lewis Pelly, the British Political Resident. Since one of the enslaved people was legally the property of an Iranian subject, Pelly could not intervene, and the enslaved person was handed over to the Iranian slave commissioner. The other enslaved person, however, was liberated.[45] Similarly, the British freed fugitive enslaved people in Gwadar who had entered via the territories under Iranian control in Makran in 1873.[46]

By 1876, the British concluded that since the number of enslaved Africans imported into Iran had decreased considerably, almost all existing enslaved people were the offspring of domestic enslaved people. While some did seek freedom (as recalled by Arnold of those choosing to escape by swimming and trying to smuggle themselves onto British ships) most enslaved people were content to stay where they were. This is proven by the fact that, despite the large number of enslaved people living in southern Iran, the number of runaway enslaved people was relatively low.[47] For those who escaped and sought refuge, however, the British assigned local telegraph stations as places of protection.[48] Reluctance to depart from the master can be found elsewhere throughout the region.[49] McMahon observes that only 15 percent of enslaved people chose emancipation in East Africa[50] and identifies several factors by way of explanation: first, the existence of a fluid enslavement to freedom continuum; second, the way slavery and freedom were understood in the context of various societal metrics like gender, age, skills, and so forth; third, the powerful economic vulnerabilities free but patronless enslaved people faced; fourth, the scope of movement and freedoms many enslaved people enjoyed. Since, these people were not the subjects of chattel slavery as in the Americas, it may be possible to draw similar conclusions to explain the situation in Iran.[51] Concerning royal enslaved people who resented the change in status they experienced when they were forcibly freed by the British in Aden, Suzanne Miers questions: "Should these highly privileged soldiers and officials really be described as slaves?" She qualifies this question by adding that while they fit the League of Nations' definition for slavery since they were legally owned, their masters did not control them.[52]

Although the suppression of the trade in enslaved Africans theoretically had no effect on internal emancipation—since slavery was still legally permitted in Iran—the authorities had difficulty adjudicating cases where the boundaries were blurred.[53] For instance, in 1877, six enslaved females of Oromo and Ethiopian descent along with two enslaved males were imported on a private British ship from Jidda to Bushehr. British officials there seized the newly imported enslaved people and handed them over to the consular East Africa court at Masqat for adjudication. The court's decision and resulting order were as follows:

> Having read the proofs and heard the evidence in this case, it appears to me that the said two male and six female slaves were being held in slavery on board the British Ship Rokeby contrary to law, and that the said eight slaves have been handed over to the Political Resident at Bushire, and I therefore pronounce the said eight slaves to have been lawfully seized and to be forfeited to our Sovereign Lady the Queen, and I condemn the same accordingly.[54]

After the ruling, the six women were sent to Basra at their request, but the two men were deported to Bombay. The case was referred to the British home government for further investigation. The law officers of the Crown stated the following:

> In our opinion Captain Prideaux, acting with the sanction of the Persian authorities, was justified in his search on board the British Steam Ship Rokeby while lying in Bushire harbor.
> Captain Prideaux would have had no authority to seize and detain the boy, Abdulla [i.e., one of the enslaved males], without the intervention of Persian authorities, and he was justified in obtaining the surrender of Abdulla through the intervention of the Persian authorities.[55]

This example clearly reveals the lengths to which the British felt they needed to justify their interference in matters of internal Iranian jurisprudence—even though international law gave them the right to intervene as per violations of the 1851 suppression legislation.

While their mandate pertained to enslaved Africans found on seaborne vessels and not on Iranian soil, the British had no authority to issue manumission certificates to enslaved people based on land. And yet, enslaved people unable to gain their freedom by any other means continued to seek consular refuge—which was problematic for both the British and their government.[56] That said, if an enslaved person's legal status was in any way questionable, the

Iranian government would assign the Investigation Council in cooperation with the British consulate to conduct an official inquiry.[57]

THE BRUSSELS ACT OF 1890

The ambivalence and uncertainty that characterized the initial period of suppressed slave-trading activities changed greatly after the Brussels Conference (1890). With the promulgation of the Brussels Act, not only did enslaved Africans become more familiar with their rights but also a concrete shift in attitudes to and policies about slavery began to develop. Moreover, the Iranian government acquiesced and accepted greater responsibility in suppressing slave trading within the country. Because it had hitherto been considered obdurate on the issue, it made significant efforts to free fugitive enslaved people:[58] "every fugitive slave arriving at the frontier of any of the powers mentioned in Article LXII shall be considered free, and shall have the right to claim letters of liberation from the competent authorities."[59] Article 63, meanwhile, stated that manumitted enslaved Africans should be returned to their native land.[60] By signing this agreement, the state was more compelled than ever to help ameliorate slavery.

Although slightly before the agreement, the eunuch Agha Bashir's request for freedom anticipated the shifting mood. Describing his life's story, he wrote in a letter to British officials on June 23, 1899:

> About fourteen, fifteen years ago, I was brought from Habash to Iran. The late Saheb Divan bought me and donated me to his daughter, the wife of Zahir al-Saltana who is my current master, and the son of 'Azad al-Mulk. He . . . mistreats and beats me. I cannot tolerate any more than this, and I am requesting my freedom from the British embassy.[61]

Two days later, a letter concerning Agha Bashir was sent to Nasrullah Mushir al-Daula, the Minister of Foreign Affairs, indicating that he had been brought to Iran by sea after the decree of *'abīd*[62] and should therefore be freed.[63] Mushir al-Daula asked for details concerning the eunuch's purchase, including the dates, his purchase price and location of sale.[64] It was revealed that twenty-two years earlier, the governor of Fars had purchased him along with five other black enslaved people in Shiraz and had brought them to Tehran.[65] After the investigation into his history was completed, Agha Bashir was granted freedom by the British embassy:

> On 26 April, 1899, Agha Bashir, the slave of Zahir al-Saltana came to the British embassy asking for his freedom from the British plenipotentiary min-

ister according to the *'Abīd* agreement on 2 March 1882. Since his master did not set any reason to demonstrate that Agha Bashir could not be freed based on the prohibition agreement, therefore, after announcing to the Iranian government, he was set free on 23 June 1899.[66]

Another example involved the *kanīz* Jamila who took refuge at the British consulate in 1905. A slave dealer had imported her from Ethiopia to Shiraz.[67] Frequently sold and transferred, she was at that time the pregnant wife of Haji Qanbar 'Ali Khan. A letter of freedom was issued swiftly by the British, underlining that her importation by sea and sale within Iran violated the anti-slave trading agreements.[68] Citing article 5 of the Brussels Act—which referred to the punishment of slave dealers and captors—the British demanded that Jamila's master be disciplined appropriately.[69]

A legal "sticking point" surrounding the granting of freedom remained in establishing a date before which an enslaved person's importation invalidated his or her claim. Even though all runaway enslaved people proclaimed their freedom based on the legislation, Iranian bureaucrats were uncertain about which agreements were applicable. Officials, such as Muhammad 'Ali in Bushehr, sent letters to the Ministry of Foreign Affairs asking for judicial clarification:

> The freedom of *kanīzān* and *ghulāmān* who were bought before the agreement is not permitted. Many governmental officers have doubts whether this [liberation] begins with the agreement of 1267 [1851], which was concluded between Iran and Britain, or with the Brussels Conference [1890].[70]

The Minister of Foreign Affairs, 'Ala' al-Saltana, reaffirmed that the trade in enslaved people became illegal within the country after the 1890 agreement, but enslaved people sold prior to this date should not be liberated.[71]

Even though the Omanis had developed a vigorous trade in enslaved Baluchis during the early twentieth century, Iranian authorities—already increasingly supportive of fugitive enslaved people at the British agency in Jask or Oman—offered them unconditional freedom. It is reported that of the ninety-five enslaved people who were manumitted at Masqat in 1904 and 1905, more than sixty were Iranians who had been imported from Makran to the Batinah coast of Oman.[72] An enslaved Iranian named Ambar, who had been sold several times, requested his freedom from the British Resident in Bushehr in 1906:

> I was born at Lingah. When 12 years old, I was sold by my first master, Syed Maseeh, to one Kerbela Bauker Lari, with whom I remained for one year. He

sold me to Mohammed Jahrumi 2 months ago. The latter has now brought me to Bushire with a view to selling me to Haji Mohamed Bauker Behbehani of this place.[73]

One month later, the Iranian Foreign Office agent in Bushehr issued his manumission certificate.[74]

In sifting through a wealth of slave narratives and official governmental reports, we are given insight into the historical stage on which the emancipation policy was built and realized. Indeed, by the early twentieth century, the Iranian government was routinely adjudicating thousands of cases. One in particular concerned the hundreds of enslaved people living in southern Iran who had been imported after the 1890 agreement. The shah wrote to the Grand Vizier and asked for an investigation into the matter; but the latter indicated that, as most of these enslaved people had been imported into Iran many years earlier, the government should not be obliged to liberate them.[75] Facing this kind of obduracy, the government was not able to do much more than liberate runaway enslaved people seeking sanctuary in government buildings in its attempt to abide by the terms of the Brussels Act.[76]

In 1905, Nasrullah Mushir al-Daula, the Minister of Foreign Affairs, instructed the government agent at Shiraz that runaway enslaved people arriving at the British consulate should first be encouraged to return to their owners, but that if an enslaved person did not accept, then the Ministry should issue a manumission certificate. If, however, the enslaved person did not meet the criteria for freedom, then a written petition should be sent to the British consulate.[77] It is reported that in the early 1900s, more than one hundred enslaved Africans escaped the homes of owners and sought their liberation.[78] Seeing the negative impact on applicants of lengthy waiting times for letters of freedom, the British consulate was forced to request the government to speed up the process.[79]

THE GOVERNMENTAL RESPONSE TO LIBERATION

Anxiety about the socioeconomic repercussions associated with the emancipation of all enslaved people was one of the reasons for the Iranian government's initial reluctance to support the abolitionist mandate. Others ranged from acknowledgment that foreign trade and domestic industry would be impacted to a deeper concern about the pernicious social consequences of liberating enslaved females in a society dominated by patriarchal and binding religious mores.

Concern that enforced manumission would lead to an exodus of merchants from Iran, taking their capital and investments with them, was not unfounded. Indeed, discontent with the financial impact of losing their en-slaved labor provoked many to relocate in India or elsewhere.[80] For instance, a group of Lar merchants in the port town of Lengeh rallied together in 1905 in response to an increase in the number of refugee enslaved Africans being liberated. In a letter to the Ministry of Foreign Affairs, they requested the re-moval of Badr Bushehri, the lawyer for the British consulate who had issued the freedom letters. They accused the lawyer of encouraging many of these en-slaved people to escape, keeping some for himself and liberating the others.[81] Other members of the community voiced concern that a departure of such a large number of discontented merchants could only negatively impact both the economy and social fabric of Lengeh.[82] Both the Iranian and British gov-ernments defended Badr's behavior as seen in Mushir al-Daula's letter, justi-fying the situation with reference to the hujjat al-Islam[83] Shari'atmadar:

> According to the international agreement, the trade in *ghulāmān* and *kanī-zān* is banned [in Iran], and if anyone buys [enslaved people], the [British] embassy will give their freedom letter immediately, once they are informed. For example, some, who were not aware of the agreement, bought several *ghulāmān* and *kanīzān* in Tehran. They [enslaved people] went to the embassy and asked for their freedom letter.[84]

What is notable here is the government's commitment to realizing all aspects of the suppression legislation.

There were some challenges with manumitting enslaved people individu-ally or as a group when they belonged to the higher social orders.[85] Although the shah himself complied with the legislation by issuing letters of freedom to his eunuchs and enslaved people,[86] complications arose when enslaved people belonged to the royal family, and members of the ruling elite escaped. Thus, when the British consulate requested a certificate of manumission for the eunuch Manuchehr Khan, Mushir al-Daula was forced to write a delicately worded letter to a female member of the royal Qajar family, who, moreover, accused the eunuch of having stolen some of her belongings. Here, Mushir al-Daula acknowledged that while there was no doubt the eunuch's original purchase complied with Islamic law, his freedom was now guaranteed by the Abolition of the Slave Trade law.[87] As to the purloined objects, a thorough investigation would be made—but not until the enslaved person had been freed.[88]

Another case was that of 'Abdulrahman Khartoumi, who had been brought from Sudan to the northern Iranian town of Damghan by Farajullah Khan Damghani. Here, he was resold and married a *kanīz* with whom he had two daughters.[89] Following his escape to the British consulate, the Minister of Foreign Affairs, Mushir al-Daula, ordered his liberation. Faced with his owner's anger, the enslaved person stated that not only did all *ghulāmān* and *kanīzān* in Iran have the right to be freed according to the treaty, but also that as a Sudanese, he was in fact a British citizen and therefore entitled to freedom.[90] The owner justified his position by suggesting that since two thousand African *ghulāmān* and *kanīzān* lived in Tehran, the treaty was obviously ineffective. He also challenged his origin of the *ghulām* and enslavement by noting that he had been purchased in Lebanon, which was under the Ottoman Empire, and then had been brought to the present day Saudi Arabia and then into Iran.[91]

Both the 1882 Convention and the Brussels Act referred to the liberation of enslaved people, but they were used in subtly different ways.[92] Thus, while the latter reinforced the liberation of every fugitive enslaved person, the former was cited usually in connection with the maltreatment of domestic enslaved people and the general importation of enslaved persons. Liberation was realized in different ways. For example, enslaved people belonging to resident Iranian masters were referred to the local governor (*kārguzār*) for their manumission certificates. However, the authorities could not intervene if a master resided in Iran but was under British protection. In such cases, the British consul associated with the enslaved person's owner was expected to be present; if not, then local authorities could assume control. However, if the enslaved person took refuge in British territories in Bas'idu, Jask, Lengeh, or Hengam, the British consul could issue a manumission certificate without involving the Iranian authorities.[93] Meanwhile, enslaved people from prominently Arab nations—like Masqat, Bahrain, Kuwait, or modern-day United Arab Emirates—were referred to the resident colonial authority who could be of any nationality.[94]

Enslaved Baluchis residing on the Makran coast posed a special concern. Lacking cohesive and effective governance, the illegal slave trade was rife in the area.[95] Thus, in spite of the momentum generated by the antislavery movement, the Arab slave trade remained firmly entrenched in this area—so much so that it became a common location for masters of other regions to dispose of superfluous or difficult domestic enslaved people. For this reason, the British took the region under its sphere of influence in 1921, as indicated in the remarks of the senior naval officer in the Persian Gulf, Captain Pearson: "The first opportunity will be taken to act as you suggest and show the [British] flag on the Makran coast and neighboring waters."[96]

And yet, slave trading of Baluchis continued well into the second decade of the twentieth century.[97] Part of the problem was that local people themselves—including the Makrani sardars and other Baluchis—fully engaged in the trafficking of enslaved people to Oman or along present-day United

Arab Emirates or the Batinah coast.[98] Sharing similar physical characteristics, it was not difficult for dealers to hide the true identities of the enslaved people they were transporting by describing them as fellow passengers or relatives.[99] As British officials confessed, it was "usually impossible
to differentiate slaves who [were] afraid to declare themselves from the ordinary crew of a dhow."[100] For this reason, many were re-enslaved after being
freed.[101] As it seemed no effective action could be taken to enforce the pre-
vention of the trade in Baluchis, the British encouraged the cooperation of
local shaykhs of the Arab countries. Without this, there was little hope for
controlling the trade; indeed, the Indian government acknowledged that the
trade in enslaved Baluchis would not end until these shaykhs were pressured
to cooperate.[102]

Crucial to the successful realization of the abolitionist mandate was the
cooperation of local authorities;[103] but in the case of Arab traders, this presented its own special challenges.[104] Due to the lack of agreements to ban the
trade in Baluchis, the shaykhs and governors of Arab countries were encouraged by the British to pursue offenders and free enslaved Baluchis according
to Islamic traditions: "Please tell Shaikh [Sharjah] from me that I look to him
to recover the two slaves from Ben Ahmad and punish latter in accordance
with Muhammadan law which does not allow enslavement of free born Mos-
lems."[105] However, the shaykhs of present-day United Arab Emirates and of
Qatar continued to trade in Baluchis because of the economic gain:

> The Shaiks of the Trucial Coast and Qatar, however, are in sympathy with the
> traders or find the traffic a source of revenue, and it is difficult to get honest
> assistance from them. I warned the Shaikhs of Abu Dhabi and Debai very
> seriously about this slave traffic and told them that the British Government
> would probably take strong exception to their conniving at it, if I reported
> the matter.[106]

These Arab countries continued to be safe haven for the buying and selling
of kidnapped enslaved people of all backgrounds for much longer than
elsewhere.[107]

THE LIBERATION OF ENSLAVED FEMALES, WIVES, AND CONCUBINES

Gender was a decisive factor in determining the practicality of freedom, as
there simply were more opportunities for enslaved males to establish new
lives for themselves than there were for their female counterparts.[108] Instead,
freeing all categories of enslaved females required that certain social and reli-

gious mores were followed—specifically in guaranteeing that no decline in traditional moral values would occur with their release. It was feared that the sudden liberation of a penniless female population might bring an increase in the number of prostitutes. This concern was not unfounded, as just such a situation had occurred in northern Nigeria and in Muslim North and East Africa.[109] The British authorities, therefore, attempted to ensure that enslaved girls and women would be freed only under guardianship: those who obtained their liberation through marriage importantly did not violate Islamic protocols regulating acceptable places for women in society.[110] However, for those without this protection, freedom was a new burden for these usually illiterate, socially isolated, and unskilled women. The *kanīz* of the late E'tezad al-Daula, for instance, was forced to seek financial assistance from the government because she had become indigent after the death of her master.[111] It was for this reason that when the British abolished slavery in Zanzibar in 1897 they treated concubines as wives in order to avoid complications.[112]

The difficulties of postliberation financial independence for enslaved people—both male and female—was an accepted reality, so much so that in some cases the British consulate required assurance of future employment before granting an enslaved person his or her letter of freedom.[113] Liberated enslaved people tended to work harder and were often absorbed into low-skilled occupations. Notably, however, it is reported that in the 1890s many liberated *kanīzān* living in Bushehr had come to earn their livelihoods as musicians and dancers.[114] The number of freed enslaved people entertainers increased which led to the formation of skilled singers and dancers, known as the *mutrebe*.[115]

But, it was not usual for freed enslaved females to find niche employment as the *kanīzān* of Bushehr. Concerns about their status abounded, as is revealed in a letter dated 1892 from the governor of Gulf Ports, Husayn Quli Khan, to his assistant and nephew, Reza Quli Khan. Describing how the Behbehani's enslaved people had demanded their freedom and the right to return to their native country at the British embassy in the south, he wrote:

> I replied that the embassy should inform the government and the 'ulama' of Bushehr and send them to a safe place and not keep them in the embassy, because all *kanīzān* who are in the ports and southern Iran are married, and according to Islam, women are not allowed to stay in a house of a stranger [i.e., someone who is not a relative]. Slaves should be sent to a safe place for two months. If they are happy with the new owner, he can take them; if not, the government will assist in releasing them.[116]

Slave masters objected to efforts to liberate runaway concubines and requested their return since, once at the British consulate, they no longer had power over their enslaved persons.[117] From an owner's perspective, an enslaved female was considered one of his concubines whose freedom not only would break hereditary links within the family but also was against the shariʿa. A letter to the British consulate from an owner reveals the anger he felt:

> The law of the British embassy concerns the black *kanīzān* imported from out of the country. This is a house-born *kanīz*, and I brought her from Tabriz. She is now in my house, and according to the shariʿa, no one can determine what I should do. I am all the rights in my house. Unless, they abolish the shariʿa orders of Muhammad, which in this case, things will change.[118]

One interesting manuscript tells of a concubine, Shirin Habashi,[119] who sought refuge at the British consulate in 1899. Her owner, Haji Zaki Behbehani, petitioned the Iranian government for her return, explaining that she was his son's wife. Although Shirin had taken refuge in the British consulate and persisted in demanding her liberation, the Ministry of Foreign Affairs decided that because she was a legal wife, she must be returned to her husband. Minister Nasrullah Mushir al-Daula stated that the 1851 convention did not provide for the liberation of *ghulāmān* or *kanīzān* who had been enslaved before Iran and Britain had signed any slave treaties.[120] As such, it was concluded that Shirin should be returned to her master.[121] In another case, when the British consulate investigated the status of Saʿida Mabrook, who took refuge in Bushehr, it was determined that she was eligible for freedom. The Iranian ministry duly processed a letter of freedom, and she was freed.[122]

RELIGIOUS INJUNCTIONS

In spite of the legislation, there remained considerable uncertainty on a case-to-case basis. In one example, an Iranian official reiterated the concern that manumitting escaped married enslaved females was against the shariʿa, adding that this action created imbalance in society:

> Many of them [*kanīzān*] have husbands and children. Once they experience a little difficulty, they run away from their husbands, come to the British consulate and make trouble. The consulate supports them and asks to issue their freedom letter. The consulate does not care that these *kanīzān* were legally married, and have husbands and children.[123]

As such, he requested the British not to issue certificates of manumission to any enslaved wives or concubines who had been bought before 1875.[124]

In 1901, the Iranian government's representative in Lengeh and 'Abbasi sent a letter to the Ministry of Foreign Affairs, stating that many enslaved Iranian *kanīzān* of Rudbar in Baluchistan had taken refuge at the British consulate and were asking for their letters of freedom. He wanted advice about how the Iranian officers should handle the situation, since the enslaved people were Muslim and their enslavement violated Islamic law.[125] In response, Mushir al-Daula issued a decree stating: "If [the enslaved people] live as . . . legally married wives, there is no problem, but if they are *kanīz* . . . they are being sold and bought, [and] then they must be liberated."[126] To the governor of Kerman and Baluchistan, the Minister highlighted specific circumstances under which enslaved people could officially be freed by differentiating between domestic enslaved people and those who were traded. As a result, an enslaved individual's personal circumstances could determine her legal status:

> I was informed about the case of the *kanīzān* and *ghulāmān*. The purpose [liberation] is not for those who are kept and treated as domestic, but according to the agreement concluded between Iran and Britain their buying and selling is prohibited. As you said, if they [enslaved people] are being kept and trained, and get married according to their wishes, there will not be any objection to this situation and no one has a right to protest.[127]

This statement reveals that the conditional liberation of enslaved people depended on Islamic injunctions. On the one hand, the government allowed the freedom of those who might be subject to exploitation, while on the other, it preserved a social structure, which—in this case—allowed for a gradual transition from slavery to freedom through marriage, ransom, or giving birth to a master's child.

The pressure on government to control fugitive *kanīzān* both was due to the need to stabilize social relationships and was deeply embedded in custom and the sharī'a. Therefore, any transitions that could disrupt socioreligious boundaries were carefully scrutinized. It is, therefore, useful to evaluate documents from the government and 'ulama' that describe the struggles and petitions of female runaway enslaved people.

Even though Qur'anic law encouraged masters to help their enslaved people find marriage partners,[128] many took their enslaved women on as concubines. The practice was viewed as a way of avoiding moral corruption, and as such was codified by the sharī'a.[129] Because the Islamic law of *istīlād* ("seeking a child") ensured that any child born to an enslaved female by her master would be eligible for emancipation, it was often viewed as a satisfactory solution for both parties.[130] The enslaved mother was called the *umm al-walad* ("mother of the child") and would be freed upon her master's death, thus altering her social status.[131]

Enslaved males could marry up to two enslaved females or a free woman who was not his owner, and an enslaved female could marry a free man who had no claims to her ownership, with the permission of her master.[132] James Baillie Fraser commented on this situation in the early nineteenth century with reference to Sayyid Sultan, the Sultan of Oman (r. 1792–1804), who had three sons, one of whom was "by an Abyssinian slave girl, manumitted for the purpose of sharing her master's bed; a custom, it seems, always observed when the master takes a fancy to a slave."[133]

In spite of these legally binding strictures, the liberation of married enslaved people remained contentious and provoked frequent investigation. In 1904, the shah issued another *firmān* (based on the shari'a) about runaway enslaved females,[134] questioning the extent to which Islamic ideology was being followed. His concerns reveal that many members of the higher echelons of Muslim society tended to adjust shari'a regulations to suit their various personal needs.

Fundamental questions about slavery were addressed by the shari'a through the direction provided by the 'ulama'. For instance, questions about whether marriage should come before or after the liberation of enslaved females were frequently raised. The response of 'Ali Akbar, one of the 'ulama', was that if a master wanted to marry one of his enslaved females, she should first be liberated; otherwise, the marriage would be unlawful.[135] Another question concerned the validity of marriages in which someone had married an enslaved person with the permission of her owner and thereafter bought her from her master. The mujtahid Husayn Razavi Qomi wrote that the priority of the marriage did not nullify the enslaved person's status but rather the reverse was the case: buying the enslaved person after marriage rendered the marriage null and void.[136]

Masters who married enslaved persons who subsequently fled considered manumission to be an imposed policy that conflicted with the shari'a. Sa'ida Nubi escaped the house of her master, Abulqasem Nilfurush, a herb merchant, and took refuge at the British consulate at Shiraz. Denied access to the embassy, Abulqasem petitioned the Ministry of Foreign Affairs and requested the return of his wife and enslaved person. He stated that Sa'ida's "liberation" was an act against Islamic law.[137] The marriage contract[138] along with testimonies notarized by dozens of 'ulama' in Shiraz indicated that Sa'ida Nubi was indeed Abulqasem's wife.[139] Responding directly to the Ministry, the British ruled that firstly, the *kanīz* denied the legality of the marriage and, secondly, the marriage was inconsequential since her importation into Iran not only violated the abolition legislation (*tijarat-i manʿ-i ʿAbīd*) but also the Brussels Act.[140] Legally entitled to her certificate of manumission,[141] she urged that her former master should instead be punished for his illegal trade.[142] Unable to decide on this complicated matter, the shah asked Mushir al-Daula to "finalize the case of the *kanīz* according to Islamic law."[143] Inquiries were subsequently sent to the ʿulamaʾ,[144] whose *fatwaha* nullified Saʿida's and Abulqasem's marriage.[145] The process of clarifying her status took several months, during which time she was sheltered at the British consulate.

LIBERATION OF ENSLAVED FEMALES IN THE SOUTH

Until full emancipation was guaranteed throughout the country in 1929, news of runaway enslaved people and their liberation spread and inspired like actions elsewhere. This was the case especially in the south where slavery was deeply ingrained in the socioeconomic structure.[146] As late as the early 1900s, officials in the province of Fars reported that not only did most families—including the ʿulamaʾ[147]—have enslaved people, but also many masters married *kanīzān* in order to have children.[148] In circumstances such as these, runaway enslaved females were particularly vulnerable.[149] For this reason, the government became especially vigilant about the liberation process for these women, ordering thorough investigations be performed in terms of their master's identity, marital status, and whether they had children by their master or not.[150] Realizing the gravity of the situation, Mushir al-Daula and the British were more cautious about these refugee *kanīzān*, often encouraging them to return to their masters, before issuing letters of freedom.[151] Two different cases illustrate this challenge. In one, the unnamed enslaved person of ʿAbdul ʿAziz's—whom he had liberated and with whom he had had a child—fell in love with and married an African in Basʿidu. It was when ʿAziz demanded her back that the British consulate became involved.[152] Meanwhile, it was more straightforward for Masrura, the *kanīz* of Muʿez al-Sultan and wife of his servant, Haji Firuz: her request for freedom was granted without hesitation by the Iranian government in 1907.[153]

As has been shown, enslaved females born outside Iran were able to obtain their freedom more easily than those born into domestic slavery, and especially if her native land was under British protection. This is apparent in a document revealing that while the Iranian government rejected giving freedom letters to three runaway concubines born in the southern port of Bandar Rig, three Sudanese concubines who accompanied them were liberated without question.[154] The case of Zaʿfaran, an Ethiopian *kanīz*, is also illuminating. Bought in 1899 in Jidda by Muhtaram al-Daula, a female Iranian returning from a pilgrimage to Mecca, Zaʿfaran was separated from her master in Suez[155] and then liberated by an abolitionist officer in Egypt.[156] Although she chose to marry there, the judge of the shari'a court would not approve the wedding unless an official freedom letter was obtained from Za'faran's master in Iran. The correspondence between the Egyptian and Iranian foreign affairs officials demonstrates how diligently the freedom of this enslaved person was pursued and obtained.[157] Some enslaved people were entitled to freedom based on several legitimate religious, international, and state laws. Thus, the enslaved Shokofa's poignant letter leaves an impression that despite having a strong case for liberation, various emotional and physical pressures locked her into slavery:

> I have been the slave of Mushir Akram, working for him for twelve years. They beat and mistreat me; I cannot tolerate [it]. I escaped several times, but they found and [brought] me [back]. I am a British citizen and want to be free. For the sake of God, give [me] my freedom letter, just [write] two words, I will pray for you.[158]

The principle mandate of the state was to guarantee the dignity of enslaved females and to ensure that their liberation would not undermine the moral fiber of society. Emphasis, therefore, was placed not on individual autonomy but rather on directing the entire nation toward social and economic security. While this "freedom" may have appeared limited to Western eyes, the government's strategy allowed social control to be maintained while the grip of former owners over enslaved people was loosened. Although preserving social norms (especially in the presence of newly freed women) was the priority, the Qajars operated more cautiously than did the Pahlavi regime. Thus, during the Qajar period, the process of liberation was characterized as one of conflict between the state and slaveholders, with governmental officials vigilantly observing Islamic law and deferring to cultural mores. As the Pahlavi regime was more attached to bureaucratic Western values than to the nuances of Islamic law, it adopted a more rigorous approach to freeing enslaved people—one not dictated by gender or culture.

LETTERS OF FREEDOM

By the early part of the twentieth century, many enslaved people were aware of the social and political developments within the country and consequently were empowered to seek their freedom. In addition to the various abolitionist laws, the establishment of the constitutional and parliamentary system in 1906 gave many a greater sense of confidence in realizing social, political, and economic self-determination. But, they also knew that being free without having a legal and formal certificate or letter of liberation meant that they were not considered free citizens in society. These documents indicated the enslaved person's name, the date of liberation and the legal basis for the liberation as well as—most importantly—his or her right to hold a job and to be treated without discrimination or prejudice.[159] (A family of enslaved people usually received one single letter.[160])

The various suppression agreements during the nineteenth century established protocols for liberating eligible enslaved people.[161] One of the first steps was taking sanctuary at the British consulate or one of the many telegraph stations located throughout the country after the 1860s. In exceptional circumstances, enslaved people took refuge at the Russian consulate.[162] But, enslaved females were also known to take sanctuary at the houses of 'ulama', who then supported and sheltered them until their letters of freedom were issued.[163] The role of the British consulate was to question the applicant before contacting the Ministry of Foreign Affairs of Iran, which then conducted a thorough investigation. If the enslaved person was entitled to freedom, the government officially ordered the owner to manumit the former enslaved person with the appropriate documentation; but if the owner opposed the decision or was deceased, then the Ministry would itself issued an official letter of freedom.[164] In many cases, the owner complied to avoid being disciplined by the government.[165] Yet, obtaining a letter of freedom did not always mean that a change in the enslaved person's status would be respected, since there were cases of liberated enslaved people being resold to slavery well into the twentieth century.[166]

Thus, Hajia Habash, who was bought in Mecca in 1891 and lived in Tehran for twenty years, complained the mistreatment of her master and demanded her freedom based on the constitutional law.[167] Baji Tafaruj, who had been liberated on religious grounds but not granted an official letter of freedom, appealed the Iranian government: "If the Constitution is freedom, free us today. . . . Give us our freedom letter to have peace of mind."[168] Protesting her maltreatment by her master, Chaman Gul stated, "The constitution has been established in our country today. Why do you mistreat me?"[169] She, too, was freed. Another case was Bashir, the enslaved person of the deceased Mustashar al-Mulk, who succeeded in gaining his freedom by referring to international laws of abolition, Iranian-British agreements, and the manumission of many enslaved people.[170] Aware of the growing numbers of newly freed enslaved people in Iran, the two enslaved females of the royal court deputy took sanctuary at the British consulate and stated that "the British government has freed all the blacks,"[171] in order to justify their liberation.

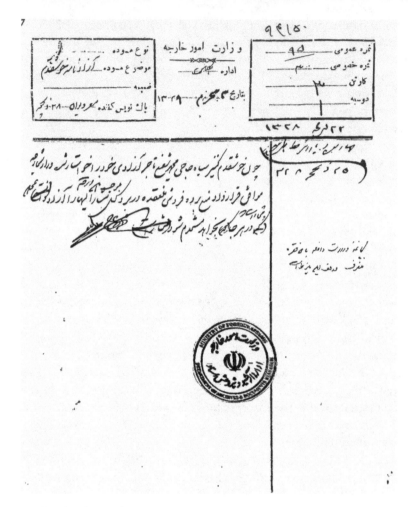

8.1. Freedom letter of a *kanīz*, Khoshgadam. Courtesy of archive of Ministry of Foreign Affairs of Iran.

FINAL STEPS TOWARD FULL EMANCIPATION

The final stage of emancipation took place during the reign of Reza Shah Pahlavi in 1929. He introduced a bill to the parliament (the *majlis-i shurā-yi millī*) that called for the full emancipation of enslaved people. With this bill, all enslaved people were legally recognized as equal to other social groups in Iranian society.[172] Importantly, legal emancipation helped condition the common people into accepting the universality of the principles of equality and freedom.

The emancipation of enslaved people took various forms, although gender divisions continued to make the transition from slavery to freedom different for men and women. That said, the socioeconomic status of freed enslaved people in Middle Eastern societies varied based on local and personal circumstances. Thus, while some were able to assume complete personal and financial independence, others saw little apparent change in their lifestyles if they became indentured laborers or servants. Some freed enslaved people obtained new lives through relocation. Others were helped by their masters, who assisted them in finding jobs and marriage partners. Overall, while in some regions enslaved people were easily absorbed into Iranian society, the stigma of slavery lasted longer in other places.[173]

PATTERNS OF LIBERATION IN AFRO-IRANIAN COMMUNITIES[174]

Liberated enslaved Africans can be categorized into two groups on the basis of settlements: those who were sent away and those who remained in Iran. Among the first group, the enslaved people were liberated by the British and transferred to other locations outside of Iran. The majority of freed adult enslaved Africans were taken directly to Bombay,[175] with their children often being sent to a branch of the Church Missionary Society at nearby Saharanpur.[176] By the 1890s, this increasingly large population of freed enslaved people forced local authorities in Bombay[177] to consider other destinations, and it was decided that East Africa would be suitable: there, they could work on plantations in Zanzibar and Pemba.[178] In the 1900s, the liberated enslaved people in Masqat were also sent to Zanzibar.[179] This scenario reflects an important transition from slavery to wage labor, as well as a meaningful shift in the demand for labor from the Persian Gulf back to East Africa.

Many of those freed along the Persian Gulf coast were also sent to the British military base at Bas'idu on Qeshm Island. Indeed, the village of Sangab was located north of Bas'idu and came to house about four hundred refugee and liberated enslaved Africans, who built an interdependent community and lived independently. By 1906, their numbers had been reduced to five men and twenty women; by the 1930s, only four elderly African women lived by mendicancy.[180]

The other group of liberated enslaved people remained in Iran. Becoming free members of society after 1929 involved the challenge of attempting to function independently. Indeed, the postemancipation era was characterized by the dismantling of traditional structures of socioeconomic protection and psychological support for both the individual and collective now considered to be autonomous and self-determining. For this reason, it is probable that perceived and real challenges often caused some newly freed citizens to delay requesting their freedom. But there is no doubt that local cultural and socioeconomic conditions also helped ease the transition for others. The process of realizing personal and group independence, therefore, was exercised in varying ways and profoundly affected future patterns of Afro-Iranian community development and identity formation.

What is perhaps most interesting about some Afro-Iranian communities is their adaptation of traditional terminologies to new social and legal realities. For example, in Bushehr, some of those whose surname is Zangoi ("from Zanzibar") are called Amu ("uncle"), and in Baluchistan, the term *ghulām*, referring to enslaved people, became the surname Ghulami in some communities.[181] In the same way, Azadi (or "liberty") was a common choice for a surname in the postemancipation period. Notably, families named Nukari (or "servant") tend to constitute the lowest social group. ʿAbid (or "enslaved person") and Kakai (or "brother") are generally associated with those living in ʿAbdulkhan communities (*ṭāʾfa*) that are comprised of descendants of enslaved Africans purchased by Arab shaykhs and brought to Khuzistan province.[182] Members of the lowest social group of the Shirani community in southwestern Baluchistan were often named Tih, indicating that they were descendants of rural enslaved people.[183] It is not surprising that words often change meaning over time. A linguistic comparison can be made with the Arabic term ʿAjam, which means "he who speaks indistinctly or mumbles." It was used by the Arab conquerors to label and mock Persians in the early Islamic period. The term continued to be used as a pejorative term of reference and an ethnolinguistic self-identification, but after the eleventh century, it gradually lost its pejorative connotation and was employed by Iranians to refer to their own ethnicity.[184]

Even though the rationalization for the hierarchical correlates of these nomenclatural differences ceased to be important with the dawn of emancipation, communal stratification was linked to the use of these names for some time. Today, however, the former enslaved people enjoy the same opportunities as the other ethnic groups. They tended to move away from endogamous marriages and entered into relationships outside their milieu. Marrying out eased the assimilation of former enslaved people within larger societies and helped to ameliorate these kinds of barriers.

CONCLUSION

The three pillars on which the liberation in Iran rested were international agreements, Islamic law, and state law. The former, including the 1882 Convention and the Brussels Act of 1890, guaranteed the prohibition of the sea-borne trade in enslaved Africans and their freedom. However, although liberation responded both to international abolitionist agreements and to Islamic injunctions, the state often could not fulfill its commitment to both laws. Faced with contradictions, in particular in the case of the liberation of enslaved females (which required specific social, economic, and religious justification), the state opted on the side of preventing social disruption. Moreover, even though racially characterized abolition injunction ensured the liberation of enslaved Africans in Iran, it still could not guarantee the freedom of the many enslaved Iranians living abroad after 1929.

This chapter has shown that the progress of liberation depended in large part on an enslaved person's self-conscious desire for freedom. Thus, as liberation laws were ratified, confidence in their own powers of self-determination increased and the liberation movement gained momentum. Slave narratives are immensely important as historical testaments, testifying not only to the circumstances of the process of liberation in terms of the behavior of the people in charge, but also in revealing the enslaved people's lives, hopes, and expectations. They show us how concepts of personal freedom grew from the germ of an idea to full acceptance. The emergence of new forms of ethnocultural identities among communities of former enslaved people and within the context of a larger national identity has also occurred over the past century, most notably in Afro-Iranian communities.

It did not take long for the reality to become as ingrained in the fiber of society as slavery had been for so many centuries. Iran had become, as the certificates of liberation for a group of runaway enslaved people in Lengeh in 1927, explained: "a country where liberty and [the] Constitution are dominant [and] no one has the right to trade [in enslaved people]."[185]

THIS BOOK IS PREMISED on the theory that the unique socioeconomic and cultural circumstances and distinct historical processes responsible for perpetuating the institution of slavery in Iran also supported its eradication over the course of the nineteenth century, culminating in the Act of 1929. It has been shown that the abolition mandate emerged within the context of a program of national cultural identity formation beginning with a gradual reconsideration of social and religious norms associated with and justifications for slavery. A coalescence of grassroots nationalist imperatives, hereafter, facilitated the passage of emancipation legislation.

Fundamental to any discussion of slavery in Iran is an understanding that the institution was a feature of Muslim religious norms in terms of legitimizing the institution as well as providing protocols for the emancipation of enslaved people. As such, it is misleading to assume the theoretical underpinnings of the abolitionist mandate—as articulated by colonialists in the region during the nineteenth century—were unheard of or had no precedent in this part of the world. Instead, established social and religious traditions helped facilitate—and also delay—the British-led legislative efforts in 1848 to suppress the trade in enslaved Africans. The final push to abolish slavery developed hereafter as a part of a greater theocratic—and latterly nationalist—imperative, principally in response to specific historical developments such as the enslavement of indigenous Iranians after 1848 and the remapping of the Middle East after World War I. These provoked public opposition against further foreign interventions and inspired a nationalist mandate that sought to eradicate slavery among other socioeconomic reforms.

The British-led abolitionist mandate was the by-product of a revolutionary fervor that swept across Europe in the late eighteenth and early nineteenth centuries, finding expression in liberal and democratic idealism. When adopted by the British based in the Middle East, however, it acquired a different agenda by focusing exclusively on the trade of people sharing certain phenotypic traits, and in particular black enslaved Africans. In doing so, however, it led to an explosion in the trade of indigenous Iranians to meet a continued market demand for enslaved people.

The backlash within the country was swift and decisive: it unleashed ideological processes that took hold within the Iranian collective consciousness, first among intellectuals and politicians but gradually trickling down to the enslaved themselves. Iranians soon recognized that full emancipation would not only guarantee democracy but also help forge a unique national identity. The emancipation process, therefore, became more than just a humanitarian movement—it helped realize a pan-Iranian identity characterized by multiethnicity. Slowly but inexorably a groundswell of Iranian nationalists emerged, one that melded religious and political identities. It was the resulting movement that first brought constitutional reform and then full emancipation. Emancipation, however, did not occur uniformly across the country. Indeed, regional variations and individual circumstances combined with socioeconomic and demographic patterns revealed the greatest differentiation between north and south as well as in rural and urban areas.

ECONOMIC TRANSFORMATIONS

Economic autonomy was not often an immediate option for the newly freed enslaved people, either on an individual or collective level in society. Thus, even though the legislation removed the enslaved person category from the social structure, the relationship between master and former enslaved person often only changed on paper. Emancipation could not alter lifelong relationships, given the depth of economic, social, and sometimes even personal dependency. The new legal status of many former enslaved people, therefore, did not immediately lead to a severing of ties with former masters. Indeed, they often recognized that full economic independence could only be achieved by relying on their former productive roles. For this reason, some former enslaved people made the transition to full citizenship only gradually, living with former masters until they had earned economic independence. A personal relationship of clientage—or voluntary subordination without fixed remuneration for services—sometimes developed after enslaved person's liberation.[1] Notably, they enjoyed a degree of security, protected by their former master's wealth and position in society, as they worked toward their future full autonomy. This was especially the case for women, given the highly stratified and gendered character of Iranian society.

In the era of slavery, former enslaved people communities developed in both rural and urban settings in Iran. Kinship[2] ties were particularly important in forging links between former masters and enslaved people in rural areas and border provinces; but landlessness and unemployment also played a role. Since some sub-societies—such as those in Baluchistan—categorized these particular enslaved people as belonging to lower social groups, kinship ties remained essential in bringing communities together. In spite of ethnic differences, however, fundamental similarities existed among the former enslaved people populations in terms of economic activities. Since their numbers had been highest in the fishery and agricultural-based south, one of the major trends of the 1930s was the migration of emancipated enslaved people to urbanized centers for employment in a range of economic activities from domestic service to the burgeoning oil industry.[3] From former owners' points of view, this transition was difficult: indeed, they already had to face labor shortages following the prohibition of the trade in enslaved Africans after 1848 and as a result of emigration. Demand for labor, therefore, was a pressing concern both before and after emancipation. Urban settings tended to offer a greater range of job opportunities than rural areas. It was most common for liberated enslaved Africans, especially in the south and in coastal areas, to be employed as entertainers and performers of religious and traditional rituals.[4] Freed enslaved people in urban areas not only worked in service, usually as domestic servants,[5] but also in the local government offices or in the consular offices.[6]

Regardless of racial, ethnic, and socioeconomic backgrounds, the lives of all Iranians were inexorably altered in the twentieth century. As a result of foreign military occupation and political pressure, the country embarked on a series of political, social, legal, and economic reforms. Sociocultural reforms not only led to the decline of traditional institutions but also transformed urban and rural settings. In particular, the postemancipation integration of rural populations (and especially liberated enslaved people) into the cities accelerated the process of the national identity formation.

There is no doubt that fewer numbers of enslaved people in Iran after the late nineteenth century eased the adjustment to liberation and its aftermath for both the former masters and the enslaved people themselves. Indeed, it may be said that the Pahlavi regime was able to realize full emancipation due to the efforts of the Qajars in brokering relations with the British as part of negotiating the realization of the abolitionist mandate. Without this initial acclimatization, the country's feudal masters would never have been able to cope with the social and economic impacts of liberation.

The Pahlavi regime was also able to direct the transition of society from slavery to wage labor as a direct result of a viable and prosperous oil industry. Indeed, by the mid-twentieth century, not only had a semi-industrial society emerged, but there also were employment opportunities for all Iranians, including the descendants of enslaved people. Similarly, economic circumstances profoundly influenced social and migratory patterns with the expansion of markets allowing former enslaved people to detach more easily from their former masters.

Modernization policies and reforms of the twentieth century radically changed traditional hierarchical social and economic structures in Iran.

Among these were the 1907 abolition of land grants (*tuyul*) and the declaration of the land reforms of the 1950s (*iṣlāḥāt-i arāżī*)[7] to distribute land among the peasants and to release indentured rural peasants. After the White Revolution in 1960s, which officially abolished the feudal system of landownership, an erosion of the feudal (*arbāb va ra'yat*) aristocratic structures allowed former enslaved people communities in rural areas greater independence. About fifteen million acres of land and about fourteen thousand villages—equal to about 15 percent of the total villages in the country—had been distributed to about 520,000 peasant families by 1966.[8]

The catalyst for realizing real change, ultimately, was the burgeoning oil industry in the early twentieth century. With the accumulation of wealth necessary to drive fully autonomous political and economic infrastructures, social reform became a real possibility. Although its manifestation has witnessed large-scale migration from the country to cities, national and ethnocultural identities have been preserved and enhanced. The exploitation of oil reserves changed the population distribution and modes of production in both rural and urban areas. With market semicapitalism replacing semifeudalism, new social and economic classes emerged. Employer–worker relationships replaced landowner–peasant/slave relationships in rural areas and slave-master relationships in urban areas. Mechanization meant that less labor was required in rural areas, but it did guarantee steady income for those agricultural workers (*kārigarān-i kishāvarz-i mozdbegīr*) remaining on the land. Meanwhile, industrial areas absorbed the huge swell of workers who migrated from the country to the cities. At the beginning of the twentieth century, 90 percent of the population was involved in the agricultural sector, but this figure stood at only 46 percent in 1966, and today only 30 percent of the population is rural.[9]

The prioritization of religion in politics after the 1979 Iranian Revolution brought further social change. Peasants fought large-scale landowners and sought further redistribution of land. By January 1982, a total of 269 million acres were made public—an increase of 1,793 percent from 1966.[10] This was further enhanced by sustained governmental efforts to undermine the regional authority of local chiefs, khans, or shaykhs by replacing them with a *dehyār* (village assistant) and an elected council. Most recently, the collapse of the Soviet Union in 1991 and the overthrow of Saddam Hussein in Iraq in 2003 has given communities of the same ethnic groups situated on both sides of the borders the opportunity to reintegrate.

Present-day descendants of all liberated enslaved people in Iran realized diverse patterns of community formation based on regional and local social structures and in response to socioeconomic and political factors. Even though many enslaved people initially chose to remain with their former masters after 1929, they gradually became integrated into society. The process of acculturation and identity formation for these individuals and communities helped unify and create shared identities that were further shaped by mainstream politics and societal mores. For Afro-Iranians, however, there is no doubt that the adoption of aspects of Iranian-Islamic culture in the early stages of acculturation helped to bridge the gap between marginalization and citizenship.

DEVELOPMENT OF CULTURAL IDENTITIES

Throughout the era of institutional slavery various diasporic communities emerged in Iran. Because the international abolitionist movement that began in the nineteenth century was realized in Iran as it was elsewhere by focusing on racial considerations, the emancipation of enslaved Africans took precedence before that of any other group—even though, here, the enslavement of individuals was not justified by reference to race or ethnicity.[11] Indeed, Iranian society was not preoccupied with racial divisions: the experiences of both black and white—enslaved people and free—testifies as much to the vulnerability of as well as opportunities available to all races. Instead, a combination of economic and sociocultural factors must be seen as the basis for slavery. Emancipation not only impacted society in various environmental and socioeconomic ways, but also it forever changed social relationships and helped forge new or transform existing cultural identities. Indeed, the identity "transformation" owed more to individual community characteristics than to the uniform mores of mainstream society.[12]

The extent to which societal inclusivity and dynamic geographical infrastructures have facilitated group affiliation—or collectively bound identity— is better observed in large cities than in the rural areas. In the latter, rigidly hierarchical kinship communities resisted the infiltration of the dominant culture and maintained unique social and ethnic characteristics. In the same way, communities along Iran's many border frontiers—the Arab states, Iraq, and Pakistan—tended to embrace transnational identities. These complex intercultural relations with neighboring countries allowed remote borderland communities to maintain close familial and cultural ties for centuries. Recent changes to international boundaries along with the forces of globalization and modernization have further impacted these groups' identities, both in terms of integration and disintegration.

AFRO-IRANIAN IDENTITY

The regional and social factors were more important in creating the diverse identities of Afro-Iranian communities since emancipation in 1929.[13] Broadly speaking, however, it is important to distinguish between the experiences of some of these communities in urban and rural areas: in the former, they tended to undergo assimilation (evidenced by the emergence of mixed-race populations) while, in the latter, integration was more usual. Specifically, assimilation was inevitable in both large port and inland cities, where ideas, technology, and migration brought people of diverse ethnic groups and nationalities into close contact. Although some urban settings provided concentrations of specific subethnic and kinship groups, these close intercommunity networks were also responsible for allowing their members to develop relationships with the rest of society. As a rule, rural communities tended to be characterized by integration; but marginalization did occur in some of those more environmentally or geographically remote areas (such as Baluchistan[14]).

It is within this context that today's Afro-Iranian communities in the southern provinces have perpetuated a range of ethnocultural rituals, including those associated with spirit possession. Even after prohibition ended the importation of enslaved Africans into Iran in the mid-nineteenth century, these ceremonies continued to be widely practiced. The belief in spirit possession and the practice of healing cults can be observed among descendants of enslaved Africans among the Hausa, Fulbe, and Bambara people, as well as among descendants of enslaved Africans in Brazil, Cuba, and Haiti.[15] Similarly, the enslaved Oromos and Gurages of Ethiopia in northeast Africa introduced into the Iranian society many unique traditions, such as the Zar,[16] Liwa, and Gowat ceremonies.[17] Such healing rituals may have been a psychological response to the natural calamities (including destructive storms, earthquakes, and drought) frequent along the coastal areas of the Indian Ocean, Gulf of Oman, and Persian Gulf.[18] Their impact on the main industries of agriculture and fishing in addition to secondary impacts (including contagious disease and pestilence) tended to increase the inhabitants' sense of vulnerability and impotence.[19] As such, practitioners often related the source of illnesses to the natural elements—water, wind, and soil—and made associations deeply rooted in the memory of mortality, fear, and anxieties connected with economic privation.

Within cities, Afro-Iranians tended to establish and congregate in separate quarters.[20] In Bandar 'Abbas, they lived in a district known as the "Black Quarter" and used specific places for religious ceremonies.[21] By 1907, the population of this district was about three hundred—some of whom were employed as entertainers. They were vibrant, tax-paying members of society.[22] Similarity can be found with the nineteenth-century residential areas in Zanzibar, the Stone Town where various ethnic groups such as Arabs, Goans, and Indian communities (Banyans)[23] lived and Ng'ambo (the other side) where African and enslaved people descendants lived. However, such city structure was not the result of segregation but a specific historical process.[24]

Political transitions and reforms were also instrumental in providing opportunities for the descendants of enslaved Africans to preserve their cultural identity. Importantly, political culture was never able to penetrate fully or significantly impact these realities. Attempts to outlaw some public festivals — such as the Liwa[25] — were unsuccessful and influenced their covert perpetuation.[26] Ironically, social and political transformations have both intensified and eased assimilation processes and have guaranteed the survival of many Afro-Iranian rituals: indeed, while the Pahlavi regime attempted to curtail Afro-Iranian cultural expressions, the Islamic Republic's encouragement of multiculturalism has seen state organization of performances of healing rituals. Transcending familial, tribal, regional, national, and even transnational boundaries, these new ethnocultural expressions have served to unify communities and create shared identities.

Various archival and anecdotal sources have sought to evaluate the extent to which various diplomatic pressures and domestic circumstances supported the processes leading to the end of slave trading and the abolition of slavery in Iran over a period from the early nineteenth century until the act of 1929 finally legislated its termination. It has been shown that contrary to the opinion of a generation of Western and Orientalist scholars, the institution of slavery was not "unique to Islam"; instead, ideological and theological tenets both provided for its perpetuation *as well as* its eradication. In the same way, the social and economic forces that both supported and restricted the institution have revealed the ease with which former enslaved people and their offspring could be integrated into society. The British-supported 1848 royal edict banning the seaborne market in enslaved Africans into Iran did inadvertently help galvanize indifferent or uncommitted support for the abolitionist mandate. Indeed, slavery became recognized as an increasingly domestic concern as greater numbers of indigenous Iranians were captured and enslaved in the second half of the nineteenth century in order to fill the resulting supply and demand vacuum. The popular reaction was decisive and explains how the Pahlavi regime was successfully able to convince both secular and religious segments of society that passage of the Act of Emancipation in 1929 supported a program of national identity formation.

Today, descendants of enslaved people from all ethnocultural backgrounds living in Iran have been integrated and/or assimilated within the society and represent examples of a single, but transmutable, collective national identity. In some areas, however, endogamous marriage practices—common in the Middle East to consolidate kindred group ties, to maintain lineage purity and to circulate wealth within a community—have helped preserve ethnic and cultural characteristics of some ethnocultural groups. Members of these communities do not view themselves within the context of slavery but rather in terms of Iranian local culture and as one of many ethnic groups within a heterogeneous state. Ending the slave trade, therefore, not only inspired the emergence of a pan-Iranian identity, but facilitated the creation of one of the few multiethnic countries in the Middle East. The goal of this book is not only to examine the history of its victims but also to demonstrate that their voices have been—and continue to be—heard.

GLOSSARY

'abīd   slave
'adālat   justice
andarūn, harem   interior, a portion of the house devoted to women and children
arbāb   master, landowner
azadi   liberty
bacha (pl. bachahā)   child
baghalahā   vessels
bāshī   chief
chādur   long veil
dada (pl. dadahā)   female nurse
darbār-i a'ẓam   supreme court
dīvān-i 'adlīya-yi a'ẓam   supreme court
dīvān khāna-yi 'adālat   justice bureau
dāyere   small round drum
fatwa (pl. fatwahā)   religious decree
firmān (pl. farāmīn)   royal decree
ghulām (pl. ghulāmān)   male servant
ghulām-i shāhīhā   royal bodyguards
hakim   ruler, governor
harām   illegal
īyālāt   provinces
kāfar   nonbeliever
kākā   brother
kanīz (pl. kanīzān)   female servant, also used to refer to a female slave
khan, shaykh   community head
khauja, Āghā   eunuch
lala (pl. lalahā)   male nurse
majlis   parliament
millī   national
mujtahidin   high-ranking religious scholar
nukar   servant
qul (pl. qullar)   refers to a male slave
ra'yat   peasant
ṣandūq-i 'idālat   Box of Justice
shari'a   Islamic law
sīāh   black
sunna   the deed and sayings of the Prophet Muhammad
tanzimat   reform
tuyul   land grants
'ulama'   religious scholar

'urf   customary
umm al-walad   mother of the child
waqf   endowment
zakat   religious tax
zangī   from Zanzibar

NOTES

A NOTE TO THE READER

1. "*Ray*" and "*man*", 'Ali Akbar Dehkhoda, *Lughatnama-yi Dehkhoda*, 14 vols. (Tehran: Daneshgah-i Tehran, 1373).

2. James Baillie Fraser, *Narrative of a Journey into Khorasan, in the Years 1821 and 1822* (London: Longman, Hurst, Rees, Orme, Brown, and Green, 1825), 9.

3. Arnold Burrowes Kemball to L. P. Willoughby, March 4, 1842, FO 84/426, NAUK, London.

4. Muhammad 'Ali Jamalzada, *Ganj-i Shaygan* (Tehran: Sukhan, 1384), 177.

5. Ibid., 173.

6. Fraser, *Narrative of a Journey into Khorasan*, 10; T1 ~ Br4; T1 ~ GC1.85.

7. C. J. Wills, *In the Land of the Lion and Sun, or Modern Persia* (London: Ward, Lock, & Co., 1891), 63.

8. Fraser, *Narrative of a Journey into Khorasan*, 10.

9. Wills, *In the Land of the Lion*, 63.

10. J. R. Wellsted, *Travels to the City of the Caliphs, along the Shores of the Persian Gulf* (London: Henry Colburn, 1840), 1:84.

11. Richard F. Burton, *Personal Narrative of a Pilgrimage to Al-Madinah & Meccah* (1893; repr., New York: Dover Publications, 1964), 2:12.

12. Wills, *In the Land of the Lion*, 63.

13. Henry Creswicke Rawlinson to Henry Wellesley, April 28, 1847, L/PS/5/450, BL; £1 = Sh13.3.

14. Wellsted, *Travels to the City of the Caliphs*, 1:279.

15. Jamalzada, *Ganj-i Shaygan*, 177.

INTRODUCTION

1. "The name Persia and Iran had both been used for the area since antiquity. Although Iran was a more correct name for the modern kingdom, westerners used Persia preferentially until 1935." Gwillim Law, *Administrative Subdivisions of Countries: A Comprehensive World Reference, 1900 through 1998* (Jefferson, North Carolina: McFarland & Company, 1999), 182. See also Houchang E. Chehabi, "Staging the Emperor's New Clothes: Dress Codes and Nation-Building under Reza Shah," *Iranian Studies* 26, no. 3/4 (1993): 226.

2. Ehud R. Toledano, *The Ottoman Slave Trade and Its Suppression, 1840–1890* (Princeton: Princeton University Press, 1982); Ehud R. Toledano, *Slavery and Abolition in the Ottoman Middle East* (Seattle: University of Washington Press, 1998).

3. Y. Hakan Erdem, *Slavery in the Ottoman Empire and Its Demise, 1800–1909* (Oxford: St. Martin's Press, 1996).

4. Madeline C. Zilfi, *Women and Slavery in the Late Ottoman Empire: The Design of Difference* (New York: Cambridge University Press, 2010).

5. Roger Owen, *The Middle East in the World Economy 1800–1914* (1981; repr., London and New York: I. B. Tauris, 2005), ix, 24.

6. Terence Walz and Kenneth M. Cuno, "The Study of Slavery in Nineteenth-Century Egypt, Sudan, and the Ottoman Mediterranean," in *Race and Slavery in the Middle East: Histories of Trans-Saharan Africans in Nineteenth-Century Egypt, Sudan, and the Ottoman Mediterranean*, ed. Terence Walz and Kenneth M. Cuno (Cairo: American University in Cairo Press, 2010), 1–3.

7. I have interviewed the descendants of enslaved Africans, visited their communities, and collected data from local historians and people (some of whom remembered enslaved people ownership in their own families). Over the last decade and a half, I have been able to film communities of descendants of enslaved Africans in the southern provinces. Although they do not have any knowledge of their ancestral homeland, their connection with Africa is strongly apparent in their perpetuation of many ethnocultural rituals. Behnaz A. Mirzai, *Afro-Iranian Lives* (Toronto: AfroIranianfilm, 2007), DVD; Behnaz A. Mirzai, *The African-Baluchi Trance Dance* (Toronto: AfroIranianfilm, 2012), DVD.

8. Jakob Eduard Polak, *Persien, das Land und seine Bewohner*, 2 vols. (Leipzig: Brockhaus, 1865).

9. Abdulghaffar Najm al-Daula, *Asar-i Najm al-Daula safarnama-yi duwwum-i Najm al-Daula be Khuzistan*, ed. Ahmad Ketabi (Tehran: Pazhuheshgah-i ʿulum-i ensani va mutaleʿat-i farhangi, 1386); Abdulghaffar Najm al-Daula, *Safarnama-yi Khuzestan* (Tehran: Anjuman-i asar-i mafakher-i farhangi, 1385).

10. Firuz Mirza Farman Farma, *Safarnamih-yi Kerman va Baluchistan* (Tehran: Nashr-i tarikh-i Iran, 1380).

11. The political division of Iran was not fixed. In the nineteenth century, Baluchistan was under Kerman, Sistan was under Khorasan, and the southern ports were part of Fars.

12. Abdulhussain Mirza Farman Farma, *Musaferat nama-yi Kerman va Baluchistan*, ed. Iraj Afshar (Tehran: Asatir, 1383).

13. Ahmad ʿAli Khan Vaziri, *Joghrafia-yi Baluchistan*, ed. Muhammad Reza Nasiri (Tehran: Anjuman-i asar va mafakher-i farhangi, 1386).

14. Muhammad ʿAli Sadid al-Saltana Kababi, *Sarzaminha-yi shumali piramun-i Khalij-i Fars va darya-yi Oman dar sad sale pish*, ed. Ahmad Eqtedari (Tehran: Amir Kabir, 1386); Muhammad ʿAli Sadid al-Saltana Kababi, *Bandar ʿAbbas va Khalij-i Fars* (Tehran: Donya-yi ketab, 1368).

15. J. G. Lorimer, *Gazetteer of the Persian Gulf, Oman and Central Arabia*, 6 vols. (Calcutta: Superintendent Government Printing, 1908–1915).

16. General Esmaʿil Khan Mirpanjeh, *Khaterat-i esarat ruznama-yi safar-i Khawrazm va Khiva*, ed. Safaʾ al-Din Tabraʿiyan (Tehran: Muʾsesa-yi pazhuhesh va mutaleʿat-i farhangi, 1370).

17. Dust ʿAli Khan Muʿayyir al-Mamalek, *Yaddashthaei az zendegani-yi khususi-yi Nasir al-Din Shah* (Tehran: Nashr-i tarikh-i Iran, 1362).

18. Muhammad Taqi Lesan al-Mulk Sepehr, *Nasekh al-tawarikh tarikh-i Qajariya*, 3 vols. (Tehran: Asatir, 1377).

19. Nazem al-Islam Kermani, *Tarikh-i bidari-yi Iranian*, 3 vols. (Tehran: Amir Kabir, 1371).

20. Hassan Arfa, *Under Five Shahs* (New York: William Morrow & Co., 1965).

21. The chapter "Iran and Britain," contains a single section entitled "The Slave Trade in the Persian Gulf." Fereydun Adamiyat, *Amir Kabir va Iran* (Tehran: Khawrazmi, 1362), 514–534.

22. See "The Slave Trade and the abolition of the Iranian navigation during the Qajar period." Esma'il Ra'in, *Daryanavardi-yi Iranian* (Tehran: Sekka, 1350), 2: 677–711.

23. Afsaneh Najmabadi, *The Story of the Daughters of Quchan* (Syracuse: Syracuse University Press, 1998).

24. Mohammed Ennaji, *Slavery, the State, and Islam*, trans. Teresa Lavender Fagan (New York: Cambridge University Press, 2013).

25. Ennaji, *Slavery, the State, and Islam*, 3.

26. J. B. Kelly, *Britain and the Persian Gulf, 1795–1880* (Oxford: Clarendon Press, 1968).

27. Frederick Cooper, *Plantation Slavery on the East Coast of Africa* (Portsmouth, NH: Heinemann, 1997), 9.

28. Cooper, *Plantation Slavery on the East Coast of Africa*, 4.

29. William Gervase Clarence-Smith, *Islam and the Abolition of Slavery* (London: Hurst & Company, 2006).

30. Toledano, *Slavery and Abolition in the Ottoman Middle East*, x, 10.

31. Ibid., 114, 116; see also Toledano, *The Ottoman Slave Trade and Its Suppression*.

32. Erdem, *Slavery in the Ottoman Empire and Its Demise*, 67.

33. Ibid., 125.

34. Zilfi, *Women and Slavery in the Late Ottoman Empire*, xii, 179.

35. Chouki El Hamel, *Black Morocco: A History of Slavery, Race, and Islam* (New York: Cambridge University Press, 2013), 9–11.

36. Jerzy Zdanowski, *Slavery and Manumission: British Policy in the Red Sea and the Persian Gulf in the First Half of the 20th Century* (Reading: Ithaca Press, 2013).

37. Suzanne Miers, *Slavery in the Twentieth Century: The Evolution of a Global Problem* (Walnut Creek, CA: AltaMira Press, 2003).

38. Miers, xiii.

39. Seymour Drescher, "Emperors of the World: British Abolitionism and Imperialism," in *Abolitionism and Imperialism in Britain, Africa, and the Atlantic*, ed. Derek R. Peterson (Athens: Ohio University Press, 2010), 132, 139.

40. Ibid., 143.

41. Robin Law, "Abolition and Imperialism: International Law and the British Suppression of the Atlantic Slave Trade," in *Abolitionism and Imperialism in Britain, Africa, and the Atlantic*, ed. Derek R. Peterson (Athens: Ohio University Press, 2010), 150.

42. Charles Issawi, *An Economic History of the Middle East and North Africa* (New York: Columbia University Press, 1982; London: Routledge, 2006), xii. Citations refer to the Routledge edition.

43. See Amartya Sen, *Development as Freedom* (New York: Alfred A. Knopf, 1999).

44. Miers, *Slavery in the Twentieth Century*, 340–342.

45. Charles Issawi, *The Middle East Economy: Decline and Recovery* (Princeton: Markus Wiener Publishers, 1995), 189.

46. There is a direct link between these trade agreements and the arms race that preceded World War I: take, for instance, the modernization of the British navy between 1904 and 1910, which saw the replacement of coal-burning ships with oil-fueled vessels. Iran became vitally important to this process especially after oil was discovered at Masjid Sulaiman in 1908. B. S. McBeth, *British Oil Policy 1919–1939* (London: Frank Cass, 1985), 1; J. E. Peterson, "Britain and the Gulf: At the Periphery of Empire," in *The Persian Gulf in History*, ed. Lawrence G. Potter (New York: Palgrave Macmillan, 2009), 284. The Middle East has one-half of

the world's oil reserves and around one-quarter of the global supplies of natural gas crucial to the world economy. Rodney Wilson, *Economic Development in the Middle East* (London: Routledge, 2013), 107.

47. Cooper, *Plantation Slavery on the East Coast of Africa*, 14–16.

48. Toledano, *Slavery and Abolition*, 166.

49. See Edward A. Alpers, *The Indian Ocean in World History* (Oxford: Oxford University Press, 2014).

50. Issawi, *The Middle East Economy*, 169–171.

51. Some of their descendants founded independent or semi-independent dynasties in Iran, such as the Ghaznavid and the Khwarezmid. Elton L. Daniel and Ali Akbar Mahdi, *Culture and Customs of Iran* (Westport, CT: Greenwood Press, 2006), 17; see also Matthew S. Gordon, "The Turkish Military Elite of Samarra and the Third Century Land Tenure System," in *Slave Elites in the Middle East and Africa*, ed. Miura Toru and John Edward Philips (London and New York: Kegan Paul International, 2000).

52. See Sussan Babaie et al., *Slaves of the Shah: New Elites of Safavid Iran* (London: I. B. Tauris, 2004).

53. See Ann Lambton, *Landlord and Peasant in Persia* (London: Oxford University Press, 1953).

54. Ugo E. M. Fabietti, *Ethnography at the Frontier: Space, Memory and Society in Southern Balochistan* (New York: Peter Lang, 2011), 49.

55. Aijaz Ahmad, "The National Question in Baluchistan," *Focus on Baluchistan* 3, no. 8/9 (May-June, 1973): 10.

56. Sadid al-Saltana Kababi, *Sarzaminha-yi shumali*, 205.

57. Abbas Amanat, "Introduction: Iranian Identity Boundaries: A Historical Overview," in *Iran Facing Others: Identity Boundaries in a Historical Perspective*, ed. Abbas Amanat and Farzin Vejdani (New York: Palgrave Macmillan, 2012), 10; Pirouz Mojtahed-Zadeh, "The Concept of Boundary and Its Origin in the Ancient Persian Tradition," in *Boundary Politics and International Boundaries of Iran: With Afghanistan, Armenia, Azerbaijan Republic, Bahrain, (the autonomous republic of Ganjah) Iraq, Kazakhstan, Kuwait, Oman, Pakistan, Qatar, Russia, Saudi Arabia, Turkey, Turkmenistan, and the United Arab Emirates*, ed. Pirouz Mojtahed-Zadeh (Boca Raton: Universal Publishers, 2006), 15.

58. H. Lyman Stebbins, "British Imperialism, Regionalism, and Nationalism in Iran, 1890–1919," in *Iran Facing Others: Identity Boundaries in a Historical Perspective*, ed. Abbas Amanat and Farzin Vejdani (New York: Palgrave Macmillan, 2012), 151.

59. Joanna de Groot, *Religion, Culture and Politics in Iran: From the Qajars to Khomeini* (New York: I. B. Tauris, 2007), 21.

60. Shlomo D. Goitein, *Studies in Islamic History and Institutions* (Leiden: Brill, 2010), 41.

61. Ehud R. Toledano, "Introduction," in *African Communities in Asia and the Mediterranean: Identities between Integration and Conflict*, ed. Ehud R. Toledano (Trenton: Africa World Press, 2012), 10.

62. Wilson, *Economic Development in the Middle East*, 111.

63. Hossein Bashiriyeh, *The State and Revolution in Iran: 1962–1982* (Oxon: Routledge, 2011), 12.

64. Khusraw Khusravi, *Jazira-yi Kharg dar dura-yi estila-yi naft* (Tehran: Danishgah-i Tehran, 1342), 110.

65. De Groot, *Religion, Culture and Politics in Iran*, 14.

66. Isma'il 'Ajami, *Shishdangi* (Tehran: Toos, 1352), 110.

67. De Groot, *Religion, Culture and Politics in Iran*, 18.

68. Eve M. Troutt Powell, "Will That Subaltern Ever Speak? Finding African Slaves in the Historiography of the Middle East," in *Middle East Historiographies: Narrating the Twentieth Century*, ed. Israel Gershoni, Amy Singer, and Y. Hakan Erdem (Seattle: University of Washington Press, 2006), 256.

69. William Francklin, *Observations Made on a Tour from Bengal to Persia: In the Years 1786-7* (London: T. Cadell, 1788), 60; Mohsen Motamedi, *Joghrafiya-yi tarikhi-yi Tehran* (Tehran: Markaz-i Nashr-i Daneshgahi, 1381), 71.

70. Geographical names associated with Africa represented the origin of Africans concentrated in these areas: the Bab Zangi village in the Hoseyn-abade Goruh district in Kerman; Zangi Kalat, located in Iranian Baluchistan near the Pakistan border; the Karmeh Zangi village in Hormozgan; Sheykh Zangi in Bushehr; the Zangi Mahalleh village, Zangian in Mazandaran; and Zangabad in the province of West Azerbaijan.

71. Also known as Twelvers, this branch of Shi'a Islam believes in the twelve imams.

72. Paul E. Lovejoy, "Slavery in the Context of Ideology," in *The Ideology of Slavery in Africa*, ed. Paul E. Lovejoy (London: Sage, 1981), 15.

73. Clarence-Smith, *Islam and the Abolition of Slavery*, 2.

74. Ehud R. Toledano, "Enslavement and Abolition in Muslim Societies," review of *Islam and the Abolition of Slavery*, by William Gervase Clarence-Smith, *Journal of African History* 48, 2007, 481.

75. El Hamel, *Black Morocco*, 9.

76. Ibid., 62.

77. Ronald Segal, *Islam's Black Slaves: The Other Black Diaspora* (New York: Farrar, Straus and Giroux, 2001), 6–7.

78. Frederick Cooper, "Islam and Cultural Hegemony: The Ideology of Slaveowners on the East African Coast," in *The Ideology of Slavery in Africa*, ed. Paul E. Lovejoy (London: Sage, 1981), 272, 273.

79. Cooper, "Islam and Cultural Hegemony," 273.

80. Ibid.

81. Troutt Powell, "Will That Subaltern Ever Speak?" 247.

82. Ibid., 249.

83. A notable exception is implementation of abolitionist practices by the Mu'tazalas and the Bateniyas of slavery following Shi'i Imam Ja'far Sadiq's (d. 756) advice. Syed Ameer Ali, *Personal Law of the Mahommedans, according to all the Schools, together with a Comparative Sketch of the Law of Inheritance among the Sunnis and the Shiahs* (London: W. H. Allen & Co., 1880), 39.

84. Ja'far ibn al-Hasan Al-Muhaqqiq al-Hilli, *Droit Musulman. Recueil de lois concernant les Musulmans Schyites*, Trans. Amédée Querry (Paris: Imprimerie nationale, 1871), vol. 2, 109; El Hamel, *Black Morocco*, 47.

85. Correspondence between the Iranian and British officials on the liberation of Delafruz, an enslaved female, Jamadi al-thani 8, 1332, Q1332.3.3, VUK, Tehran.

86. Zilfi, *Women and Slavery in the Late Ottoman Empire*, 98. Notwithstanding, most of the tens of thousands of foreigners enslaved outside the Ottoman Empire were actually organized into social groupings based on religion, wealth, and skin color. By contrast, the situation in Moroccan society was more strictly differentiated according to race and skin color in order to privilege the Arabs and Berbers, as El Hamel has noted (*Black Morocco*, 10).

87. *Ghulām* is an Arabic word meaning boy or servant.

88. *Kanīz* is derived from kanīg, the Pahlavi word (the pre-Islamic Iranian language), meaning girl or maid. D. N. MacKenzie, *A Concise Pahlavi Dictionary* (London: Oxford University Press, 1971), 49.

89. *Ḥājī* and *ḥajīa* applied to those who had made the hajj—the pilgrimage to Mecca.

90. 'Abdullah Mustaufi, *Sharh-i zendegani-yi man: Tarikh-i ejtema'i va edari-yi daura-yi Qajar* (Tehran: Zavvar, 1377), 1:214.

91. See Aliakbar Dehkhoda, *Lughatnama-yi Dehkhoda* (Tehran: Daneshgah-i Tehran, 1373); for information on names referring to Africans in Asia, see Shihan De Silva jayasuriya, "Identifying Africans in Asia: What's In a Name?" in *Uncovering the History of Africans in Asia*, ed. Shihan de Silva Jayasuriya and Jean-Pierre Angenot (Leiden: Brill, 2008).

CHAPTER 1. COMMERCE AND SLAVERY ON IRAN'S FRONTIERS, 1600–1800

1. Reza Quli Khan Hedayat, *Tarikh-i ruzat al-safa-yi Naseri* (Qom: Hekmat, 1339), 8:431; Joaquim Veríssimo Serrão, *Un voyageur Portugais en Perse au début du XVIIe siècle: Nicolau de Orta Rebelo* (Lisbon: Comité National Portugais, 1972), 47.

2. Rudolph P. Matthee, *The Politics of Trade in Safavid Iran: Silk for Silver, 1600–1730* (Cambridge: Cambridge University Press, 1999), 27.

3. João Teles e Cunha, "The Portuguese Presence in the Persian Gulf," in *The Persian Gulf in History*, ed. Lawrence G. Potter (New York: Palgrave Macmillan, 2009), 208.

4. Haj Mirza Hasan Husayni Fasa'i, *Farsnama-yi Naseri*, ed. Mansur Rastgar Fasa'i (Tehran: Amir Kabir, 1382), 1:444; Lorimer, *Gazetteer of the Persian Gulf*, 1: pt. 1A, 9; Serrão, *Un voyageur Portugais en Perse*, 47.

5. Husayni Fasa'i, *Farsnama-yi Naseri*, 1:466; J. B. Kelly, *Britain and the Persian Gulf, 1795–1880* (Oxford: Clarendon Press, 1968), 185.

6. Arnold T. Wilson, *The Persian Gulf* (1928; repr., London: George Allen & Unwin, 1959), 151; John R. Jenson, ed., *Journal and Letter Book of Nicholas Buckeridge, 1651–1654* (Minneapolis: University of Minnesota Press, 1973), 7.

7. See Jenson, *Journal and Letter Book*; Timothy Walker, "Slaves or Soldiers? African Conscripts in Portuguese India, 1857–1860," in *Slavery in South Asian History*, ed. Indrani Chatterjee and Richard M. Eaton (Bloomington: Indiana University Press, 2006); Mohammad Bagher Vosoughi, "The Kings of Hormuz: From the Beginning until the Arrival of the Portuguese," in *The Persian Gulf in History*, ed. Lawrence G. Potter (New York: Palgrave Macmillan, 2009), 98; See also M. N. Pearson, *The Portuguese in India* (Cambridge: Cambridge University Press, 1987), 94–96.

8. The term "Galla" was widely used in the older texts, but today is considered to be pejorative. For this reason, I have replaced it with "Oromo" throughout the book. See Yohannes K. Mekonnen, ed., *Ethiopia: The Land, Its People, History and Culture* (Dar es Salaam: New Africa Press, 2013), 277.

9. Lorimer, *Gazetteer of the Persian Gulf*, 1: pt. 1A, 4.

10. Thomas Vernet, "Slave Trade and Slavery on the Swahili Coast, 1500–1750," in *Slavery, Islam and Diaspora*, ed. Behnaz A. Mirzai, Ismael Musah Montana, and Paul E. Lovejoy (Trenton, NJ: Africa World Press, 2009), 50; Joseph Harris, "Africans in Asian History," in *Global Dimensions of the African Diaspora*, ed. Joseph Harris (Washington, DC: Howard University Press, 1993), 328.

11. Vosoughi, "The Kings of Hormuz," 89.

12. Cunha, "The Portuguese Presence in the Persian Gulf," 207.

13. G. Bondarevsky, "Turning the Persian Gulf into a British Lake: British Domination in the Indian Ocean in the Nineteenth and Twentieth Century," in *The Indian Ocean: Explorations in History, Commerce and Politics*, ed. Satish Chandra (New Delhi: Sage Publications, 1987), 318.

14. Wilson, *The Persian Gulf*, 147; Matthee, *The Politics of Trade*, 105.

15. Lorimer, *Gazetteer of the Persian Gulf*, 1: pt. 1A, 70.

16. Ibid., 13; Sugata Bose and Ayesha Jalal, *Modern South Asia: History, Culture, Political Economy* (New York: Routledge, 2004), 34; see also K. N. Chaudhuri, *Trade and Civilization in the Indian Ocean: An Economic History from the Rise of Islam to 1750* (Cambridge: Cambridge University Press, 1985), 90.

17. Mehdi Quli Khan Hedayat (Mukhber al-Saltana), *Guzaresh-i Iran, Qajariya va mashrutiyat* (Tehran: Nuqra, 1363), 145; Lorimer, *Gazetteer of the Persian Gulf*, 2: pt. 1A, 341.

18. See Jamalzada, *Ganj-i Shaygan*.

19. Owen, *The Middle East in the World Economy*, 92.

20. See Eric Williams, *Capitalism and Slavery* (Chapel Hill: University of North Carolina Press, 1944); also see Hilary McD. Beckles, *Britain's Black Debt: Reparations for Caribbean Slavery and Native Genocide* (Kingston: University of the West Indies Press, 2012).

21. Robin Law, "Slave-Raiders and Middlemen, Monopolists and Free-Traders: The Supply of Slaves for the Atlantic Trade in Dahomey c. 1715–1850," *Journal of African History* 30, no. 1 (1989): 45–68. For more information on the British and French involvement in the slave trade, see Philip Curtin, *The Atlantic Slave Trade: A Census* (Madison: University of Wisconsin Press, 1969); see also Paul E. Lovejoy, *Transformations in Slavery: A History of Slavery in Africa*, 3rd ed. (Cambridge: Cambridge University Press, 2012); and also see Herbert S. Klein and Ben Vinson III, *African Slavery in Latin America and the Caribbean*, 2nd ed. (Oxford: Oxford University Press, 2007).

22. Joseph E. Harris, "Return Movements to West and East Africa: A Comparative Approach." in *Global Dimensions of the African Diaspora*, ed., Joseph E. Harris (Washington, DC: Howard University Press, 1993), 56.

23. Lorimer, *Gazetteer of the Persian Gulf*, 1: pt. 1A, 88–89.

24. Ibid., 105.

25. Ibid., pt. 2, 1780; for instance, in 1763, Shaykh Sa'dun of Bushehr signed a treaty with the British. Interestingly, the ninth article of this treaty referred to the enslaved persons of the British "who may desert, are not to be protected, or entertained by the Shaykh or his people, but bona fide secured and returned." Sultan Muhammad al-Qasimi, *The Myth of Arab Piracy in the Gulf* (London: Croom Helm, ca. 1986), 24.

26. Ibid., pt. 2, 2475.

27. Entrepreneurial activities by the Dutch, English, and French meant that Bandar 'Abbas was to become an important trading hub throughout the seventeenth century. One of its main commercial activities was shipbuilding.

28. The Dutch controlled the spice trade in the region and were exempt from import taxes. Wilson, *The Persian Gulf*, 163; Engelbert Kaempfer, *Safarnama-yi Kaempfer*, trans. Keykavus Jahandari (Tehran: Khawrazmi, 1363), 115.

29. Willem Floor, "Dutch Relations with the Persian Gulf," in *The Persian Gulf in History*, ed. Lawrence G. Potter (New York: Palgrave Macmillan, 2009), 254.

30. Lorimer, *Gazetteer of the Persian Gulf*, 1: pt. 1A, 130.

31. Mirza Muhammad Sadeq Musavi Nami Isfahani, *Tarikh-i giti gusha dar tarikh-i khan-dan-i Zand*, ed. Azizullah Bayat (Tehran: Amir Kabir, 1368), 62; Floor, "Dutch Relations with the Persian Gulf," 250.

32. Wilson, *The Persian Gulf*, 169.

33. See Patricia Risso, *Oman and Muscat: An Early Modern History* (London: Croom Helm, 1986).

34. Throughout the eighteenth century, the ports of the Gulf of Oman and the southern Persian Gulf were either ruled by independent shaykhs and were the protectorates of the British (such as Abu Dhabi, Dubai, Sharjah, Umm al Qaywayn, Ra's al Khaymah, and 'Ajman) or were under the control of the rulers of Masqat (such as Sohar, Suwaiq, and Masna'a). Muhammad 'Ali Sadid al-Saltana Kababi, *al-Menas fi ahval-i al-ghaus va al-ghavas* (Tehran: Modern, 1308), 3.

35. Lorimer, *Gazetteer of the Persian Gulf*, 1: pt. 2, 2494; See Erik Gilbert, "Oman and Zanzibar: The Historical Roots of a Global Community," in *Cross Currents and Community Networks: The History of the Indian Ocean World*, ed. Himanshu Prabha Ray and Edward A. Alpers (New Delhi, Oxford University Press, 2007).

36. Lorimer, *Gazetteer of the Persian Gulf*, 1: pt. 1A, 79.

37. George N. Curzon, *Persia and the Persian Question* (1892; repr., New York: Barnes & Noble, 1966), 2:232.

38. Lorimer, *Gazetteer of the Persian Gulf*, 1: pt. 1A, 107–109; see also pt. 2, 1914. Indeed, the Omanis often acted independently, making alliances as necessary.

39. Husayni Fasa'i, *Farsnama-yi Naseri*, 1:495.

40. Sir Percy Molesworth Sykes, *A History of Persia*, 3rd ed. (1915; repr., London: Macmillan & Co., 1963), 2:352; Curzon, *Persia and the Persian Question*, 2:422.

41. Sadid al-Saltana Kababi, *Sarzaminha-yi shumali*, 202; Kelly, *Britain and the Persian Gulf*, 19. The term *Qawasem* refers to all of the tribes of the coast of northwestern Oman known to be engaged in piracy. In 1808, they possessed sixty-three large vessels and a very large fleet of small ones, keeping about nineteen thousand men afloat. Lorimer, *Gazetteer of the Persian Gulf*, 1: pt. 1A, 178, 183.

42. Kelly, *Britain and the Persian Gulf*, 19.

43. Lorimer, *Gazetteer of the Persian Gulf*, 1: pt. 1A, 110.

44. Kelly, *Britain and the Persian Gulf*, 416–417.

45. Ibid., 10.

46. For the political, military, and commercial expansions of the Omani Arabs in the Indian Ocean see M. Reda Bhacker, *Trade and Empire in Muscat and Zanzibar: The Roots of British Domination* (London: Routledge, 1994).

47. Al-Qasimi, *The Myth of Arab Piracy*, 9.

48. Lorimer, *Gazetteer of the Persian Gulf*, 1: pt. 1A, 602, 603, and pt. 2, 2153.

49. Sadid al-Saltana Kababi, *Bandar 'Abbas*, 201.

50. Lorimer, *Gazetteer of the Persian Gulf*, 1: pt. 1A, 421–422, 148; Kelly, *Britain and the Persian Gulf*, 13. See also J. S. Buckingham, *Travels in Assyria, Media, and Persia*, 2 vols. (London: Henry Colburn and Richard Bentley, 1830); Fraser, *Narrative of a Journey into Khorasan*; M. Niebuhr (1733–1815), *Travels through Arabia and Other Countries in the East*, trans. Robert Heron (1764–1807), 2 vols. (Beirut: Librairie du Liban, 1968); and Kelly, *Britain and the Persian Gulf*, 185, 533.

51. Lorimer, *Gazetteer of the Persian Gulf*, 1: pt. 2, 1911, and pt. 1A, 180.

52. Abdul Sheriff, *Slaves, Spices, and Ivory in Zanzibar: Integration of an East African Com-*

mercial Empire into the World Economy, 1770–1873 (Athens: Ohio University Press, 1987), 2; Beatrice Nicolini, *Makran, Oman and Zanzibar: Three-Termianl Cultural Corridor in the Western Indian Ocean* (1799–1856), trans. Penelope-Jane Watson (Leiden: Brill, 2004), 32; see also Matthew S. Hopper, *Slaves of One Master: Globalization and Slavery in Arabia in the Age of Empire* (New Haven: Yale University Press, 2015).

53. Vincenzo Maurizi, *History of Seyd Said, Sultan of Muscat*, 2nd ed. (1819; repr., Cambridge: Oleander Press, 1984), 29, 36.

54. Lorimer, *Gazetteer of the Persian Gulf*, 1: pt. 1A, 434, and 2: pt. B, 1041.

55. Nicolini, *Makran, Oman and Zanzibar*, 116–122.

56. Mohammad Hassan Ganji, "The Historical Development of the Boundaries of Azerbaijan," in *The Boundaries of Modern Iran*, ed. Keith S. McLachlan (New York: St. Martin's Press, 1994), 39.

57. Issawi, *The Middle East Economy*, 91–93.

58. Ganji, "The Historical Development," 39.

59. Lorimer, *Gazetteer of the Persian Gulf*, 1: pt. 1A, 82; Mehdi Quli Khan Hedayat, *Guzaresh-i Iran*, 39. For the history of Russian expansion in Iran, see Muriel Atkin, *Russia and Iran, 1780–1828* (Minneapolis: University of Minnesota Press, 1980).

60. Mehdi Quli Khan Hedayat, *Guzaresh-i Iran*, 44; Atkin, *Russia and Iran, 1780–1828*, 25; Sykes, *A History of Persia*, 2:310.

CHAPTER 2. SLAVERY AND FORGING NEW IRANIAN FRONTIERS, 1800–1900

1. Ganji, "The Historical Development," 37.

2. Bahram Amirahmadian, "Evolution of Russo-Iranian Boundaries in the Caucasus," in *Boundary Politics and International Boundaries of Iran: With Afghanistan, Armenia, Azerbaijan Republic, Bahrain (the autonomous republic of Ganjah), Iraq, Kazakhstan, Kuwait, Oman, Pakistan, Qatar, Russia, Saudi Arabia, Turkey, Turkmenistan, and the United Arab Emirates*, ed. Pirouz Mojtahed-Zadeh (Boca Raton: Universal Publishers, 2006), 51.

3. Atkin, *Russia and Iran 1780–1828*, 6.

4. Ganji, "The Historical Development," 40.

5. Ibid., 41.

6. For a discussion of the meaning of the term *jihad*, see Majid Khadduri, *The Islamic Conception of Justice* (Baltimore: Johns Hopkins University Press, 1984), 161–173.

7. Lesan al-Mulk, *Nasekh al-tawarikh*, 1:181.

8. Notably, this treaty did not demarcate the Talesh district frontier.

9. Jamalzada, *Ganj-i Shaygan*, 63.

10. Mehdi Quli Khan Hedayat, *Guzaresh-i Iran*, 57–59.

11. Captain R. Mignan, *Winter Journey through Russia, the Caucasian Alps, and Georgia* (London: Richard Bentley, 1839), 1:63, 68, 235.

12. John Macdonald Kinneir (1782–1830) described the sale of enslaved Georgians in his publication *A Geographical Memoir of the Persian Empire* (1813; repr., London: Arno Press, a New York Times Company, 1973), 27. Similarly, those Georgians captured in a military campaign by the Qajar Aqa Muhammad Khan were sold in Shiraz. John Malcolm, *Sketches of Persia* (London: John Murray, Albemarle Street, 1827), 1:117.

13. Kinneir, *A Geographical Memoir of the Persian Empire*, 27.

14. At that time, an enslaved female cost between one hundred (eighty tomans) and four hundred pounds (320 tomans) in Medina. Burton, *Personal Narrative of a Pilgrimage*, 2:13.

15. Muhammad Hasan Khan E'temad al-Saltana, *Tarikh-i muntazam-i Naseri*, ed. Muhamad Esma'il Razavi (Tehran: dunya-yi ketab, 1363), 3: 1513; Lesan al-Mulk, *Nasekh al-tawarikh*, 1:243.

16. Aleksandr Sergeyevich Griboyedov, *Nameha-yi Aleksandr Giribayduf dar bara-i Iran, marbut be saltanat-i Fath 'Ali Shah Qajar*, trans. Reza Farzana (Isfahan: Neshat, 2536), 34–38.

17. Mignan, *Winter Journey through Russia*, 1:73.

18. Mirza Mas'ud Ansari, *Safarnama-yi Khusru Mirza be Petersburg va tarikh-i zendegi-yi 'Abbas Mirza*, ed. Farhad Mirza Mu'tamed al-Daula (Tehran: Mustaufi, 1349), 35–39; Atkin, *Russia and Iran 1780–1828*, 145.

19. Fatemeh Qaziha, ed., *Asnadi az ravand-i ejra-yi mu'ahede-yi Turkomanchai (1245–1250)* (Tehran: Sepehr, 1891), 26, 247; Edvin Arvidovich Grantovski et al., *Tarikh-i Iran az zaman-i bastan ta emruz*, trans. Kaykhusru Keshavarz (Tehran: Puyesh, 1359), 324; Lorimer, *Gazetteer of the Persian Gulf*, 1: pt. 2, 1879.

20. Those discovered to have been brought into Iran secretly were immediately reclaimed by the Russian embassy. Polak, *Persien*, 1:249.

21. Jahangir Mirza, *Tarikh-i nu* (Tehran: 'Ali Akbar 'Elmi, 1327), 120.

22. For comparison with the Russian-forced dislocation of the Circassians into the Ottoman Empire see Toledano, *The Ottoman Slave Trade*, 148–191.

23. See "Reza Shah Pahlavi," Iran Chamber Society, http://www.iranchamber.com/history/reza_shah/reza_shah.php.

24. Ganji, "The Historical Development," 43.

25. There is no doubt that the Russians sought to influence Armenian, Georgian, and Circassian populations in order to expand their authority further into Iran. For example, it was believed that Russia played a role in the appointment of Manuchehr Khan, a Georgian, as governor of Khuzistan in 1839. Lorimer, *Gazetteer of the Persian Gulf*, 1: pt. 2, 1962.

26. Mirza, *Tarikh-i nu*, 120–123; Reza Quli Khan Hedayat, *Tarikh-i ruzat al-safa*, 9:705–711; George A. Bournoutian, *From Tabriz to St. Petersburg: Iran's Mission of Apology to Russia in 1829* (California: Mazda Publishers, 2014), 9. The enslaved women belonged to Muhammad Shah's maternal uncle.

27. John F. Baddeley, *The Russian Conquest of the Caucasus* (1908; repr., New York: Russell & Russell, 1969), 202–205; Sykes, *A History of Persia*, 2:322; Lesan al-Mulk, *Nasekh al-tawarikh*, 1:418–421; Reza Quli Khan Hedayat, *Tarikh-i ruzat al-safa*, 9:705–710; E'temad al-Saltana, *Tarikh-i muntazam-i Naseri*, 3:1594–1596.

28. Mehdi Quli Khan Hedayat, *Guzaresh-i Iran*, 51; Lesan al-Mulk, *Nasekh al-tawarikh*, 1:427; Mignan, *Winter Journey through Russia*, 4; Adamiyat, *Amir Kabir va Iran*, 54–57.

29. Griboyedov, *Nameha-yi Aleksandr Giribayduf dar bara-i Iran*, 106.

30. Mustaufi, *Sharh-i zendegani-yi man*, 1:33.

31. Sa'id Nafisi, *Tarikh-i ejtema'i va siasi-yi Iran dar daura-yi mu'aser* (Tehran: Bunyad, 1376), 2:282; see also David M. Lang, "Griboedov's Last Years in Persia," *American Slavic and East European Review* 7, no. 4 (Dec 1948): 327.

32. Circassians were Muslim.

33. Sykes, *A History of Iran*, 2:355.

34. John Clark Marshman, *The History of India* (London: Longmans, Green, Reader & Dyer, 1867), 3:157.

35. James Bassett, *Persia, the Land of the Imams: A Narrative of Travel and Residence, 1871–1885* (London: Blackie & Son, 1887), 244–247.

36. Russian forces were evacuated from the island by Amir Kabir in 1850. See 'Ali Asghar

Shamim, *Iran dar daura-yi saltanat-i Qajar* (Tehran: Ibn Sina, 1342), 193; Lorimer, *Gazetteer of the Persian Gulf*, 1: pt. 2, 1969.

37. In the same vein, the Turcoman raid of the Russian naval station of Ashuradeh in 1851 was blamed on the incompetency of the governor of Mazandaran, Nasir al-Din Shah's brother, and used as justification to demand his removal.

38. Lorimer, *Gazetteer of the Persian Gulf*, 1: pt. 2, 2040.

39. Arminius Vambéry, *Arminius Vambéry: His Life and Adventures* (London: T. Fisher Unwin, 1889), 172; Firuz Kazemzadeh, *Russia and Britain in Persia, 1864–1914: A Study in Imperialism* (New Haven: Yale University Press, 1968), 12.

40. Kazemzadeh, *Russia and Britain in Persia*, 12.

41. Frederick Burnaby, *A Ride to Khiva: Travels and Adventures in Central Asia* (1876; repr., Oxford: Oxford University Press, 2005), 408.

42. Mehdi Quli Khan Hedayat, *Guzaresh-i Iran*, 89, 90.

43. Ibid., 91–92; Sykes, *A History of Iran*, 2:359.

44. Mirpanjeh, *Khaterat-i esarat*, 121–124.

45. Charles Marvin, *Merv, the Queen of the World and the Scourge of the Man-Stealing Turcomans* (London: W.H. Allen & Co., 1881), 250. In 1870–1871, an estimated 1.5 million Iranians perished due to famine and political instability in the north (Okazaki, "Great Persian Famine," 183–192).

46. Julian Bharier, *Economic Development in Iran, 1900–1970* (London: Oxford University Press, 1971), 4; Grantovski et al., *Tarikh-i Iran*, 371.

47. Nicolini, *Makran, Oman and Zanzibar*, 100; The Italian physician Vincenzo Maurizi described buying an African female in Masqat in 1809. *History of Seyd Said*, 131.

48. Arnold Burrowes Kemball, resident in the Persian Gulf, to Syed Soweynee, governor of Muscat, April 18, 1853, AA3/12, ZNL, Zanzibar; reports on Bandar Lengeh, 1266, Q1263.6.15, VUK, Tehran; Arfa, *Under Five Shahs*, 238; Moses D. E. Nwulia, *Britain and Slavery in East Africa* (Washington, DC: Three Continents Press, 1975), 42; Mignan, *Winter Journey through Russia*, 239; Arfa, *Under Five Shahs*, 240; M. R. Izady, "The Gulf's Ethnic Diversity: An Evolutionary History," in *Security in the Persian Gulf: Origins, Obstacles, and the Search for Consensus*, ed. Lawrence G. Potter and Gary G. Sick (New York: Palgrave Macmillan, 2003), 64.

49. Mehdi Quli Khan Hedayat, *Guzaresh-i Iran*, 146.

50. Sadid al-Saltana Kababi, *Sarzaminha-yi shumali*, 202–204; Lorimer, *Gazetteer of the Persian Gulf*, 1: pt. 1A, 180, 421–422; Kelly, *Britain and the Persian Gulf*, 105; see Shahnaz Razieh Nadjmabadi, "The Arab Presence on the Iranian Coast of the Persian Gulf," in *The Persian Gulf in History*, ed. Lawrence G. Potter (New York: Palgrave Macmillan, 2009), 130–145.

51. Vessels could land on the sandy shore on the east side of the port and at a number of its villages, such as Bostaneh and Shenas, but large boats needed to anchor between twelve hundred and eighteen hundred meters from the coast. Lorimer, *Gazetteer of the Persian Gulf*, 1: pt. 1A, 289, 366; Sadid al-Saltana Kababi, *Sarzaminha-yi shumali*, 201, 194.

52. Kelly, *Britain and the Persian Gulf*, 660; see also Chhaya Goswami, *The Call of the Sea: Kachchhi Traders in Muscat and Zanzibar, C. 1800–1880* (New Delhi: Orient Blackswan, 2011).

53. Badr was regent and ruled jointly with Sayyid Sultan's son Sayyid Sa'id from 1804 to 1806.

54. Lorimer, *Gazetteer of the Persian Gulf*, 1: pt. 1A, 439.

55. Curzon, *Persia and the Persian Question*, 2:423.

56. Muhammad Ja'far Khurmuji, *Haqa'q al-akhbar Naseri* (Tehran: Ney, 1363), 131; Lorimer, *Gazetteer of the Persian Gulf*, 1: pt. 1A, 449.

57. Izady, "The Gulf's Ethnic Diversity," 62.

58. Lorimer, *Gazetteer of the Persian Gulf*, 1: pt. 2, 1915.

59. Curzon, *Persia and the Persian Question*, 2: 437.

60. Lorimer, *Gazetteer of the Persian Gulf*, 1: pt. 2, 469; Mehdi Quli Khan Hedayat, *Guzaresh-i Iran*, 148.

61. Sheriff, *Slaves, Spices and Ivory in Zanzibar*, 208–217.

62. Abdulhussain Mirza Farman Farma, *Musaferat nama-yi Kerman va Baluchistan*, 300, 369.

63. This included Qeshm and Hormuz Islands along with Tazian, Shamil, and Minab on the mainland, from Bandar 'Abbas to Cape Jask and beyond to the Sudaij River. Mehdi Quli Khan Hedayat, *Guzaresh-i Iran*, 78; Kelly, *Britain and the Persian Gulf*, 530–533.

64. The sixteen thousand tomans Sa'id agreed on with Iran in 1856 included an honorarium of two thousand tomans. The arrangement was valid only with him and his sons, and was terminable at the will of Iran after twenty years or a change in Omani rulership. Khurmuji, *Haqa'q al-akhbar Naseri*, 164–168; Fasa'i, *Farsnama-yi Naseri*, 1:801–807; Charles Belgrave, *The Pirate Coast* (London: G. Bell and Sons Ltd., 1966), 179; Lorimer, *Gazetteer of the Persian Gulf*, 1: pt. 1A, 460; Reza Quli Khan Hedayat, *Tarikh-i ruzat al-safa*, 10:574–577.

65. Lorimer, *Gazetteer of the Persian Gulf*, 1: pt. 2, 1941.

66. Fasa'i, *Farsnama-yi Naseri*, 1:830–831.

67. This lease was for eight years at the annual rate of thirty thousand tomans. Ibid., 833, 834.

68. Lorimer, *Gazetteer of the Persian Gulf*, 1: pt. 1A, 246; Sadid al-Saltana Kababi, *Bandar 'Abbas*, 155, 205–209.

69. Salem also claimed Larak and Hengam as dependencies of Oman. Lorimer, *Gazetteer of the Persian Gulf*, 1: pt. 1A, 480; Kelly, *Britain and the Persian Gulf*, 661.

70. Sadid al-Saltana Kababi, *Sarzaminha-yi shumali*, 205, 301; Sadid al-Saltana Kababi, *Bandar 'Abbas*, 614; Kelly, *Britain and the Persian Gulf*, 663; Lorimer, *Gazetteer of the Persian Gulf*, 1: pt. 2, 2045–2047, pt. 1A, 521.

71. Kelly, *Britain and the Persian Gulf*, 557.

72. Peasants of Kurdistan to the Iranian government, Rabi' al-Awwal 15, 1285, Q1284.12.24, VUK, Tehran; Lorimer, *Gazetteer of the Persian Gulf*, 2: pt. B, 1137.

73. For instance, Lorimer reported that the port town of Chabahar's entire revenue of five thousand rupees was paid to the sultan of Oman. *Gazetteer of the Persian Gulf*, 1: pt. 1A, 603; see also 2: pt. 1A, 591.

74. For instance, the reliance on enslaved labor in the clove and grains plantations of East Africa not only transformed the region but also brought great wealth. Sheriff, *Slaves, Spices and Ivory in Zanzibar*, 2; Robert Harms, "Introduction: Indian Ocean Slavery in the Age of Abolition," in *Indian Ocean Slavery in the Age of Abolition*, ed. Robert Harms, Bernard K. Freamon, and David W. Blight (New Haven: Yale University Press, 2013), 7; Anne K. Bang, "Cosmopolitanism Colonised? Three Cases From Zanzibar 1890–1920," in *Struggling With History: Islam and Cosmopolitanism in the Western Indian Ocean*, ed. Edward Simpson and Kai Kresse (New York: Columbia University Press, 2008), 168; see also Gill Shepherd, "The Comorians and the East African Slave Trade," in *Asian and African Systems of Slavery*, ed. James L. Watson (Berkeley: University of California Press, 1980), 73–99.

75. Sadid al-Saltana Kababi, *al-Menas fi ahval-i al-ghaus*, 26; Cooper, *Plantation Slavery on the East Coast of Africa*, 34–38; Sheriff, *Slaves, Spices and Ivory in Zanzibar*, 37.

76. Lorimer, *Gazetteer of the Persian Gulf*, 1: pt. 1A, 435.

77. Reza Quli Khan Hedayat, *Tarikh-i ruzat al-safa*, 10:575.

78. Colonel C. P. Rigby, consul and British agent, Zanzibar, to H. L. Anderson, chief secretary to the government, Bombay, dated Zanzibar, May 14, 1861, AA3/20, ZNL, Zanzibar.

79. Maurizi, *History of Seyd Said, Sultan of Muscat*, 29.

80. Lorimer, *Gazetteer of the Persian Gulf*, 1: pt. 1A, 2493; see also Hopper, *Slaves of One Master*.

81. Maurizi, *History of Seyd Said, Sultan of Muscat*, 30. According to Lorimer, many of Sa'id's Baluchi and Jadgal mercenary troops were killed during a battle with the Wahhabis in 1811 (*Gazetteer of the Persian Gulf*, 1: pt. 1A, 444.)

82. Fraser, *Narrative of a Journey into Khorasan*, 5.

83. Lorimer, *Gazetteer of the Persian Gulf*, 2: pt. 1A, 585, 588. For instance, in exchange for challenging his authority at Gwadar in 1857, the ruler of Kalat, Nasir Khan II, was bought off by the Omani governor with enslaved people, money, and a sword (ibid., 1: pt. 1A, 604).

84. Kelly, *Britain and the Persian Gulf*, 556. Sadid al-Saltana Kababi, *Sarzaminha-yi shumali*, 302, 309; Lorimer, *Gazetteer of the Persian Gulf*, 1: pt. 1A, 607; Jamalzada, *Ganj-i Shaygan*, 113.

85. For instance, around 1868, the annual tribute from Dashtyari and Bahu was five thousand rupees; Lorimer, *Gazetteer of the Persian Gulf*, 1: pt. 1A, 2166. Baluchistan was formally annexed by 1867. Ibid., 2011.

86. In 1864, the yearly revenue of Chabahar was six thousand rupees, of which the Arab governor Rashid ibn Hamad retained one thousand for administrative purposes. Additionally, two local chiefs, Mir Din Muhammad (a Jadgal of Dashtyari) and Mir 'Abdullah (ruler of Geh, now Nikshahr), received nine hundred rupees and two hundred rupees a year, respectively, from the sultan of Oman from the revenue of Chabahar for protecting the towns. Lorimer, *Gazetteer of the Persian Gulf*, 1: pt. 1A, 606, 609, and pt. 2, 2162.

87. Ibid., pt. 1A, 484; Vaziri, *Joghrafia-yi Baluchistan*, 5.

88. Sadid al-Saltana Kababi, *Sarzaminha-yi shumali*, 302.

89. Abdulhussain Mirza Farman Farma, *Musaferat nama-yi Kerman*, 258.

90. Lorimer, *Gazetteer of the Persian Gulf*, 1: pt. 1A, 611. See also Sykes, *A History of Iran*, 2:361.

91. Lorimer, *Gazetteer of the Persian Gulf*, pt. 2, 2190. See Firuz Mirza Farman Farma, *Safarnamih-yi Kerman*.

92. Lorimer, *Gazetteer of the Persian Gulf*, 1: pt. 1A, 612.

93. For instance, the chief officer of a passing Turkish vessel purchased four enslaved persons at Masqat in 1878. Ibid., 467, 522.

94. Ibid., 513.

95. The British government to the Iranian government, Shawwal 25, 1266, Q1263.6.15, VUK, Tehran; Colonel C. P. Rigby, consul and British agent, Zanzibar, to A. K. Forbes, acting secretary to the government, Bombay, September 5, 1861, AA3/20, ZNL, Zanzibar; O. A. Scott, Foreign Office, March 27, 1930, "Memorandum concerning the existence of slavery and slave trading along the Eastern and South-Eastern coasts of Arabia," FO 371/14475, NAUK, London; see Beatrice Nicolini, "The 19th Slave Trade in the Western Indian Ocean: The Role of the Baloch Mercenaries," in *The Baloch and Others: Linguistic, Historical and Socio-*

Political Perspectives on Pluralism in Balochistan, ed. Carina Jahani, Agnes Korn, and Paul Titus (Wiesbaden: Reichert, 2008), 327–344; Izady, "The Gulf's Ethnic Diversity," 62.

96. Lorimer, *Gazetteer of the Persian Gulf*, 1: pt. 1A, 596; Major General Christopher P. Rigby to secretary of Bombay government, July 15, 1859, AA12/2, ZNL, Zanzibar.

97. Lorimer, *Gazetteer of the Persian Gulf*, 1: pt. 1A, 531.

98. Ibid., 545.

99. Ibid., pt. 2, 2505.

100. Ibid., pt. 2, 2500–2501. See also his description of the Portuguese capturing many Suri slave traders in East Africa. Ibid., 580; José Capela, *O Tráfico de Escravos nos Portos de Moçambique 1733–1904* (Porto: Edições Afrontamento, 2002), 121–122.

101. Ibid., pt. 2, 2503.

102. Mojtahed-Zadeh, "The Concept of Boundary," 13; see also Firoozeh Kashani-Sabet, *Frontier Fictions: Shaping the Iranian Nation, 1804–1946* (Princeton: Princeton University Press, 1999).

103. Mohammad Hassan Ganji, "Stages in the Shaping of Iran's North-Western Boundaries," in *Boundary Politics and International Boundaries of Iran: With Afghanistan, Armenia, Azerbaijan Republic, Bahrain, (the autonomous republic of Ganjah) Iraq, Kazakhstan, Kuwait, Oman, Pakistan, Qatar, Russia, Saudi Arabia, Turkey, Turkmenistan, and the United Arab Emirates*, ed. Pirouz Mojtahed-Zadeh (Boca Raton: Universal Publishers, 2006), 41.

104. Pirouz Mojtahed-Zadeh, "The Eastern Boundaries of Iran," in *The Boundaries of Modern Iran*, ed. Keith S. McLachlan (New York: St. Martin's Press, 1994), 128. For more information on the Great Game and the creation of Afghanistan and the formation of Central Asian states see Pirouz Mojtahed-Zadeh, *Small Players of the Great Game: The Settlement of Iran's Eastern Borderlands and the Creation of Afghanistan* (New York: Routledge, 2004).

105. The province had been divided into two chiefdoms—British-protected Baluchistan (Kalat) and Iranian Baluchistan—by the late eighteenth century. Mojtahed-Zadeh, "The Eastern Boundaries of Iran," 131; see also Ellsworth Huntington, "The Depression of Sistan in Eastern Persia," *Bulletin of the American Geographical Society* 37, no. 5 (1905): 279.

106. Peterson, "Britain and the Gulf," 279. See Jamalzada, *Ganj-i Shaygan*.

107. The significance of this area was recognized in a report by Captain N. P. Grant of Brigadier-General Malcolm's Royal Asiatic Society mission to Iran's toured the region in 1809. Lorimer, *Gazetteer of the Persian Gulf*, 1: pt. 1A, 176.

108. Reports on southern ports, 1311–1317, 293004045, SAM, Tehran, 8.

109. Lorimer, *Gazetteer of the Persian Gulf*, 1: pt. 2, 2160, 2161; Sadid al-Saltana Kababi, *Sarzaminha-yi shumali*, 303; Mehdi Quli Khan Hedayat, *Guzaresh-i Iran*, 87.

110. Lorimer, *Gazetteer of the Persian Gulf*, 1: pt. 2A, 606.

111. Ibid., pt. 2, 2034, and pt. 1A, 240.

112. Ibid., pt. 2, 2120; Sykes, *A History of Iran*, 2:363; the Ministry of Customs of Iran to the grand vizier, 1319, Q1319.16.3.13, VUK, Tehran.

113. Sykes, *A History of Iran*, 2:323.

114. Marshman, *The History of India*, 3:121.

115. Lorimer, *Gazetteer of the Persian Gulf*, 1: pt. 2, 1962, 1971.

116. Ibid., 2010.

117. Sykes, *A History of Iran*, 2:325.

118. Khurmuji, *Haqa'q al-akhbar Naseri*, 27.

119. Mojtahed-Zadeh, "The Eastern Boundaries of Iran," 130; Lorimer, *Gazetteer of the Persian Gulf*, 1: pt. 1A, 223.

120. Lorimer, *Gazetteer of the Persian Gulf*, 1: pt. 2, 1973. This period of withdrawal is also known as the first Afghan war, 1838–1842. Hedayat, *Guzaresh-i Iran*, 65.

121. Lorimer, *Gazetteer of the Persian Gulf*, 1: pt. 2, 2007–2011.

122. Mehdi Quli Khan Hedayat, *Guzaresh-i Iran*, 80; Mojtahed-Zadeh, "The Eastern Boundaries of Iran," 130.

123. Mustaufi, *Sharh-i zendegani-yi man*, 1:85. See Jamalzada, *Ganj-i Shaygan*.

124. Lesan al-Mulk, *Nasekh al-tawarikh*, 3:1412.

125. Ibid., 1385; Reza Quli Khan Hedayat, *Tarikh-i ruzat al-safa*, 10:726; Khurmuji, *Haqa'q al-akhbar Naseri*, 203; minutes of evidence presented before the royal commission on enslaved people fugitive, Major General Christopher P. Rigby examined, March 11, 1875, AA12/2, ZNL, Zanzibar.

126. Mustaufi, *Sharh-i zendegani-yi man*, 1:85; see also Denis Wright, *The English amongst the Persians during the Qajar Period, 1787–1921* (London: I. B. Tauris, 1977), 113–116; Lorimer, *Gazetteer of the Persian Gulf*, 1: pt. 2, 2030.

127. Mustaufi, *Sharh-i zendegani-yi man*, 1:85.

128. Mehdi Quli Khan Hedayat, *Guzaresh-i Iran*, 81.

129. Lesan al-Mulk, *Nasekh al-tawarikh*, 3:1454.

130. Lorimer, *Gazetteer of the Persian Gulf*, 1: pt. 1A, 273.

131. Mojtahed-Zadeh, "The Eastern Boundaries of Iran," 137–138.

132. Peterson, "Britain and the Gulf," 277, 279.

133. Pirouz Mojtahed-Zadeh, "Iran's Maritime Boundaries in the Persian Gulf: The Case of Abu Musa Island," in *The Boundaries of Modern Iran*, ed. Keith S. McLachlan (New York: St. Martin's Press, 1994), 103.

134. Edward A. Alpers, "On Becoming a British Lake: Piracy, Slaving, and British Imperialism in the Indian Ocean during the First Half of the Nineteenth Century," in *Indian Ocean Slavery in the Age of Abolition*, ed. Robert Harms, Bernard K. Freamon, and David W. Blight (New Haven: Yale University Press, 2013), 46.

135. Al-Qasimi, *The Myth of Arab Piracy in the Gulf*, 15; Peterson, "Britain and the Gulf," 279.

136. Lorimer, *Gazetteer of the Persian Gulf*, 1: pt. 1A, 200; Mehdi Quli Khan Hedayat, *Guzaresh-i Iran*, 148. The prevailing view at the time was that problems with the drinking water in Ra's al Khaymah occasioned the relocation: that is, Sir William Grant Keir suggested that the British transfer the garrison in Ra's al Khaymah in what is now the United Arab Emirates to Qeshm. See also Kelly, *Britain and the Persian Gulf*, 183.

137. Lorimer, *Gazetteer of the Persian Gulf*, 1: pt. 2, 1937–1939.

138. Ibid., pt. 1A, 198.

139. Sadid al-Saltana Kababi, *Sarzaminha-yi shumali*, 55–57.

140. Climate has often been cited as a reason for this move and the impetus for relocating to Bas'idu, which consisted of two small ports: one was known as the British Bas'idu situated at the south of Qeshm Island, which when occupied turned into a coal depot for the British warships. The other was the Iranian Bas'idu or Customs Bas'idu, which was located at the northern side of the island. Reports on southern ports, 1311–1317, 293004045, SAM, Tehran, 4. The British briefly relocated to Moghu but returned to Bas'idu by order of the government of Bombay. See Lorimer, *Gazetteer of the Persian Gulf*, 1: pt. 1A, 253, 677, and pt. 2, 1945, 1949.

141. Sadid al-Saltana Kababi, *Bandar 'Abbas*, 103; Kelly, *Britain and the Persian Gulf*, 197.

142. G. Jenkins, commander of the Persian Gulf squadron, Bushire, November 1, 1858, L/PS/20/C246, BL, London; Lorimer, *Gazetteer of the Persian Gulf*, 1: pt. 2, 2105–2106.

143. Ibid., pt. 1A, 285, 366; Sadid al-Saltana Kababi, *Sarzaminha-yi shumali*, 323. The British conveyed their forces to other bases, including Bahrain, Masqat, and Sharjah, so their presence was insignificant in this area in 1909, when Bas'idu was used to store coal for British ships. Ra'in, *Daryanavardi-yi Iranian*, 2:848. In 1877, the coal agent, Haji 'Abbas, was dismissed by order of the British resident for possessing several enslaved persons. Initially, he was deposed from his post by the government of India, but in 1878, he was reinstated because he was an Iranian subject, and slavery was still legal in Iran. Lorimer, *Gazetteer of the Persian Gulf*, 1: pt. 2, 2106–2107, 2512. See also G. Jenkins, Bushire, November 1, 1858, L/PS/20/C246, BL

144. Lorimer, *Gazetteer of the Persian Gulf*, 1: pt. 2, 2441, 2451, 2454.

145. Ibid., 2037.

146. Ibid., pt. 1A, 310–317.

147. Ibid., 364; Sadid al-Saltana Kababi, *Sarzaminha-yi shumali*, 166–173. Lorimer, *Gazetteer of the Persian Gulf*, 2: pt. 1A, 148. Through the Bakhtiari Oil Company, the British agreed to pay three percent of their revenue to the khans: two thousand pounds (five thousand tomans) as a subsidy and one thousand pounds (twenty five hundred tomans) for safeguarding the pipelines annually. Jamalzada, *Ganj-i Shaygan*, 70, 108; Arash Khazeni, *Tribes and Empire on the Margins of Nineteenth-Century Iran* (Seattle: University of Washington Press, 2009), 123.

148. Lorimer, *Gazetteer of the Persian Gulf*, 1: pt. 1A, 366.

149. Mehdi Quli Khan Hedayat, *Guzaresh-i Iran*, 197.

150. Lorimer, *Gazetteer of the Persian Gulf*, 1: pt. 1A, 164, and 2: pt. 1A, 1957; Jamalzada, *Ganj-i Shaygan*, 17; Sadid al-Saltana Kababi, *Sarzaminha-yi shumali*, 180.

151. For more information see Sabri Ateş, *Ottoman-Iranian Borderlands: Making a Boundary, 1843–1914* (New York: Cambridge University Press, 2013).

152. Into the Arvandrud flowed Khuzistan's three important tributaries: the Karun, Jarrahi, and Hendiyan rivers. Lorimer, *Gazetteer of the Persian Gulf*, 2: pt. 1A, 95.

153. Ibid., 129, 140; Najm al-Daula, *Asar-i Najm al-Daula*, 79.

154. Mehdi Quli Khan Hedayat, *Guzaresh-i Iran*, 65.

155. Justin Sheil to Lord Palmerston, June 27, 1847, L/PS/5/451, BL, London.

156. Justin Sheil to the shah, June 21, 1847, L/PS/5/451, BL, London.

157. Justin Sheil to Lord Palmerston, May 31, 1847, L/PS/5/451, BL, London.

CHAPTER 3. THE TRADE IN ENSLAVED PEOPLE FROM AFRICA TO IRAN, 1800–1900

1. Reports on southern ports, 1311–1317, the immigration of people, Khordad 25, 1317, 293004045, SAM, Tehran, 1; Lorimer, *Gazetteer of the Persian Gulf*, 1: pt. 2, 2179.

2. A parallel network of recruiting enslaved Africans existed also from the same ports to the Ottoman Empire. For more information see Toledano, *The Ottoman Slave Trade*, 14–54.

3. The senior naval officer in the Gulf, H. W. Dowding, noted that enslaved people were sent from the Persian Gulf into the interior of Iran, the Ottoman Empire, and as far as India (Dowding to E. C. Ross, political resident in the Persian Gulf and consul general for Fars, dated at Basra, November 11, 1885, L/PS/20/246, BL, London). See also Arnold

Burrowes Kemball to Colonel H. D. Robertson and Justin Sheil, July 8, 1842, FO 84/426, NAUK, London.

4. S. B. Haines to A. Malet, December 15, 1847, L/PS/5/456, BL, London.

5. Historically known as Abyssinia or Habesha.

6. In the mid-nineteenth century, the journey could take anywhere from two weeks to two months. M. Lambert to Brigadier W. M. Coghlan, political resident at Aden, May 22, 1856, L/PS/5/487, BL, London; Timothy Fernyhough, "Slavery and the Slave Trade in Southern Ethiopia in the 19th Century," *Slavery and Abolition* 9, no. 3 (1988): 103–130.

7. The mortality rate was as high as 60 percent within twenty-four hours of operation: "[D]uring a heavy sleep produced by the smoke of burning leaves of a poisonous plant (the *datura Stramonium*) and infusions of certain other plants (probably the poppy) the genital organs were completely removed. On the wound, after a preliminary application of butter, boiling hot, the operator placed a poultice of crushed plant leaves. If an infection of the bladder did not carry off the victim within six days after the operation, he was considered out of danger, and for a month was fed on raw meat and honey." Henri De Monfried, *Pearls, Arms and Hashish: Pages from the Life of a Red Sea Navigator*, compiled, Ida Treat (London: Victor Gollancz, 1930), 126.

8. Ibid.

9. Major General Christopher P. Rigby to secretary to Bombay government, April 18, 1861, AA12/2, ZNL, Zanzibar.

10. A voyage from the interior of Africa to Zanzibar could take between fifteen and thirty days, and from there to Masqat by sea, the voyage could take between thirty to thirty-five days. Ibid.; M. H. Lambert to Brigadier William Marcus Coghlan, May 20, 1856, AA3/15B, ZNL, Zanzibar.

11. S. B. Haines to A. Malet, December 15, 1847, L/PS/5/456, BL, London; See also Richard F. Burton (d. 1890), *First Footsteps in East Africa* (London: J. M. Dent & Sons, 1910), 268–270; James Edwards to Arnold Burrowes Kemball, 1842, FO 84/426, NAUK, London.

12. Lambert to Coghlan, May 20, 1856, AA3/15B, ZNL; Rigby to secretary to Bombay government, April 18, 1861, AA12/2, ZNL; G. L. Sulivan, *Dhow Chasing in Zanzibar Waters* (1873; repr., London: Dawsons of Pall Mall, 1967), 203; Burton, *First Footsteps in East Africa*, 268–270.

13. Lorimer described that enslaved people remaining in Oman tended to end up on the Batinah coast or Trucial Oman. Lorimer, *Gazetteer of the Persian Gulf*, 1: pt. 2, 2498.

14. Sur was particularly appealing as an easily navigable port. Dowding to Ross, dated at Basra, November 11, 1885, L/PS/20/246, BL.

15. C. Forjett, esquire, deputy commissioner of police, to William Crawford, esquire, commissioner of police, Bombay, November 27, 1857, AA3/17, ZNL, Zanzibar. Lorimer, *Gazetteer of the Persian Gulf*, 1: pt. 2, 2497.

16. Alan Hyde Gardner, commander, to I. P. Porter, commander of the Indian navy, July 11, 1849, L/PS/5/463, BL, London; see also Willem Floor, *A Fiscal History of Iran in the Safavid and Qajar Periods, 1500–1925* (New York: Bibliotheca Persica Press, 1998), 373–400.

17. Nastaran Baji Habashia to the British consulate, 1328, Q1328.3.1.39, VUK, Tehran; Mahmud Zand-i Muqadam, *Hekayat-i Baluch* (Tehran: Karun, 1370), 1: 169.

18. Malcolm, *Sketches of Persia*, 1: 17.

19. William Heude, *A Voyage Up the Persian Gulf and a Journey Overland from India to England in 1817* (London: Longman, Hurst, Rees, Orme, and Brown, 1819), 24.

20. Belgrave, *The Pirate Coast*, 63.

21. Fraser, *Narrative of a Journey into Khorasan*, 6.

22. Major David Wilson, resident in the Persian Gulf, to the government, January 28, 1831, FO 84/426, NAUK, London.

23. Ibid.; Lorimer, *Gazetteer of the Persian Gulf*, 1: pt. 2, 2508 and 2509.

24. Kemball to Robertson and Sheil, July 8, 1842, FO 84/426, NAUK, 190–198; Rigby to Anderson, dated Zanzibar, May 14, 1861, AA3/20, ZNL. Kemball was assistant resident from 1841 to 1852 and resident from 1852 to 1855.

25. H. D. Robertson to L. P. Willoughby, March 4, 1842, FO 84/426, NAUK, London, 198–201; Denis de Rivoyre described the living conditions of these enslaved people in *Obock, Mascate, Bouchire, Bassorah* (Paris: Imprimeurs, 1883), 220.

26. H. C. Rawlinson, consul at Baghdad, to Henry Wellesley, minister plenipotentiary, April 28, 1847, L/PS/5/450, BL, London. Mecca was a center for enslaved Sudanese. Bassett, *Persia, the Land of the Imams*, 287.

27. Locals conducted the piloting of vessels from Basra to Kharg Island, as this was the only revenue that the shaykh received. Edward Scott Waring, *A Tour to Sheeraz by the Route of Kazroon and Feerozabad* (1807; repr., New York: Arno Press, 1973), 130.

28. Hennell was resident from 1838 to 1841 and again from 1843 to 1852.

29. Samuel Hennell to Sir Justin Sheil, dated Bushire, January 11, 1850, L/PS/5/463, BL, London.

30. In 1925, Reza Shah changed the Arabic name of the town (Muhammara) to the Persian Khorramshahr.

31. Sir Justin Sheil, dated Tehran, February 8, 1853, FO 84/919, NAUK, London.

32. Kemball to Robertson and Sheil, July 8, 1842, FO 84/426, NAUK.

33. Najm al-Saltana to the Ministry of Foreign Affairs, Rajab 5, 1332, Q1332.3.3, VUK, Tehran.

34. Bassett, *Persia, the Land of the Imams*, 4.

35. Burton, *Personal Narrative of a Pilgrimage*, 2:13.

36. Ibid., 252.

37. Haj Mirza Muhammad Husayn Husayni Farahani, *Safarnamih-yi Haj Mirza Muhammad Husayn Husayni Farahani* (Tehran: Ferdusi, 1362), 197.

38. Kemball to Soweynee, April 18, 1853, AA3/12, ZNL; Major General Christopher P. Rigby to Commander J. C. Wilson, September 2, 1861, AA12/2, ZNL, Zanzibar; Elisabeth McMahon, *Slavery and Emancipation in Islamic East Africa: From Honor to Respectability* (New York: Cambridge University Press, 2013), 2.

39. Slave Trade report to A. Malet, secretary to the government of Bombay, dated Zanzibar, April 29, 1847, AA3/8, ZNL, Zanzibar; Lorimer, *Gazetteer of the Persian Gulf*, 1: pt. 2, 2498; Wilson to the government, January 28, 1831, FO 84/426, NAUK.

40. The British government to the Iranian government, Rabi' al-Awwal 1267, Q1263.6.24.3, VUK, Tehran; Mirza Muhammad 'Ali Khan, minister of foreign affairs, to Mirza Aqa Khan, prime minister, 1268, Q1268.6.40, VUK, Tehran.

41. Lorimer, *Gazetteer of the Persian Gulf*, 1: pt. 2, 2494.

42. Précis on the slave trade in the Gulf of Oman and the Persian Gulf, 1873–1905, "Capture of Slave Dhows by the Philomel," dated Muscat, October 31, 1884, L/PS/20/C246, BL, London, no. 172, 75.

43. Moolla Ahmed to Felix Jones, August 17, 1857, FO 248/168, NAUK, London. The

importer usually made profits of between 20 and 30 percent. Wilson to the government, January 28, 1831, FO 84/426, NAUK.

44. Lorimer, *Gazetteer of the Persian Gulf*, 1: pt. 1A, 252. The slave trade was also hindered by tribal rivalries. Indeed, in October 1884, the sultan of Oman imprisoned an Arab captain when he was found to have transported 128 enslaved males and 26 enslaved females of the Wazaramo tribe from Ra's al Hadd (Lorimer, *Gazetteer of the Persian Gulf*, 1: pt. 2, 2496). In early 1893, a Ra's al Khaymah boat was attacked by pirates on Khargu Island (ibid., 2048).

45. Reports on Bandar Lengeh, 1266, Q1263.6.15, VUK; Rigby to Anderson, dated Zanzibar, May 14, 1861, AA3/20, ZNL.

46. Translated extract of a letter from Mollah Houssein, agent at Sharjah, to Major Hennell, resident in the Persian Gulf, signed A. B. Kemball, June 25, 1849, AA3/9, ZNL, Zanzibar.

47. Lorimer, *Gazetteer of the Persian Gulf*, 1: pt. 2, 2498; Rigby to Anderson, dated Zanzibar, May 14, 1861, AA3/20, ZNL. In the first decade of 1900, an estimated one thousand enslaved Africans were brought annually by Suri vessels flying the French flag. Lorimer, *Gazetteer of the Persian Gulf*, 1: pt. 2, 2499.

48. Lorimer, *Gazetteer of the Persian Gulf*, 1: pt. 2, 2497. These searches responded to the increased number of enslaved people coming from Africa into the Persian Gulf after 1884 following a severe famine in the African interior.

49. Ibid., pt. 1A, 391.

50. O. A. Scott, Foreign Office, March 27, 1930, "Memorandum concerning the existence of slavery and slave trading along the Eastern and South-Eastern coasts of Arabia," FO 371/14475, NAUK, London; see also Hopper, *Slaves of One Master*.

51. Kemball to Robertson and Sheil, July 8, 1842, FO 84/426, NAUK; Arnold Burrowes Kemball, report on the Persian Gulf, 1847, FO 84/692, NAUK, London; Robertson to Willoughby, March 4, 1842, FO 84/426, NAUK.

52. Lorimer, *Gazetteer of the Persian Gulf*, 1: pt. 2, 2494.

53. Kemball to Robertson and Sheil, July 8, 1842, FO 84/426, NAUK; Kemball, report on the Persian Gulf, 1847, FO 84/692, NAUK; Edwards to Kemball, 1842, FO 84/426, NAUK, 207–211.

54. Lorimer, *Gazetteer of the Persian Gulf*, 1: pt. 2, 2494.

55. Rigby to Anderson, dated Zanzibar, May 14, 1861, AA3/20, ZNL.

56. Wilson, *The Persian Gulf*, 225.

57. Husayn Quli Khan Nezam al-Saltana Mafi, *Khatirat va asnad-i Husayn Quli Khan*, ed. Mansureh Ettehadieh, Sirus Sa'dvandian, and Hamid Rampisha (Tehran: Nashr-i tarikh-i Iran, 1361), 1:139; Lorimer, *Gazetteer of the Persian Gulf*, 1: pt. 1A, 167.

58. Lorimer, *Gazetteer of the Persian Gulf*, 1: pt. 1A, 166. In the mid-nineteenth century, Masqat had fifteen ships (of four hundred to seven hundred tons), three brigs, fifty large dhows, and fifty small dhows. Kelly, *Britain and the Persian Gulf*, 15–16.

59. Kemball, report on the Persian Gulf, 1847, FO 84/692, NAUK.

60. Robertson to Willoughby, March 4, 1842, FO 84/426, NAUK.

61. J. G. Taylor, British agent at Basra, to A. B. Kemball, July 24, 1853, L/PS/5/478, BL, London.

62. Ahmed ben Hussein, agent at Lengah, to Samuel Hennell, June 6, 1850, FO 84/815, NAUK, London.

63. Kemball, report on the Persian Gulf, 1847, FO 84/692, NAUK; Robertson to Willoughby, March 4, 1842, FO 84/426, NAUK.

64. Justin Sheil to Lord Palmerston, dated Tehran, February 7, 1851, FO 248/144, NAUK, London, 179–187; Justin Sheil to Lord Palmerston, dated Ispahan, September 1, 1851, FO 84/144, NAUK, London; Justin Sheil to Ameer-i-Nezam, March 3, 1851, FO 84/857, NAUK, London; Justin Sheil to Mirza Taqi Khan Amir Kabir, Rabi' al-Awwal 29, 1267, Q1267.6.24, VUK, Tehran.

65. Kemball to Robertson and Sheil, July 8, 1842, FO 84/426, NAUK.

66. Reports on Bandar Lengeh, 1266, Q1263.6.15, VUK, Tehran.

67. In various correspondences, Sheil suggested numbers between twenty and forty-five. Sheil to Palmerston, dated Tehran, February 7, 1851, FO 248/144, NAUK; Sheil to Palmerston, dated Ispahan, September 1, 1851, FO 84/144, NAUK; Sheil to Ameer-i-Nezam, March 3, 1851, FO 84/857, NAUK.

68. Colonel Francis Farrant to Lord Palmerston, September 5, 1849, FO 84/737, NAUK, London.

69. Rawlinson to Wellesley, April 28, 1847, L/PS/5/450, BL.

70. Felix Jones to Charles Alison, envoy of philanthropy at the Persian court, December 7, 1860, FO 248/189, NAUK, London.

71. In 1850, Hennell gave information on the importation of enslaved Africans traveling on Iranian ships from Zanzibar into the Persian Gulf. Samuel Hennell to Justin Sheil, dated Bushire, December 12, 1850, R/15/1/123, BL, London.

72. Lorimer, *Gazetteer of the Persian Gulf*, 1: pt. 1A, 339.

73. Ibid., 548–550.

74. Gwyn Campbell, *An Economic History of Imperial Madagascar, 1750–1895: The Rise and Fall of an Island Empire* (New York: Cambridge University Press, 2005), 227. Shepherd, "The Comorians and the East African Slave Trade," 79.

75. Ibid., pt. 2, 2495.

76. Ibid., 548–550; "Précis of Maskat Affairs, 1892–1905," report from the political resident, December 1891, L/PS/20/C245, BL, London.

77. Lorimer, *Gazetteer of the Persian Gulf*, 1: pt. 1A, 563–564.

78. Edward A. Alpers, *Ivory and Slaves in East Central Africa* (Berkeley: University of California Press, 1975), 192.

79. Rigby to Anderson, dated Zanzibar, May 14, 1861, AA3/20, ZNL.

80. Lady Mary Sheil, *Glimpses of Life and Manners in Persia* (1856; repr., New York: Arno Press, 1973), 245.

81. Lambert to Coghlan, May 20, 1856, AA3/15B, ZNL.

82. Rigby to Anderson, dated Zanzibar, May 14, 1861, AA3/20, ZNL.

83. David Eltis, "Assessing the Slave Trade," *Voyages: The Trans-Atlantic Slave Trade Database*, 2007, accessed December 30, 2015, http://www.slavevoyages.org/assessment/estimates.

84. It is based on Sheil's estimate that in the mid-nineteenth century the number of enslaved Africans disembarked at Iranian ports did not exceed 2,000 to 3,000 annually.

85. Martin B. Esmond and T. C. I. Ryan, "A Quantitative Assessment of the Arab Slave Trade of East Africa, 1770–1896," *Kenya Historical Review* 5, no. 1 (1977): 79; Lovejoy, *Transformations in Slavery*, 151; Behnaz A. Mirzai, "African Presence in Iran: Identity and Its Reconstruction in the 19th and 20th Centuries," *Revue française d'histoire d'outre-mer* 89, no. 336–337 (2002): 234; Ahmed to Jones, August 17, 1857, FO 248/168, NAUK. At the first sale, an importer might make a profit of 20 to 30 percent. Wilson to government, January 28, 1831, FO 84/426, NAUK.

86. Brazil's economy was dependent on enslaved people procured by the Portuguese,

Arabs, and Swahilis for its plantations and cattle farms; the French brought enslaved people to sugar colonies in the Mascarenes; and the Omani Arabs established clove plantations in Zanzibar and on the island of Pemba. For further discussion on the expansion of the East African slave trade, see Jane Hooper and David Eltis, "The Indian Ocean in Transatlantic Slavery," *Slavery and Abolition* 34, no. 3 (2013): 353–375; Richard B. Allen, *European Slave Trading in the Indian Ocean, 1500–1850* (Athens: Ohio University Press, 2014); Patrick Manning, *Slavery and African Life: Occidental, Oriental, and African Slave Trades* (Cambridge: Cambridge University Press, 1995), 136–148; and Sheriff, *Slaves, Spices and Ivory in Zanzibar*.

87. Rawlinson to Wellesley, April 28, 1847, L/PS/5/450, BL.

88. Samuel Hennell to Henry Richard Charles Wellesley, chargé d'affaires at the Ottoman ports, May 8, 1847, FO 248/129, NAUK, London; this number excludes the number of enslaved people brought by Iranian pilgrims on their return from Mecca and Karbalā'. See ibid., May 8, 1847, L/PS/5/450, BL.

89. Translated extract of a letter from Mollah Houssein, agent at Sharjah, to Samuel Hennell, resident in the Persian Gulf, June 25, 1849, L/PS/5/463, BL, London. Translated extract of a letter from Mollah Houssein, agent at Sharjah, to Major Hennell, resident in the Persian Gulf, signed A. B. Kemball, June 25, 1849, AA3/9, ZNL, Zanzibar.

90. Samuel Hennell, resident in the Persian Gulf, to Arthur Malet, chief secretary to the government, Bombay, dated Bushire, September 20, 1847, L/PS/5/456, BL, London; Arthur Malet, July 4, 1848, R/15/1/111, BL, London; Samuel Hennell to Justin Sheil, dated Bushire, September 16, 1847, R/15/1/111, BL, London. This number agrees with Lorimer's estimate of three hundred enslaved people being imported into the Gulf by Suri vessels each year. Lorimer, *Gazetteer of the Persian Gulf*, 1: pt. 2, 2499.

91. Robert B. M. Binning, *A Journal of Two Years' Travel in Persia, Ceylon, Etc.* (London: W.H. Allen & Co., 1857), 1:144; Charles Issawi, *The Economic History of Iran, 1800–1914* (Chicago: University of Chicago Press, 1971), 27. In 1870, Iran's population was just under five million. Augustus H. Mounsey, *A Journey through the Caucasus and the Interior of Persia* (London: Smith, Elder & Co., 1872), 97.

92. Kemball to Robertson and Sheil, July 8, 1842, FO 84/426, NAUK.

93. Gregor Grant, senior magistrate of police, to Arthur Malet, chief secretary to the government of Bombay, November 19, 1847, L/PS/5/452, BL, London.

94. J. R. Wellsted, *Travels to the City of the Caliphs*, 1:58; Belgrave, *The Pirate Coast*, 63.

95. Clive Alfred Spinage, *African Ecology: Benchmarks and Historical Perspectives* (Berlin: Springer-Verlag, 2012), 129.

96. Wilson to the government, January 28, 1831, FO 84/426, NAUK. Notably, enslaved males from Zanzibar were cheaper than the women, selling for thirty-five German crowns; the enslaved females could earn forty German crowns.

97. Edwards to Kemball, 1842, FO 84/426, NAUK.

98. Kemball to Robertson and Sheil, July 8, 1842, FO 84/426, NAUK; Kemball, report on the Persian Gulf, 1847, FO 84/692, NAUK. See also Robertson to Willoughby, March 4, 1842, FO 84/426, NAUK. for slave prices see Sheriff, *Slaves, Spices and Ivory in Zanzibar*, 70.

99. Wilson to the government, January 28, 1831, FO 84/426, NAUK.

100. "Précis on the Slave Trade in the Gulf of Oman and the Persian Gulf," 1885, L/PS/20/C246, BL.

101. Kemball to Robertson and Sheil, July 8, 1842, FO 84/426, NAUK; Kemball, report on the Persian Gulf, 1847, FO 84/692, NAUK.

102. "Précis on the Slave Trade in the Gulf of Oman and the Persian Gulf," 1885, L/PS/20/

C246, BL. Like Ethiopians, Sudanese women could earn more than Sudanese men, ranging in one report of 1831 from forty to eighty German crowns. Wilson to the government, January 28, 1831, FO 84/426, NAUK.

103. Wilson to the government, January 28, 1831, FO 84/426, NAUK.

104. Edwards to Kemball, 1842, FO 84/426, NAUK.

105. Burton, *Personal Narrative of a Pilgrimage*, 2:13. According to another report, pretty enslaved Ethiopians sold for 100 to 150 Bombay rupees. Robertson to Willoughby, March 4, 1842, FO 84/426, NAUK.

106. Kemball to Robertson and Sheil, July 8, 1842, FO 84/426, NAUK; Kemball, report on the Persian Gulf, 1847, FO 84/692, NAUK.

107. Marriage contract of Saheb Beygum Khanum and Aqa Abulhasan, 1263, 296/16904, SAM, Tehran.

108. Kemball to Robertson and Sheil, July 8, 1842, FO 84/426, NAUK.

109. Mordechai Abir, "The Ethiopian Slave Trade and Its Relation to the Islamic World," in *Slaves and Slavery in Muslim Africa*, ed. John Ralph Willis (London: Frank Cass, 1985), 2:128.

110. E. A. Floyer, "Journal of a Route from Jask to Bampur," *Journal of the Royal Geographical Society* 47 (1877): 192.

111. Binning, *A Journal of Two Years' Travel*, 1:272.

112. Polak, *Persien*, 1:254.

113. Marriage contract of Mirza Muhamad Kazem Nezam al-Mulk and Nimtaj Khanum, 1289, no. 9149, film, 4946, Nusakh-i Khatti, KMDT, Tehran; Muhammad from Malayer to the Council for the Investigation of Grievances, the reign of Nasir al-Din Shah, 1301, 2929/018, summary of requests, Majlis-i tahqiq-i Mazalem, KMDT, Tehran; marriage contract of Sultan Muhammad Mirza, the son of Mirza Muhammad Khan Qajar and Zarrin Kullah Khanum, the daughter of Mu'tamed al-Sultan, Jamadi al-Akbar 18, 1279, no. 9553, KMDT, Tehran.

114. Arthur Arnold, *Through Persia by Caravan* (New York: Harper & Brothers, 1877), 361.

115. Wills, *In the Land of the Lion*, 326–327.

116. Sulayman at Isfahan to the minister of foreign affairs in Tehran, 1298, Q1298.16.18, VUK, Tehran.

117. C. J. Wills, *Persia as It Is* (London: Sampson Low, Marston, Searle, & Rivington, 1886), 75–76.

118. Abir, "The Ethiopian Slave Trade," 2:128. In spite of the legislation, enslaved people were still available at the southern ports, and it is reported that some government officials continued to purchase them. For example, Ahmad Khan, an agent in Bushehr, purchased three young *khānazād* (born in the house) *kanīzān* in the south for a government official in Tehran. Ahmad Khan, agent at Bushehr, Dhi al-Qa'dah 9, 1288, Q1288.13.29, VUK, Tehran.

119. The modern name of Saudi Arabia has been used throughout the book instead of the former name Arabia.

120. Henry-René D'Allemagne, *Du Khorassan au pays des Backhtiaris: Trois mois de voyage en Perse* (Paris: Hachette, 1911), 1:193.

121. Burton, *Personal Narrative of a Pilgrimage*, 2:12–14.

122. Husayni Farahani, *Safarnamih-yi Haj Mirza Muhammad Husayn Husayni*, 197. The cost of transporting one enslaved person along the Mecca-Syria-Tehran route was about thirty tomans.

123. Lorimer, *Gazetteer of the Persian Gulf*, 1: pt. 2, 2499.

124. An epidemic of cholera from 1821 to 1823 spread from Bushehr, Burazjan, and Iran's southern coasts into Iran's interior, killing many. Bushehr was hit by cholera again in 1832, and the bubonic plague killed five hundred in 1851. In 1865, cholera spread from India to Makran and from there across Iran's southern coasts to various ports and islands, such as Minab and Bandar 'Abbas, Qeshm, and Lengeh. In 1867 and 1877, bubonic plague spread from Iraq to Khuzistan by pilgrims returning from Karbalā', killing more than twenty-seven hundred; indeed, one-quarter of the population of the village of Jallakan on the Karun River died. In 1889 and 1904, cholera spread from Basra to Khuzistan, across to the Iranian coast, and then throughout the regions located along the road Bushehr–Shiraz as well as Kermanshah and Tangestan. Over seven thousand died in Shiraz alone. Smallpox was responsible for a considerable number of deaths in Khorramshahr in 1901 and in Bushehr from 1902 to 1903. In 1904, cholera broke out first in Dezful and Shushtar and then spread to Naseri, bringing an end to the slave trade. That same year, the bubonic plague spread to Lengeh and Lar, killing more than 146 people. See Lorimer, *Gazetteer of the Persian Gulf*, 1: pt. 2, 1739, 1864, 1913, 1954, 2052, 2517–2520, 2530, 2532, 2539, and 2555. For the spread of the bubonic plague throughout southern ports in the Persian Gulf, see also Sh. 1302, 290005769, SAM, Tehran.

125. Disability was prevalent among their children, and many died before adulthood. Polak, *Persien*, 1:250; Edwards to Kemball, 1842, FO 84/426, NAUK.

126. Najm al-Saltana to the Ministry of Foreign Affairs, Rajab 5, 1332, Q1332.3.3, VUK.

127. Charles M. Doughty, *Travels in Arabia Deserta* (1888; repr., London: Jonathan Cape and the Medici Society Limited, 1923), 2:348.

128. Arnold Burrowes Kemball to Commodore G. Robinson, January 28, 1853, FO 84/919, NAUK, London.

129. Sheil, *Life and Manners in Persia*, 244.

130. Shiraz was considered to be the main hub in this network. Polak, *Persien*, 1:254; Fraser, *Narrative of a Journey into Khorasan*, 103; Percy Molesworth Sykes, "The Geography of Southern Persia As Affecting Its History," *Scottish Geographical Magazine* 18, no. 12 (December 1902), 625.

131. In 1850, Robert Binning observed that most of the enslaved people in Shiraz had come from or were the progeny of enslaved people from Zanzibar. *A Journal of Two Years' Travel*, 1:152; Arnold, *Through Persia by Caravan*, 272, 283. See also Edwards to Kemball, 1842, FO 84/426, NAUK, 207–211.

132. Isabella Bird, *Journeys in Persia and Kurdistan* (London: John Murray, 1891), 1:3; Bassett, *Persia, the Land of the Imams*, 4. Express-post horsemen traveled the seven-hundred-mile distance straight from Bushehr to Tehran in ten days. Kinneir, *A Geographical Memoir of the Persian Empire*, 44. See Jamalzada, *Ganj-i Shaygan*, and Lorimer, *Gazetteer of the Persian Gulf*, 1: pt. 2, 2455.

133. Issawi, *The Economic History of Iran*, 196.

134. The Saho are a Cushitic-speaking group in northern Ethiopia.

135. Presumably Oromo.

136. The statement of Jamila, Shawwal 8, 1323, Q1323.3.2, VUK, Tehran.

137. Edwards to Kemball, 1842, FO 84/426, NAUK.

138. Binning, *A Journal of Two Years' Travel*, 1:272.

139. Polak, *Persien*, 1:248; Samuel Hennell to Justin Sheil, June 14, 1850, FO 84/815, NAUK, London.

140. The British government to the Iranian government, Dhi al-Hajja 9, 1266, Q.1263.6.15, VUK, Tehran; Wills, *Persia as It Is*, 75.

141. Waring, *A Tour to Sheeraz*, 79.

142. Samuel Hennell to Justin Sheil, September 10, 1850, FO 84/815, NAUK, London, 209–212; Justin Sheil to Ameer-i-Nizam, October 16, 1850, FO 84/815, NAUK, London; Kemball, report on the Persian Gulf, 1847, FO 84/692, NAUK.

143. Edwards to Kemball, 1842, FO 84/426, NAUK.

144. Wills, *Persia as It Is*, 75.

145. The entire southern region of Fars, which borders the Persian Gulf, is called the Garmsir, or "hot region." Herein, the enslaved people were taken to places such as Dashti, Tangestan, Dalaki, Burazjan, Bandar Deylam, and Bandar Rig. See Hennell to Sheil, September 10, 1850, FO 84/815, NAUK; Sheil to Ameer-i-Nizam, October 16, 1850, FO 84/815, NAUK; Arnold Burrowes Kemball to Arthur Malet, chief secretary to the government of Bombay, August 2, 1853, L/PS/5/479, BL, London.

146. Kemball to Robertson and Sheil, July 8, 1842, FO 84/426, NAUK; Hennell to Sheil, dated Bushire, January 11, 1850, L/PS/5/463, BL.

147. Bassett, *Persia, the Land of the Imams*, 288; Arnold, *Through Persia by Caravan*, 361, 431.

148. The Iranian government to the British government, Shawwal 8, 1278, Q1278.9.20, VUK, Tehran.

149. Muhammad ibn Sabzʿali Esfahani, *Vajizat al-tahrir: dar chegonegi-yi tanzim-i asnad-i sharʿi, meli va hoqoqi dar dore-yi Safavi va Qajar*, ed. Rasul Jafariyan (Qom: Movarekh, 1393), 45, 178–179; See slave purchase contract in which Hesam al-Sadat sold his *kaniz* to Khadija Khanum, the sister of Sepahsalar, 1285, 296001068, SAM, Tehran; Iranian Ministry of Foreign Affairs to the British Consul, Q1317.3.4, VUK, Tehran.

150. Slave transaction contract and the guarantee of an enslaved person between Aqa Ebrahim, slave seller, and Nimtaj, slave buyer, 1292, 296/7135/2, SAM, Tehran; slave transaction contract and the guarantee of an enslaved person between Hashem Khan, slave dealer, and Haji ʿAlaʾ al-Mulk, the minister of the Great Council, slave buyer, Shaʿban 23, 1304, 296/1812/1and 2, SAM, Tehran; slave transaction contract and the guarantee of Fazeh, an enslaved black female and her two children, Sulayman and Arghavan, 1290, 296/2398/1, SAM, Tehran.

151. Kemball, report on the Persian Gulf, 1847, FO 84/692, NAUK.

152. Basset, *Persia, the Land of the Imams*, 288. One such slave broker was Karbalaʾi ʿAli Dad, who lived in Shiraz and Tehran. Extract from a French letter from Monsieur Castelli, British agent at Shiraz, to Captain Felix Jones, political resident in the Persian Gulf, August 12, 1859, FO 248/183, NAUK, London.

153. For example, Aqa Ebrahim, a native of Qazvin who was based in Shiraz, and Sayyid Esmaʿil of Quchan were identified in the buying and selling of girls in Lutfabad and Quchan to Turcomans, The report of the customs office in Lutfabad, Mizan 29, 1329, 293001104, SAM, Tehran; Malcolm, *Sketches of Persia*, 1:114–116.

154. The rental contract of Firuze, Rabiʿ al-Awwal 1329, Q1332.3.3, VUK, Tehran.

155. Polak, *Persien*, 1:254.

156. The buying and selling of girls in Lutfabad and Quchan to Turcomans, Mizan 29, 1329, 293001104, SAM, Tehran.

157. Polak, *Persien*, 1:254.

158. The British government to the Iranian government, Rabiʿ al-Awwal 27, 1266, Q1263.6.15, VUK, Tehran; Lorimer, *Gazetteer of the Persian Gulf*, 1: pt. 2, 1682.

159. Taylor to Kemball, July 24, 1853, L/PS/5/478, BL.

160. Sadid al-Saltana Kababi, *Sarzaminha-yi shumali*, 346.

161. Slave purchase contract, Hesam al-Sadat, 1285, 296001068, SAM, Tehran; slave transaction contract, Fazeh, Sulayman, and Arghavan, 1290, 296/2398/1, SAM, Tehran.

162. Iranian government agent in Sistan to the Ministry of Foreign Affairs of Iran, the sale of Iranian women as *kaniz* to Afghans in Sistan, Ramadan 5, 1335, 293001109, SAM, Tehran; the sale of Za'feran, the *kaniz* of Mahpare Baygum Khanum, to Mahrukh Khanum Tabataba'i, 1284, 110000141, SAM, Tabriz.

163. The trade in enslaved Africans in the Americas, by contrast, began in response to the decline in population of aboriginal peoples due to the ravages of war, disease and pestilence, and legislation by the Spanish restricting their captivity in the 1540s. Robin Blackburn, *The Overthrow of Colonial Slavery, 1776–1848* (London: Verso, 1990), 39.

CHAPTER 4. PATTERNS OF ENSLAVEMENT

1. Musavi Nami Isfahani, *Tarikh-i giti gusha*, 108; Ahmad 'Ali Khan Vaziri, *Tarikh-i Kerman*, ed. Muhammad Ebrahim Bastani Parizi (Tehran: 'Elmi, 1364), 2:744–750; Mehdi Quli Khan Hedayat, *Guzaresh-i Iran*, 40; Henry Savage Landor, *Across Coveted Lands* (New York: Charles Scribner's Sons, 1903), 1:451; Curzon, *Persia and the Persian Question*, 2:243.

2. Nafisi, *Tarikh-i ejtema'i va siasi-yi Iran*, 1:66; Lesan al-Mulk, *Nasekh al-tawarikh*, 1:80.

3. Kinneir, *A Geographical Memoir of the Persian Empire*, 27; Atkin, *Russia and Iran 1780–1828*, 110.

4. Reza Quli Khan Hedayat, *Tarikh-i ruzat al-safa*, 9:271; Malcolm, *Sketches of Persia*, 1:78–79; Muhammad Fathullah ibn Muhammad Taqi Sarvi, *Tarikh-i Muhammadi, ahsan al-tawarikh*, ed. and annot. Ghulamreza Tabataba'i Majd (Tehran: Sepehr, 1371), 276; Lesan al-Mulk, *Nasekh al-tawarikh*, 1:77; Polak, *Persien*, 1:249; Mehdi Quli Khan Hedayat, *Guzaresh-i Iran*, 40; Mignan, *Winter Journey through Russia*, 1:71.

5. Lorimer, *Gazetteer of the Persian Gulf*, 1: pt. 2, 1858; Atkin, *Russia and Iran 1780–1828*, 121.

6. Nafisi, *Tarikh-i ejtema'i va siasi-yi Iran*, 1:66; Kinneir, *A Geographical Memoir of the Persian Empire*, 339.

7. The inhabitants of Semnan to the Council for the Investigation of Grievances, the reign of Nasir al-Din Shah, 1301, 2929-246, summary of requests, Majlis-i tahqiq-i Mazalem, KMDT, Tehran; J. P. Ferrier, *Caravan Journeys and Wanderings in Persia, Afghanistan, Turkistan, and Beloochistan* (London: John Murray, Albemarle Street, 1857), 87.

8. Adamiyat, *Amir Kabir va Iran*, 599.

9. A report on the enslavement of Iranian salt buyers at Ashuradeh by Turcomans, Rabi' al-Awwal 18, 1272, Q1272.7.47, VUK, Tehran.

10. A report by the Iranian government's agent in Khorasan and Sistan, Rabi' al-Thani 29, 1325, Q1325.11.7, VUK, Tehran.

11. The report of the Iranian government's agent to the Russian consulate, Dhi al-Qa'da 16, 1324, Q1324.3.3, VUK, Tehran; Mirza Rahim to the Council for the Investigation of Grievances, Damghan, the reign of Nasir al-Din Shah, 1301, 2929-189, summary of requests, Majlis-i tahqiq-i Mazalem, KMDT, Tehran; Polak, *Persien*, 1:68; Nikolay Murav'yov, *Journey to Khiva through the Turkoman Country* (1822; repr., London: Oguz Press, 1977), 13.

12. Edward B. Eastwick, *Three Years' Residence in Persia* (London: Smith, Elder, & Co., 1864), 1:251.

13. Kinneir, *A Geographical Memoir of the Persian Empire*, 115.

14. Fraser, *Narrative of a Journey into Khorasan*, 256; Marvin, *Merv, the Queen of the World*, 244.

15. Ferrier, *Caravan Journeys*, 80.

16. Vambéry, *Arminius Vambéry*, 181; Bassett, *Persia, the Land of the Imams*, 244–247. Ferrier also noted the harshness of the conditions: if slaves committed offenses, their owners would "gratify their revenge by cutting off their ears, putting out an eye, or stab[bing] them with their knives in a part which is not mortal. . . . At the second attempt he is nailed by the ear to the street-door of his master's house, and remains in this state for three days." *Caravan Journeys*, 81; see also *Vaqay'e Ettefaqiye*, no. 445 (24 Safar 1276): 4, no. 465 (11 Shawwal 1276): 4, no. 114. (27 Jamadi al-Thani 1269): 3.

17. Murav'yov, *Journey to Khiva*, 31, 56–59, 113.

18. Haj Sultan Husayn Tabanda Gunabadi, *Nabegha-yi 'elm va 'erfan* (Tehran: Taban, 1350), 13.

19. Marvin, *Merv, the Queen of the World*, 239.

20. Ibid., 148–150.

21. Murav'yov, *Journey to Khiva*, 75.

22. Fraser, *Narrative of a Journey into Khorasan*, 331.

23. Najmabadi, *The Story of the Daughters of Quchan*, 97. Women also worked in the hotels in Tiflis. Parliamentary discussions, *Muzakerat-i Majlis-i Shuray-i Melli-yi Iran*, hereafter referred to as Majlis, Muharram 6, 1325.

24. Vambéry, *Arminius Vambéry*, 251.

25. Marvin, *Merv, the Queen of the World*, 250.

26. Najmabadi, *The Story of the Daughters of Quchan*, 21.

27. Parliamentary discussions, Majlis, Muharram 6, 1325, Safar 2, 1325; Fereydun Adamiyat, *Ide'uluzhi-yi nehzat-i mashrutiyat-i Iran* (Tehran: Payam, 2535 [1355]), 406; parliamentary discussions, Majlis, Muharram 6, 1325; Lorimer, *Gazetteer of the Persian Gulf*, 1: pt. 2, 1997.

28. Polak, *Persien*, 1:31.

29. Murav'yov, *Journey to Khiva*, 164.

30. Lesan al-Mulk, *Nasekh al-tawarikh*, 2:690.

31. Lord Palmerston to Sir John McNeil, July 9, 1841, FO 84/373, NAUK, London; Ronald F. Thomson to Earl Granville, October 27, 1881, FO 84/1592, NAUK, London.

32. Taylour Thomson to the earl of Derby, February 29, 1876, FO 84/1450, NAUK, London; Ferrier, *Caravan Journeys*, 90.

33. Taylour Thomson to the earl of Derby, Tehran, February 29, 1876, FO 84/1450, NAUK, London; Mustaufi, *Sharh-i zendegani-yi man*, 1:20.

34. Murav'yov, *Journey to Khiva*, 58; James Hutton, *Central Asia: From the Aryan to the Cossack* (1875; repr., New Delhi: Manas Publications, 2005), 205.

35. A report by the official of the Ministry of Foreign Affairs of Iran at Bujnurd, Jamadi al-Thani 29, 1324, Q1324.3.3, VUK, Tehran.

36. Grantovski et al., *Tarikh-i Iran*, 370.

37. Najmabadi, *The Story of the Daughters of Quchan*, 20.

38. Report from Hussain, the Iranian government's agent in Sarakhs, Safar 6, 1325, Q1325.11.3, VUK, Tehran; the agent of the Ministry of Foreign Affairs in Qa'enat to the Ministry of Foreign Affairs in Tehran, Sha'ban 23, 1335, Q1335.3.13, VUK, Tehran; see Gwyn Campbell and Alessandro Stanziani, eds., *Bonded Labour and Debt in the Indian Ocean World* (London: Pickering and Chatto, 2013).

39. Nasrullah Mushir al-Daula to the Iranian government's agent in Kurdistan, Sha'ban

14, 1319, Q1319.12.6.27, VUK, Tehran; Mushir al-Daula to the Russian embassy, Ramadan 26, 1325, Q1325.11.7, VUK, Tehran; Mushir al-Daula to Taqarub al-Mulk, the governor of Sanandaj, Ramadan 26, 1325, Q1325.11.7, VUK, Tehran; Bassett, *Persia, the Land of the Imams*, 287; Polak, *Persien*, 1:249.

40. A large number of enslaved Iranian women in Marv were from Sarakhs, Bujnurd, Kalat, Darreh Jaz, Quchan. Report of Mirza Sadeqkhan, the Iranian government's official in Marv, to the minister of foreign affairs, Safar 19, 1322, Q1323.3.2, VUK, Tehran; Najmabadi, *The Story of the Daughters of Quchan*, 7–20, 36; A report on the buying and selling of girls in Lutfabad and Quchan to Turcomans, Mizan 12, 1329, 293001104, SAM, Tehran; report from Ashgabat, Sha'ban 21, 1322, Q1322.3.4, VUK, Tehran.

41. The report of Ebrahim, the assistant to the Iranian agent in Ashgabat, on the enslavement of Iranians by the Turcomans, Q1319.11.8, VUK, Tehran; report from Hussain, Safar 6, 1325, Q1325.11.3, VUK; the agent of the Ministry of Foreign Affairs in Qa'enat to the Ministry of Foreign Affairs in Tehran, Sha'ban 23, 1335, VUK.

42. Report of Mirza Sadeqkhan to the Minister of Foreign Affairs, Safar 19, 1322, Q1323.3.2, VUK; the agent of the Ministry of Foreign Affairs of Iran, Bujnurd, and Guklan, Sha'ban 19, 1324, Q1324.3.3, VUK, Tehran.

43. Ansari, *Safarnama-yi Khusru Mirza*, 119; Marvin, *Merv, the Queen of the World*, 241.

44. The report of Ebrahim on the enslavement of Iranians by the Turcomans, Q 1326 .57.15, VUK.

45. Habib Ajez to the Council for the Investigation of Grievances, Bandar Jaz, the reign of Nasir al-Din Shah, 1301, 2929-272, summary of requests, Majlis-i tahqiq-i Mazalem, KMDT, Tehran; Murav'yov, *Journey to Khiva*, 17, 29, 43–44, 58, 82, 113, 134, 135. See also Fraser, *Narrative of a Journey into Khorasan*, 257.

46. Vambéry indicated that the price ranged between two and three pounds. *Arminius Vambéry*, 252, 271; Mirpanjeh, *Khaterat-i esarat*, 101.

47. Murav'yov, *Journey to Khiva*, 58, 148.

48. Ansari, *Safarnama-yi Khusru Mirza*, 121; Murav'yov, *Journey to Khiva*, 58.

49. Vambéry, *Arminius Vambéry*, 181.

50. Report of Mirza Sadeqkhan to the minister of foreign affairs, Safar 19, 1322, Q1323.3.2, VUK.

51. Report of the Iranian government's agent at Ashgabat, Muharram 27, 1323, Q1323.3.2, VUK, Tehran; A telegram from Mashhad to the government of Khorasan, Rabi' al-Thani 21, 1323, Q1323.3.2, VUK, Tehran.

52. Lorimer, *Gazetteer of the Persian Gulf*, 1: pt. 2, 1858.

53. Nafisi, *Tarikh-i ejtema'i va siasi-yi Iran*, 1:66; Lesan al-Mulk, *Nasekh al-tawarikh*, 1:80.

54. Kinneir, *A Geographical Memoir of the Persian Empire*, 170.

55. Hutton, *Central Asia*, 205; Ferrier, *Caravan Journeys*, 81–83; British agent at Astarabad to Taylour Thomson, June 25, 1846, FO 60/380, NAUK, London. Those British who were captured in Bukhara in 1846 were ransomed for fifteen thousand tomans. Colonel Justin Sheil to the ameer of Bokhara, 1846, FO 60/125, NAUK, London; Murav'yov, *Journey to Khiva*, 17, 49.

56. Lesan al-Mulk, *Nasekh al-tawarikh*, 1:82.

57. Murav'yov, *Journey to Khiva*, 58, 113.

58. Mirza Muhammad Hadi 'Alavi Shirzai, *Safarnama-yi Mirza Abulhasan Khan Shirazi (Ilchi) be Russia*, ed. Muhammad Gulbun (Tehran: Donya-yi ketab, 1363), 62.

59. Lesan al-Mulk, *Nasekh al-tawarikh*, 2:682–690.

60. Fereydun Adamiyat, *Fekr-i azadi* (Tehran: Sukhan, 1340), 39.

61. Lorimer, *Gazetteer of the Persian Gulf*, 1: pt. 2, 1865; Sykes, *A History of Iran*, 2:324.

62. Marvin, *Merv, the Queen of the World*, 430–432.

63. Each *farsang* is equal to three miles.

64. They were usually sold at the markets in Bukhara and Khiva. Polak, *Persien*, 2:334; Ehtesham al-Vuzara' to the Ministry of Foreign Affairs of Iran, from Astarabad to Tehran, Sha'ban 2, 1317, Q1317.15.23, VUK, Tehran. In 1883, about one hundred Georgian families were living in 'Abbasabad. Mirza Qahraman Amin Lashkar, *Roozname-yi safar-i Khorasan be hamrahi-yi Nasir al-Din Shah (1300)*, ed. Iraj Afshar and Mohamad Rasuldarya gasht (Tehran: Asatir, 1374), 206.

65. Mirpanjeh wrote the memoir of his captivity; see Mirpanjeh, *Khaterat-i esarat*.

66. Lorimer, *Gazetteer of the Persian Gulf*, 1: pt. 2, 2010.

67. Sykes, *A History of Iran*, 2:358.

68. Lorimer, *Gazetteer of the Persian Gulf*, 1: pt. 2, 2011.

69. Murav'yov, *Journey to Khiva*, 130.

70. Mirpanjeh, *Khaterat-i esarat*, 92.

71. Report from Hussain, the Iranian government's agent in Sarakhs, Rajab 19, 1325, Q1325.11.3, VUK, Tehran.

72. Reports by Muhamad Isma'il, the Iranian government's agent in Ashgabat, Shawwal 17, 1325, Q1325.11.7, VUK, Tehran; Isma'il, the Iranian government's agent in Ashgabat, Rabi' al-Awwal 18, 1325, Q1325.11.7, VUK, Tehran; the order of Muhamad 'Ali 'Ala' al-Saltana from Mashhad to Tehran, Rabi' al-Awwal 29, 1325, Q1325.11.7, VUK, Tehran.

73. The order of Muhamad 'Ali 'Ala' al-Saltana from Mashhad to Tehran, Rabi' al-Awwal 29, 1325, Q1325.11.7, VUK, Tehran; A report by Isma'il, the Iranian government's agent in Ashgabat, Shawwal 8, 1325, Q1325.11.7, VUK, Tehran; Isma'il to the minister of foreign affairs, Ashgabat, Dhi al-Hajja 3, 1325, Q1325.11.7, VUK, Tehran; 'Ali Akbar, the Iranian government's agent in Sistan, to the Ministry of Foreign Affairs, Ramadan 5, 1335, Q1335.3.13.1, VUK, Tehran.

74. R. E. L. Wingate, political agent and H. B. Miles's consul in Muscat, to the political resident in the Persian Gulf, Bushire, dated in Muscat, February 6, 1921, R/15/1/221, BL, London.

75. The Makran coast was a particular focus for these traders and local chiefs. Kinneir, *A Geographical Memoir of the Persian Empire*, 203.

76. Abdul Sheriff, "The Persian Gulf and the Swahili Coast: A History of Acculturation Over the Longue Durée," in *The Persian Gulf in History*, ed. Lawrence G. Potter (New York: Palgrave Macmillan, 2009), 183; Lorimer, *Gazetteer of the Persian Gulf*, 1: pt. 2, 2500–2501.

77. The Buzdars, Hots, Kalmats, Latts, Mullas, Raises, Rinds, Sangurs, Shaizadahs, and Jadgals (the British assumed the latter to be the same as Jats) were the principal ethnic groups. Lorimer, *Gazetteer of the Persian Gulf*, 2: pt. 1A, 258.

78. R. H. Clive to Arthur Henderson, November 9, 1929, FO 248/1387, NAUK, London.

79. Report of the customs bureau in 'Arabistan [the Khuzistan province] to Muhamad 'Ali 'Ala' al-Saltana, the minister of foreign affairs, January 23, 1907, Q1325.3.8, VUK, Tehran. So long had this system been used that already by the mid-seventeenth century, Baluchis were considered to be one of the most important elements of the Omani royal army in East Africa. J. S. Mangat, *A History of the Asians in East Africa c. 1886 to 1945* (Oxford: Clarendon Press, 1969), 13. See Walter Brown, "Pre-colonial History of Bagamoyo: Aspects of the Growth of an East African Coastal Town" (PhD diss., University of Boston, 1971), 255–274. See also Lorimer, *Gazetteer of the Persian Gulf*, 1: pt. 1A, 406.

80. H. B. Miles's consul general for Fars to the British resident and consulate general, Bu-

shire, August 13, 1929, FO 248/1387, NAUK, London; statement made by Muhammad, son of Jan Muhammad, son-in-law of Salih al-Din, resident of Lashar in Makran, July 8, 1926, R/15/1/203, BL, London; C. C. J. Barrett, Political Resident in the Persian Gulf and Consul-General for Fars, to Robert Clive, Bushire, August 13, 1929, FO 371/13791, NAUK, London.

81. The Ministry of Foreign Affairs to Hesam al-Sadat, the Iranian government's agent in Lengeh, Sh.1300, 293001106, SAM, Tehran; Reports from the Ministry of the Interior, the government of Bandar ʿAbbas and Minab, Aban 19, Sh. 1309, 293/6626, SAM, Tehran.

82. Report of the customs bureau in ʿArabistan [the Khuzistan province] to Muhamad ʿAli ʿAlaʾ al-Saltana, January 23, 1907, Q1325.3.8, VUK.

83. Correspondance on the liberation of slaves, the Ministry of Foreign Affairs to the Ministry of the Interior, Sh. 1300, 293001106, SAM, Tehran; Lorimer, *Gazetteer of the Persian Gulf*, 1: pt. 2, 2510.

84. H. B. Miles's consul general to the British resident and consulate general, Bushire, October 15, 1929, FO 248/1387, NAUK, London.

85. Lorimer, *Gazetteer of the Persian Gulf*, 1: pt. 2, 2503.

86. Rupee, the currency of India, was also used in Baluchistan. *Nedā-yi Vatan*, no. 31 (May 21, 1907): 3.

87. Lorimer, *Gazetteer of the Persian Gulf*, 1: pt. 2, 2228.

88. Issawi, *The Economic History of Iran*, 126.

89. Consular memorandum, Muscat, August 23, 1921, R/15/1/221, BL, London.

90. Statement made by Shanbeh, son of Chawash of Tutan of Karavan, aged about fourteen, October 31, 1929, FO 248/1387, NAUK, London.

91. H. B. Miles's consul general for Fars to the British resident and consulate general in Tehran, dated in Bushire, October 15, 1929, FO 248/1387, NAUK.

92. Lorimer, *Gazetteer of the Persian Gulf*, 1: pt. 2, 2221; H. B. Miles's consul general to the British resident and consulate general, Bushire, October 15, 1929, FO 248/1387, NAUK.

93. Sadid al-Saltana Kababi, *al-Menas fi ahval-i al-ghaus*, 11; Lorimer, *Gazetteer of the Persian Gulf*, 1: pt. 2, 2228.

94. Arnold, *Through Persia by Caravan*, 433.

95. From the Secretary to the Government of India in the Foreign and Political Department to L. D. Wakely, Secretary, Political Department, India Office, London, dated Delhi, Januray 17, 1924, FO 371/9531, NAUK, London.

96. The inhabitants of Rudavar to the Council for the Investigation of Grievances, Toyserkan, the reign of Nasir al-Din Shah, 1301, 2929-492, summary of requests, Majlis-i tahqiq-i Mazalem, KMDT, Tehran; *Nedā-yi Vatan*, no. 31 (May 21, 1907): 3.

97. Iraj Afshar Sistani, *Ilha, chadurneshinan va tavaʾf ʿashayr-i Iran* (Tehran: Huma, 1366), 2:896.

98. Reza Mukhtari Isfahani, ed., *Guzareshha-yi iyalat va velayat az auzaʿ-i ejtemaʿi eqtesadi-yi Iran dar sal-i 1310 H. Sh.* (Tehran: Markaz-i asnad-i riyasat-i jumhuri, 1383), 321; Lorimer, *Gazetteer of the Persian Gulf*, 1: pt. 1A, 323; From Lieut-Colonel A. P. Trevor, Political Resident, Persian Gulf, to E. B. Howell, Foreign Secretary to the Government of India, Foreign and Political Department, Delhi, Bushire, December 16, 1923, FO 371/9531, NAUK, London.

99. "Slave Trade: Kidnapping of Baluchis and Indians on the Mekran Coast of Oman and Trucial Coast," January 1921–July 1922, R/15/1/221, BL, London.

100. Lorimer, *Gazetteer of the Persian Gulf*, 1: pt. 2, 2503.

101. He also allied with Mir Barkat, the chief of Jask, in the enslavement of free Muslim Baluchis. Report of the customs bureau in ʿArabistan [the Khuzistan province] to Muhamad

'Ali 'Ala' al-Saltana, January 23, 1907, Q1325.3.8, VUK; Lorimer, *Gazetteer of the Persian Gulf*, 1: pt. 2, 2192.

102. Lorimer, *Gazetteer of the Persian Gulf*, 1: pt. 2, 2511.

103. Ibid.; Sadid al-Saltana Kababi, *Sarzaminha-yi shumali*, 302.

104. Reports on southern ports, 1311–1317, the immigration of people, 293004045, SAM, 1. In the 1930s, about two hundred thousand Iranian immigrations were recorded to India, Oman, and the Arab states in the Persian Gulf. The emigration of inhabitants from the Gazik village in Khorasan to Afghanistan was a result of poverty, "the immigration of some inhabitants of Khorasan to Afghanistan," Sh. 1316, 240000604, SAM, Tehran; see Arnold T. Wilson, "Notes on a Journey from Bandar Abbas to Shiraz via Lar, in February and March, 1907," *Geographical Journal* 31 (February 1908), 169. See also *Vaqay'e Ettefaqiye*, no. 381 (Shawwal 6, 1274): 4.

105. Sadid al-Saltana Kababi, *Bandar 'Abbas*, 36; Sistani, *Ilha*, 2:1017. A report on the poverty of peasants in Qa'enat and Quchan as a result of the tyrannical feudal system and the stagnation in imports and exports. Sh. 1315, Khorasan, 240006012, SAM, Tehran.

106. 'Ali Akbar, the Iranian government's agent in Sistan, to the Ministry of Foreign Affairs in Tehran, Sha'ban 2, 1335, Q1335.47.29.6, VUK, Tehran; A report on the sale of Iranian women as *kaniz* to Afghans in Sistan, 1335, 293001109, SAM, Tehran; A report by the Iranian government's agent in Khorasan and Sistan, Jamadi al-Thani 19, 1325, Q1324.3.3, VUK, Tehran; report from Hussain, the Iranian government's agent in Sarakhs, Ramadan 9, 1325, Q1325.11.3, VUK, Tehran; report from Hussain, the Iranian government's agent in Sarakhs, Sha'ban 3, 1325, Q1325.11.3, VUK, Tehran.

107. Statements of enslaved Baluchis, January 27, 1921, R/15/1/221, BL. London; resident agent in Shargah [Sharjah] to the political resident in the Persian Gulf, Bushire, August 3, 1921, R/15/1/221, BL, London.

108. "Slave Trade," political [agent] in Muscat to resident in Bushire, January 1921, R/15/1/221, BL.

109. The Minister of the Interior to the Minister of War, Sh.1303, 293001107, SAM, Tehran.

110. Arfa, *Under Five Shahs*, 254.

111. Guity Nashat, *The Origins of Modern Reform in Iran, 1870–1880* (Urbana: University of Illinois Press, 1982), 9.

112. Mehdi Quli Khan Hedayat, *Guzaresh-i Iran*, 48.

113. The inhabitants of Manjil, Talesh, Rasht, and Nahavand to the Council for the Investigation of Grievances, the reign of Nasir al-Din Shah, 1301, 2929-131 and 189, summary of requests, Majlis-i tahqiq-i Mazalem, KMDT, Tehran; local chiefs of Baluchistan to E'tedal al-Daula, the governor of 'Arabistan [the Khuzestan province] and Shatt al Arab [Arvandrud], 1323, Q1323.15.5, VUK, Tehran.

114. The peasants of Jaghatai to the Council for the Investigation of Grievances, Jovain, the reign of Nasir al-Din Shah, 1301, 2929-286, summary of requests, Majlis-i tahqiq-i Mazalem, KMDT, Tehran.

115. Reports on southern ports, 1311–1317, Chabahar, Khordad 3, 1317, 293004045, SAM, Tehran, 2.

116. The summary of the Kerman report, 1319, Q1319.2.3.48, VUK, Tehran.

117. Ahmad Majd al-Islam Kermani, *Enhelal-i majlis* (Isfahan: Daneshgah-i Isfahan, 1351), 113; Willem Floor, *Agriculture in Qajar Iran* (Washington, DC: Mage Publishers, 2003), 111. See also Stephen Pastner and Carroll McC. Pastner, "Agriculture, Kinship and Politics in Southern Baluchistan," *Man* 7 (March 1972), 129.

118. F. J. Goldsmid, "Journey from Bandar Abbas to Mash-had by Sistan, with Some Account of the Last-Named Province," *Journal of the Royal Geographical Society of London* 43 (1873), 67.

119. Vaziri, *Joghrafia-yi Baluchistan*, 52, 53.

120. Ibid., 4.

121. The head of the customs bureau in the south of Iran to Muhamad ʿAli ʿAlaʾ al-Saltana, the minister of foreign affairs, January 23, 1907, Q1325.3.8, VUK, Tehran. The local governors used military force to collect taxes from the Baluchis.

122. ʿAbdulhamid Mirza Naser al-Daula, *Safarnama-yi Baluchistan: Az Mahan ta Chabahar* (Kerman: Markaz-i Kermanshenasi, 1370), 22; Vaziri, *Joghrafia-yi Baluchistan*, 50–55; Vaziri, *Tarikh-i Kerman*, 2:759.

123. Vaziri, *Joghrafia-yi Baluchistan*, 56.

124. Naser al-Daula, *Safarnama-yi Baluchistan*, 25; Lesan al-Mulk, *Nasekh al-tawarikh*, 2:765.

125. Report of the Iranian government's agent in Bujnurd, Rabiʿ al-Awwal 10, 1323, Q1323.3.2, VUK, Tehran; the Ministry of War to the Ministry of the Interior, Sh. 1303, 293001107, SAM, Tehran.

126. Firuz Mirza Farman Farma, *Safarnamih-yi Kerman*, 80–83; the Ministry of Foreign Affairs to the government of Khorasan, Rabiʿ al-Thani 24, 1323, Q1323.3.2, VUK, Tehran; the Ministry of Foreign Affairs to the governor of Darreh Jaz, Rabiʿ al-Thani 24, 1323, Q1323.3.2, VUK, Tehran; A telegraph sent from Bujnurd on the trade in Iranian women by the Russian Turcomans to Mushir al-Daula in Tehran, Rabiʿ al-Thani 2, 1323, Q1323.3.2, VUK, Tehran.

127. Lorimer, *Gazetteer of the Persian Gulf*, 1: pt. 2, 2191.

128. Vaziri, *Joghrafia-yi Baluchistan*, 16, 26; Percy Sykes, *Ten Thousand Miles in Persia or Eight Years in Iran* (London: John Murray, Albemarle Street, 1902), 106.

129. Najmabadi, *The Story of the Daughters of Quchan*, 16.

130. Parliamentary discussions, Majlis, Muharram 22, 1325. The slave trade was organized by local agents under Sardar Ahmad Khan, Sardar Islam Khan, Sardar Saʿid Khan, and Asʿad al-Daula, the governor of Baluchistan (see the head of the customs bureau in the south of Iran to Muhamad ʿAli ʿAlaʾ al-Saltana, January 23, 1907, Q1325.3.8, VUK).

131. Firuz Mirza Farman Farma, *Safarnamih-yi Kerman*, 60, 118; Mukhtari Isfahani, *Guzareshha-yi iyalat va velayat*, 102, 124. In fact, the prevalence of a feudal system of landownership meant that peasants had to give at least four-fifths of their produce to the landowners. Peasants to the Council for the Investigation of Grievances, Kerman, and peasants of the governmental lands (*khalisijat*) in Nazar Abad Ulya to the Council for the Investigation of Grievances, Savjublagh, the reign of Nasir al-Din Shah, 1301, 2929-088, summary of requests, Majlis-i tahqiq-i Mazalem, KMDT, Tehran.

132. Famine provoked revolts in 1897 and 1898 against the British exportation of grain. And yet, in spite of the negative feelings, it was ironic that some slaves sought the protection of the British consulate at Bandar ʿAbbas to avoid being sold to strangers. See Grantovski et al., *Tarikh-i Iran*, 375, and Lorimer, *Gazetteer of the Persian Gulf*, 1: pt. 2, 2002, 2052, 2079, 2514.

133. Reports on southern ports, 1311–1317, the Ministry of the Interior, political office, Day 26, 1317, and reasons for immigration, 293004045, SAM, Tehran, 1–12.

134. Colonel A. P. Trevor, political resident in the Persian Gulf, to Denys de S. Bray, CIE, CBE, foreign secretary to the government of India in the Foreign and Political Department, Delhi, December 31, 1921, R/15/1/221, BL, London.

135. Ibid.

136. Ibid.

137. Hugh Tothill, commander in chief stationed in the East Indies, to senior naval officer in the Persian Gulf, June 22, 1921, R/15/1/221, BL, London.

138. "Slave Traffic between the Mekran Coast and the Oman," June 22, 1921, R/15/1/221, BL, London; "Slave Traffic on the Mekran Coast," extract from report of commanding officer, H.M.S. Cyclanen, October 21, 1921, FO 371/7831, NAUK, London; The Secretary to the Government of India in the Foreign and Political Department to L. D. Wakely, Secretary, Political Department, Indian Office, London, dated August 23, 1922, FO 371/7831, NAUK, London.

139. H. B. Miles's consul general to the British resident and consulate general, Bushire, October 15, 1929, FO 248/1387, NAUK; Lorimer, *Gazetteer of the Persian Gulf*, 1: pt. 2, 2511. An example that illustrates this phenomenon is that of a slave dealer named Sarfaraz, who was described in 1921 as having "returned from Bint [in Makran] after selling rifles . . . with him two females and one male slave . . . to his home at Gooshki Birkat's village." A.S. in Jask to the director in Karachi, June 12, 1921, R/15/1/221, BL, London; Viceroy, Foreign and Political Department, to Secretary of State for India, New Delhi, Dated November 12, 1929, FO 371/13791, NAUK, London.

140. Navarra at Jask to D.P.G. at Karachi, August 23, 1921, R/15/1/221, BL, London.

141. Lorimer, *Gazetteer of the Persian Gulf*, 1: pt. 2, 2556.

142. Ibid., pt. 1A, 295.

143. Political Department, General Act of the Brussels Conference, Bombay Castle, June 8, 1891, R/15/1/199, BL, London.

144. R. W. Beachey, "The Arms Trade in East Africa in the Late Nineteenth Century," *Journal of African History* 3, no. 3 (1962), 457; Lorimer, *Gazetteer of the Persian Gulf*, 1: pt. 2, 2558. See also Lorimer, *Gazetteer of the Persian Gulf*, 1: pt. 2199; the head of the customs bureau in the south of Iran to Muhamad 'Ali 'Ala' al-Saltana, January 23, 1907, Q1325.3.8, VUK; report of the customs bureau in 'Arabistan [the Khuzistan province] to Muhamad 'Ali 'Ala' al-Saltana, the minister of foreign affairs, January 23, 1907, Q1325.3.8, VUK, Tehran.

145. Lorimer, *Gazetteer of the Persian Gulf*, 1: pt. 1A, 303, and pt. 2, 2498.

146. Emrys Chew, *Arming the Periphery: The Arms Trade in the Indian Ocean during the Age of Global Empire* (Basingstoke, Hampshire: Palgrave Macmillan, 2012), 38. See Lorimer, *Gazetteer of the Persian Gulf*, 1: pt. 2, 2559.

147. Ibid., 42.

148. Lorimer, *Gazetteer of the Persian Gulf*, 1: pt. 2194.

149. Lorimer, *Gazetteer of the Persian Gulf*, 1: pt. 1A, 316; Charles Hardinge to Mushir al-Daula, Tehran, December 11, 1897, FO 371/13790, NAUK, London.

150. Report on the arms trade and the order to the prime minister, Rajab 1, 1315, Q1315.31.3, VUK, Tehran.

151. Similarly, Malek al-Tujjar successfully confiscated a large shipment of rifles and ammunition from a British steamer. Lorimer, *Gazetteer of the Persian Gulf*, 1: pt. 2, 2561.

152. Ibid., 2573.

153. A telegraph from the Ministry of the Interior sent to the southern office, the sale of Baluchis to the neighboring countries by the local chiefs, the purchase of arms and conflicts of local chiefs, Tir 4, Sh. 1303, 293001568, SAM, Tehran; from the officer in charge, Jask telegraph sub-division, to the director, Persian Gulf section, Indo-European Telegraph department, Karachi, copy of a report, dated July 3, 1928, FO 371/13065, NAUK, London.

154. Chew, *Arming the Periphery*, 24, 104–105.

155. From the Lieutenant Colonel Sir Armine Dew, K.C.I.E., C.S.I., Agent to the Governor General and Chief Commissioner in Baluchistan, to Denys De S. Bray, Esq., C.I.E., C.B.E., Foreign Secretary to the Government of India in the Foreign and Political Department, Simla, dated Quetta, May 18, 1922, FO 371/7831, NAUK, London.

CHAPTER 5. SLAVES IN NINETEENTH-CENTURY IRAN

1. See, for example, Bassett, *Persia, the Land of the Imams*, 288; Sirus Sa'dvandian and Mansureh Ettehadieh, eds., *Amar-i dar al-khalafa-yi Tehran* (Tehran: Nashr-i tarikh-i Iran, 1368).

2. Spinage, *African Ecology*, 129.

3. Sheil, *Life and Manners in Persia*, 243–244.

4. Kemball, report on the Persian Gulf, 1847, FO 84/692, NAUK; Kemball to Robertson and Sheil, July 8, 1842, FO 84/426, NAUK.

5. Hennell to Wellesley, May 8, 1847, FO 248/129, NAUK; Samuel Hennell to Henry Richard Charles Wellesley, May 8, 1847, L/PS/5/450, BL, London.

6. Arnold Burrowes Kemball to Justin Sheil, July 8, 1842, FO 84/426, NAUK, London.

7. Ibid. Kemball noted that the children born to these enslaved people became free. Edwards to Kemball, 1842, FO 84/426, NAUK, 207–211.

8. Edwards to Kemball, 1842, FO 84/426, NAUK, 207–211.

9. Kemball to Robertson and Sheil, July 8, 1842, FO 84/426, NAUK.

10. The name "Mombasan" is very commonly used by European Orientalists, however, its usage raises many questions for it is not clear to whom they refer, and also Mombasa itself was not a major slavery port.

11. Wills, *In the Land of the Lion*, 326–327.

12. Edward E. Oliver, *Across the Border: Or, Pathán and Biloch* (London: Chapman and Hall, 1890), 9.

13. Sheil, *Life and Manners in Persia*, 243–244; Wills, *In the Land of the Lion*, 326–327. See also Kemball to Sheil, July 8, 1842, FO 84/426, NAUK; Edwards to Kemball, 1842, FO 84/426, NAUK, 207–211; and Kemball to Robertson and Sheil, July 8, 1842, FO 84/426, NAUK.

14. Kemball to Robertson and Sheil, July 8, 1842, FO 84/426, NAUK.

15. Edwards to Kemball, 1842, FO 84/426, NAUK, 207–211.

16. Sulivan, *Dhow Chasing in Zanzibar Waters*, 154–156, 263. Ethnic preferentialism was also common among the American slave markets (Curtin, *The Atlantic Slave Trade*, 155).

17. McMahon, *Slavery and Emancipation in Islamic East Africa*, 12; Nicolini, "The 19th Century Slave Trade," 329; Kai Kresse, "The Uses of History: Rhetorics of Muslim Unity and Difference On the Kenyan Swahili Coast," in *Struggling with History: Islam and Cosmopolitanism in the Western Indian Ocean*, ed. Edward Simpson and Kai Kresse (New York: Columbia University Press, 2008), 228. For classification of enslaved people on the Swahili coast, see Jonathon Glassman, *Feasts and Riot: Revelry, Rebellion, and Popular Consciousness on the Swahili Coast, 1856–1888* (Portsmouth, NH: Northwestern University, 1995), 85–90.

18. Jeremy Prestholdt, "Portuguese Conceptual Categories and the 'Other' Encounter on the Swahili Coast," in *Conceptualizing/Re-Conceptualizing Africa: The Construction of African Historical Identity*, ed. Maghan Keita (Leiden: Brill, 2002), 56.

19. Bang, "Cosmopolitanism Colonised?," 172.

20. Ibid.

21. Doughty, *Travels in Arabia Deserta*, 1:553.

22. Sulivan, *Dhow Chasing in Zanzibar Waters*, 177–179. Notably, enslaved Africans in Mecca had darker skin than those in Medina. This may have been the result, according to Burton, of enslaved females from the Swahili coast, Zeila, Tadjoura, and Berbera marrying into the local populations of Jidda and Mecca. Burton, *Personal Narrative of a Pilgrimage*, 2:233.

23. Wilson to the government, January 28, 1831, FO 84/426, NAUK, extract. Indeed, it is noted that four to five hundred of them were acquired for this purpose.

24. Seymour Drescher, *Capitalism and Antislavery: British Mobilization in Comparative Perspective* (London: Macmillan Press, 1986), 5.

25. Segal, *Islam's Black Slaves*, 4.

26. Issawi, *An Economic History of the Middle East*, 3.

27. William H. McNeill, *Europe's Steppe Frontier, 1500–1800* (Chicago: University of Chicago Press, 1964), 28. See also Troutt Powell, "Will That Subaltern Ever Speak?," 253.

28. McNeill, *Europe's Steppe Frontier, 1500–1800*, 27.

29. Zilfi, *Women and Slavery in the Late Ottoman Empire*, 99. For a case study of the social mobility of enslaved people in the Indian Ocean, see Abdul Sheriff, "Social Mobility in Indian Ocean Slavery: The Strange Career of Sultan bin Aman," in *Indian Ocean Slavery in the Age of Abolition*, ed. Robert Harms, Bernard K. Freamon, and David W. Blight (New Haven: Yale University Press, 2013).

30. Harms, "Introduction," 13.

31. Zilfi, *Women and Slavery in the Late Ottoman Empire*, 101–103.

32. Wills, *In the Land of the Lion*, 326.

33. Ibid.; Edwards to Kemball, 1842, FO 84/426, NAUK.

34. Malcolm, *Sketches of Persia*, 1:18.

35. Polak, *Persien*, 1:252.

36. Mustafa Husayni, *Bardegi az didgah-i Islam* (Tehran: Bunyad-i da'rat al-ma'aref-i Islami, 1372), 29–31.

37. Abdul Sheriff, *Dhow Cultures of the Indian Ocean: Cosmopolitanism, Commerce, and Islam* (New York: Columbia University Press, 2010), 219.

38. Ameer Ali, *Personal Law of the Mahommedans*, 219.

39. Moreover, while Hanafi law dictates that a man may marry four enslaved females (if he has not already taken a free wife), an enslaved person can only have two wives. By contrast, the Shafa'i and Maliki sects allow a free man to marry only one enslaved female; but it does not prohibit the marriage of a free woman thereafter. An enslaved male in these sects can have as many as four wives. Ameer Ali, *Personal Law of the Mahommedans*, 264–266, 277.

40. Correspondence between the Iranian and British officials on the liberation of Delafruz, an enslaved female, Jamadi al-thani 8, 1332, Q1332.3.3, VUK, Tehran; Ja'far ibn al-Hasan Al-Muhaqqiq al-Hilli, *Droit Musulman. Recueil de lois concernant les Musulmans Schyites*, trans. Amédée Querry (Paris: Imprimerie nationale, 1871), vol. 2, 109; El Hamel, *Black Morocco*, 47.

41. In Sunni law, the emancipator of an enslaved person is entitled to inherit from his former enslaved person. Shi'i regulations, by contrast, allow the former enslaved person more autonomy and rights over the disposition of his or her property. Ameer Ali illustrates multiple examples and circumstances (*Personal Law of the Mahommedans*, 54–58, 62, 100).

42. Polak, *Persien*, 1:251.

43. A governmental order on the issue of the trade in *kanīzān* and *ghulāmān*, Rabi' al-Thani 15, 1319, Q1319.3.4.3, VUK, Tehran.

44. The decree of Aqa Sayyid Ahmad Mujtahid Behbehani, the general consulate of the

Iranian government in Baghdad, 1332, Q1332.12.21.10, VUK, Tehran; the Ministry of Foreign Affairs of Iran, the interrogation of the *kaniz* dealer Mirza Aqa, 1332, Q1332.3.3, VUK, Tehran.

45. The British consulate to the Iranian government, Dhi al-Qaʿda 26, Q1328.3.1.40, VUK, Tehran. Survival could be complicated, however, if the master died without leaving a direct relative or an income behind—especially for enslaved females. Jamal to Mushir al-Daula, the minister of foreign affairs of Iran, Safar 26, 1322, Q1322.4.11.58, VUK, Tehran.

As discussed above, many enslaved people were entitled to inherit from their masters. See, for instance, Heirs of the deceased Haji Muhammad Hussain Khan Qaraquzlu to the Council for the Investigation of Grievances, Hamedan, the reign of Nasir al-Din Shah, 1301, 2929-164, summary of requests, Majlis-i tahqiq-i Mazalem, KMDT, Tehran.

The offspring of enslaved people and their masters also had rights. See Hujjat al-Islam ʿElm al-Huda to Hujjat al-Islam ʿAbdullah Mutahid Behbehani, 1324, Q1324.13.3, VUK, Tehran; Hujjat al-Islam ʿElm al-Huda to Mushir al-Daula, Bushehr to Tehran, 1324, Q1324.13.3, VUK, Tehran.

46. The decree of Aqa Sayyid Ahmad Mujtahid Behbehani, 1332, Q1332.12.21.10, VUK.

47. Malcolm, *Sketches of Persia*, 1:18.

48. The Bab (Sayyid ʿAli Muhammad) claimed to be the long-awaited Mahdi in 1844.

49. Abuʾl-Qasim Afnan, *Black Pearls: Servants in the Households of the Báb and the Baháʾuʾlláh* (Los Angeles: Kalimát Press, 1988), 35–42.

50. Sheil, *Life and Manners in Persia*, 61. See Lesan al-Mulk, *Nasekh al-tawarikh*, 1:219.

51. Ferrier, *Caravan Journeys*, 23.

52. Abbas Amanat, *Pivot of the Universe: Nasir al-Din Shah Qajar and the Iranian Monarchy, 1831–1896* (Berkeley: University of California Press, 1997), 438.

53. For comparison with Zanzibar see Jeremy Prestholdt, *Domesticating the World: African Consumerism and the Genealogies of Globalization* (Berkeley: University of California Press, 2008), 122.

54. Troutt Powell, "Will That Subaltern Ever Speak?," 251.

55. Report to the Iranian government about Jamila, Dhi al-Hajja 4, 1328, Q1328.3.1.49, VUK, Tehran.

56. Muhammad to the Council for the Investigation of Grievances, Malayer, the reign of Nasir al-Din Shah, 1301, 2929-018, summary of requests, Majlis-i tahqiq-i Mazalem, KMDT, Tehran; marriage contract of Mirza Muhamad Taqi and Mahrukh Baygum Khaum and a black *kaniz* as dowry, 1265, 110000141, SAM, Tabriz.

57. Wills, *In the Land of the Lion*, 326.

58. Polak, *Persien*, 1:252.

59. Ennaji, *Slavery, the State, and Islam*, 22.

60. Kemball to Robertson and Sheil, July 8, 1842, FO 84/426, NAUK; Kemball, report on the Persian Gulf, 1847, FO 84/692, NAUK; Edwards to Kemball, 1842, FO 84/426, NAUK, 207–211.

61. Muhammad Hasan Khan Eʿtemad al-Saltana, *Yaddashtha-yi Eʿtemad al-Saltana marbut be sal-i 1300 H.Q.* (Tehran: Vahid, 1350), 45.

62. Saʿidi Sirjani, annot., *Vaqayʿ-i ettefaqiya* (Tehran: Nuvin, 1362), 139.

63. Zilfi, *Women and Slavery in the Late Ottoman Empire*, 15.

64. Ehud R. Toledano, *As If Silent and Absent: Bonds of Enslavement in the Islamic Middle East* (New Haven: Yale University Press, 2007), 17–19.

65. Zilfi, *Women and Slavery in the Late Ottoman Empire*, 120.

66. See Behnaz A. Mirzai, "Qajar Haram: Imagination or Reality," in *Slavery, Islam and Diaspora*, ed. Behnaz A. Mirzai, Ismael Musah Montana, and Paul E. Lovejoy (Trenton, NJ: Africa World Press, 2009).

67. See Haleh Afshar, "Age, Gender and Slavery in and out of the Persian Harem: A Difference Story," *Ethnic and Racial Studies* 23, no. 5 (2000): 905–916; see also J. D. Gurney, "A Qajar Household and Its Estates," *Iranian Studies* 16, no. 3/4 (1983): 137–176.

68. Nomads and members of the middle classes were considered wealthy if they had two or three wives. Polak, *Persien*, 1:209.

69. Jean Baptiste Feuvrier, *Trois ans a la cour de Perse* (Paris: F. Juven, 1900), 146.

70. D'Allemagne, *Du Khorassan au pays des Backhtiaris*, 3:229.

71. *Quruq* is a Turkish word meaning forbidden.

72. Polak, *Persien*, 1:235.

73. *Quruq* was also practiced in public to clear the way for the shah.

74. The report of the eunuch Agha 'Anbar on the people who came and left the *andarūn*, 1282, 295005926, SAM, Tehran.

75. Letters of women in the harem to Nasir al-Din Shah about their long waiting period during the *quruq* time, 1287, 295000146, SAM, Tehran.

76. Indeed, details of visitors and their times of arrival and departure were assiduously recorded. Reports on the arrival and departure from the harem, Muharram 1291, 295004506, SAM, Tehran.

77. Samuel Greene Wheeler Benjamin, *Persia and the Persians* (London: John Murray, 1887), 104, 130; James Baillie Fraser, *Historical and Descriptive Account of Persia, from the Earliest Ages to the Present Time* (New York: Harper & Brothers, 1834), 290; Kinneir, *A Geographical Memoir of the Persian Empire*, 26.

78. For this reason, members had to request to be discharged from the harem. Request letter of a woman in the harem to the shah, 1287, 295000133, SAM, Tehran.

79. D'Allemagne, *Du Khorassan au pays des Backhtiaris*, 3:230; Gaspard Drouville, *Voyage en Perse, pendant les années 1812 et 1813* (St. Petersburg: Imprimé chez Pluchart, 1819), 1:49.

80. The order purchase of three enslaved Turcoman women for Nasir al-Din Shah, 1286, Tehran, 295.2155 and 295/709/1, SAM, Tehran.

81. Taj al-Saltana, *Khaterat-i Taj al-Saltana*, ed. Mansureh Ettehadia and Sirus Sa'dvandian (Tehran: Nashr-i tarikh-i Iran, 1361), 8.

82. Mirza Husayn ibn Muhammad Ebrahim Khan, *Jughrafiya-yi Isfahan* (Tehran: Danishgah-i Tehran, 1342), 91.

83. N. M. Penzer, ed., *Sir John Chardin's Travels in Persia* (New York: AMS Press, 1927), 184.

84. Segal, *Islam's Black Slaves*, 125.

85. Zilfi, *Women and Slavery in the Late Ottoman Empire*, xii.

86. Zilfi, *Women and Slavery in the Late Ottoman Empire*, 137.

87. Wills, *In the Land of the Lion*, 77.

88. Lesan al-Mulk, *Nasekh al-tawarikh*, 1:523–565; James B. Fraser, *Narrative of a Journey into Khorasan in the Years 1821 and 1822* (London: Longman, 1824), 219; Malcolm, *Sketches of Persia*, 2:147.

89. Jane Dieulafoy, *Une Amazone en Orient: Du Caucase à Ispahan, 1881–1882* (Paris: Phébus, 1989), 117. The shah's harem children were known as *shāhzādagān* (descendants of the king), and some could expect to be posted to important governmental positions. D'Allemagne, *Du Khorassan au pays des Backhtiaris*, 3:156.

90. Atkin, *Russia and Iran, 1780–1828*, 115; Ferrier, *Caravan Journeys*, 23.

91. Mu'ayyir al-Mamalek, *Yaddashthaei az zendegani-yi khususi*, 26.

92. Qahraman Mirza 'Ayn al-Saltana, *Ruznama-yi khaterat-i 'Ayn al-Saltana*, ed. Mas'ud Salvar and Iraj Afshar (Tehran: Asatir, 1378), 1:872 and 2:1022; Curzon, *Persia and the Persian Question*, 1:408.

93. Babaie et al., *Slaves of the Shah*, 20.

94. Muhammad Sami' Mirza Sami'a, *Tazkarat al-muluk*, annot. Dabir Siaqi (Tehran: Sepehr, 1368), 8.

95. Griboyedov, *Nameha-yi Aleksandr Giribayduf*, 32–36.

96. Guy Le Strange, *Don Juan of Persia: A Shi'ah Catholic, 1590–1609* (New York: Harper & Brothers, 1926), 217.

97. Military and administrative reorganization was necessary to defend the regime against constant threat from the Turcoman Qezelbash (Red Heads).

98. D'Allemagne, *Du Khorassan au pays des Backhtiaris*, 1:128.

99. Kinneir, *A Geographical Memoir of the Persian Empire*, 32; Fraser, *Historical and Descriptive Account of Persia*, 254; Ann Lambton, *Qajar Persia* (London: I. B. Tauris, 1987), 97; Jeremy Black, *Beyond the Military Revolution: War in the Seventeenth-Century World* (Basingstoke: Palgrave Macmillan, 2011), 182.

100. Sami'a, *Tazkarat al-muluk*, 19. In 1850, Mihr 'Alikhan Nuri was the *yūzbāshī* overseeing eighty enslaved people. Khurmuji, *Haqa'q al-akhbar Naseri*, 86, 187; Ebrahim Khan, *Jughrafiya-yi Isfahan*, 75.

101. Lesan al-Mulk, *Nasekh al-tawarikh*, 1:128.

102. Kinneir, *A Geographical Memoir of the Persian Empire*, 32; Fraser, *Historical and Descriptive Account of Persia*, 254.

103. Fraser, *Historical and Descriptive Account of Persia*, 254.

104. Similarly, the Georgian father of Sepahdar was so trusted by the shah that he became the commander of his troops in 1833. Fraser, *A Winter's Journey*, 2:19.

105. D'Allemagne, *Du Khorassan au pays des Backhtiaris*, 1:128.

106. Fraser, *Narrative of a Journey into Khorasan*, 103.

107. Fraser, *Historical and Descriptive Account of Persia*, 254; Fraser, *Narrative of a Journey into Khorasan*, 224.

108. Waring, *A Tour to Sheeraz*, 84, 98.

109. Wills, *In the Land of the Lion*, 50.

110. Lesan al-Mulk, *Nasekh al-tawarikh*, 2:645.

111. Majd al-Islam Kermani, *Enhelal-i majlis*, 291.

112. The grievance of the mother of the shah concerning two eunuchs in the harem, 1287, 295002440, SAM, Tehran.

113. Mustaufi, *Sharh-i zendegani-yi man*, 1:410; Polak, *Persien*, 1:43.

114. In 1860, Muhammad Mehdikhan was the *kishīkchī bāshī*. See Khurmuji, *Haqa'q al-akhbar Naseri*, 265.

115. In 1851, Khalil Khan was the *yūzbāshī* of Nasir al-Din Shah's enslaved people. See ibid., introduction, 12.

116. Mu'ayyir al-Mamalek, *Rejal-i 'ahd-i Naseri*, 225.

117. Lorimer, *Gazetteer of the Persian Gulf*, 2: pt. 1A, 164. Enslaved Africans and members of other ethnic groups constituted another group of soldiers known as the *ghulāmān*.

118. Mirza Ghulam Husayn Afzal al-Mulk, *Afzal al-tavarikh* (Tehran: Nashr-i tarikh-i Iran, 1361), 42. See Khurmuji, *Haqa'q al-akhbar Naseri*, 265.

119. Polak, *Persien*, 1:258; Bassett, *Persia, the Land of the Imams*, 287.

120. Polak, *Persien*, 1:204; A royal eunuch to the shah, request for a *khal'at*, 1289, 295002589, SAM, Tehran; Agha Faraj to Nasir al-Din Shah, request for a *khal'at*, 1292, 295003603, SAM, Tehran.

121. Jan Hogendorn notes, "Castration can be partial (removal of the testicles only or removal of the penis only) or total (removal of both)." "The Location of the 'Manufacture' of Eunuchs," in *Slave Elites in the Middle East and Africa*, ed. Miura Toru and John Edward Philips (London and New York: Kegan Paul International, 2000). Johnston revived a claim that French monks mutilated the impoverished children in order to sell them to the Moors in Spain. J. H. Johnston, "The Mohammedan Slave Trade," *The Journal of Negro History* 13, no. 4 (October 1928), 486.

122. Wills, *Persia as It Is*, 77; Polak observed that eunuchs tended to live longer than other enslaved males (*Persien*, 1:257).

123. Feuvrier, *Trois ans a la cour de Perse*, 157; Mu'ayyir al-Mamalek, *Yaddashthaei az zendegani-yi khususi*, 12; 'Ayn al-Saltana, *Ruznama-yi khaterat*, 1:872.

124. Bird, *Journeys in Persia and Kurdistan*, 1:181; Le Strange, *Don Juan of Persia*, 13; Mu'ayyir al-Mamalek, *Yaddashthaei az zendegani-yi khususi*, 46; Polak, *Persien*, 2:208.

125. Penzer, *Sir John Chardin's Travels*, 53. See the reports of Agha Yusuf about the princesses, princes, women, and staff in the harem and the construction of the Saltanat Abad palace, 1286, 295004639 and 295004752, SAM, Tehran.

126. Feuvrier wrote about the duties of Ethiopian eunuchs, when he visited the king's palace, one of which was to protect the privacy of women. *Trois ans a la cour de Perse*, 155–156.

127. 'Ayn al-Saltana, *Ruznama-yi khaterat*, 1:794; Mu'ayyir al-Mamalek, *Yaddashthaei az zendegani-yi khususi*, 50, 70; Polak, *Persien*, 1:254.

128. Polak, *Persien*, 1:258. See also 'Ayn al-Saltana, *Ruznama-yi khaterat*, 2:1020.

129. Mu'ayyir al-Mamalek, however, stated that Nasir al-Din Shah had ninety eunuchs. *Yaddashthaei az zendegani-yi khususi*, 17; *Persien*, 1:256.

130. Mu'ayyir al-Mamalek, *Yaddashthaei az zendegani-yi khususi*, 18, 23; Taj al-Saltana, *Khaterat-i Taj al-Saltana*, 14, 18.

131. 'Ayn al-Saltana, *Ruznama-yi khaterat*, 2:1034.

132. Mehdi Malekzada, *Tarikh-i enqelab-i mashrutiyat-i Iran* (Tehran: Ibn Sina, 1335), 2:118.

133. Arfa, *Under Five Shahs*, 102.

134. Polak, *Persien*, 1:261.

135. Polak, *Persien*, 1:258; Bassett, *Persia, the Land of the Imams*, 287.

136. See Khurmuji, *Haqa'q al-akhbar Naseri*, 94; Muhammad Hasan Khan E'temad al-Saltana, *al-Ma'aser va al-a'sar* (Tehran: Ketabkhana-yi Sana'i, 1307), 24, 35.

137. See Khurmuji, *Haqa'q al-akhbar Naseri*, 120; Jahangir Qa'emmaqami, *Yeksad va panjah sanad-i tarikhi* (Tehran: Artish, 1348), 263–264; see also Polak, *Persien*, 1:230.

138. Polak, *Persien*, 1:256.

139. Lesan al-Mulk, *Nasekh al-tawarikh*, 3:1480; Khurmuji, *Haqa'q al-akhbar Naseri*, 112.

140. Griboyedov, *Nameha-yi Aleksandr Giribayduf*, 57.

141. Polak, *Persien*, 1:261; James Baillie Fraser, *A Winter's Journey from Constantinople to Tehran* (1838; repr., New York: Arno Press, 1973), 2:16–17.

142. Griboyedov, *Nameha-yi Aleksandr Giribayduf*, 57; Lorimer, *Gazetteer of the Persian Gulf*, 1: pt. 2, 1657; Other enslaved people who rose in this way include 'Ali Akbar Khan,

who commanded the *ghulāmān* at the court of the prince of Shiraz in 1821. Fraser, *Narrative of a Journey into Khorasan*, 105.

143. Khurmuji, *Haqa'q al-akhbar Naseri*, 148, 263.

144. Ibid., 300.

145. Polak, *Persien*, 1:256.

146. Kemball reported in 1847 that only one in ten survived the operation (Report on the Persian Gulf, 1847, FO 84/692, NAUK). See also the Sadr Azim to Meerza Mahmood Khan, October 19, 1853, FO 84/919, NAUK, London, 167–170. It was typical for boys to be selected and castrated at their point of captivity, prior to embarkation and transit to market.

147. Polak, *Persien*, 1:255. A eunuch child was usually the most expensive (Wills, *Persia as It Is*, 77). See also Wilson to the government, January 28, 1831, FO 84/426, NAUK; Albertine Jwaideh and J. W. Cox, "The Black Slaves of Turkish Arabia during the 19th Century," *Slavery and Abolition* 9, no. 3 (1988), 55; and Ehud R. Toledano, "The Imperial Eunuchs of Istanbul: From Africa to the Heart of Islam," *Middle Eastern Studies* 20, no.3 (July 1984), 379–390.

148. Wilson reported in 1831 that a mere ten to fifteen eunuchs came through Masqat annually. Since they appear not to have been mutilated there, it would seem that they were mutilated either in their own countries or in parts of Yemen. Wilson to the government, January 28, 1831, FO 84/426, NAUK, 211–217.

149. Shirley Foster, "Colonialism and Gender in the East: Representations of the Harem in the Writings of Women Travellers," *The Yearbook of English Studies* 34 (2004), 9.

150. Wills, *In the Land of the Lion*, 41–43.

151. Bird, *Journeys in Persia and Kurdistan*, 2:181.

152. 'Ayn al-Saltana, *Ruznama-yi khaterat*, 1:1021.

153. In addition to being the head of the harem, the shahs' mothers were often politically influential.

154. Among her servants were two African children, a girl named Mahbuba and a boy named Salim, who—we are told—were well dressed and respected in the harem. Dust 'Ali Khan Mu'ayyir al-Mamalek, *Rijal-i 'ahd-i Naseri* (Tehran, Nashr-i tarikh, 1361), 234.

155. While legal marriage—which could only be terminated through divorce—was based on Qur'anic (4:3) strictures, which indicated that a man could marry up to four wives at the same time, temporary marriages tended to last for only a specific period of time; 'Ayn al-Saltana, *Ruznama-yi khaterat*, 1:1021; *Du Khorassan au pays des Backhtiaris*, 1:199.

156. The shah cared so much for this concubine that he sent her to Vienna for a surgical procedure. Curzon, *Persia and the Persian Question*, 2:410.

157. Letters of some women of the *andarūn* to the shah requesting his attention, 1286, 295000053 and 295000058, SAM, Tehran.

158. Curzon, *Persia and the Persian Question*, 1:408; 'Ayn al-Saltana, *Ruznama-yi khaterat*, 1:1021.

159. D'Allemagne, *Du Khorassan au pays des Backhtiaris*, 3:228–232.

160. A report on the list of the salary of the servants of women in the harem, such as Anis al-Daula and Shams al-Daula, paid from the tax of the Fars customs house, 1281, 295005351, SAM, Tehran.

161. 'Ayn al-Saltana, *Ruznama-yi khaterat*, 2:1018–1020.

162. Mu'ayyir al-Mamalek, *Yaddashthaei az zendegani-yi khususi*, 18.

163. Taj al-Saltana, *Khaterat-i Taj al-Saltana*, 66; D'Allemagne, *Du Khorassan au pays des Backhtiaris*, 1:198.

164. ʿAyn al-Saltana, *Ruznama-yi khaterat*, 2:1024, 1037.

165. ʿAyn al-Saltana, *Ruznama-yi khaterat*, 1:26; the shah's order for acquiring a *kanīz* for his wife, Gelin Khanum, 296001405, SAM, Tehran; Wills, *In the Land of the Lion*, 326; Polak, *Persien*, 1:236.

166. Polak, *Persien*, 1:207.

167. ʿAyn al-Saltana, *Ruznama-yi khaterat*, 2:1753.

168. Muʿayyir al-Mamalek, *Rejal-i ʿahd-i Naseri*, 240.

169. ʿAyn al-Saltana, *Ruznama-yi khaterat*, 2:1753.

170. Waring, *A Tour to Sheeraz*, 51.

171. Kaempfer, *Safarnama-yi Kaempfer*, 227.

172. Ibid., 53.

173. Eʿtemad al-Saltana, *Yaddashtha-yi Eʿtemad al-Saltana*, 43.

174. Malcolm, *Sketches of Persia*, 2:149; Mustaufi, *Sharh-i zendegani-yi man*, 1:214.

175. Mustaufi, *Sharh-i zendegani-yi man*, 1:214; John Chardin, a French traveller, noted that during the seventeenth century, almost all adult enslaved females wore a thin ring passed through one of their nostrils as a form of status identification. Penzer, *Sir John Chardin's Travels*, 217.

176. Muʿayyir al-Mamalek, *Yaddashthaei az zendegani-yi khususi*, 49.

177. Malek al-Shuʿaraʾ Bahar, *Tarikh-i ahzab-i siyasi-yi Iran* (Tehran: Amir Kabir, 1371), 2:370–400.

178. Najm al-Daula, *Safarnama-yi Khuzestan*, 79.

179. Ibid., 82.

180. Najm al-Daula, *Asar-i Najm al-Daula*, 118.

181. Bird, *Journeys in Persia and Kurdistan*, 1:333.

182. Ibid., 353.

183. Muhammad Hasan Khan Eʿtemad al-Saltana, *Khalsa* (Tehran: Tahuri, 1348), 11.

184. Among the enslaved people were two Habashis: a man by the name of Mubarak and a woman by the name of Fazzeh. Both had been acquired when they were very young and became trusted members of the household. Afnan, *Black Pearls*, 5; see also Anthony A. Lee, "Half the Household Was African: Recovering the Histories of Two Enslaved Africans in Iran, Haji Mubarak and Fezzeh Khanum," *UCLA Historical Journal* 26, no. 1 (2015).

185. Ibid., 3.

186. Ghulam Husain Zargari Nejad, ed. *Rasaʾel mashrutiyat* (Tehran: Kavir, 1374), 68.

187. See C. B. Fisher, "The Feudal System in Persia," *Journal of Farm Economics* 13, no. 4 (October 1931): 621–629.

188. Sistan was under the jurisdiction of Khorasan Province.

189. Baluchistan was under the jurisdiction of Kerman Province; in the 1930s, this division was called the *hukumat-i nizāmī-yi Baluchistan* (military government of Baluchistan).

190. Mukhtari, *Guzareshha-yi iyalat va velayat*, introduction, 7, 131; Curzon, *Persia and the Persian Question*, 1:437, 2:470.

191. See Abdulhussain Mirza Farman Farma, *Musaferat nama-yi Kerman*; Ismail Ajami, *Iran: Past, Present and Future* (New York: Aspen Institute for Humanistic Studies, 1975), 5. Julian Bharier estimated that 90 percent of the working population was engaged in agriculture and related tasks. *Economic Development in Iran, 1900–1970* (London: Oxford University Press, 1971), 5.

192. Majd al-Islam Kermani, *Enhelal-i majlis*, 113; Sykes, *A History of Persia*, 2:389.

193. See Firuz Mirza Farman Farma, *Safarnamih-yi Kerman*; Khusru Khusravi,

Jamaʻshenasi-yi deh dar Iran (Tehran: Markaz-i Nashr-i daneshgahi, 1372), 50. In the absence of more traditional networks of protection and governmental support, those working on the land were badly exploited. Ajami, *Iran: Past, Present and Future*, 10.

194. Lambton, *Landlord and Peasant*, 170.

195. Lutfullah Ehteshami, *Naqsh-i kalantaran va kadkhudayan dar mudiriyat-i shahr va rusta* (Isfahan: Mehrqaʾm, 1384), 203. This tax was not revoked until the Constitutional Revolution in the early twentieth century, when it was deemed a violation of fundamental human rights. See Jamalzada, *Ganj-i Shaygan*, 121.

196. Baqer Muʻmeni, *Masʾala-yi arzi va jang-i tabaqati dar Iran* (Tehran: Payvand, 1359), 28. See also Bharier, *Economic Development in Iran*, 8.

197. Bharier, *Economic Development in Iran*, 136.

198. Firuz Mirza Farman Farma, *Safarnamih-yi Kerman*, 68.

199. Khusru Khusravi, *Dehqan-i khurdepa* (Tehran: ʻElmi, [1985?]), 32. The main date plantations were located in Bushehr, Dashtestan, Dashti, Lengeh, and Bandar ʻAbbas.

200. Minutes of evidence presented before the royal commission, March 11, 1875, AA12/2, ZNL.

201. Arnold, *Through Persia by Caravan*, 226

202. Curzon, *Persia and the Persian Question*, 2:409.

203. See Jamalzada, *Ganj-i Shaygan*; Lorimer, *Gazetteer of the Persian Gulf*, 2: pt. B, 1227.

204. For instance, the shaykh of Bushehr is known to have generated much revenue from this industry. See Lorimer, *Gazetteer of the Persian Gulf*, 1: pt. 2, 2221; Sadid al-Saltana Kababi, *Sarzaminha-yi shumali*, 180.

205. For instance, timber and other building materials for Bushehr were imported from Zanzibar, and the matting produced in Bushehr was sent to Khorramshahr. Lorimer, *Gazetteer of the Persian Gulf*, 2: pt. 1A, 80.

206. Arthur Malet, summary, July 4, 1848, L/PS/5/456, BL, London.

207. Jamalzada, *Ganj-i Shaygan*, 63; Lorimer, *Gazetteer of the Persian Gulf*, 1: pt. 2, 2321. *Baghalahā* were large trading ships that traveled between Iran and Bombay and as far away as Zanzibar, whereas *bagharahā* were smaller boats used for traveling short distances and for pearl fishing in the Persian Gulf.

208. Arfa, *Under Five Shahs*, 239.

209. The dialect associated with Bandar ʻAbbas, ʻAbbasi, was a hybrid of Persian, Baluchi, Arabic, and Swahili. Lorimer, *Gazetteer of the Persian Gulf*, 2: pt. 1A, 10; Arnold, *Through Persia by Caravan*, 226.

210. Arfa, *Under Five Shahs*, 240.

211. Lorimer, *Gazetteer of the Persian Gulf*, 2: pt. 1A, 923.

212. Abdulhussain Mirza Farman Farma, *Musaferat nama-yi Kerman*, 359–361.

213. Lorimer, *Gazetteer of the Persian Gulf*, 2: pt. 1A, 929.

214. Ibid., 931.

215. Abdulhussain Mirza Farman Farma, *Musaferat nama-yi Kerman*, 343.

216. Lorimer, *Gazetteer of the Persian Gulf*, 2: pt. 1A, 916, 918.

217. See Vaziri, *Joghrafia-yi Baluchistan*.

218. Lorimer, *Gazetteer of the Persian Gulf*, 2: pt. 1A, 925. See also his discussion of the villages of Jagin and Luran (ibid., 927, 928).

219. Curzon, *Persia and the Persian Question*, 2:260.

220. Sadid al-Saltana Kababi, *Sarzaminha-yi shumali*, 301–310; Lorimer, *Gazetteer of the Persian Gulf*, 1: pt. 2, 2193, 2318.

221. Lorimer, *Gazetteer of the Persian Gulf*, 1: pt. 2, 2219; reports on southern ports, 1311–1317, reasons for immigration, 293004045, SAM, Tehran, 5, 25, 26.

222. Notably, during the American Civil War (1861–1865), Iran became a main exporter of cotton, exporting twelve million pounds per year. Jamalzada, *Ganj-i Shaygan*, 17.

223. Vaziri, *Joghrafia-yi Baluchistan*, 4; Sadid al-Saltana Kababi, *Sarzaminha-yi shumali*, 302; Kinneir, *A Geographical Memoir of the Persian Empire*, 203.

224. Fraser, *Historical and Descriptive Account of Persia*, 67.

225. Landowners of Baluchistan to Nasir al-Daula, 1289, Q1289.14.19, VUK, Tehran.

226. Vaziri, *Joghrafia-yi Baluchistan*, 8.

227. Ibid., 26.

228. Mukhtari, *Guzareshha-yi iyalat va velayat*, 48; Mirza Naser al-Daula, *Safarnama-yi Baluchistan*, 67, 71.

229. Mukhtari, *Guzareshha-yi iyalat va velayat*, 43, 47. In the 1950s, more than 70 percent of the land in Sistan was farmed by tenant farmers, about 86 percent of whom did so under the sharecropping system. See Okazaki Shōkō, *The Development of Large-Scale Farming in Iran* (Tokyo: Institute of Asian Economic Affairs, 1968), 5.

230. Vaziri, *Joghrafia-yi Baluchistan*, 7.

231. Firuz Mirza Farman Farma, *Safarnamih-yi Kerman*, 129.

232. Mukhtari, *Guzareshha-yi iyalat va velayat*, 48, 49.

233. Ibid., 50; The Ministry of War to the Ministry of Finance, on the poverty of the Qa'enat and Quchan peasants due to the tyrannical feudal system, Sh. 1315, Khorasan, 240006012, SAM, Tehran.

234. Mukhtari, *Guzareshha-yi iyalat va velayat*, 371.

235. Afshar Sistani, *Ilha*, 2:747.

236. In Kermanshah, Kerman, and Baluchistan, for instance. Arnold T. Wilson, *Persia* (New York: Charles Scribner's Sons, 1933), 34.

237. Keith Edward Abbott, "Notes on Various Cities and Countries of Southern Persia, 1849–50," in *Cities and Trade: Consul Abbott on the Economy and Society of Iran, 1847–1866*, ed. Abbas Amanat (London: Ithaca Press, 1983), 164.

238. Mahmud Khan Tabataba'i Ala' al-Mulk, *Safarnama-yi Baluchistan* (Tehran: Vahid, 1364), 80.

239. Fraser, *Narrative of a Journey into Khorasan*, 18.

240. Floyer, "Journal of a Route from Jask to Bampur," 192.

241. Firuz Mirza Farman Farma, *Safarnamih-yi Kerman*, 59, 62.

242. Even in 1897, when the harvest was not especially large, about 5,310 tons of dates were produced. Lorimer, *Gazetteer of the Persian Gulf*, 1: pt. 2, 2303.

243. It is reported that the export of dates in the late nineteenth century brought in about one hundred thousand tomans annually. Najm al-Daula, *Asar-i Najm al-Daula*, 91.

244. Lorimer described the density of the date groves and plantations on both sides of the Karun River between Barah and Khorramshahr. *Gazetteer of the Persian Gulf*, 1: pt. B, 95.

245. A few of these enslaved people, however, were forced into hard labor at a few ports, according to Sir John Malcolm. *Sketches of Persia*, 1:18.

246. Mignan, *Winter Journey through Russia, the Caucasian Alps, and Georgia*, 1:182.

247. Sa'dvandian and Ettehadieh, *Amar-i dar al-khalafa-yi Tehran*, 347; Mansureh Ette-hadieh, "The Social Condition of Women in Qajar Society," in *Society and Culture in Qajar Iran*, ed. Elton L. Daniel (Costa Mesa, CA: Mazda Publishers, 2002), 82.

248. Ebrahim Khan, *Jughrafiya-yi Isfahan*, 65, 122; Malcolm, *Sketches of Persia*, 1:19. See

the marriage contract of the Black Almas and Kokab Khanum, Rajab 22, 1311, 296012411, SAM, Tehran; the report to the Iranian government about Jamila, Dhi al-Hajja 4, 1328, Q1328.3.1.49, VUK; and Del Afrooz, freedom letter, Jamadi al-Thani 7, 1332, Q1332.3.3, VUK, Tehran.

249. Arnold, *Through Persia by Caravan*, 367.

250. Ibid., 226.

251. *British and Foreign Anti-Slavery Reporter*, London, March-May, 1903, 70; ibid., January-February, 1898, 57; Julian Bharier, "A Note on the Population of Iran, 1900–1966," *Population Studies* 22, no. 2 (July 1968): 275.

252. See Ebrahim to 'Ala' al-Saltana, the minister of foreign affairs, from Shiraz to Tehran, Rabi' al-Akhar 5, 1325, Q1325.3.8, VUK, Tehran; Lorimer, *Gazetteer of the Persian Gulf*, 1: pt. 2, 2510; and Majd al-Islam Kermani, *Enhelal-i majlis*, 289. During his commission in Qazvin, F. A. C. Forbes-Leith met Yadullah, an inhabitant of the city who had just married his own enslaved African. *Checkmate: Fighting Tradition in Central Persia* (New York: Robert M. McBride & Co., 1927), 86.

253. Polak, *Persien*, 2:361.

254. The inhabitants of Lengeh to the Iranian government, 1323, Q1323.14.4, VUK, Tehran.

255. Landor, *Across Coveted Lands*, 2:80–81.

256. Najm al-Daula, *Asar-i Najm al-Daula*, 57. Isabella Bird, who traveled to Kermanshah in 1890, described some African servants dressed elegantly in high black lambskin caps, tight black trousers, and tight coats with full skirts who were employed at the governor's office. *Journeys in Persia and Kurdistan*, 1:104.

257. Minutes of evidence presented before the royal commission, March 11, 1875, AA12/2, ZNL.

258. Charles Pellat, *The Life and Works of Jāḥiz*, trans. D. M. Hawke (London: Routledge & Kegan Paul, 1969), 195.

259. The author's father, Mahmoud Mirzai, remembered occasions as a child in Tabriz when groups of Africans regularly passed the streets singing and dancing. Residents invited them inside their homes for the performance and offered them a gratuity.

260. The inhabitants of Lengeh to the Iranian government, 1323, Q1323.14.4, VUK.

261. Henri Massé described some common elements in the Zar ceremony: a veil to cover the sick individual, a *māmā* ("mother") or *bābā* ("father"), a *khyzarān* ("stick") with which to gently beat the sick individual, the prevalence of chanting, and a *qalyān* (a water pipe for the smoking of tobacco). *Persian Beliefs and Customs* (New Haven, CT: Human Relations Area Files, 1954), 755; For African cultural performances in the Ottoman Empire, see Ehud R. Toledano, "The Fusion of *Zar-Bori* and Sufi *Zikr* as Performance: Enslaved Africans in the Ottoman Empire," in *Medieval and Early Modern Performance in the Eastern Mediterranean*, ed. A. Öztürkmen, E. B. Vitz (Turnhout, Belgium: Brepols Publishers, 2014), 216–240.

262. Arfa, *Under Five Shahs*, 241.

263. They sing: "Am I Haji Firuz? Yes. Am I once a year? Yes" or "Hello my master, raise your head, my master. My master is sweet. Why do not you laugh my master?"

264. This practice popularized and celebrated African culture rather than denigrated it, as did the "blackface" minstrel performers in American culture, whose acts were deliberately mocking and racist, and their roots stretched back to the 1440s Portuguese slave trade. For more information see: John Strausbaugh, *Black Like You: Blackface, Whiteface, Insult and Imitation in American Popular Culture* (New York: Jeremy P. Tarcher/Penguin, 2006), 36.

CHAPTER 6. SLAVE-TRADE SUPPRESSION LEGISLATION

1. Ehud R. Toledano, "Abolition and Anti-Slavery in the Ottoman Empire: A Case to Answer," in *A Global History of Anti-Slavery Politics in the Nineteenth Century*, ed. William Mulligan and Maurice Bric (Houndmills, Basingstoke, Hampshire: Palgrave Macmillan, 2013), 118.

2. See James Onley, *The Arabian Frontier of the British Raj: Merchants, Rulers, and the British in the Nineteenth-Century Gulf* (Oxford: Oxford University Press, 2007).

3. Bushehr was chosen for its geographical importance since the coastal Arab shaykhs did not possess suitable hinterland. Glen Balfour-Paul, *The End of Empire in the Middle East: Britain's Relinquishment of Power in her Last Three Arab Dependencies* (Cambridge: Cambridge University Press, 1991), 98.

4. Peterson, "Britain and the Gulf," 278, 279.

5. See Percy Molesworth Sykes, "Ten Thousand Miles in Persia," *Scottish Geographical Magazine* 18, no. 12 (1902), 626–631; Ronald Robinson and John Gallagher, *Africa and the Victorians*, 2nd ed. (London: Macmillan Press, 1981), 35; Sugata Bose, *A Hundred Horizons: The Indian Ocean in the Age of Global Empire* (Cambridge, MA: Harvard University Press, 2006), 36–71.

6. Ameer Ali, *Personal Law of the Mahommedans*, 36.

7. See Williams, *Capitalism and Slavery*.

8. Drescher, *Capitalism and Antislavery*, 5.

9. Ibid., 12.

10. Blackburn, *The Overthrow of Colonial Slavery*, 58.

11. Ibid., 138–156.

12. Law, "Abolition and Imperialism," 150.

13. Blackburn, *The Overthrow of Colonial Slavery*, 138–156.

14. It was not until 1838 that enslaved people were legally emancipated. See Lorimer, *Gazetteer of the Persian Gulf*, 1: pt. 2, 2475.

15. Harms, "Introduction," 1.

16. A first step was to order the pasha of Baghdad to return any Indians who had been sold in Basra. Lorimer, *Gazetteer of the Persian Gulf*, 1: pt. 2, 2481.

17. See Behnaz A. Mirzai, "The Persian Gulf and Britain: The Suppression of the African Slave Trade," in *Abolitions as a Global Experience*, ed. Hideaki Suzuki (Singapore: National University of Singapore, 2016), 113–129.

18. Ibid., pt. 1A, 688.

19. Much of this was due to a weakening by the early 1800s of the Qawasem navy. Ibid., 673; the British government to the Iranian government, Rabiʿ al-Awwal 23, 1267, Q1263.6.24.3, VUK, Tehran. See Alpers, "On Becoming a British Lake," 45–58.

20. Indeed, it is estimated that it cost the sultanate one hundred thousand dollars a year. Lorimer, *Gazetteer of the Persian Gulf*, 1: pt. 2, 2477.

21. Ibid., 2479.

22. Ibid., 2477, and pt. 1A, 702.

23. Ibid., pt. 2, 2478.

24. Ibid., pt. 1A, 702.

25. Ibid., 679.

26. Wright, *The English amongst the Persians*, 69.

27. Palmerston to McNeil, July 9, 1841, FO 84/373, NAUK; Lord Aberdeen to Sir John

McNeil, December 1841, FO 84/373, NAUK, London. As a physician, McNeil was uniquely positioned to collect political information, as he was permitted access to the shah's harems. Griboyedov, *Nameha-yi Aleksandr Giribayduf*, 92.

28. Palmerston to McNeil, July 9, 1841, FO 84/373, NAUK.

29. Lorimer, *Gazetteer of the Persian Gulf*, 1: pt. 2, 2512.

30. Palmerston to McNeil, July 9, 1841, FO 84/373, NAUK.

31. Erdem, *Slavery in the Ottoman Empire*, 85.

32. The attempted secession of Herat brought Iran and Afghanistan to the brink of war in 1838–1839 and actual war in 1856. With support from Britain, the Treaty of Paris (1857) recognized the province's short-lived independence. See Lambton, *Qajar Persia*, 21; Adamiyat, *Amir Kabir va Iran*, 516; and Kelly, *Britain and the Persian Gulf*, 594.

33. Ra'in, *Daryanavardi-yi Iranian*, 2:685.

34. Justin Sheil to Haji Mirza Aqasi, 1263, Q1263.6.5, VUK, Tehran.

35. Justin Sheil to Lord Palmerston, June 7, 1847, L/PS/5/451, BL, London.

36. The French were skeptical of this argument, viewing the commercial interests of Britain in India as the main reason for the British abolitionist policy in the Persian Gulf. M. de Sartiges à le ministre des affaires étrangères, July 31, 1848, v. 24, MAE, Paris.

37. Hajee Meerza Aghassee to Justin Sheil, May 31, 1847, FO 84/692, NAUK, London.

38. Justin Sheil to Meerza Aghassee, August 29, 1847, FO 84/692, London; Henry Rawlinson to Francis Farrant, Baghdad, January 15, 1848, FO 84/737, NAUK, London.

39. Justin Sheil to Lord Palmerston, September 22, 1847, FO 84/692, NAUK, London; the British government to the Iranian government, Shawwal 5, 1263, Q1263.6.5, VUK, Tehran; Justin Sheil to Meerza Aghassee, September 15, 1847, FO 84/692, NAUK, London; Sheil to Aqasi, 1263, Q1263.6.5, VUK, Tehran.

40. Meerza Aghassee to Justin Sheil, September 17, 1847, FO 84/692, NAUK, London.

41. Lorimer, *Gazetteer of the Persian Gulf*, 1: pt. 2, 1975.

42. Francis Farrant to Meerza Aghassee, May 28, 1848, L/PS/5/457, BL, London.

43. Francis Farrant to Meerza Aghassee, June 12, 1848, L/PS/5/457, BL, London.

44. Kelly, *Britain and the Persian Gulf*, 587. The general suppression of the trade in enslaved Africans in the Ottoman states took place in 1857. See Erdem, *Slavery in the Ottoman Empire*, 99–113; Ehud R. Toledano, "Ottoman Concepts of Slavery in the Period of Reform, 1830s–1880s," in *Slavery, Bondage, and Emancipation in Modern Africa and Asia*, ed. Martin A. Klein (Madison: University of Wisconsin Press, 1993), 47; Justin Sheil to Lord Palmerston, February 23, 1847, FO 84/692, NAUK, London.

45. Meerza Aghassee to Sheil, translation, Til Hijjeh 9, 1846, FO 84/647, NAUK, London.

46. This was particularly clear by the proximity of towns like Khorramshahr and Basra on the Arvandrud, since it was a simple matter of crossing the river into another jurisdiction in order to trade slaves. Justin Sheil to the shah, June 2, 1847, L/PS/5/451, BL, London; Justin Sheil to the shah, June 21, 1847, FO 84/692, NAUK, London.

47. Samuel Hennell to Commodore J. C. Hawkins, senior officer in the Indian navy in the Persian Gulf, July 13, 1848, L/PS/5/457, BL, London.

48. Justifying British maritime policy was another argument that was specifically detailed in a letter to the shah's successor, Nasir al-Din Shah. Justin Sheil to Ameer-i Nizam, March 1850, FO 84/815, NAUK, London.

49. Erdem, *Slavery in the Ottoman Empire*, 94. This policy was first implemented when they reacted against the Russian enslavement of Christian Georgians and Muslim Circassians in Ottoman territory in 1854 during the Crimean War, arguing that this action was

beyond the pale of normal religious injunction and thus appeasing their ally Britain. Ibid., 94, 102–107.

50. Meerza Aghassee to Justin Sheil, December 20, 1846, FO 84/647, NAUK, London.

51. Sheil to Palmerston, May 31, 1847, L/PS/5/451, BL.

52. Justin Sheil to Lord Palmerston, Tehran, April 27, 1847, FO 84/692, NAUK, London.

53. Kemball to Soweynee, April 18, 1853, AA3/12, ZNL; reports on Bandar Lengeh, 1266, Q1263.6.15, VUK; Lorimer, *Gazetteer of the Persian Gulf*, 1: pt. 2, 2478.

54. Sheil to Aqasi, 1263, Q1263.6.5, VUK; see also Sheil's earlier letters to Mirza Aqasi, especially in which he had underlined the moral implications of the religious justification: Justin Sheil to Meerza Aghassee, November 16, 1846, FO 84/647, NAUK, London, and Justin Sheil to Meerza Aghassee, December 13, 1846, FO 84/647, NAUK, London.

55. Meerza Aghassee to Justin Sheil, "Moherrem 1, 1263," December 20, 1846, FO 84/647, NAUK, London; Justin Sheil to Henry Rawlinson, September 18, 1847, FO 84/692, NAUK, London.

56. The mujtahid is a religious authority that may act according to his own judgment in matters relating to religious law. For further information on the position of mujtahidin in Iran, see Azar Tabari, "The Role of the Clergy in Modern Iranian Politics," in *Religion and Politics in Iran: Shi'ism from Quietism to Revolution*, ed. Nikki R. Keddie (New Haven: Yale University Press, 1983), 47–72.

57. See Nikki R. Keddie, "The Roots of the 'Ulamā''s Power in Modern Iran," in *Scholars, Saints, and Sufis: Muslim Religious Institutions in the Middle East since 1500*, ed. Nikki R. Keddie (Berkeley: University of California Press, 1972), 216–229. See also A. Sepsis, "Quelque mots sur l'état religieux actuel de la Perse," *Revue de l'Orient* 3 (1844), 97–114. In Iran, the *marja'-i taqlid* was the supreme spiritual leader of the twelve Shi'a, who exercised independent legal reasoning and delivered judicial opinion when consulted by an official or individual. See Lawyers Committee for Human Rights, *Islam and Justice* (New York: Lawyers Committee for Human Rights, 1997), 115–125.

58. Kermani, *Tarikh-i bidari-yi Iranian* 1:429–430. One of the biggest *bast*s (taking refuge) took place in 1905, when about three hundred constitutionalists took refuge at the British consulate in Tabriz for over one week. See Wright, *The English amongst the Persians*, 46.

59. It was the policy of Haji Mirza Aqasi to reduce the authority of the 'ulama' through prohibiting use of these refuges (*basthā*). See A. Sepsis, "De l'état administrative et politique de la Perse," *Revue de l'Orient* 4 (1844), 105; Zargari Nejad, *Rasa'el mashrutiyat*, 71; and Eugène Aubin, *La Perse d'aujourd'hui* (Paris: Librairie Armand Colin, 1908), 182–183.

60. The *waqf* was a charitable trust, land, or property endowment, while *zakat* was legal almsgiving.

61. During the Qajar period, the religious capital and the center of Shi'a leadership was transferred to Najaf in Iraq, close to the shrine of 'Ali (the Shi'as' first imam and the Sunnis' fourth caliph).

62. Sheil to Palmerston, Tehran, April 27, 1847, FO 84/692, NAUK. Aghassee to Sheil, December 20, 1846, FO 84/647, NAUK.

63. The customary practices of the Prophet.

64. Adamiyat, *Amir Kabir va Iran*, 517. In fact, linguistic and cultural differences along with the Shi'i doctrine did contribute to distinguishing Iran from its Muslim neighbors.

65. Autographed note from Muhammad Shah to Haji Mirza Aqasi, 1263, Q1262.5.38, VUK, Tehran.

66. Sheil to Palmerston, Tehran, April 27, 1847, FO 84/692, NAUK.

67. Questions to various priests in Tehran relative to the slave trade with their replies, translated by Justin Sheil, 1847, FO 84/692, NAUK, London.

68. Ibid. The hadith (sayings of the Prophet) specified, "The worst people are those who sell human beings." Husayni, *Bardegi az didgah-i Islam*, 85.

69. Questions to various priests, 1847, FO 84/692, NAUK.

70. Ibid.

71. Ibid.

72. Ibid.

73. Husayni, *Bardegi az didgah-i Islam*, 19.

74. Sheil to Rawlinson, September 18, 1847, FO 84/692, NAUK; Henry Rawlinson to Justin Sheil, Baghdad, November 8, 1847, L/PS/5/453, BL, London; Justin Sheil in Tehran to Henry Rawlinson, political resident in Baghdad, September 18, 1847, L/PS/5/452, BL, London.

75. Sheil to Rawlinson, September 18, 1847, FO 84/692, NAUK.

76. Francis Farrant to Lord Palmerston, Tehran, December 18, 1847, FO 84/692, NAUK, London; Francis Farrant to Lord Palmerston, Tehran, December 18, 1847, L/PS/5/453, BL, London.

77. Rawlinson to Sheil, Baghdad, November 8, 1847, L/PS/5/453, BL.

78. Rawlinson to Farrant, Baghdad, January 15, 1848, FO 84/737, NAUK.

79. Foreign Office to Francis Farrant, draft, March 30, 1848, FO 84/737, NAUK, London.

80. Sheil to Palmerston, February 23, 1847, FO 84/692, NAUK.

81. Rawlinson to Sheil, Baghdad, November 8, 1847, L/PS/5/453, BL.

82. Ra'in, *Daryanavardi-yi Iranian*, 2:685.

83. Justin Sheil to Hajee Meerza Aghassee, May 11, 1847, L/PS/5/451, BL, London.

84. Sheil to Haji Mirza Aqasi, 1263, Q1263.6.5, VUK.

85. In order to support his argument, he obtained another decree from 'ulama' Aqa Mahmud referring only to the enslavement of unbelievers. Autographed note of the shah to Hajee Meerza Aghassee, translation, L/PS/5/451, BL, London; Hajee Meerza Aghassee to Justin Sheil, May 12, 1847, L/PS/5/451, BL, London.

86. Justin Sheil to Hajee Meerza Aghassee, June 4, 1847, L/PS/5/451, BL, London.

87. Rawlinson to Sheil, Baghdad, November 8, 1847, L/PS/5/453, BL.

88. Muhammad Shah to Haji Mirza Aqasi, 1263, Q1263.6.5, VUK, Tehran.

89. Muhammad Shah's order, Rajab 23, 1263, Q1264.6.6, VUK, Tehran.

90. Aqa Khan Mahallati, the leader of the Esma'ili (a sect of Shi'i Islam), was appointed as the governor of Kerman in 1835 or 1836. He was supported by Britain to fight against the central government.

91. Sheil to Palmerston, Tehran, April 27, 1847, FO 84/692, NAUK.

92. Lord Palmerston to Justin Sheil, February 12, 1847, FO 84/692, NAUK, London.

93. Sheil to Palmerston, June 27, 1847, L/PS/5/451, BL; Justin Sheil to Lord Palmerston, June 27, 1847, FO 84/692, NAUK, London.

94. The shah to Haji Mirza Aqasi, 1264, Q1264.5.38, VUK, Tehran; the shah to Meerza Aghassee, June 12, 1848, L/PS/5/457, BL, London; Lorimer, *Gazetteer of the Persian Gulf*, 1: pt. 2, 1974.

95. Farrant acknowledged the important role of Mirza Aqa and another official in garnering the imperial *firmān* (Francis Farrant to Lord Palmerston, June 17, 1848, camp near

Tehran, L/PS/5/457, BL, London). The British government subsequently presented one hundred pounds (T250) to Mirza Aqa for his efforts. Lord Palmerston to Francis Farrant, chargé d'affaires in Persia, September 25, 1848, FO 84/737, NAUK, London.

96. Meerza Aghassee to Francis Farrant, June 12, 1848, L/PS/5/457, BL, London.

97. The British government to the Iranian government, Jamadi al-Awwal 16, 1264, Q1264.6.6, VUK, Tehran.

98. Justin Sheil to Lord Palmerston, August 31, 1847, FO 84/692, NAUK, London; Farrant to Palmerston, June 17, 1848, L/PS/5/457, BL.

99. Farrant to Palmerston, June 17, 1848, L/PS/5/457, BL.

100. The shah's farman to Hosein Khan, governor of Fars, Rajab 1264, L/PS/5/457, BL, London.

101. Samuel Hennell to Arthur Malet, Bushire, July 12, 1848, L/PS/5/457, BL, London; His Excellency Houssein Khan Nizam ood Dowleh, governor of Fars, to Shaik Nasir Khan Duureya Beggee, governor of Bushire, July 1848, L/PS/5/457, BL, London.

102. Among these were the shaykhs of Bandar Kangan, 'Asaluyeh, Lengeh, Charak, Chiru, and Moghuyah. Hennell realized that they had traditionally enjoyed the immunity of Iranian ports before distributing enslaved people throughout the Persian Gulf. Hennell to Hawkins, July 13, 1848, L/PS/5/457, BL.

103. The shah's farman to Mirza Nabi Khan, governor of Isfahan and Arabia, Rajab 1264, L/PS/5/457, BL, London.

104. The governor of Persian Arabia to the authorities of Mohamrah and Arabistan, Ramadan 1264, L/PS/5/459, BL, London. Samuel Hennell to Francis Farrant, chargé d'affaires at the court in Persia, September 1, 1848, L/PS/5/459, BL, London.

105. Samuel Hennell to T. G. Carless, Bushire, September 21, 1848, L/PS/5/459, BL, London; Samuel Hennell to T. G. Carless, September 21, 1848, L/PS/9/136, BL, London.

106. Hennell to Carless, Bushire, September 21, 1848, L/PS/5/459, BL.

107. Lord Palmerston to Justin Sheil, December 31, 1849, R/15/1/123, BL, London.

108. After the shah's death, the British focused their attention on his heir, Nasir al-Din Shah. Gardner to Porter, July 11, 1849, L/PS/5/463, BL.

109. Justin Sheil to Ameer-i-Nizam, July 5, 1850, L/PS/5/465, BL, London.

110. Nasir al-Din Shah's order, Safar 3, 1265, Q1263.6.12.4, VUK, Tehran; Nasir al-Din Shah's order, Jamai al-Awwal 9, 1266, Q1264.6.6, VUK, Tehran.

111. Mirza Mahmoud Ali Khan to Francis Farrant, February 1, 1849, FO 84/774, NAUK, London; Ameer-i Nizam to Justin Sheil, March 25, 1850, FO 84/815, NAUK, London; Amir Kabir to the British minister plenipotentiary, Jamadi al-Awwal 9, 1266, Q1264.6.9, VUK, Tehran.

112. The British government to the Iranian government, 1266, Q1263.6.15, VUK, Tehran.

113. Justin Sheil to Ameer-i Nezam, June 8, 1850, FO 84/815, NAUK, London.

114. Justin Sheil to Lord Palmerston, December 1, 1850, L/PS/5/469, BL, London.

115. Taylour Thomson to Lord Palmerston, Tehran, November 21, 1849, FO 84/774, NAUK, London; Justin Sheil to Lord Palmerston, camp near Tehran, August 26, 1850, FO 84/815, NAUK, London. Astarabad was situated along the Caspian Sea and was the main route between Mashhad and Tehran (M. de Sartiges à le ministre des affaires étrangères, July 31, 1848, v. 24, MAE, Paris). Indeed, Russia was also already attempting to gain permission to build a military hospital in Astarabad. Justin Sheil to Ameer-i Nizam, February 1851, L/PS/5/469, BL, London.

116. Justin Sheil to Lord Palmerston, December 24, 1850, L/PS/5/469, BL, London.

NOTES TO PAGES 148–152 265

117. Mirpanjeh, *Khaterat-i esarat*, 112.

118. Justin Sheil to Lord Palmerston, Tehran, March 26, 1850, FO 84/815, NAUK, London. The communications were apparently being copied to Prince Nicolas Dolgorouki, the Russian minister at Tehran.

119. Justin Sheil to Lord Palmerston, Tehran, February 20, 1850, FO 84/815, NAUK, London.

120. Francis Farrant to Lord Palmerston, January 26, 1848, FO 84/737, NAUK, London.

121. Sheil to Ameer-i Nezam, June 8, 1850, FO 84/815, NAUK.

122. Issawi, *The Economic History of Iran*, 266.

123. Justin Sheil to Lord Palmerston, camp near Tehran, September 16, 1850, FO 84/815, NAUK, London; Justin Sheil to Amir Kabir, Shawwal 23, 1266, Q1266.6.15, VUK, Tehran.

124. Justin Sheil to Lord Palmerston, camp near Tehran, June 17, 1850, FO 84/815, NAUK, London; Justin Sheil to Ameer-i Nizam, September 1, 1850, FO 84/815, NAUK, London.

125. Adamiyat, *Amir Kabir va Iran*, 527.

126. Justin Sheil to Lord Palmerston, September 16, 1850, L/PS/5/466, BL, London; Major General Christopher P. Rigby to the secretary to the Bombay government, September 14, 1860, AA12/2, ZNL, Zanzibar; Lorimer, *Gazetteer of the Persian Gulf*, 1: pt. 1A, 725, and pt. 2, 2480.

127. The British determined that between 1847 and 1859, 997 enslaved people had been smuggled into the country. Of these, nearly 26 percent had arrived in 1850 alone. Indeed, the numbers peaked between 1849 and 1851; thereafter, no more than one hundred came in each year. The data are based on various archival sources collected for this study (see chart 6.1).

128. The khan paid about sixteen thousand tomans annually to the governor of Fars. Lorimer, *Gazetteer of the Persian Gulf*, 2: pt. 1A, 371, 552. See also British government to the Iranian government, Rabi' al-Awwal 27, 1266, Q1263.6.15, VUK.

129. The British government to the Iranian government, Shawwal 23, 1266, Q1263.6.15, VUK, Tehran.

130. Lorimer, *Gazetteer of the Persian Gulf*, 1: pt. 2, 2514.

131. W. M. Taylour Thomson to the earl of Derby, Tehran, March 20, 1877 (received April 25, 1877), AA1/22, ZNL, Zanzibar.

132. Justin Sheil to Ameer-i Nizam, May 27, 1851, FO 84/857, NAUK, London; Justin Sheil to Lord Palmerston, Ispahan, July 4, 1851, FO 84/857, NAUK, London.

133. The 1851 agreement between the British and Iranian governments, Isfahan, Shawwal 1267, Q1263.6.24.2, VUK, Tehran. The British considered the role of the Iranian secretaries of the mission, Mirza Aqa and Mirza Husayn Quli, to have been so important in achieving the agreement that they rewarded them with one hundred pounds. No doubt that the monetary rewards Britain presented to its allies in the Iranian government had important implications to further their political and economic ambitions in the region. Sheil to Palmerston, Ispahan, July 4, 1851, FO 84/857, NAUK; Lord Palmerston to Justin Sheil, December 17, 1851, FO 84/857, NAUK, London; the translation of agreement between Colonel Justin Sheil and Mirza Taqi Khan Amir Kabir for the detention and search of Persian vessels by British and East India Company cruisers, August 1851, R/15/1/127, BL, London.

134. Sheil to Amir Kabir, 1267, Q1267.6.24, VUK; Lorimer, *Gazetteer of the Persian Gulf*, 1: pt. 2, 2483.

135. Minutes of evidence presented before the royal commission, March 11, 1875, AA12/2, ZNL; the British government to the Iranian government, Muharram 21, 1288, Q1286.13.29, VUK, Tehran; Wilson, *The Persian Gulf*, 228.

136. Justin Sheil to Samuel Hennell, Tehran, December 27, 1851, L/PS/5/473, BL, London.

137. Instructions to Mirza Mahmud, the commissioner in the Bushehr port, regarding the abolition of slavery, 1268, Q1268.6.40, VUK, Tehran.

138. Palmerston to Sheil, December 17, 1851, FO 84/857, NAUK.

139. Reports on the slave trade in the Persian Gulf, 1852–1859, L/PS/20/C246, BL, London.

140. Arnold Burrowes Kemball to Commodore Robinson, April 11, 1854, FO 248/157, NAUK, London.

141. Treaty of Peace between Her Majesty, the Queen of the United Kingdom of Great Britain and Ireland, and His Majesty, the Shah of Persia, March 4, 1857, FO 60/371, NAUK, London; Reza Quli Khan Hedayat, *Tarikh-i ruzat al-safa*, 10:752.

142. Erdem, *Slavery in the Ottoman Empire*, 107–113; Toledano, *The Ottoman Slave Trade*, 135–138.

143. The 'ulama', Shaykh Jamal of Mecca's fatwa denouncing this ban whipped up public unrest, led to riots and resulted in massacre. Hadjia Georjee Kastanti of Hodeida to William Marcus Coghlan, Rabeel awal 25, 1272, L/PS/5/486, BL, London; Erdem, *Slavery in the Ottoman Empire*, 86; Toledano, *The Ottoman Slave Trade*, 129–135.

144. The British embassy to Mirza Ahmad Munshi Sulati, Shawwal 4, 1278, Q1278.9.20, VUK, Tehran.

145. Felix Jones to H. Anderson, Bushire, August 24, 1859, FO 248/183, NAUK, London.

146. There were several reports regarding the fifty-one enslaved people who disembarked at Lengeh in 1859: Meerza Saeed Khan to William Doria, September 13, 1859, R/15/1/177, BL, London; Felix Jones to Mirza Abdul Karim, slave commissioner, Bushire, October 28, 1858, R/15/1/177, BL, London.

147. *Gazetteer of the Persian Gulf*, 1: pt. 2, 2493.

148. The Iranian government to the British embassy, Rabi' al-Awwal 9, 1278, Q1278.9.20, VUK, Tehran. Mirza Mahmud Khan's poor health was cited as the reason for his ineptitude; since 1858, he had temporarily been replaced by Mirza 'Abdul Karim. Felix Jones to W. Murray, minister at the court in Persia, July 1, 1858, FO 248/176, NAUK, London; Taylour Thomson, Tehran, May 17, 1876, FO 84/1450, NAUK, London; Felix Jones to William Doria, Tehran, Bushire, September 7, 1859, R/15/1/177, BL, London; Felix Jones to C. Alison, HBM's envoy and minister of philanthropy at the court in Persia, Tehran, Bushire, June 6, 1860, R/15/1/177, BL, London; Felix Jones to C. Alison, Tehran, Bushire, December 7, 1860, R/15/1/177, BL, London; Felix Jones to C. Alison, Tehran, Bushire, January 16, 1862, R/15/1/177, BL, London; Taylour Thomson to Arnold Burrowes Kemball, Tehran, April 13, 1853, L/PS/5/478, BL, London; Taylour Thomson to Lord Clarendon, camp near Tehran, July 14, 1853, L/PS/5/478, BL, London; Taylour Thomson to W. Murray, February 18, 1856, FO 84/1000, NAUK, London.

149. The Persian minister for foreign affairs to Ahmed Khan, governor of Bushire, January 6, 1859, R/15/1/177, BL, London; the Persian minister for foreign affairs to Meerza Mahmood Khan, January 6, 1859, R/15/1/177, BL, London; C. Alison to Meerza Saeed Khan, September 7, 1861, R/15/1/168, BL, London; C. Alison to Meerza Saeed Khan, camp near Tehran, September 9, 1861, FO 84/1144, NAUK, London.

150. Mirza Saeed Khan to Alison, September 16, 1861, FO 84/1144, NAUK, London; Mirza Saeed Khan, Persian minister of foreign affairs, to C. Alison, September 16, 1861,

R/15/1/168, BL, London; Taylour Thomson to Captain Prideaux, Tehran, May 7, 1876, FO 84/1450, NAUK, London.

151. Taylour Thomson to Prideaux, Tehran, May 7, 1876, FO 84/1450, NAUK.

152. Lorimer, *Gazetteer of the Persian Gulf*, 1: pt. 2, 2483.

153. Taylour Thomson to Earl Granville, Tehran, December 30, 1873, FO 84/1369, NAUK, London.

154. Lorimer, *Gazetteer of the Persian Gulf*, 1: pt. 2, 2495, and pt. 1A, 271.

155. Benjamin, *Persia and the Persians*, 170.

156. Taylour Thomson to the earl of Derby, May 23, 1876, FO 84/1450, NAUK, London.

157. Wilson, *The Persian Gulf*, 221.

158. Report to the Iranian government, Mirza Sultan Khan from the British consulate, 1292, Q1292.15.26.5, VUK, Tehran.

159. Ronald Thomson to Earl Granville, Tehran, October 29, 1881, FO 84/1592, NAUK, London.

160. Mu'in al-Mulk to the embassy of the Ottoman Empire, Safar 21, 1299, Q1299.17.9, VUK, Tehran.

161. Lorimer, *Gazetteer of the Persian Gulf*, 1: pt. 2, 2036. The treaty was signed by the British envoy Ronald Thomson and the minister of foreign affairs Mirza Sa'id Khan.

162. Ra'in, *Daryanavardi-yi Iranian*, 2:705.

163. The Ministry of Foreign Affairs of Iran in Bushehr to the British agent in Tehran, Rabi' al-Thani 29, 1300, Q1300.17.21.2, VUK, Tehran.

164. J. Kirk, the agent and consul general at Zanzibar, to the secretary to the government of India, Foreign Department, dated at Zanzibar, March 3, 1885, L/PS/20/C246, BL, London, no. 2; Lorimer, *Gazetteer of the Persian Gulf*, 1: pt. 2, 2496.

165. H. D. Wolff, April 22, 1890, FO 84/2040, NAUK, London. Article 85 stipulated the responsibility of signatories to share the expenses of the conference, paid annually to the agency of the Department of the Foreign Office in Brussels (Political Department, General Act of the Brussels Conference, June 8, 1891, R/15/1/199, BL, article 85). And, into the early twentieth century, Iran dutifully sent its share of the expenses to the Belgian embassy. Legation de Belgique, Shawwal 24, 1316, Q1316.32.10, VUK, Tehran; Mushir al-Daula, at the Ministry of Foreign Affairs, to the Belgian embassy, Sha'ban 19, 1317, Q1317.3.4, VUK, Tehran; the Ministry of Foreign Affairs to Mustufi al-Mamalek, the finance minister, Sha'ban 25, 1327, Q1327.7.5, VUK, Tehran.

166. Suzanne Miers and Richard Roberts, eds., *The End of Slavery in Africa* (Madison: University of Wisconsin Press, 1988), 16; Lorimer, *Gazetteer of the Persian Gulf*, 1: pt. 2, 2485.

167. Political Department, General Act of the Brussels Conference, June 8, 1891, R/15/1/199, BL.

168. Correspondence on the liberation of enslaved people imported after the 1890 agreement, Muharram 26, 1324, Q1324.3.3, VUK, Tehran.

169. Political Department, General Act of the Brussels Conference, June 8, 1891, R/15/1/199, BL.

170. British resident and consulate to the residency agent in Lingah, dated Bushire, April 25, 1892, R/15/1/199, BL, London; see Hideaki Suzuki, "Baluchi Experiences Under Slavery and the Slave Trade of the Gulf of Oman and the Persian Gulf, 1921–1950," in "The Baluch and Baluchistan," ed. Behnaz A. Mirzai, Special issue, *The Journal of the Middle East and Africa* 4, no. 2 (2013).

171. Indeed, this phenomenon is not dissimilar to the situation found in the Americas when anti-slave-trade policy in the 1830s resulted in a new stream of unfree labor in the form of indentured labor from India. Bose, *A Hundred Horizons*, 75. As Drescher notes: "The British government allowed its West Indian colonies to turn to India for the recruitment of indentured servants. For a very brief period British abolitionists were able to brand this system a 'new slave trade.'" Drescher, "Emperors of the World," 144. Similarly, Indians were imported across the Indian Ocean to work as indentured laborers in countries such as Mauritius. See Richard B Allen, *Slaves, Freedmen, and Indentured Laborers in Colonial Mauritius* (Cambridge: Cambridge University Press, 1999). See also Marina Carter and Khal Torabully, *Coolitude: An Anthology of the Indian Labour Diaspora* (London: Anthem Press, 2002).

172. R. H. Clive, the British minister, contacted Mirza Ghaffar Khan Jalal of the English section of the Ministry of Foreign Affairs and Ghaffari, the director general of the ministry, concerning the issue of buying and selling Iranians, minutes sheet, "Slaves in the Gulf," December 9, 1929, FO 248/1387, NAUK, London.

173. The British Resident in Bushire to the shaikh of Abu Dhabi, November 29, 1921, R/15/1/221, BL, London.

174. Trevor to Bray, Delhi, December 31, 1921, R/15/1/221, BL.

175. Miers, *Slavery in the Twentieth Century*, 306. Balfour-Paul, *The End of Empire in the Middle East*, 107.

176. Suzanne Miers, "Slave Rebellion and Resistance in the Aden Protectorate in the Mid-Twentieth Century," in *Slavery and Resistance in Africa and Asia*, ed. Edward Alpers, Gwyn Campbell, and Michael Salman (London and New York: Routledge, 2005), 99–101.

177. Gwyn Campbell and Edward A. Alpers, "Slavery, Forced Labour and Resistance in Indian Ocean Africa and Asia," in *Slavery and Resistance in Africa and Asia*, ed. Edward Alpers, Gwyn Campbell, and Michael Salman (London and New York: Routledge, 2005), 13.

178. Drescher, "Emperors of the World," 146; 'Abdullahi Ahmed An-Na'im, "Shari'a and Basic Human Rights Concerns," in *Liberal Islam: A Sourcebook*, ed. Charles Kurzman (Oxford: Oxford University Press, 1998), 231.

CHAPTER 7. ANTISLAVERY DEBATES WITHIN IRAN

1. El Hamel, *Black Morocco*, 42. El Hamel also notes that the word 'abd (commonly referring to slaves) is usually only used in connection with descriptions of God's relationship to his creation. Ibid., 34.

2. Ibid., 17.

3. Ameer Ali, *Personal Law of the Mahommedans*, 37.

4. Ibid., 39.

5. The followers of the Babi movement came under severe attack and persecution after 1852 but continued their social and messianic practices. See Lambton, *Qajar Persia*, 104.

6. Bahá'u'lláh, *The Kitáb-i-Aqdás* (Pakistan: Bāhā'ī, 1997), 68. For further information on Babism, see Peter Smith, *The Babi and Baha'i Religions: From Messianic Shi'ism to a World Religion* (Cambridge: Cambridge University Press, 1987).

7. Bahá'u'lláh and 'Abdu'l-bahá, *Bahá'í World Faith* (Wilmette, IL: Bahá'í, 1956), 53.

8. Abdul-Hadi Hairi, *Shi'ism and Constitutionalism in Iran* (Leiden: Brill, 1977), 71.

9. Mírzá Maḥmúd-i-Zarqání, *Maḥmúd's Diary: The Diary of Mírzá Maḥmúd-i-Zarqání chronicling Ábdu'l-Bahá's Journey to America*, trans. Mohi Sobhani (Oxford: George Ronald, 1998), 70.

10. Zarqání, *Maḥmúd's Diary*, 70.

11. Ibid., 189, 190.

12. For further information on Sufism, see Spencer Trimingham, *The Sufi Orders in Islam* (Oxford: Clarendon, 1971); see also Nile Green, *Sufism: A Global History* (Oxford: Wiley-Blackwell, 2012).

13. After the death of Zayn al-ʿAbidin Rahmat ʿAli Shah in 1861, the Niʿmatullahi Sufi order was divided into three factions led separately by Saʿadat ʿAli Shah (d. 1876)—known as Gunabadi—Zulriyasatayn Munavvar ʿAli Shah (d. 1884), and Safi ʿAli Shah (d. 1899). The Gunabadi line developed into the most powerful branch of the Niʿmatullahi order under the direction of Mulla Muhammad Sultan ʿAli Shah. Aubin, *La Perse d'aujourd'hui*, 185.

14. Abbas Amanat, *Resurrection and Renewal: The Making of the Babi Movement in Iran, 1844–1850* (Ithaca: Cornell University Press, 1989), 77.

15. Lesan al-Mulk, *Nasekh al-tawarikh*, 1:317.

16. Indeed, there was a marked increase in Sufi influence in official government circles during the reign of Muhammad Shah. See Husayn Saʿadat Nuri, "Haji Mirza Aqasi," *Yaghma* 16, no. 5 (1342), 231; ʿAbdul Rafiʿ Haqiqat, *Vaziran-i Irani az Buzurgmehr ta Amir Kabir* (Tehran: Koshesh, 1374), 387; Shamim, *Iran*, 96; and Amanat, *Resurrection and Renewal*, 20.

17. He studied under Mulla ʿAbdulsamad Hamedani, one of the prominent Sufis who was the follower of Mirza Muhammad ʿAli Nur ʿAli Shah Isfahani—a celebrated Niʿmatullahi Sufi. Saʿadat Nuri, "Haji Mirza Aqasi," 231. See also Haqiqat, *Vaziran-i Irani*, 387.

18. Lesan al-Mulk, *Nasekh al-tawarikh*, 2:650. See also Shamim, *Iran*, 96.

19. Adamiyat, *Fekr-i azadi*, 40; Huma Nateq, *Iran dar rahyabi-yi farhangi* (Paris: Abnus, 1990), 30.

20. Nateq, *Iran dar rahyabi-yi farhangi*, 47, 141.

21. Ibid., 29.

22. Sheil to Palmerston, February 23, 1847, FO 84/692, NAUK.

23. Nateq, *Iran dar rahyabi-yi farhangi*, 31. France abolished slavery during the French Revolution in 1794, but Napoleon reinstated slavery in the French colonies in 1802. During the Second Republic, slavery was finally abolished in 1848. For more information on the abolition of slavery in France, see Sue Peabody, "France's Two Emancipations in Comparative Context," in *Abolitions as a Global Experience*, ed. Hideaki Suzuki (Singapore: National University of Singapore, 2016), 25–49.

24. Haj Sultan Husayn Tabanda Gunabadi, *Nazar-i mazhabi ba eʿlamiʾa-yi huquq-i bashar* (Tehran: Piruz, 1354), 45–46.

25. Ibid., 51. In other Muslim societies, similar arguments were used to end slavery. For example, in November 1962, Prince Faisal, the prime minister of Saudi Arabia, issued a decree to end slavery: "Any slavery existing at the present time fails to fulfill many of the Shariʿa conditions laid down by Islam for slavery." See John Laffin, *The Arabs as Master Slavers* (Englewood, NJ: SBS, 1982), 71.

26. Amir Kabir gained important insight into successful imperial infrastructures while in Russia (1828–1829), Yerevan (1837), and the Ottoman Empire (1843–1847). See Stanford J. Shaw, *History of the Ottoman Empire and Modern Turkey* (Cambridge: Cambridge University Press, 1976); Nashat, *The Origins of Modern Reform in Iran*, 20.

27. The independent military and political power of nomadic tribes, Iran's mountainous topography, and the distance between centers of population were factors that prolonged the process of centralization in Iran as compared to Egypt. See Keddie, "The Roots of the ʿUlamā'ʾs Power," 215.

28. L. Carl Brown, *The Tunisia of Ahmad Bey 1837–1855* (Princeton: Princeton University Press, 1974), 321; Ismael M. Montana, *The Abolition of Slavery in Ottoman Tunisia* (Gainesville: University Press of Florida, 2013), 85.

29. Willem Floor, "Change and Development in the Judicial System of Qajar Iran (1800–1925)," in *Qajar Iran: Political, Social and Cultural Change, 1800–1925*, ed. Edmund Bosworth and Carole Hillenbrand (Edinburgh: Edinburgh University Press, 1983), 120.

30. The six ministers were the ministers of justice, the interior, finance, war, foreign affairs, and pensions (Mustaufi, *Sharh-i zendegani-yi man*, 1:88). For the development of cabinets and councils, see Shaul Bakhash, *Iran, Monarchy, Bureaucracy, & Reform under the Qajars, 1858–1896* (London: Ithaca Press for the Middle East Centre, St. Antony's College, 1978), 133–186; Lambton, *Qajar Persia*, 100.

31. Taylour Thomson to the earl of Derby, Tehran, May 13, 1874, FO 84/1397, NAUK, London.

32. Nashat, *The Origins of Modern Reform in Iran*, 44, 49.

33. Mirza Ja'far Khan had been the ambassador to the Ottoman Empire from 1836 to 1842. Ibid., 21.

34. One key reform was the removal of the legal distinctions describing enslaved people, freed people, and free people. Esma Durugönül, "Construction of Identity and Integration of African-Turks," in *African Communities in Asia*, 286.

35. Mirza Husayn Khan's reforms did attract criticism, principally from the 'ulama' (including Haji Mulla 'Ali and Aqa Sayyid Saleh 'Arab) who accused him of heresy for introducing Western-style institutions and reforms. Although their vociferous opposition forced him to resign, the shah had him reappointed. Kermani, *Tarikh-i bidari*, 1:105–108.

36. Adamiyat, *Fekr-i azadi*, 57–59. The nine ministers were accountable to the prime minister and the shah. Mustaufi, *Sharh-i zendegani-yi man*, 1:120–124; Kasravi Tabrizi, *Tarikh-i mashruta-yi Iran* (Tehran: Amir Kabir, 1370), 8; Adamiyat, *Fekr-i azadi*, 79–85.

37. Mustaufi, *Sharh-i zendegani-yi man*, 1:135.

38. Nashat, *The Origins of Modern Reform in Iran*, 52, 72.

39. Lorimer, *Gazetteer of the Persian Gulf*, 1: pt. 2, 2179.

40. Ibid., 2052.

41. Adamiyat, *Ide'uluzhi-yi nehzat-i mashrutiyat-i Iran*, 4.

42. Nikki R. Keddie and Mehrdad Amanat, "Iran under the Later Qajars, 1848–1922," in *The Cambridge History of Iran*, ed. Peter Avery, Gavin Hambly, and Charles Melville (Cambridge: Cambridge University Press, 1991), 7:199.

43. Kermani, *Tarikh-i bidari*, 3:436–443, 481.

44. In 1893, at the age of fifteen, Reza Khan joined the Cossack infantry brigade in Tehran, becoming a lieutenant colonel in Kermanshah around 1916. In 1921, he organized a coup d'état against the Qajars. In 1923, Reza Khan became prime minister, and two years later, the Majlis-i Shuray-i Melli deposed Ahmad Shah Qajar, and Reza Khan (1878–1944) took power as Reza Shah Pahlavi.

45. Mehdi Quli Khan Hedayat (Mukhber al-Saltana), *Khatirat va khatarat* (Tehran: Zavar, 1375), 388; Arfa, *Under Five Shahs*, 201. For political reforms in the late Qajar period, see Nikki R. Keddie, *Qajar Iran and the Rise of Reza Khan, 1796–1925* (Costa Mesa, CA: Mazda Publishers, 1999); Donald N. Wilber, *Riza Shah Pahlavi: The Resurrection and Reconstruction of Iran* (New York: Exposition Press, 1975), 6–11; and Keddie, "The Roots of the 'Ulamā''s Power," 227.

46. Dāvar, a graduate of the University of Geneva and one of the shah's ablest and most intelligent modernizers, began the task of shaping a lay judiciary. See Gavin R. G. Hambly,

"The Pahlavī Autocracy: Muḥammad Riża Shāh, 1921–1941," in *The Cambridge History of Iran*, ed. Peter Avery, Gavin Hambly, and Charles Melville (Cambridge: Cambridge University Press, 1991), 7:231; and Arfa, *Under Five Shahs*, 218.

47. See Afsaneh Najmabadi, *Land Reform and Social Change in Iran* (Salt Lake City: University of Utah Press, 1987), 206–209; Hadi Enayat, *Law, State, and Society in Modern Iran: Constitutionalism, Autocracy, and Legal Reform, 1906–1941* (New York: Palgrave Macmillan, 2013).

48. Notably, the British gave Iranian vessels partial immunity from search-and-seizure efforts. And yet, in a communiqué to Lord Palmerston, Justin Sheil noted that in spite of these efforts, Arab traders were wont to hire Iranian vessels from the opposite shore to import enslaved Africans. Tehran, January 22, 1851, FO 84/857, NAUK, London; Sheil to Ameer-i Nizam, October 16, 1850, FO 84/815, NAUK, London.

49. Felix Jones, political resident in the Persian Gulf, to Commodore Griffith Jenkins, commander of the Persian Gulf squadron, Bushire Road, November 18, 1858, FO 248/176, NAUK, London.

50. Infractions of the legislation were met with harsh penalties. See, for instance, Ameer-i-Nizam to Justin Sheil, January 28, 1850, L/PS/5/465, BL, London; and a letter to Mirza Sa'id, the minister of foreign affairs, Muharram 11, 1270, Q1270.7.22, VUK, Tehran.

51. Samuel Hennell to Justin Sheil, Bushire, December 15, 1849, L/PS/5/463, BL, London.

52. Agent in Shiraz to Justin Sheil, February 3, 1851, L/PS/5/469, BL, London.

53. Ameer-i Nizam to the prince, government of Fars, Moherrem 2, 1266, November 18, 1849, FO 84/774, NAUK, London.

54. Samuel Hennell to Justin Sheil, Bushire, December 12, 1850, FO 84/857, NAUK, London. We also read of Bin Shams being forced to swear an oath before the mujtahid of Bushehr that he had not been involved in the trafficking of enslaved people in 1850. Samuel Hennell to Justin Sheil, Bushire, August 14, 1850, FO 84/815, NAUK, London.

55. Arnold Kemball to Meerza Fuzloollah, agent at Shiraz, December 14, 1852, L/PS/5/477, BL, London.

56. Arnold Kemball to Taylour Thomson, chargé d'affaires at the court of Persia, March 29, 1854 (Jamadi al-Tani 29, 1270), FO 248/157, NAUK, London; ibid., concerning receipt of Meerza Mahmood Khan, Jamadi al-Tani 29, 1270; Reza Quli Khan Hedayat, *Tarikh-i ruzat al-safa*, 10:575.

57. Arnold Kemball to Justin Sheil, February 1, 1853, L/PS/5/477, BL, London; H. R. H. Feerooz Mirza, prince, governor of Fars, to Arnold Kemball, Rubeeool Awal 1269 (January 24, 1853), L/PS/5/477, BL, London. 'Alireza Khan, the Iranian *moḥaṣṣil* (an official or a tax collector) sent by Firuz Mirza to Bushehr to punish the offending Arab chiefs and exact fines from them, was given T30 by Kemball as a gift for his efforts.

58. Arnold Kemball, in a letter to Taylour Thomson, chargé d'affaires at the Persian court, described how enslaved people were still being imported into Khorramshahr and that Shaykh Jaber was involved (May 23, 1853, L/PS/5/478, BL, London). See also Samuel Hennell to Taylour Thomson at the court of Persia, Bushire, December 5, 1849, L/PS/5/463, BL, London; Ameer-i Nizam to the prince, government of Fars, Moherrem 2, 1266 (November 18, 1849), FO 84/774, NAUK, London.

59. Nasir al-Din Shah's order, Shawwal 2, 1268, Q1264.6.6.5, VUK, Tehran; Sadid al-Saltana Kababi, *Sarzaminha-yi shumali*, 202–206.

60. Hennell to Sheil, Bushire, January 11, 1850, L/PS/5/463, BL. Notably, some of these boats belonged to Shaykh Jaber, the governor of Khorramshahr.

61. The districts of southern Khuzistan were Ahwaz, Fallahiya, Hawiza, Hendiyan,

Jarraji, and Khorramshahr. Northern Khuzistan comprised Dezful, Shushtar, Aqili, and Ramuz. See Lorimer, *Gazetteer of the Persian Gulf*, 2: pt. 1A, 158.

62. Ameer-i Nizam to Justin Sheil, July 18, 1850, L/PS/5/465, BL, London; Ameer-i Nizam to Colonel Justin Sheil, February 18, 1850, FO 84/815, NAUK, London.

63. The response of the Iranian government to Taylour Thomson, Ramadan 1270, Q1270.7.22, VUK, Tehran.

64. Iran had neither the ability to build vessels nor the wood to do so; indeed, their ships had to be sent to Bombay in order to be repaired. Issawi, *The Economic History of Iran*, 265.

65. The British squadron patrolled the coast between Basra and Bushehr and was based at Basʿidu on the island of Qeshm. Denis Wright, *The English amongst the Persians: Imperial Lives in the Nineteenth Century* (London: Heinemann, 1977), 74.

66. To the Ministry of Foreign Affairs, 1295, Q1295.15.26.7, VUK, Tehran.

67. Davud Khan had actually gone to Austria and Prussia to recruit teachers for the Dar al-Funun school. Adamiyat, *Amir Kabir va Iran*, 305–306; Eʿtemad al-Saltana, *al-Maʿaser va al-aʿsar*, 127.

68. The chargé d'affaires of Britain to Mirza Saʿid Khan, Dhi al-Hajjah 20, 1275, Q1275.8.34, VUK, Tehran.

69. Mirza Saʿid Khan's response to the chargé d'affaires of Britain, Dhi al-Hajjah 25, 1275, Q1275.8.34, VUK, Tehran.

70. Compared to the total tax received at the port of Lengeh (four hundred tomans), this fine represented 7.5 percent. Sadid al-Saltana Kababi, *Sarzaminha-yi shumali*, 203.

71. The testimony of local people, Dhi al-Hajjah 10, 1277, Q1277.9.2, VUK, Tehran.

72. Précis on the slave trade in the Gulf of Oman and the Persian Gulf, 1873–1905, January 1891, L/PS/20/C246, BL, London, 43.

73. The resident agent at Lingah to Colonel Ross, February 3, 1890, NAUK, FO 84/2040.

74. Sadid al-Saltana Kababi, *Sarzaminha-yi shumali*, 204, 205.

75. Ibid., 206.

76. Indeed, he estimated the number of enslaved Africans residing in this area to be about two thousand, some of whom had wives and children. The head of the customs bureau in the south of Iran to ʿAlaʾ al-Saltana, January 23, 1907, Q1325.3.8, VUK.

77. Evidence like this persuasively disproves the Thomas Ricks's claim that, by 1900, enslaved people were no longer politically and economically important in Iran. Thomas Ricks, "Slaves and Slave Trading in Shiʿi Iran, AD 1500–1900," in *Conceptualizing/Re-conceptualizing Africa: The Construction of African Historical Identity*, ed. Maghan Keita (Leiden: Brill, 2002), 85.

78. See, for instance, reports of free Baluchis being kidnapped—even children being sold by parents—in the interior and shipped to countries like Oman and Saudi Arabia: the Ministry of War to the Ministry of the Interior, Sh. 1303, 293001107, SAM; the government of Lengeh and the annexed regions to the Ministry of the Interior, Tir 6, 1306, 293/1105/1, SAM, Tehran; Sadid al-Saltana Kababi, *al-Menas fi ahval-i al-ghaus*, 26; Ebrahim Khan, *Jughrafiya-yi Isfahan*, 65, 122.

79. The decree of the shah to the grand vizier, Jamadi al-Awwal 16, 1322, Q1322.3.4.35, VUK, Tehran. Again, in 1917, the Ministries of the Interior and Foreign Affairs of Iran instructed all of the government agents in the provinces of Kerman and Baluchistan to implement the order forthwith. The Ministry of the Interior to the Ministry of Foreign Affairs, the office in the east, Shawwal 15, 1335, Q1335.3.13, VUK, Tehran; ʿAyn al-Daula, the prime minister, to the Ministry of Foreign Affairs, Ramadan 5, 1335, Q1335.3.13, VUK, Tehran.

80. Nasir al-Daula, the Iranian government agent in Sistan, to the Iranian Ministry of Foreign Affairs concerning the sale of Iranian women as *kanīzān* to Afghans in Sistan, Shaʿban 1335, 293001109, SAM, Tehran.

81. Mansur al-Mulk to the Iranian government's agent in Sistan, Shaʿban 4, 1335, Q1335.47.29.7, VUK, Tehran.

82. Akbar to the Ministry of Foreign Affairs in Tehran, Shaʿban 2, 1335, Q1335.47.29.6, VUK; see Indrani Chatterjee, *Gender, Slavery and Law in Colonial India* (New Delhi: Oxford University Press, 2002).

83. What this meant in practice was that enslaved people owners in the parts of India under direct British rule could no longer use East India Company courts to recover runaway enslaved people. Harms, "Introduction," 11.

84. Nasrullah Mushir al-Daula, the minister of foreign affairs, to the government of Bushehr, Rajab 8, 1322, Q1322.3.4, VUK, Tehran.

85. Sayyid Jaʿfar to Hesam al-Sadat, governor of Lengeh, Sh. 1300, 293001106, SAM, Tehran.

86. The Ministry of Foreign Affairs of Iran to the government agent in Lengeh, Sh. 1300, 293001106, SAM, Tehran; a letter from the Ministry of the Interior to the southern ports, 293001106, SAM, Tehran.

87. See the Ministry of the Interior to the Ministry of War, Sh. 1303 293001107, SAM, Tehran. These efforts brought to an end the independent rule of Sardar Dost Muhammad Khan in Bampur and Saravan. Arfa, *Under Five Shahs*, 254.

88. ʿAbbas Eram, the Ministry of Interior, the government of Lengeh, to the government of the Persian Gulf ports, Sh. 1306, 293001105, SAM, Tehran.

89. Lesan al-Mulk, *Nasekh al-tawarikh*, 2:682–690.

90. Ibid., 1:135.

91. Lambton, *Landlord and Peasant in Persia*, 139.

92. Fraser, *A Winter's Journey*, 2:26; Lesan al-Mulk, *Nasekh al-tawarikh*, 1:485. See also request to the shah for the liberation of an enslaved Iranian, 1252–1255, 295000476, SAM, Tehran.

93. Lesan al-Mulk, *Nasekh al-tawarikh*, 1:496.

94. Arfa, *Under Five Shahs*, 1; Mustaufi, *Sharh-i zendegani-yi man*, 1:28, 101.

95. Muhammad Hasan Khan Eʿtemad al-Saltana, *Sadr al-tawarikh* (Tehran: Vahid, 1349), 130.

96. Lorimer, *Gazetteer of the Persian Gulf*, 1: pt. 2, 1968, 1997; Eʿtemad al-Saltana, *Sadr al-tawarikh*, 173; Mehdi Quli Khan Hedayat, *Guzaresh-i Iran*, 71.

97. Lesan al-Mulk, *Nasekh al-tawarikh*, 3:976–1056, 1101; Reza Quli Khan Hedayat, *Tarikh-i ruzat al-safa*, 10:393–395; Muhammad Yusuf Riyazi Heravi, *ʿAyn al-waqayah*, ed. Muhammad Asef Fekrat (Tehran: Sahand, 1372), 44, 52; see also *Vaqayʿe Ettefaqiye*, no. 409 (25 Rabiʿ al-Thani, 1275): 4.

98. Mehdi Quli Khan Hedayat, *Guzaresh-i Iran*, 76.

99. Mirpanjeh, *Khaterat-i esarat*, 91; Lesan al-Mulk, *Nasekh al-tawarikh*, 3:1129. See Tabanda Gunabadi, *Nabegha-yi ʿelm va ʿerfan*, 13. For a comparison with the enslavement of Muslims in Africa, see Humphrey Fisher, *Slavery in the History of Muslim Black Africa* (London: Hurst, 2001).

100. Lesan al-Mulk, *Nasekh al-tawarikh*, 3:1129; Reza Quli Khan Hedayat, *Sefarat nama-yi Khawrazm* (Tehran: Tahuri, 1356), 66; Reza Quli Khan Hedayat, *Tarikh-i ruzat al-safa*, 10:24.

101. Lesan al-Mulk, *Nasekh al-tawarikh*, 3:1129.

102. Ibid.

103. Muhamad ʿAli ʿAla' al-Saltana to the Minister of the Interior, Safar 22, 1325, Q1325.11.7, VUK, Tehran.

104. Mushir al-Daula to Mustufi al-Mamalek, the minister of war, Ramadan 30, 1325, Q1325.11.3, VUK, Tehran.

105. Mushir al-Daula to the Russian embassy, Ramadan 26, 1325, Q1325.11.7, VUK, Tehran; Mushir al-Daula to Taqarub al-Mulk, the governor of Sanandaj, Ramadan 26, 1325, Q1325.11.7, VUK, Tehran; the Iranian government's agent in Quchan to the central government, Shaʿban 7, 1325, Q1325.11.7, VUK, Tehran; a letter from Ismaʿil, the Iranian government's agent in Ashgabat, Rabiʿ al-Awwal 18, 1325, Q1325.11.7, VUK, Tehran.

106. Najd al-Saltana to the minister of the interior, Mashhad, Rabiʿ al-Awwal 1325, Q1325.11.7, VUK, Tehran.

107. A letter from the Iranian government's agent in Khorasan and Sistan, Rabiʿ al-Thani 29, 1325, Q1325.11.7, VUK, Tehran; Mushir al-Daula to the Iranian government's agent in ʿArabistan [Khuzistan], Shawwal 17, 1325, Q1325.11.7, VUK, Tehran.

108. On one occasion, after a group of sold Iranian women were returned to their families, the two principal slave dealers, Mirza Baluch and Hasan Kermanshahani, were captured and handed over to the Iranian government. The embassy of the Russian Empire at the Iranian court to the prime minister, Shaʿban 22, 1326, Q1326.23.47, VUK, Tehran; the Ministry of Foreign Affairs to the prime minister, Shaʿban 22, 1326, Q1326.23.47, VUK, Tehran; the Iranian government's agent to Rokn al-Daula, the governor of Khorasan, Shaʿban 26, 1326, Q1326.23.47, VUK, Tehran.

109. Eʿtezam al-Mulk, the Iranian government's agent in Sarakhs, to the Ministry of Foreign Affairs of Iran in Tehran, Shawwal 28, 1327, Q1327.22.12, VUK, Tehran.

110. For instance, fortifications were built around the villages in Kerman. Benjamin, *Persia and the Persians*, 51. See also Riyazi Heravi, *ʿAyn al-waqayah*, 99.

111. See Homa Katouzian, *State and Society in Iran: The Eclipse of the Qajars and the Emergence of the Pahlavis* (London: I.B. Tauris, 2000), 29–33. The girls were often sold to Armenian and Turcoman traders, who took them to slave markets in Central Asia.

112. See Ann Lambton, "Secret Societies and the Persian Revolution of 1905–1906," *St Antony's Paper* 4 (1958): 43–63; Fereydun Adamiyat, *Fekr-i demokrasi-yi ejtemaʿi dar nehzat-i mashrutiyat-i Iran* (Tehran: Payam, 1363), 11; Mikhail Sergeevich Ivanov, *Enqelab-i mashrutiyat-i Iran*, trans. Kazem Ansari (Tehran: Amir Kabir, 2537), 38; Ghulamreza Varahram, *Nezam-i siasi va sazmanha-yi ejtemaʿi-yi Iran dar ʿasre Qajar* (Tehran: Muʿin, 1367), 397–402; and Esmaʿil Ra'in, *Anjumanha-yi serri dar enqelab-i mashrutiyat-i Iran* (Tehran: Javidan, 2535), 157.

113. Toledano, "Ottoman Concepts of Slavery," 48.

114. Adamiyat, *Ide'uluzhi-yi nehzat-i mashrutiyat-i Iran*, 28; Hamid Algar, *Religion and State in Iran, 1785–1906: The Role of the Ulama in the Qajar Period* (Berkeley: University of California Press, 1969), 184–204. See also Nikki R. Keddie, *An Islamic Response to Imperialism: Political and Religious Writings of Sayyid Jamal ad-Din "al-Afghani"* (Berkeley: University of California Press, 1968).

115. Hairi, *Shīʿism and Constitutionalism in Iran*, 13.

116. Fereydun Adamiyat, *Andisheha-yi Mirza Fathʿali Akhundzada* (Tehran: Khawrazmi, 1349), 157.

117. Hairi, *Shī'ism and Constitutionalism in Iran*, 26. Mirza Fath 'Ali Akhund Zadeh (1812–1878) came from an Iranian-Caucasian family in Shaki.

118. Ibid., 27.

119. Ibid., 37.

120. Erdem, *Slavery in the Ottoman Empire*, 125.

121. Hairi, *Shī'ism and Constitutionalism in Iran*, 38–43.

122. Hamid Algar, *Mīrzā Malkum Khān* (Berkeley: University of California Press, 1973), 29, 187; Hairi, *Shī'ism and Constitutionalism*, 38.

123. Toledano, *As If Silent and Absent*, 16.

124. Habl al-Matin was one such author. Najmabadi, *The Story of the Daughters of Qu-chan*, 35, 39, 79.

125. Ervand Abrahamian, *A History of Modern Iran* (Cambridge and New York: Cambridge University Press, 2008), 46.

126. *Iran-i No*, no. 45 (20 October, 1909): 2.

127. Ibid., no. 46 (21 October, 1909): 2.

128. Ibid., no. 47 (23 October, 1909): 2.

129. Mongol Bayat, *Iran's First Revolution: Shi'ism and the Constitutional Revolution of 1905–1909* (New York and Oxford: Oxford University Press, 1991), 168.

130. *Nedā-yi Vatan*, no. 12 (February 26, 1907): 1–7, and no. 18 (March 26, 1907): 1–5, and no. 23 (April 16, 1907): 5–7, and no. 25 (April 27, 1907): 6, 7, and no. 36 (June 15, 1907): 7,8, and no. 44 (July 17, 1907): 2, and no. 58 (September 17, 1907): 3, and no. 104 (November 12, 1907): 3.

131. Ibid., no. 21 (April 9, 1907): 1–3, and no. 22 (April 13, 1907): 1–3.

132. 'Abdulkarim Sultan, in Qa'enat, to Mirza Ja'far Khan, Dhi al-Qa'da 1324, Q1324.3.3, vuk, Tehran.

133. Kermani, *Tarikh-i bidari*, 2:339, 376; Malekzada, *Tarikh-i enqelab*, 2:120–122.

134. Kermani, *Tarikh-i bidari*, 1:376.

135. Zargari Nejad, *Rasa'el mashrutiyat*, 304.

136. Ibid., 339–348.

137. Ibid., 435.

138. Ibid., 434.

139. Erdem, *Slavery in the Ottoman Empire*, 113–120.

140. The order of the shah, Ramadan 12, 1322, Q1322.3.4, vuk, Tehran.

141. The National Consultative Assembly of Iran to the minister of foreign affairs of Iran, Dhi al-Hajja 14, 1324, Q1324.3.3, vuk, Tehran; A letter from the Ministry of Foreign Affairs of Iran, the office in Russia, Dhi al-Hajja 18, 1324, Q1324.3.3, vuk, Tehran.

142. Nasrullah Mushir al-Daula, the minister of foreign affairs, to the Iranian government's agent at Bujnurd, Jamadi al-Awwal 5, 1323, Q1323.3.2, vuk, Tehran; Nasrullah Mushir al-Daula, the minister of foreign affairs, to the government of Khorasan, Dhi al-Qa'da 4, 1322, Q1322.3.4, vuk, Tehran; the Ministry of Foreign Affairs to the governor of Darreh Jaz, Rabi' al-Thani 24, 1323, Q1323.3.2, vuk.

143. Nasrullah Mushir al-Daula to Mushir al-Mulk, Rabi' al-Awwal 8, 1323, Q1323.3.2, vuk, Tehran; the Ministry of Foreign Affairs to the government of Khorasan, Rabi' al-Thani 24, 1323, Q1323.3.2, vuk; the Ministry of Foreign Affairs to the Iranian agents at Darreh Jaz and Kalat, Rabi' al-Awwal 1323, Q1323.3.2, vuk, Tehran; Nazem al-Mulk to the Iranian government's agent in Khorasan, Q1323.3.2, vuk, Tehran.

276 NOTES TO PAGES 173-175

144. Parliamentary discussions, Majlis, Ṣafar 18, 1325 (March 31, 1907); the report of the Iranian government's agent in Bujnurd, Shaʿban 19, 1324, Q1324.3.3, VUK, Tehran.

145. *Nedā-yi Vatan*, no. 27 (May 4, 1907): 1–3; Najmabadi, *The Story of the Daughters of Quchan*, 23; parliamentary discussions, Majlis, Rabi al-Awwal 13, 1325 (April 26, 1907).

146. Report on the sale of five Iranian women, and the order of the shah, Dhi al-Hajja 1323, Q1323.3.2, VUK, Tehran.

147. Najmabadi, *The Story of the Daughters of Quchan*, 5.

148. Parliamentary discussions, Majlis, Muharram 6, 1325 (February 19, 1907).

149. For instance, congregational imams stated that anyone who sold Muslims must be punished immediately. Parliamentary discussions, Majlis, Jamadi al-Thani 19, 1325 (July 30, 1907).

150. Parliamentary discussions, Majlis, Rabiʿ al-Awwal 13, 1325 (April 26, 1907).

151. Parliamentary discussions, Majlis, Rabiʿ al-Thani 1326 (May 1908).

152. Parliamentary discussions, Majlis, Muharram 13, 1325 (February 26, 1907); Parliamentary discussions, Majlis, Muharram 4, 1325 (February 17, 1907). This included a testimony of five thousand Iranian inhabitants from Ashgabat who confirmed that Quchani children were sold to Turcomans in the city.

153. Asef al-Daula was reported to have allowed the sale of 160 Quchani girls in a single day. Kermani, *Tarikh-i bidari*, 1:91–92; Ahmad Kasravi, *Tarikh-i mashruta-yi Iran* (Tehran: Amir Kabir, 1370), 226–228.

154. Najmabadi, *The Story of the Daughters of Quchan*, 95.

155. The representatives were Sayyid Hasan Taqizada, Aqa Muhammad Yazdi, Vakil al-Tujjar, Aqa Sayyid Mahdi, Aqa Mirza Mahmud Khaunsari, Aqa Sayyid Husayn Burujirdi, and Aqa Mirza Baba (see ibid., 98). A thousand people marched on the assembly in June 1907 to protest the situation and to demand action. Malekzada, *Tarikh-i enqelab*, 3:65.

156. Kasravi, *Tarikh-i mashruta-yi Iran*, 480. Asef al-Daula's son, Amir Husayn Khan, was also dismissed from his governmental post for a period of two years and was ordered to pay three thousand tomans. Similarly, Sardar Afkham, the governor of Astarabad, was also condemned for his negligence in turning a blind eye to the Turcomans' activities, fined five thousand tomans, and dismissed from his position for a year. Adamiyat, *Ide'uluzhi-yi nehzat-i mashrutiyat-i Iran*, 406; Najmabadi, *The Story of the Daughters of Quchan*, 25–26, 112.

157. Malekzada, *Tarikh-i enqelab*, 5:102; the minister of justice to ʿAla' al-Saltana, the minister of foreign affairs, Jamadi al-Awwal 6, 1325, Q1325.11.7, VUK, Tehran; the minister of justice to Shojaʿ al-Daula, Jamadi al-Awwal 13, 1325, 298001380, SAM, Tehran; the minister of justice to Asef al-Daula, Jamadi al-Awwal 4, 1325, 298001380, SAM, Tehran; the minister of justice to Sardar Mufakham, Jamadi al-Awwal 13, 1325, SAM, Tehran.

158. The practice of *tuyul* was the allocation of a tax to a person in lieu of salary by the government that often led to the extortion from the people and their enslavement. *Nedā-yi Vatan*, no. 20 (April 2, 1907): 1–4.

159. Muʿmeni, *Mas'ala-yi arzi va jang-i tabaqati dar Iran*, 87, 128.

160. Ibid., 129; Hundreds of groups like the democratic Reformist Society of Rasht (Firqi-yi Mujadidin-i Rasht) and the Society of Free Slaves in Jiruft and Kerman (*anjuman-i ghulāmān-i āzād-i Jīruft va Kirmān*) were meeting regularly to discuss issues pertaining to freedom, justice, and increasingly, nationalism. Grantovski et al., *Tarikh-i Iran*, 390.

161. Parliamentary discussions, Majlis, Rabiʿ al-Thani 1326 (May 1908).

162. Mehdi Quli Khan Hedayat, *Guzaresh-i Iran*, 221–224.

163. Chair of Majlis-i Shura-yi Melli to the Ministry of Finance concerning the release

of enslaved Quchanis from Russia, Jamadi al-Akhar 6, 1329, 240007042, SAM, Tehran. See *Iran-i No* (October 20, 1909): 2, (August 27, 1909): 3, (September 8, 1909): 3, (September 12, 1909): 2, (December 26, 1909): 2, (December 30, 1909): 2.

164. Arfa, *Under Five Shahs*, 167; Keith S. McLachlan, "Traditional Regions and National Frontiers of Iran: A General Overview," in *Boundary Politics and International Boundaries of Iran: With Afghanistan, Armenia, Azerbaijan Republic, Bahrain (the autonomous republic of Ganjah), Iraq, Kazakhstan, Kuwait, Oman, Pakistan, Qatar, Russia, Saudi Arabia, Turkey, Turkmenistan, and the United Arab Emirates*, ed. Pirouz Mojtahed-Zadeh (Boca Raton: Universal Publishers, 2006), 30.

165. Arfa, *Under Five Shahs*, 172–183.

166. Shōkō, *The Development of Large-Scale Farming*, 7–9.

167. Suzanne Miers, "The Anti-Slavery Game: Britain and the Suppression of Slavery in Africa and Arabia, 1890–1975," in *Slavery, Diplomacy and Empire: Britain and the Suppression of the Slave Trade, 1807–1975*, ed. Keith Hamilton and Patrick Salmon (Brighton: Sussex Academic Press, 2009), 207. See also Government of India to India Office, Whitehall, London, S.W.I., February 25, 1924, FO 371/9531, NAUK, London.

168. Mohamad Tavakoli-Targhi, *Refashioning Iran: Orientalism, Occidentalism and Historiography* (Basingstoke: Palgrave Macmillan, 2001), x.

169. Tavakoli-Targhi, *Refashioning Iran*, xi, xiv, 96.

170. Robert Clive to Austen Chamberlain, Tehran, received February 4, 1929, FO 371/13791, NAUK, London. Although earlier, the decision to implement abolitionist policies by Mustafa Kemal Ataturk in 1925 was informed by a similar desire to establish a cohesive national identity. Durugönül, "Construction of Identity and Integration of African-Turks," in *African Communities in Asia*, 287; From Foreign Office, "Slavery in Arabia," dated April 11, 1930, FO 371/14475, NAUK, London.

171. In 1904, 1910, and 1921, Iran signed international agreements on the abolition of the trade of women and children (agreement to ban the trade of women, Ministry of Foreign Affairs, 21,1,1313, 310000092, SAM, Tehran). Iran was one of the thirty-six signatories of the 1926 Slavery Convention signed at Geneva. See Miers, *Slavery in the Twentieth Century*, 128–130.

172. From Sir R. Clive, Anglo-Persian relations in Persian Gulf, Tehran, dated January 8, 1929, FO 371/13775, NAUK, London; From H. M.'s Minister, Tehran to H. M.'s Secretary of State for Foreign Affairs, London, dated January 15, 1929, R/15/1/225, BL, London.

173. Foreign Office, memorandum, Anglo-Persian Slavery Convention of 1882, September 27, 1929, FO 371/13791, NAUK, London.

174. "By that Convention, British cruisers are allowed to visit and detain merchant vessels under the Persian flag, or belonging to Persian subjects, who are suspected of carrying slaves; and if any slaves are found on board, the vessels, with all on board, is taken before the nearest Persian authorities for trial." From India Office, "Slavery in Persian Gulf as affected by Anglo-Persian treaty negotiations," dated April 21, 1928, FO 371/13068, NAUK, London; From Foreign Office minute, Mr. Baxter, "Possibility of cancelling or replacing Anglo-Persian slavery convention of 1882," dated June 6, 1928, FO 371/13068, NAUK, London.

175. Zdanowski, *Slavery and Manumission*, 294.

176. From the Undersecretary of State for India, Political Department, to Austen Chamberlain, Foreign Office, London, January 26, 1929, FO 371/13791, NAUK, London.

177. From Viceroy, Foreign & Political Department, to Secretary of State for India, dated July 10, 1928, FO 371/13068, NAUK, London.

178. Foreign Office, memorandum, "Anglo-Persian Slavery Convention of 1882," September 27, 1929, FO 371/13791, NAUK, London; Pirouz Mojtahed-Zadeh, "Iran's Maritime Boundaries in the Persian Gulf: The Case of Abu Musa Island," in *The Boundaries of Modern Iran*, ed. Keith McLaclan (New York: St. Martin's Press, 1994), 103.

179. Telegram from Sir Robert Clive, Tehran, "Proposed revision of Anglo-Persian Slavery Convention," dated January 15, 1929, FO 371/13791, NAUK, London.

180. Zdanowski, *Slavery and Manumission*, 296.

181. Teymurtash was not convinced this new agreement differed fundamentally from the 1882 iteration. Abdulhusain Teymurtash to Robert Clive, Tehran, January 13, 1929, FO 371/13791, NAUK, London.

182. Telegram from Robert Clive, "Revision of Anglo-Persian slavery convention: right of search," Tehran, dated February 14, 1929, FO 371/13791, NAUK, London; Cypher telegram to Robert Clive, Tehran, Foreign Office, March 15, 1929, FO 371/13791, NAUK, London.

183. Parliamentary discussions, the seventh period, Majlis, Bahman 18, 1307 (February 7, 1929).

184. Robert Clive to Austen Chamberlain, His Majesty's Principal Secretary of State for Foreign Affairs, Foreign Office, Tehran, February 23, 1929, FO 371/13791, NAUK, London.

185. Parliamentary discussions, the seventh period, Majlis, Bahman 18, 1307 (February 7, 1929). Ra'in, *Daryanavardi-yi Iranian*, 2:706–710.

186. The decree of the Ministry of the Interior, 25, 12, 1307, 290/8034/3 (March 16, 1929), SAM, Tehran.

187. The Ministry of the Interior, South Office, to the government of Isfahan, 25/12/1307 (March 16, 1929), 291/2472/2, SAM, Tehran.

188. The Ministry of the Interior to the government of the ports and islands of the Persian Gulf and Dashti and Dashtestan, 16/6/1310 (September 8, 1931), 290/8034/1, SAM, Tehran.

189. Erdem, *Slavery in the Ottoman Empire and Its Demise*, 94.

190. Nasrine Abiad, *Sharia, Muslim States and International Human Rights Treaty Obligations: A Comparative Study* (London: British Institute of International and Comparative Law, 2008), 32.

191. See Madia J. A. Thomson, *The Demise of Slavery in Southwestern Morocco, 1860–2000: Economic Modernization and the Transformation of Social Hierarchy* (Lewiston: The Edwin Mellen Press, 2010). In Tazerwalt, the imposition of capitalism by the French protectorate created a wage economy that "released" enslaved people from agricultural bondage. As the "number of slaves . . . dwindled, . . . the institution eventually died a natural death," describes El Hamel (*Black Morocco*, 268).

192. Hilary Charlesworth, "The Challenges of Human Rights Law for Religious Traditions," in *Religion and International Law*, ed. Mark W. Janis and Carolyn Evans (Boston: M. Nijhoff, 1999), 405.

193. Zdanowski, *Slavery and Manumission*, 250.

194. Toledano, "Abolition and Anti-Slavery in the Ottoman Empire," 133.

CHAPTER 8. EMANCIPATION

1. It has been suggested that some of these conventions may have been influenced by non-Arabic pre-Islamic precedents such as the Roman law of debt slavery and the patron-client relationship in which the freed person and his or her descendants are bound forever to the manumitter. Ulrike Mitter, "Unconditional Manumission of Slaves in Early Islamic

Law: A Ḥadīth Analysis," in *The Formation of the Classical Islamic World*, ed. Wael B. Hallaq (Aldershot: Ashgate Publishing, 2004), 27:117–149; Patricia Crone, *Roman, Provincial and Islamic Law* (Cambridge: Cambridge University Press, 1987), 64–76; see Qur'an 9:60 (Tehran: Salihi, 1354).

2. Polak, *Persien*, 1:250.

3. The interrogation of the *kanīz* dealer Mirza Aqa by the Ministry of Foreign Affairs of Iran, 1332, Q1332.3.3, VUK, Tehran; Sabzʿali Esfahani, *Vajizat al-tahrir*, 67–68.

4. The daughter of the Prophet Muhammad.

5. Munavar al-Saltana, freedom letter, 1302, 296/11036/1, SAM, Tehran.

6. Governments guided by the shariʿa were entitled to use zakat, or alms, in eight situations, one of which was the payment of ransom for enslaved people. Qur'an 9:60.

7. See Qur'an 24:33; Joseph Schacht, *An Introduction to Islamic Law* (Oxford: Clarendon Press, 1964), 127; Husayni, *Bardegi az didgah-i Islam*, 28.

8. Ennaji, *Slavery, the State, and Islam*, 23–26; Erdem, *Slavery in the Ottoman Empire*, 152–154.

9. There were various Qur'anic verses (58:3, 5:89, and 4:92) that provided justification for emancipation, usually in terms of a penalty against masters. For instance, liberation was obligatory as religious expiation (*kaffāra*) for not fulfilling a Ramadan fast or not acting on undertaken vows (the law of *ṣadaqa*). An enslaved person was to be freed if owned by an unmarriageable relative or *maḥram* (the law of *tamalluk arḥām*, or of being in a degree of consanguinity precluding marriage). The *umm walad*, or an enslaved female who gives birth to the child of her owner, would become free after the death of her master (the law of *istilād*). According to chapter 24, verse 33 of the Qur'an, enslaved people also had the right to purchase their freedom through work (the law of *mukātibah*). Schacht, *An Introduction to Islamic Law*, 129; Muhammad Hamidullah, *Introduction to Islam* (Paris: Centre Culturel Islamique, 1957), 127; and Husayni, *Bardegi az didgah-i Islam*, 39–43; see also Thomas F. McDow, "Deeds of Freed Slaves: Manumission and Economic and Social Mobility in Pre-Abolition Zanzibar," in *Indian Ocean Slavery in the Age of Abolition*, ed. Robert Harms, Bernard K. Freamon, and David W. Blight (New Haven: Yale University Press, 2013); Zdanowski, *Slavery and Manumission*, 65.

10. Gwyn Campbell, "Female Bondage and Agency in the Indian Ocean World," in *African Communities in Asia*, 56. See also Erdem, *Slavery in the Ottoman Empire*, 152–184.

11. Durugönül, "Construction of Identity and Integration of African-Turks," in *African Communities in Asia*, 285.

12. Segal, *Islam's Black Slaves*, 9.

13. McMahon, *Slavery and Emancipation in Islamic East Africa*, 3.

14. By contrast, it was common practice for Europeans to own enslaved people in other Middle Eastern societies such as Egypt. See George Michael La Rue, "'My Ninth Master was a European': Enslaved Blacks in European Households in Egypt, 1798–1848," in *Race and Slavery in the Middle East: Histories of Trans-Saharan Africans in Nineteenth-Century Egypt, Sudan, and the Ottoman Mediterranean*, ed. Terence Walz and Kenneth M. Cuno (Cairo: American University in Cairo Press, 2010).

15. Schacht, *An Introduction to Islamic Law*, 127; Husayni, *Bardegi az didgah-i Islam*, 28. See Qur'an 24:33.

16. Ennaji, *Slavery, the State, and Islam*, 4, 22.

17. Minutes of evidence presented before the royal commission, March 11, 1875, AA12/2, ZNL.

18. Sheil, *Life and Manners in Persia*, 244. In the case of newly arrived enslaved Africans, it is possible they did not request their freedom because of linguistic barriers, social isolation, and unfamiliarity with the new society. By the end of the century, most of these enslaved people would have lived in the country long enough to have assimilated and be familiar with their rights.

19. Ameer Ali, *Personal Law of the Mahommedans*, 38; Husayni, *Bardegi az didgah-i Islam*, 42.

20. The statement of Firuz ibn Almas, May 26, 1927, 293001105, SAM, Tehran.

21. In another example, the enslaved Masʿud was treated well by his first master, but his second master's maltreatment forced him to flee. The statement of Masʿud, May 26, 1927, 293001105, SAM, Tehran.

22. Mrima refers to the coast in Kiswahili, in this case, the coast from about Tanga to Dar es Salaam.

23. Statement of a woman named Khyzaran, age twenty-two, seized by the agent at Lingah as an enslaved person, July 24, 1856, FO 248/168, NAUK, London.

24. Husayni, *Bardegi az didgah-i Islam*, 46.

25. A report by W. A. Smart, British legation, Tehran, Dhi al-Qaʿda 7, 1326, Q1326.3.25, VUK, Tehran.

26. A letter by Nasrullah Mushir al-Daula, the minister of foreign affairs, Muharram 4, 1323, Q1323.3.2, VUK, Tehran.

27. Schacht, *An Introduction to Islamic Law*, 130.

28. Minutes of evidence presented before the royal commission, March 11, 1875, AA12/2, ZNL.

29. The statement of Zivar ibn Mabruk, May 26, 1927, 293001105, SAM, Tehran.

30. Aghassee to Sheil, May 12, 1847, L/PS/5/451, BL; Muhammad Shah to Haji Mirza Aqasi, 1263, Q1263.6.5, VUK, Tehran; Justin Sheil to Hajee Meerza Aghassee, May 15, 1847, L/PS/5/451, BL, London.

31. The British government to the Iranian government, Ramadan 21, 1266, Q1263.6.15, VUK, Tehran.

32. Justin Sheil to Meerza Aghassee, December 13, 1846, FO 84/647, NAUK, London. The extent to which the situation was complicated is revealed in correspondence from the khan of Khiva to John McNeil in May 1842: "If the Shah of Persia possessed with royal dignity had been submissively desirous and anxious for peace and union, doubtless he would first have released our captives and he would have issued imperative orders to his own commanders to desist" (FO 60/90, NAUK, London). See also Mirpanjeh, *Khaterat-i esarat*, 79.

33. ʿArez Muhammad ibn ʿAlinaqi, an inhabitant of Sang Sefid, to the Council for the Investigation of Grievances, Sabzvar, the reign of Nasir al-Din Shah, 1301, 2929-447, summary of requests, Majlis-i tahqiq-i Mazalem, KMDT, Tehran; Fraser, *Narrative of a Journey into Khorasan*, 276, 278.

34. Fraser, *Narrative of a Journey into Khorasan*, 276–277. Vambéry described the sad circumstances of one Iranian family: his "wife and the two smallest of the children as well as his sister had perished from the hardships of slavery, and of the four remaining children he could purchase the freedom of only the two younger ones." *Arminius Vambéry*, 270.

35. And if fears of re-enslavement were not enough, many were required to pay customs tolls on the way home. Vambéry, *Arminius Vambéry*, 269–271; Mirpanjeh, *Khaterat-i esarat*, 90.

36. Mirpanjeh, *Khaterat-i esarat*, 79; the Iranian government to the British government, Shawwal 8, 1278, Q1278.9.20, VUK.

37. Edward Granville Browne, *A Year amongst the Persians* (1893; repr., London: Adam and Charles Black, 1959), 399.

38. Najm al-Saltana to the Ministry of Foreign Affairs, Rajab 5, 1332, Q1332.3.3, VUK.

39. '*Itq*, or *i'tāq*, is the Arabic term for manumission.

40. Samuel Hennell, resident in the Persian Gulf, to Arthur Malet, September 25, 1849, L/PS/5/462, BL, London.

41. Sheik Nasir, the governor of Bushire, to Major Samuel Hennell, resident in the Persian Gulf, September 25, 1849, L/PS/5/462, BL, London.

42. A. Le Messurier, advocate general, to Arthur Malet, November 19, 1849, L/PS/5/462, BL, London.

43. Sedr Azim to Taylour Thomson, October 13, 1854, L/PS/5/483, BL, London.

44. The Iranian government to the British embassy, Shawwal 24, 1278, Q1278.9.20, VUK, Tehran.

45. Précis on the slave trade in the Gulf of Oman and the Persian Gulf, 1873–1905, "Reception of Fugitive Slaves on Board Her Majesty's Ships of War and Other British Vessels," January 1874, L/PS/20/C246, BL, London.

46. Landowners of Baluchistan to Naser al-Daula, 1289, Q1289.14.19, VUK; Lorimer, *Gazetteer of the Persian Gulf*, 1: pt. 2, 2511, and pt. 1A, 615; see also a letter by Ahmad Khan, the agent at Bushehr, Dhi al-Qa'dah 9, 1288, Q1288.13.29, VUK.

47. Arnold, *Through Persia by Caravan*, 432.

48. The British had consulates, navy offices, telegraph stations, and commercial centers throughout the southern ports and islands in Iran to which fugitive enslaved people escaped. Reports on southern ports, 1311–1317, 293004045, SAM, 1; Lorimer, *Gazetteer of the Persian Gulf*, 1: pt. 2, 2514.

49. The Foreign Office describes enslaved people voluntarily returning to their masters after being exiled during the Hijaz war of 1924–1925. Foreign Office, "Slavery in Arabia," dated April 11, 1930, FO 371/14475, NAUK, London.

50. McMahon, *Slavery and Emancipation in Islamic East Africa*, 4, 51.

51. Ibid., 4; see also Harms, "Introduction."

52. Miers, "Slave Rebellion and Resistance in the Aden Protectorate," 104–106.

53. Thomson to Earl of Derby, May 23, 1876, FO 84/1450, NAUK.

54. Précis on the slave trade in the Gulf of Oman and the Persian Gulf, 1873–1905, "The Rokeby case," 1877, L/PS/20/C246, BL, London.

55. Ibid.

56. Wright, *The English amongst the Persians*, 70.

57. A letter from Farhad in Shiraz to Sepahsalar A'zam in Tehran, Rabi' al-Thani 19, 1294, Q1292.15.22, VUK, Tehran.

58. 'Ala' al-Saltana, the minister of foreign affairs, to Nezam al-Saltana, the Iranian government's agent in Shiraz, Ramadan 2, 1325, Q1325.3.8, VUK, Tehran.

59. Political Department, General Act of the Brussels Conference, June 8, 1891, R/15/1/199, BL, article 64. Article 62 was titled "Countries Whose Institutions Recognized Domestic Slavery."

60. Ibid., article 63.

61. The statement of Agha Bashir, June 23, 1899, Q1317.3.4, VUK, Tehran.

62. *'Abīd* means enslaved people, but here it refers to the abolitionist *firmān*s.

63. The minister plenipotentiary to Mushir al-Daula, Dhi al-Hajjah 1316, Q1317.3.4, VUK, Tehran.

64. Correspondence of the minister of foreign affairs regarding Agha Bashir, Safar 25, 1317, Q1317.3. 4, VUK, Tehran.

65. Ibid.

66. The freedom letter of Agha Bashir issued by the British embassy, Safar 14, 1317, Q1317.3.4, VUK, Tehran.

67. The British consulate to the Iranian government, Shawwal 23, 1323, Q1323.3.2, VUK, Tehran.

68. The British consulate to the agent of the Ministry of Foreign Affairs in Fars, Shawwal 8, 1323, Q1323.3.2, VUK, Tehran; Manshur al-Saltana in Shiraz to Mushir al-Daula, the minister of foreign affairs in Tehran, Shawwal 9, 1323, Q1323.3.2, VUK, Tehran.

69. Correspondence regarding Jamila, Muharram 26, 1324, Q1324.3.3, VUK, Tehran.

70. A telegraph on the issue of *kanīz* and *ghulām* by Muhammad 'Ali, the officer in Bushehr, Sha'ban 5, 1319, Q1319.3.4, VUK, Tehran.

71. 'Ala' al-Saltana to the Iranian government's agent in Shiraz, Rabi' al-Thani 26, 1325, Q1325.3.8, VUK, Tehran.

72. Wilson, *The Persian Gulf*, 224.

73. The statement of an enslaved named Ambar, January 26, 1906, R/15/1/203, BL, London.

74. The Persian Foreign Office agent to HBM's consul general, February 15, 1906, R/15/1/203, BL, London.

75. The shah to Atabak-i A'zam, Muharram 26, 1324, Q1324.3.3, VUK, Tehran.

76. For instance, in 1909, the Iranian government issued a freedom letter to Firuz Khan, an enslaved eunuch, indicating that thereafter he could be involved in any social and economic activity in Iran he desired. Sa'd al-Daula, the letter of freedom issued by the Ministry of Foreign Affairs, Jamadi al-Thani 14, 1327, Q1327.3.18, VUK, Tehran.

77. Nasrullah Mushir al-Daula to Manshur al-Saltana, the government agent at Shiraz, Jamadi al-Awwal 15, 1323, Q1323.13.12, VUK, Tehran.

78. The inhabitants of Lengeh to the Iranian government, 1323, Q1323.14.4, VUK.

79. The British consulate in Shiraz to the Iranian government, Sha'ban 1324, Q1324.3.3, VUK, Tehran; Nasrullah Mushir al-Daula to Musaddeq al-Saltana, Safar 1324, Q1324.3.3, VUK, Tehran.

80. Nastaran Baji Habashia to the British consulate, 1328, Q1328.3.1.39, VUK.

81. Lar merchants to the Iranian government, Jamadi al-Awwal 24, 1323, Q1323.14.4, VUK, Tehran. One report went so far as to suggest that Badr "liberated" enslaved Ethiopians and Georgians for his own sexual gratification, subsequently releasing the pregnant ones and selling the others back to their owners.

82. Sir Charles Harding at the British embassy in London to the Iranian government, Rabi' al-Akhar 14, 1324, Q1323.14.4, VUK, Tehran.

83. An honorific title meaning the proof of Islam, referring to religious scholars and leaders.

84. Nasrullah Mushir al-Daula to the hujjat al-Islam Shari'atmadar, Dhi al-Hajja 16, 1323, Q1323.14.4, VUK, Tehran; extract from the telegraph from London to Mushir al-Daula, Rabi' al-Awwal 14, 1324, Q1323.14.4, VUK, Tehran.

85. The Ministry of Foreign Affairs to the deputy of the royal court, Rabiʻ al-Awwal 26, 1335, Q1335.3.13, VUK, Tehran.

86. The shah's eunuchs who escaped were Agha Juhar Khan, Eqbal Khan, Surur Khan, Bashir Khan, Saʻid Khan, Yaqut Khan, and Bahram Khan. Mushir al-Daula, the eunuchs' letters of freedom, Dhi al-Qaʻda 29, 1325, VUK, Tehran; Mushir al-Daula to the British consulate, Dhi al-Hajja 2, 1325, Q1325.3.8, VUK, Tehran.

87. The British consulate to the Iranian government, Ramadan 5, 1323, Q1323.3.2, VUK, Tehran.

88. Nasrullah Mushir al-Daula to the Grand Lady in Tehran, Shaʻban 19, 1323, Q1323.3.2, VUK, Tehran. For similar stories, see the inhabitants of Lengeh to the Iranian government, 1323, Q1323.14.4, VUK.

89. ʻAbbasquli, on the issue of Haji ʻAbdulrahman Khartoumi, Muharram 16, 1323, Q1323.3.2, VUK, Tehran.

90. Nasrullah Mushir al-Daula to Sadr al-Mamalek, Muharram 4, 1323, Q1323.3.2, VUK, Tehran.

91. ʻAbdulrahman's master to Nasrullah Mushir al-Daula, Q1323.3.2, VUK, Tehran.

92. The British government to the Iranian government, Jamadi al-Thani 19, 1325, Q1325.3.8, VUK, Tehran.

93. "Slave Trade," the manumission of slaves and rules regarding cases arising out of the pearling industry, November 1918, R/15/1/234, BL, London; From W. F. Johnston, Political Resident, Persian Gulf and H. B. M.'s Consul General for Fars, British Residency and Consulate General to the Government of India, Bushire, April 26, 1929, FO 371/13791, NAUK, London.

94. Indeed, there were numerous cases of runaway enslaved people from the Arabian states who took refuge in British consulates in Iran. Sadid al-Saltana Kababi, *Sarzaminha-yi shumali*, 100.

95. The political resident in the Persian Gulf to the senior naval officer, Persian Gulf division, Bushire, January 31, 1921, R/15/1/221, BL, London.

96. Captain B. Pearson, senior naval officer in the Persian Gulf, to the political resident in the Persian Gulf, February 18, 1921, R/15/1/221, BL, London.

97. The British Resident in Masqat, for example, released Paishu Ramazan, but upon his arrival in Jask, he was resold in the Arabian Peninsula. A. S. in Jask to the director in Karachi, May 23, 1921, R/15/1/221, BL, London; see issue of manumission certificate to certain enslaved people on the Trucial Coast by the political agent, Bahrain; slavery: cases reported by British agency, Sharjah, 1947–1950, 143996 (British Library R/15/2/1840); and slave trade on the Trucial Coast, 1937–1938, 143997 (British Library R/15/2/1852), Juma Al Majid Centre for Culture and Heritage, Dubai, United Arab Emirates; From Samuel Hoare, Secretary at Tehran, Anglo-Persian treaty negotiations: Article X Slavery, dated February 24, 1932, FO 371/16075, NAUK, London.

98. "Slave Trade—Kidnapping of Baluchis on the Mekran Coast and Exporting Them for Sale on Oman and Trucial Coast," January 1921, R/15/1/221, BL, London. Religious injunctions were often cited as justification for this activity.

99. Trevor to Bray, Delhi, December 31, 1921, R/15/1/221, BL.

100. HBM's consul general to the British resident and consulate general, Bushire, October 15, 1929, FO 248/1387, NAUK.

101. See, for instance, the case of kidnapped Baluchis sold in Oman who escaped and re-

ceived a freedom letter at Bandar ʿAbbas but were re-enslaved after returning to the Arab states. The Ministry of Foreign Affairs of Iran to the government agent at Lengeh, Sh. 1300, 293001106, SAM.

102. The deputy secretary to the government of India in the Foreign and Political Department to the political resident in the Persian Gulf, Bushire, March 27, 1922, R/15/1/221, BL, London; Isa ben Abdol Latif, resident agent in Sharjah, to A. P. Trevor in Bushire, January 13, 1921, R/15/1/221, BL, London; Trevor to Bray, Delhi, December 31, 1921, R/15/1/221, BL. See also the Iranian Ministry of Foreign Affairs to the Ministry of the Interior regarding the British consulate's consent for liberating an Iranian who was enslaved by the Arabs in Dubai, Sh. 1306, 290001670, SAM, Tehran; "Slave Traffic on the Mekran Coast, Extract from Report of Commanding Officer, H.M.S. Cyclamen," October 21, 1921, R/15/1/221, BL, London.

103. It was not uncommon for *kadkhudās* (heads of villages) to challenge the liberation of enslaved people. "Statement of Shirin, Daughter of Firuz of Village Muhammadi, Rohilla, Dashtistan, Aged about 45 Years," January 2, 1937, R/15/1/203, BL, London.

104. Zdanowski, *Slavery and Manumission*, 255–310.

105. Resident agent in Bushire to the resident agent in Sharjah, November 29, 1921, R/15/1/221, BL, London.

106. Trevor to Bray, Delhi, December 31, 1921, R/15/1/221, BL.

107. For example, they signed an agreement with Shaykh Ahmad ibn ʿAbid, the ruler of Hengam, according to which they agreed not to liberate any runaway enslaved people from his territory in return for the safeguarding of their telegraph lines. Sadid al-Saltana Kababi, *Sarzaminha-yi shumali*, 355; *Bandar ʿAbbas*, 135.

108. The stories of enslaved female runaways, however, do provide valuable insight into the complex ways gender intersected with the process of emancipation.

109. John H. Sinclair, records on slavery, 1897, AB71/1, ZNL, Zanzibar. For a discussion on the emancipation of enslaved females in Sudan, see Ahmad A. Sikainga, "Shariʿa Courts and the Manumission of Female Slaves in the Sudan, 1898–1939," *International Journal of African Historical Studies* 28, no. 1 (1995).

110. Paul E. Lovejoy and Jan S. Hogendorn, *Slow Death for Slavery* (Cambridge: Cambridge University Press, 1993), 98–119; see also Firuz the black *ghulām* to the British consulate, Rabiʿ al-Thani, 1333, Q1332.3.3, VUK, Tehran.

111. Request by a *kanīz* for pension, 1287, 295002935, SAM, Tehran.

112. These women were only released in cases of cruelty. McMahon, *Slavery and Emancipation in Islamic East Africa*, 50; Harms, "Introduction," 12. Harms has suggested, "The practical result of Britain's delegalization policy was that emancipation in the western Indian Ocean came to be seen as something bestowed upon certain favored individuals and not as a right that applied to an entire category of people" ("Introduction," 12).

113. A report from Abdullah, an agent of the British consulate on Firuz, 1333, Q1332.3.3, VUK, Tehran.

114. Najm al-Daula, *Asar-i Najm al-Daula*, 116.

115. Sadid al-Saltana Kababi, *Sarzaminha-yi shumali*, 50. During the author's fieldwork in several villages located in Bushehr Province (2000–2012), it became clear that entertaining at weddings is still one of the main occupations of Afro-Iranians. Here, groups of up to fifteen liberated *kanīzān* played round drums (*dayerehā*), sang, and danced at weddings and other festivities.

116. Mafi, *Khatirat va asnad*, 2:123–124.

117. Report on two refugee enslaved women at the British consulate, 1315, Q1315.31.3, VUK, Tehran. See also Iranian government report on a runaway enslaved female with her eleven-year-old daughter, Ramadan 28, 1317, Q1315.31.3, VUK, Tehran. Notably, when they escaped with children conceived by their masters, manumission certificates were issued for both the mother and her children.

118. The owner of Gulchehreh, a *kanīz*, to the Ministry of Foreign Affairs, the British office, Rabiʿ al-Awwal 1332, Q1331.3.5.13, VUK, Tehran.

119. The name Habashi denotes that she was from Habash, which today is Ethiopia.

120. The Ministry of Foreign Affairs to Vaseq al-Mulk, 1317, Q1317 3.4, VUK, Tehran.

121. Mushir al-Daula, the decree of the Ministry of Foreign Affairs to Vaseq al-Mulk, 1317, Q1317.3.4, VUK, Tehran. Around this time, four African *kanīzān* who belonged to Muʿddel al-Saltana took sanctuary at the holy shrine of Hazrat-i ʿAbdul ʿAzim in Ray. Mushir al-Mulk (Mushir al-Daula) to Muʿyyd al-Daula, Rabiʿ al-Awwal 13, 1317, Q1317.20.25, VUK, Tehran.

122. Captain Richard Birdwood, assistant to the British consulate, to the Persian Foreign Office agent, Bushire, August 29, 1913, 1 (86), BISB, Bushehr.

123. ʿAli to Mushir al-Daula, Muharram 17, 1317, Q1317.3.4, VUK, Tehran.

124. ʿAli to Mushir al-Daula, Rabiʿ al-Thani 13, 1317, Q1317.3.4, VUK, Tehran.

125. The agency of ʿAbbasi and Lengeh, report, Dhi al-Qaʿdah 6, 1319, Q1319.3.4, VUK, Tehran.

126. Nasrullah Mushir al-Daula to Abdulmalek, the governor of Kerman and Baluchistan, Dhi al-Hajjah 25, 1319, Q1319.3.4, VUK, Tehran.

127. Nasrullah Mushir al-Daula to ʿAbdulmalek, the governor of Kerman and Baluchistan, Jamadi al-Awwal 28, 1319, Q1319.3.4, VUK, Tehran.

128. Qurʾan 24:32.

129. Qurʾan 4:25.

130. Husayni, *Bardegi az didgah-i Islam*, 40.

131. Ibid.; John Hunwick, "African Slaves in the Mediterranean World: A Neglected Aspect of the African Diaspora," in Harris, *Global Dimensions of the African Diaspora*, 308–314.

132. Schacht, *An Introduction to Islamic Law*, 127.

133. Fraser, *Narrative of a Journey into Khorasan*, 13.

134. The shah to the grand vizier, Jamadi al-thani 1322, Q1322.3.4, VUK, Tehran.

135. The decree of ʿAli Akbar, 1322, Q1322.3.4, VUK, Tehran.

136. The decree of Husayn Razavi Qomi, 1322, Q1322.3.4, VUK, Tehran.

137. ʿAbulqasem Nilfurush to Nasrullah Mushir al-Daula, the minister of foreign affairs, Rabiʿ al-Awwal 3, 1319, Q1319.3.4, VUK, Tehran; Abulqasem Nilfurush in Shiraz to Nasrullah Mushir al-Daula, the minister of foreign affairs, in Tehran, Rabiʿ al-Awwal 3 and 27, Rabiʿ al-Thani 5, 1322, Q1322.3.4, VUK, Tehran.

138. Nasrullah Mushir al-Daula to Abulqasem Nilfurush, Rabiʿ al-Thani 9, 1322, Q1322. 3.4, VUK, Tehran; Abulqasem Nilfurush to Sadr-i ʿAzam, Shiraz, Rajab 10, Safar 16, 1322, Q1322.3.4, VUK, Tehran.

139. The testimonies of the ʿulamaʾ of Shiraz, Safar 30, 1322, Rabiʿ al-Thani 1, 1322, Q1322.3.4, VUK, Tehran.

140. The British consulate to the Iranian government, Jamadi al-Thani 10, 1322, Q1322. 3.4, VUK, Tehran.

141. The British consulate to the Iranian government, Rajab 11, 1322, Q1322.3.4, VUK, Tehran.

142. The British consulate to the Iranian official in Fars, Rabi' al-Thani 29, 1322, Q1322.3.4, VUK, Tehran; the British consulate to Haji 'Ezzulmulk, an official of the Foreign Affairs office at Fars, Jamadi al-Awwla 25, 1322, Q1322.3.4, VUK, Tehran.

143. The order of the shah, Jamadi al-Thani 13, 1322, Q1322.3.4, VUK, Tehran.

144. The inquiry of the Iranian government and the decree of 'Ali Akbar, Rajab 1322, Q1322.3.4, VUK, Tehran; see also the inquiry of the Iranian government and the decree of Husayn Razavi Qomi, 1322, Q1322.3.4, VUK, Tehran.

145. Nasrullah Mushir al-Daula to the Iranian official of the Foreign Affairs office in Fars, Sha'ban 15, 1322, Q1322.3.4, VUK, Tehran.

146. Indeed, even liberated enslaved people risked being sold back into slavery. Hujjat al-Islam 'Elm al-Huda to Mushir al-Daula, 26, 1324, Q1324.13.3, VUK, Tehran.

147. Iranian local officials to the Ministry of Foreign Affairs of Iran, Rabi' al-Awwal 3, 1324, Q1324.3.3, VUK, Tehran.

148. Report to the Iranian government, Dhi al-Qa'da 13, 1326, Q1324.13.2, VUK, Tehran.

149. Report on the runaway enslaved females, Rajab 6, 24, 1322, Q1322.3.4, VUK, Tehran; local Iranian official to the Ministry of Foreign Affairs of Iran, Muharram 6, 1324, Q1324.3.3, VUK, Tehran.

150. Nasrullah Mushir al-Daula to the Iranian official of the Foreign Affairs office in Fars, Dhi al-Qa'da 11, 1322, Q1322.3.4, VUK, Tehran.

151. The British consulate in Shiraz to the Iranian government, Muharram 1324, Q1324.3.3, VUK, Tehran; the British consulate in Shiraz to the Iranian government, Sha'ban 1324, Q1324.3.3, VUK.

152. Sadid al-Saltana Kababi, *Sarzaminha-yi shumali*, 285.

153. 'Abdullah, the Ministry of Foreign Affairs, freedom letter, 1326, Q1326.3.25, VUK, Tehran.

154. Malek Mansur to Mushir al-Daula, 1323, Q1323.3.2, VUK, Tehran.

155. One of the pilgrimage routes from Iran to Mecca was the land-sea route of Tehran-Anzali-Tiflis-Istanbul-Suez-Jidda. The people of southern Iran usually traveled along the Bushehr-Bandar-'Abbas-Baghdad-Jidda route. See Husayni Farahani, *Safarnamih-yi Haj Mirza Muhammad*.

156. Nasrullah Mushir al-Daula to Amin al-Daula, Rabi' al-Awwal 21, 1318, Q1318. 23.26.23, VUK, Tehran; Nasrullah Mushir al-Daula to the Ministry of Foreign Affairs of Egypt, freedom letter, Safar 14, 1318, Q1318.3.8, VUK, Tehran.

157. The letter of freedom for Za'faran, Rabi' al-Thani 24, 1318, Q1318.3.8, VUK, Tehran.

158. Shokofa to the British consulate, 1329, Q1329.1.3, VUK, Tehran.

159. The eunuch Safar's letter of freedom, 10, 1324, Q1324.3.3, VUK, Tehran; the letter of freedom for Sa'ida, Shiraz, Rabi' al-Thani 25, 1323, Q1324.3.3, VUK, Tehran.

160. Patrick Owen, British legation, the letter of freedom for Chaman Ara and her grandchild, Tehran, Rabi' al-Thani 13, 1329, Q1329.1.3, VUK, Tehran.

161. The guidelines of the Ministry of Foreign Affairs of Iran to Manshur al-Saltana, the governor of Shiraz, Jamadi al-Awwal 15, 1323, Q1323.13.12.25, VUK, Tehran.

162. The Russian consulate to the Ministry of Foreign Affairs of Iran, 1331, Q1331.3.5.15, VUK, Tehran.

163. Guhar and Taj Gul to the British consulate, 1328, Q1328.3.1.29, VUK, Tehran.

164. The Ministry of Foreign Affairs, the British office, to Mustashar al-Mulk, the master of the *kaniz* Chaman Ara, Rabi' al-Awwal 19, 1329, Q1329.1.3, VUK, Tehran.

165. The Ministry of Foreign Affairs, the British office, Rajab 21, 1335, Q1335.3.13, VUK, Tehran.

166. Nastaran Baji Habashia to the British consulate, 1328, Q1328.3.1.39, VUK.

167. Hajia Habash to the British consulate, 1328, Q1328.3.1.3, VUK, Tehran.

168. Baji Tafaruj to the Iranian government, 1329, Q1329.1.3, VUK, Tehran.

169. Chaman Gul to the British consulate, Rabiʿ al-Thani 1328, Q1328.3.1.17, VUK, Tehran.

170. Bashir to the British embassy, Muharram 8, 1329, Q1329.1.3, VUK, Tehran; the *ghulām* Bashir's letter of freedom from the deceased Mustashar al-Mulk, Muharram 7, 1329, Q1329.1.3, VUK, Tehran.

171. The statement of two enslaved females of the royal court, Zaʿfaran Baji and Chaman Baji, to the British consulate, 1335, Q1335.3.13, VUK, Tehran.

172. The decree issued by the assembly of Shura-yi Milli, 1929, 291/2472/3, SAM, Tehran.

173. The author visited different villages in Baluchistan and discovered that the descendants of enslaved people chose family names for themselves when they obtained their identity cards; poignantly, their choices tended to reflect their heritage, with names like Shanba Azadi (Saturday Freedom) and Jumaʿ Azadi (Friday Freedom). Author's interviews, 2004–2012.

174. I developed the term *Afro-Iranian* in 1998 within the context of a graduate "Nigerian Hinterland Project," which was directed by Paul E. Lovejoy at York University in Canada. See Behnaz A. Mirzai, "Identity Transformations of African Communities in Iran," in *The Persian Gulf in Modern Times: People, Ports and History*, ed. Potter, Lawrence (New York: Palgrave Macmillan, 2014), 535.

175. Report to the Iranian government, Dhi al-Qaʿda 13, 1326, Q1324.3.3, VUK, Tehran. Notably, those enslaved Rindi Baluchis who had sought refuge at the telegraph station in Gwadar were sent to British India in order to prevent conflict with the local enslaved people's owners. Lorimer, *Gazetteer of the Persian Gulf*, 1: pt. 1A, 620, and pt. 2, 2512.

176. Lorimer, *Gazetteer of the Persian Gulf*, 1: pt. 2, 2491; Wilson, *The Persian Gulf*, 230.

177. These freed enslaved Africans in India were known as the "Bombay Africans," about three thousands of whom were sent back to Freetown in Mombasa and Rabai in Khilifi to work. See Anna Greenwood and Harshad Topiwala, *Indian Doctors in Kenya, 1895–1940: The Forgotten History* (New York: Palgrave Macmillan, 2015), 34; see also Arnold J. Temu, "The Role of the Bombay Africans on the Mombasa Coast, 1874–1904," in *Hadith 3*, ed. Bethwell Ogot (Nairobi: East African Publishing House, 1971), 53–81; and see Joe Khamisi, *Dash before Dusk: A Slave Descendant's Journey in Freedom* (Nairobi: Kenway Publications, 2014), 243–250.

178. Lorimer, *Gazetteer of the Persian Gulf*, 1: pt. 1A, 620, and pt. 2, 2512; Wilson, *The Persian Gulf*, 230.

179. Lorimer, *Gazetteer of the Persian Gulf*, 1: pt. 2, 2491.

180. These former *ghulāmān* and *kanīzān* owned fifty goats. Sadid al-Saltana Kababi, *Bandar ʿAbbas*, 105, and *Sarzaminha-yi Shumali*, 322, 326; reports on southern ports, 1311–1317, 293004045, SAM, 4.

181. Information about Afro-Iranian communities relies extensively on observations made by the author and interviews conducted during the author's fieldwork in the southern provinces of Iran beginning in 2000.

182. Afshar Sistani, *Ilha, Chadurneshinan va Tavaʾf*, 1:417.

183. Ibid., 2:930.

184. Amanat, "Introduction: Iranian Identity Boundaries," 12.

185. The statement of Salum ibn Firuz, May 26, 1927, 293001105, SAM, Tehran; the government of Lengeh and the annexed regions to the Ministry of the Interior, Tir 6, 1306, 293/1105/1, SAM.

FINAL THOUGHTS

1. Schacht, *An Introduction to Islamic Law*, 130.

2. I use the term *kinship* instead of *tribe* to refer to the words *taife* and *tireh* applied in Iran.

3. Reports on the economic, hygiene, cultural, and social conditions in Khuzistan and Bandar 'Abbas, Sh. 1320, 293005555, SAM, Tehran.

4. Sadid al-Saltana Kababi, *Sarzaminha-yi shumali*, 50.

5. Ibid., 284.

6. Reports on southern ports, 1311–1317, 293004045, SAM, Tehran, 3, 6.

7. Much of this reform followed a 1950 resolution of the General Assembly of the United Nations. See Doreen Warriner, *Land Reform and Development in the Middle East: A Study of Egypt, Syria, and Iraq*, 2nd ed. (London: Oxford University Press, 1962); and United Nations, *Land Reform Defects in Agrarian Structure as Obstacles to Economic Development* (New York: United Nations, Department of Economic Affairs, 1951); Mu'meni, *Mas'ala-yi arzi va jang-i tabaqati dar Iran*, 276; Hung-Chao Tai, *Land Reform and Politics: A Comparative Analysis* (Berkeley: University of California Press, 1974), 76; Mohammad Javad Amid, *Agriculture, Poverty and Reform in Iran* (Oxon: Routledge, 2011), 70.

8. Bharier, *Economic Development in Iran*, 138; Khusravi, *Dehqan-i khurdepa*, 40.

9. Bharier, *Economic Development in Iran*, 131.

10. Khusravi, *Dehqan-i khurdepa*, 47, 102.

11. Many of these attitudes can be found in Islamic teachings and culture, which emphasize the equality of all races before God.

12. See Mirzai, "Identity Transformations of African Communities in Iran," 351–376.

13. See Behnaz A. Mirzai, "Identity Transformations of African Communities in Iran," in *The Persian Gulf in Modern Times: People, Ports and History*, ed. Lawrence Potter (New York: Palgrave Macmillan, 2014).

14. Sistan va Baluchistan is among several other provinces, officially recognized as "deprived regions" by the Iranian government after the Islamic Revolution.

15. John Hunwick and Eve Troutt Powell, *The African Diaspora in the Mediterranean Lands of Islam* (Princeton: Markus Wiener, 2002), xxiii; I. M. Lewis, "Zar in Context: The Past, the Present and Future of an African Healing Cult," in *Women's Medicine*, ed. I. M. Lewis, Ahmed Al-Safi, and Sayyid Hurreiz (Edinburgh: Edinburgh University Press, 1991), 2. The main participants of the Bori cult in Hausaland are women (Ismail H. Abdalla, "Neither Friend nor Foe: The *Malam* Practitioner–*Yan Bori* Relationship in Hausaland," in *Women's Medicine*, eds. Lewis, Al-Safi, and Hurreiz, 41; Lewis, "Zar in Context," 6). The practice of the Candomblé religion in Bahia, Brazil, can be traced to the Yoruba culture of the Bight of Benin; Toledano, *As If Silent and Absent*, 204–254.

16. Mirzai, "African Presence in Iran," 240–246; Richard Natvig, "Oromos, Slaves, and the Zar Spirits: A Contribution to the History of the Zar Cult," *International Journal of African Historical Studies* 20, no. 4 (1987), 679.

17. Although some are still practiced today, genuine Zar ceremonies are rarely witnessed by non-believers; however, the author was granted permission by community trustees

(shaykhs) and local elders to witness and film several. Usually, theatrical performances based on the rituals are performed for the public.

18. The "Swahili," for instance, is a southwest winter wind coming off the Gulf coast that routinely causes considerable damage. Lorimer, *Gazetteer of the Persian Gulf*, 1: pt. 2, 2207 and 2218.

19. Apart from the uncontrollable, some of the psychological illnesses can also be traced to very real, chemical imbalances, such as those prevalent among sailors and pearl divers whose illnesses were ascribed to possession by evil spirits and jinns. Sadid al-Saltana Kababi, *al-Menas fi ahval-i al-ghaus*, 76.

20. Hassan Arfa, who visited Bandar 'Abbas in 1934, stated that "most of the inhabitants were living in reed huts, about one-third of them being Negroes who had been imported by the Masqatis" (*Under Five Shahs*, 240).

21. Sadid al-Saltana Kababi, *Bandar 'Abbas*, 157, 158, 167. Kababi reported that the total population of Bandar 'Abbas in 1907 was just over ten thousand; thus, we can conclude that about 3 percent of the total population comprised liberated enslaved Africans.

22. Indeed, the tax paid by the African entertainers in Lengeh totaled 150 rupees in 1911. Sadid al-Saltana Kababi, *Sarzaminha-yi shumali*, 213.

23. The "Banyans" is a blanket label ascribed to the various Indian communities by British officials and some historians. See Bhacker, *Trade and Empire in Muscat and Zanzibar*, 69.

24. Bang, "Cosmopolitanism Colonised?" 170. See Abdul Sheriff, "The Spatial Dichotomy of Swahili Towns: The Case of Zanzibar in the Nineteenth Century," *Azania* 36–37 (January 2001). See also Garth Myers, *African Cities: Alternative Visions of Urban Theory and Practice* (London: Zed Books, 2011).

25. The Liwa ceremony was practiced during healing rituals, weddings, and festivals.

26. Taghi Modarressi, "The Zar Cult in South Iran," in *Trance and Possession States*, ed. Raymond Prince (Montreal: R. M. Bucke Memorial Society, 1966), 151; Ghulam Husayn Sa'edi, *Ahl-i hava* (Tehran: Amir Kabir, 2535), 93. In the case of spirit possession, healers continued to perform their ceremonies secretly. By contrast, the Liwa ceremony has either been modified or has disappeared altogether in some areas.

BIBLIOGRAPHY

ARCHIVAL SOURCES

British Library (BL), London
  Oriental and India Office L/PS/5, enclosures from Bombay (L/PS/5)
  Oriental and India Office L/PS/9, enclosures from Persia (L/PS/9)
  Oriental and India Office L/PS/20, précis on the Persian Gulf region (L/PS/20)
  Oriental and India Office R/15, Persian Gulf States Collection (R/15)
Bonyad-i Iranshenasi—Sho'be-yi Bushehr (BISB) [Centre of Iranian Studies—the Bushehr
    Branch], Bushehr, Iran
  Captain Birdwood, assistant to the British consulate, to the Persian Foreign Office agent.
    Bushire. August 29, 1913. 1 (86)
  Album SH (13)
Gulestan Palace, Albumkhana-yi Kakh-i Gulestan [The Photo Collection Center of the Gule-
    stan Palace], Tehran, Iran
  Albums 133, 210, 215, 289, 297, 302, 362
Juma Al Majid Centre for Culture and Heritage, Dubai, United Arab Emirates
  Slavery: Cases Reported by the British Agency, Sharjah, 1947–1950, 143996 (British
    Library R/15/2/1840)
  Slave Trade on the Trucial Coast, 1937–1938, 143997 (British Library R/15/2/1852)
Ketabkhana-yi Markazi-yi Danishgah-i Tehran (KMDT) [The Central Library of the Univer-
    sity of Tehran], Nusakh-i Khatti [Manuscript Collection], Tehran, Iran
  Reports to Nasir al-Din Shah, Majlis-i Tahqiq-i Mazalem [The council for the investiga-
    tion of grievances] Collection (2929)
  Marriage contract between Mirza Muhamad Kazem Nezam al-Mulk and Nimtaj
    Khanum, 1289, no. 9149, film (4946)
  Marriage contract between Sultan Muhammad Mirza, the son of Mirza Muhammad
    Khan Qajar, and Zarrin Kullah Khanum, the daughter of Mu'tamed al-Sultan,
    Jamadi al-Akbar 18, 1279 (9553)
Ministère des Affaires Étrangères (MAE) [Ministry of Foreign Affairs], Paris, France
  M. de Sartiges à le ministre des affaires étrangères [Mr. de Sartiges to the minister of for-
    eign affairs], July 31, 1848. V. 24
National Archives of the United Kingdom (NAUK), Kew, London
  Foreign Office 60, Persia Collection (FO 60)
  Foreign Office 84, Slave Trade Collection (FO 84)
  Foreign Office 248, Persian Consular Collection (FO 248)
  Foreign Office 371, Persia Collection (FO 371)
Sazman-i Asnad va Ketabkhana-yi Milli-yi Jomhuri-yi Islami-yi Iran (SAM) [The National
    Archive and Library of the Islamic Republic of Iran], Tehran, Iran
  Marriage contract of Saheb Beygum Khanum and Aqa Abulhasan, 1263 (296/16904)
  The emigration of inhabitants of Khorasan to Afghanistan (240000604)
  The poverty of the peasants of Qa'enat and Quchan due to the exploitative feudal system
    (240006012)

Permission of the payment of expenses for repatriation of Quchani slaves from Russia (240007042)

The British consulate's acceptance to help free Iranians enslaved by the Dubai Arabs (290001670)

The spread of plague in southern ports on the Persian Gulf (290005769)

The proclamation of the abolition of the slave trade law in Isfahan and its surrounding areas (290/8034)

The abolition of the slave trade law in Iran (291/2472)

The sale of girls in Lutfabad and the silence of the governor (293001104)

The sale of two Iranians to the Arabs in Oman ports by Baluchis (293001106)

The sale of Baluchi children to the Arabs of the Oman coasts (293001107)

The sale of Iranian women to the Afghans in Sistan (293001109)

The sale of Baluchis to neighboring countries by local rulers, and the purchase of weapons (293001568)

Reports on southern ports (293004045)

Reports about the economic, social, cultural, and health conditions of cities in Khuzistan (293005555)

The kidnapping of two Iranians by the Arabs in Dubai (293/6626)

The sale of eleven *ghulāmān* and *kanīzān* who took refuge at the British consulate; their story (293/1105)

Letters by women in the shah's harem asking for his attention (295000053)

A letter by a woman in the harem to Nasir al-Din Shah regarding how she had missed him (295000058)

The letter of a woman in the shah's harem requesting her freedom (295000133)

Request to free the people enslaved by the Turcomans (295000476)

The complaints of two eunuchs in the shah's harem (295002440)

The request of the *kanīz* of E'tezad al-Daula for pension after his death (295002935)

Request by Agha Faraj, one of the eunuchs, to Nasir al-Din Shah (295003603)

Reports on the arrival to and departure from the harem and events in the harem (295004506)

The reports of Agha Yusuf on princes and the harem women (295004639)

The letter of Agha Yusuf to the shah regarding the situation in the harem, princes, and women in the harem (295004752)

The salary of the servants of the women in the harem (295005351)

The strict rules by Agha Anbar regarding the arrival to and departure from the haram during the shah's hunting trip to Jajrud (295005926)

The purchase of a *kanīz* for Nasir al-Din Shah (295.2155)

Request for sixty tomans for purchasing a *kanīz*, Tehran, 1281 (295/709)

The marriage contract between a *ghulām* and a *kanīz* (the Black Almas and Kokab Khanum) (296012411)

The contract selling Hesam al-Sadat's *kanīz* to the sister of Sepahsalar (296001068)

The consideration of the purchase of a *kanīz* for Gelin Khanum (296001405)

Commitment to pay back the price of the sold *kanīz* to Haji 'Ala' al-Mulk in case of her robbery or escape from home—the *kanīz* agreement with him for about fifty tomans (296/1812)

A letter regarding the sale of a *kanīz* and her children (296/2398)

A contract selling a *kanīz* belonging to Aga Muhammad Husain to Nimtaj Khanum, the
wife of Nezam al Mulk (296/7135)

The agreement of a sale of a *ghulām* between Mirza Ahmad Khan Mustufi and Munavar
al-Saltana for thirty-five tomans (296/11036)

The complaints of the Bashqanlu community of Asef al-Dula, the governor of Khorasan, regarding the sale of their girls [first trial after the Constitutional Revolution]
(298001380)

An agreement banning the sale of women (310000092)

Sazman-i Asnad-i Milli-yi Iran (SAM) [National Archive of Iran], Tabriz, Iran

Marriage contract and the sale of a *kanīz* 1265; 1284 (110000141)

Vezarat-i Umur-i Khareja-yi Iran (VUK) [Ministry of Foreign Affairs of Iran], Markaz-i
Asnad [Center of Documents], Tehran, Iran

Correspondence with the British and Russians on the trade in *ghulām* and *kanīz*; on the
abolition of the slave trade (Q1262.5.38)

The British protest to Iran regarding the trade in blacks (Q1263.6.5)

The abolition of the trade in blacks (Q1263.6.15)

The trade in blacks; the agreement between Iran and Britain (Q1263.6.24)

On the agreement of the abolition of the slave trade (Q1264.6.6)

The trade in slaves (Q1264.6.9)

On slave transportation and the slave trade (Q1266.6.15)

On the abolition of the slave trade and slave transportation (Q1267.6.24)

On the abolition of the slave trade and slave transportation (Q1268.6.40)

On the abolition of the slave trade (Q1270.7.22)

Letter to the chargé d'affaires of Russia about Ashuradeh and its salt mines (Q1272.7.47)

On the abolition of the slave trade (Q1275.8. 34)

On the abolition of the slave trade and slave transportation (Q1277.9.2)

Correspondence on the abolition of the slave trade (Q1278.9.20)

Aggressions of border tribes and the problems regarding the Iran and Ottoman frontiers (Q1284.12.24)

The order of slave purchases to the governor of Bushehr (Q1286.13.29)

The agreement of the abolition of the slave trade (Q1288.13.29)

Letter from the people of Baluchistan (Q1289.14.19)

Letter regarding the replacement of officers from Fars to Bushehr, telegram about the
trade in blacks (Q1292.15.22)

The importation of slaves (Q1292.15.26)

On the agreement of the abolition of the slave trade (Q1295.15.26)

The purchase of Haji Muhammad Baqir khan's slaves (Q1298.16.18)

On the abolition of the slave trade (Q1299.17.9)

On the agreement of the abolition of the slave trade and several of its legal sections
(Q1300.17.21)

Regarding two runaway *kanīzān* at the British consulate (Q1315.31.3)

On the abolition of the slave trade (Q1316.32.10)

Correspondence between the Ministry of Foreign Affairs and the Belgium embassy on
the abolition of the slave trade (Q1317.3.4)

Telegram from Sa'ed al-Dawlah (Q1317.15.23)

The escape of four black *kanīzān* from the Mu'ddel al-Saltana's house (Q1317.20.25)

The abolition of the slave trade (Q1318.3.8)

Letter regarding the freedom of Za'faran (Q1318.23.26.23)

Enslavement of the Baluchi people (Q1319.2.3)

Rudbari girls and their freedom (Q1319.3.4)

The raids of the Yamut Turcomans and the killing, plundering, and enslavement of the inhabitants of Mashhad (Q1319.11.8)

Payment for the purchase of a *kanīz* (Q1319.12.6)

Determining the border between Iran and British Baluchistan (Q1319.16.3)

Enslavement of a Makrani Baluch (Q1322.3.4)

Determining the salary for a *kanīz* (Q1322.4.11)

The abolition of the slave trade (Q1323.3.2)

The escape of slaves (Q1323.13.12)

The misuse of slave women by Badr, the lawyer of the British consulate (Q1323.14.4)

Enslavement of a family (Q1323.15.5)

Freedom letters (Q1324.3.3)

Protests regarding the return of slave women (Q1324.13.2)

Complaint against the Shiraz consulate for the return of slave women (Q1324.13.3)

Slave refugees at the Shiraz consulate and request from the Shiraz officials for issuing their freedom letters; the trade in the Baluchis in the Persian Gulf (Q1325.3.8)

The trade in Iranian women (Q1325.11.3)

The sale of a wife and girls to the Turcomans (Q1325.11.7)

The freedom letters of Masrura and Zebar Jad (Q1326.3.25)

The sale of Iranian women to the Turcomans (Q1326.23.47)

The enslavement of Iranian women by the Turcomans and the shah's order to liberate them (Q1326.57.15)

Name change of the slave woman Gul Bahar to Khush Qadam, her refuge at the consulate, and freedom (Q1327.3.18)

The abolition of the slave trade (Q1327.7.5)

Sale of a wife to the Turcomans (Q1327.22.12)

Freedom letters (Q1328.3.1)

Freedom letters (Q1329.1.3)

Freedom letters (Q1331.3.5)

Freedom letters (Q1332.3.3)

The death of Fazeh Baji—a *kanīz*—and the question of inheritance (Q1332.12.21)

The trade in slaves; freedom letters (Q1335.3.13)

The trade in Sistani girls (Q1335.47.29)

Zanzibar National Library (ZNL), Zanzibar, Tanzania

Foreign Office Confidential Print: Correspondence with British Representatives & Agents Abroad & Reports from Naval Officers regarding the Slave Trade, 1877, AA1/22 (1877)

Outward: Political & Finance, 1847, AA3/8 (1846–1851)

Bombay Government Circulars & Copy Correspondence, 1849, AA3/9 (1849)

Inward: 1853, AA3/12 (1853–1855)

Outward: Political & Finance, 1856, AA3/15B (1856)

Outward: 1857, AA3/17 (1858–1859)

Letters, Inward & Outward: 1861, AA3/20 (1862–1863)

Lt. Col. C. P. Rigby: Extracts from Official Correspondence; Rigby's Evidence to Select Committee on the Slave Trade, 1859, AA12/2 (1857–1864, 1871, 1875) The Slavery Decree No. 11 of 1909, 1897, AB71/1 (1897–1909)

PERSIAN AND ARABIC SOURCES

Adamiyat, Fereydun. *Amir Kabir va Iran*. Tehran: Khawrazmi, 1362.

———. *Andisheha-yi Mirza Fathʿali Akhundzada*. Tehran: Khawrazmi, 1349.

———. *Fekr-i azadi*. Tehran: Sukhan, 1340.

———. *Fekr-i demokrasi-yi ejtemaʿi dar nehzat-i mashrutiyat-i Iran*. Tehran: Payam, 1363.

———. *Ideʾuluzhi-yi nehzat-i mashrutiyat-i Iran*. Tehran: Payam, 2535 [1355].

Afshar Sistani, Iraj. *Ilha, chadurneshinan va tavaʾf ʿashayr-i Iran*. 2 vols. Tehran: Huma, 1366.

Afzal al-Mulk, Mirza Ghulam Husayn. *Afzal al-tavarikh*. Tehran: Nashr-i tarikh-i Iran, 1361.

ʿAjami, Ismaʿil. *Shishdangi*. Tehran: Toos, 1352.

ʿAlavi Shirzai, Mirza Muhammad Hadi. *Safarnama-yi Mirza Abulhasan Khan Shirazi (Ilchi) be Russia*. Edited by Muhammad Gulbun. Tehran: Donya-yi ketab, 1363.

Amin Lashkar, Mirza Qahraman. *Roozname-yi safar-i Khorasan be hamrahi-yi Nasir al-Din Shah (1300)*. Edited by Iraj Afshar and Mohamad Rasuldarya gasht. Tehran: Asatir, 1374.

Ansari, Mirza Masʿud. *Safarnama-yi Khusru Mirza be Petersburg va tarikh-i zendegi-yi ʿAbbas Mirza*. Edited by Farhad Mirza Muʿtamed al-Daula. Tehran: Mustaufi, 1349.

ʿAyn al-Saltana, Qahraman Mirza. *Ruznama-yi khaterat-i ʿAyn al-Saltana*. Edited by Masʿud Salvar and Iraj Afshar. 7 vols. Tehran: Asatir, 1378.

Bahar, Malek al-Shuʿaraʾ. *Tarikh-i ahzab-i siyasi-yi Iran*. 2 vols. Tehran: Amir Kabir, 1371.

Dehkhoda, Aliakbar. *Lughatnama-yi Dehkhoda*. 14 vols. Tehran: Daneshgah-i Tehran, 1373.

Ebrahim Khan, Mirza Husayn ibn Muhammad. *Jughrafiya-yi Isfahan*. Tehran: Daneshgah-i Tehran, 1342.

Ehteshami, Lutfullah. *Naqsh-i kalantaran va kadkhudayan dar mudiriyat-i shahr va rusta*. Isfahan: Mehrqaʾm, 1384.

Eʿtemad al-Saltana, Muhammad Hasan Khan. *al-Maʿaser va al-aʿsar*. Tehran: Ketabkhana-yi Sanaʾi, 1307.

———. *Khalsa*. Tehran: Tahuri, 1348.

———. *Sadr al-tawarikh*. Tehran: Vahid, 1349.

———. *Tarikh-i muntazam-i Naseri*. Edited by Muhamad Esmaʿil Razavi. 3 vols. Tehran: dunya-yi ketab, 1363.

———. *Yaddashtha-yi Eʿtemad al-Saltana marbut be sal-i 1300 H.Q*. Tehran: Vahid, 1350.

Farman Farma, Abdulhussain Mirza. *Musaferat nama-yi Kerman va Baluchistan*. Edited by Iraj Afshar. Tehran: Asatir, 1383.

Farman Farma, Firuz Mirza. *Safarnamih-yi Kerman va Baluchistan*. Tehran: Nashr-i tarikh-i Iran, 1380.

Grantovski, Edvin Arvidovich, M. A. Dandamaev, G. A. Koselenko, I. P. Petrashevsky, M. S. Ivanov, L. K. Blavy. *Tarikh-i Iran az zaman-i bastan ta emruz*. Translated by Kaykhusru Keshavarz. Tehran: Puyesh, 1359.

Griboyedov, Aleksandr Sergeyevich. *Nameha-yi Aleksandr Giribayduf dar bara-i Iran, marbut be saltanat-i Fath ʿAli Shah Qajar*. Translated by Reza Farzana. Isfahan: Neshat, 2536.

Haqiqat, ʿAbdul Rafiʿ. *Vaziran-i Irani az Buzurgmehr ta Amir Kabir*. Tehran: Koshesh, 1374.

Hedayat (Mukhber al-Saltana), Mehdi Quli Khan. *Guzaresh-i Iran, Qajariya va mashrutiyat*. Tehran: Nuqra, 1363.

————. *Khatirat va khatarat*. Tehran: Zavar, 1375.

Hedayat, Reza Quli Khan. *Sefarat nama-yi Khawrazm*. Tehran: Tahuri, 1356.

————. *Tarikh-i ruzat al-safa-yi Naseri*. 10 vols. Qom: Hekmat, 1339.

Husayni Farahani, Haj Mirza Muhammad Husayn. *Safarnamih-yi Haj Mirza Muhammad Husayn Husayni Farahani*. Tehran: Ferdusi, 1362.

Husayni Fasa'i, Haj Mirza Hasan. *Farsnama-yi Naseri*. Edited by Mansur Rastgar Fasa'i. 2 vols. Tehran: Amir Kabir, 1382.

Husayni, Mustafa. *Bardegi az didgah-i Islam*. Tehran: Bunyad-i da'rat al-ma'aref-i Islami, 1372.

Ivanov, Mikhail Sergeevich. *Enqelab-i mashrutiyat-i Iran*. Translated by Kazem Ansari. Tehran: Amir Kabir, 2537.

Jamalzada, Muhammad 'Ali. *Ganj-i Shaygan*. Tehran: Sukhan, 1384.

Kaempfer, Engelbert. *Safarnama-yi Kaempfer*. Translated by Keykavus Jahandari. Tehran: Khawrazmi, 1363.

Kasravi, Ahmad. *Tarikh-i mashruta-yi Iran*. Tehran: Amir Kabir, 1370.

Kermani, Nazem al-Islam. *Tarikh-i bidari-yi Iranian*. 3 vols. Tehran: Amir Kabir, 1371.

Khurmuji, Muhammad Ja'far. *Haqa'q al-akhbar Naseri*. Tehran: Ney, 1363.

Khusravi, Khusru. *Dehqan-i khurdepa*. Tehran: 'Elmi, [1985?].

————. *Jama'shenasi-yi deh dar Iran*. Tehran: Markaz-i nashr-i daneshgahi, 1372.

————. *Jazira-yi Kharg dar dura-yi estila-yi naft*. Tehran: Danishgah-i Tehran, 1342.

Lesan al-Mulk Sepehr, Muhammad Taqi. *Nasekh al-tawarikh tarikh-i Qajariya*. 3 vols. Tehran: Asatir, 1377.

Mafi, Nezam al-Saltana, Husayn Quli Khan. *Khatirat va asnad-i Husayn Quli Khan*. Edited by Mansureh Ettehadieh, Sirus Sa'dvandian, and Hamid Rampisha. 3 vols. Tehran: Nashr-i tarikh-i Iran, 1361.

Majd al-Islam Kermani, Ahmad. *Enhelal-i majlis*. Isfahan: Daneshgah-i Isfahan, 1351.

Malekzada, Mehdi. *Tarikh-i enqelab-i mashrutiyat-i Iran*. 7 vols. Tehran: Ibn Sina, 1335.

Mirpanjeh, Esma'il Khan. *Khaterat-i esarat ruznama-yi safar-i Khawrazm va Khiva*. Edited by Safa' al-Din Tabra'iyan. Tehran: Mu'sesa-yi pazhuhesh va mutale'at-i farhangi, 1370.

Mirza, Jahangir. *Tarikh-i nu*. Tehran: 'Ali Akbar 'Elmi, 1327.

Mirza Naser al-Daula, 'Abdulhamid. *Safarnama-yi Baluchistan: Az Mahan ta Chabahar*. Kerman: Markaz-i Kermanshenasi, 1370.

Motamedi, Mohsen. *Joghrafiya-yi tarikhi-yi Tehran*. Tehran: Markaz-i Nashr-i Daneshgahi, 1381.

Mu'ayyir al-Mamalek, Dust 'Ali Khan. *Rejal-i 'ahd-i Naseri*. Tehran, Nashr-i tarikh, 1361.

————. *Yaddashthaei az zendegani-yi khususi-yi Nasir al-Din Shah*. Tehran: Nashr-i tarikh-i Iran, 1362.

Mu'meni, Baqer. *Mas'ala-yi arzi va jang-i tabaqati dar Iran*. Tehran: Payvand, 1359.

Mukhtari Isfahani, Reza, ed. *Guzareshha-yi iyalat va velayat az auza'-i ejtema'i eqtesadi-yi Iran dar sal-i 1310 H. Sh.* [Governmental reports on Iran's socioeconomic situation in 1931]. Tehran: Markaz-i asnad-i riyasat-i jumhuri, 1383.

Musavi Nami Isfahani, Mirza Muhammad Sadeq. *Tarikh-i giti gusha dar tarikh-i khandan-i Zand*. Edited by Azizullah Bayat. Tehran: Amir Kabir, 1368.

Mustaufi, 'Abdullah. *Sharh-i zendegani-yi man: Tarikh-i ejtema'i va edari-yi daura-yi Qajar*. 3 vols. Tehran: Zavvar, 1377.

Nafisi, Sa'id. *Tarikh-i ejtema'i va siasi-yi Iran dar daura-yi mu'aser*. 2 vols. Tehran: Bunyad, 1376.

Najm al-Daula, Abdulghaffar. *Asar-i Najm al-Daula safarnama-yi duwwum-i Najm al-Daula be Khuzistan*. Edited by Ahmad Ketabi. Tehran: Pazhuheshgah-i 'ulum-i ensani va mutale'at-i farhangi, 1386.

———. *Safarnama-yi Khuzestan*. Tehran: Anjuman-i asar-i mafakher-i farhangi, 1385.

Nateq, Huma. *Iran dar rahyabi-yi farhangi*. Paris: Abnus, 1990.

Qa'emmaqami, Jahangir. *Yeksad va panjah sanad-i tarikhi*. Tehran: Artish, 1348.

Qaziha, Fatemeh, ed. *Asnadi az ravand-i ejra-yi mu'ahede-yi Turkomanchai (1245–1250)*. Tehran: Sepehr, 1891.

Qur'an. Tehran: Salihi, 1354.

Ra'in, Esma'il. *Anjumanha-yi serri dar enqelab-i mashrutiyat-i Iran*. Tehran: Javidan, 2535.

———. *Daryanavardi-yi Iranian*. 2 vols. Tehran: Sekka, 1350.

Riyazi Heravi, Muhammad Yusuf. *'Ayn al-waqayah*. Edited by Muhammad Asef Fekrat. Tehran: Sahand, 1372.

Sa'adat Nuri, Husayn. "Haji Mirza Aqasi." *Yaghma* 16, no. 5 (1342): 231–236.

Sabz'ali Esfahani, Muhammad ibn. *Vajizat al-tahrir: dar chegonegi-yi tanzim-i asnad-i shar'i, meli va hoqoqi dar dore-yi Safavi va Qajar*. Edited by Rasul Jafariyan. Qom: Movarekh, 1393.

Sadid al-Saltana Kababi, Muhammad 'Ali. *al-Menas fi ahval-i al-ghaus va al-ghavas*. Tehran: Modern, 1308.

———. *Bandar 'Abbas va Khalij-i Fars*. Tehran: Donya-yi Ketab, 1368.

———. *Sarzaminha-yi shumali piramun-i Khalij-i Fars va darya-yi Oman dar sad sale pish*. Edited by Ahmad Eqtedari. Tehran: Amir Kabir, 1386.

Sa'dvandian, Sirus, and Mansureh Ettehadieh, eds. *Amar-i dar al-khalafa-yi Tehran*. Tehran: Nashr-i Tarikh-i Iran, 1368.

Sa'edi, Ghulam Husayn. *Ahl-i hava*. Tehran: Amir Kabir, 2535.

Mirza Sami'a, Muhammad Sami'. *Tazkarat al-muluk*. Annotated by Dabir Siaqi. Tehran: Sepehr, 1368.

Sarvi, Muhammad Fathullah ibn Muhammad Taqi. *Tarikh-i Muhammadi, ahsan al-tawarikh*. Edited and annotated by Ghulamreza Tabataba'i Majd. Tehran: Sepehr, 1371.

Semsar, Mohammad Hasan, and Fatemeh Saraiyan, eds. *Kakh-i Gulestan (Albumkhana): fehrest-i 'aksha-yi barguzideh-yi 'asre-i Qajar*. Tehran: Vezarat-i Farhang va Ershad-i Eslami, 1382.

Shamim, 'Ali Asghar. *Iran dar daura-yi saltanat-i Qajar*. Tehran: Ibn Sina, 1342.

Sirjani, Sa'idi, annot. *Vaqay'-i ettefaqiya*. Tehran: Nuvin, 1362.

Tabanda Gunabadi, Haj Sultan Husayn. *Nabegha-yi 'elm va 'erfan*. Tehran: Taban, 1350.

———. *Nazar-i mazhabi ba e'lami'a-yi huquq-i bashar*. Tehran: Piruz, 1354.

Tabataba'i Ala' al-Mulk, Mahmud Khan. *Safarnama-yi Baluchistan*. Tehran: Vahid, 1364.

Taj al-Saltana, *Khaterat-i Taj al-Saltana*. Edited by Mansureh Ettehadia and Sirus Sa'dvandian. Tehran: Nashr-i tarikh-i Iran, 1361.

Varahram, Ghulamreza. *Nezam-i siasi va sazmanha-yi ejtema'i-yi Iran dar 'asre Qajar*. Tehran: Mu'in, 1367.

Vaziri, Ahmad 'Ali Khan. *Joghrafia-yi Baluchistan*. Edited by Muhammad Reza Nasiri. Tehran: Anjuman-i asar va mafakher-i farhangi, 1386.

———. *Tarikh-i Kerman*, ed. Muhammad Ebrahim Bastani Parizi. 2 vols. Tehran: 'Elmi, 1364.

Zand-i Muqadam, Mahmud. 4 vols. *Hekayat-i Baluch*. Tehran: Karun, 1370.

Zargari Nejad, Ghulam Husain, ed. *Rasa'el mashrutiyat*. Tehran: Kavir, 1374.

PERIODICALS

Iran-i No. August 27, 1909.
———. September 8, 1909.
———. September 12, 1909.
———. October 20, 1909.
———. October 21, 1909.
———. October 23, 1909.
———. December 26, 1909.
———. December 30, 1909.

Nedā-yi Vatan. No. 12. February 26, 1907.
———. No. 18. March 26, 1907.
———. No. 20. April 2, 1907.
———. No. 21. April 9, 1907.
———. No. 22. April 13, 1907.
———. No. 23. April 16, 1907.
———. No. 25. April 27, 1907.
———. No. 27. May 4, 1907.
———. No. 31. May 21, 1907.
———. No. 36. June 15, 1907.
———. No. 44. July 17, 1907.
———. No. 58. September 17, 1907.
———. No. 104. November 12, 1907.

Muzakerat-i Majlis-i Shuray-i Melli-yi Iran [Parliamentary discussions]. Sept. 1906–June
    1908, May 1909–May 1911, February 7, 1929, Tehran.

Vaqayʿe Ettefaqiye. No. 381. Shawwal 6, 1274.
———. No. 409. Rabiʿ al-Thani 25, 1275.
———. No. 445. Safar 24, 1276.
———. No. 465. Shawwal 11, 1276.
———. No. 114. Jamadi al-Thani 27, 1269.

ENGLISH, FRENCH, AND GERMAN SOURCES

Abbott, Keith Edward. "Notes on Various Cities and Countries of Southern Persia, 1849–
    50." In *Cities and Trade: Consul Abbott on the Economy and Society of Iran, 1847–1866*, edited
    by Amanat, 121–209.
Abdalla, Ismail H. "Neither Friend nor Foe: The *Malam* Practitioner–*Yan Bori* Relation-
    ship in Hausaland." In *Women's Medicine*, edited by Lewis, Al-Safi, and Hurreiz, 37–48.
Abiad, Nasrine. *Sharia, Muslim States and International Human Rights Treaty Obligations:
    A Comparative Study*. London: British Institute of International and Comparative Law,
    2008.
Abir, Mordechai. "The Ethiopian Slave Trade and Its Relation to the Islamic World." In
    Slaves and Slavery in Muslim Africa, edited by Willis, 121–133.

Abrahamian, Ervand. *A History of Modern Iran*. Cambridge and New York: Cambridge University Press, 2008.

Afnan, Abu'l-Qasim. *Black Pearls, Servants in the Households of the Báb and the Bahá'u'lláh*. Los Angeles: Kalimát Press, 1988.

Afshar, Haleh. "Age, Gender and Slavery in and out of the Persian Harem: A Difference Story." *Ethnic and Racial Studies* 23, no. 5 (2000): 905–916.

Ahmad, Aijaz. "The National Question in Baluchistan." In *Focus on Baluchistan*, 3: 8/9 (May-June 1973): 4–37.

Ahmed An-Na'im, 'Abdullahi. "Shari'a and Basic Human Rights Concerns." In *Liberal Islam: A Source Book*, edited by Kurzman, 222–238.

Ajami, Ismail. *Iran: Past, Present and Future*. New York: Aspen Institute for Humanistic Studies, 1975.

Algar, Hamid. *Mīrzā Malkum Khān*. Berkeley: University of California Press, 1973.

———. *Religion and State in Iran, 1785–1906: The Role of the Ulama in the Qajar Period*. Berkeley: University of California Press, 1969.

Allen, Richard B. *European Slave Trading in the Indian Ocean, 1500–1850*. Athens: Ohio University Press, 2014.

———. *Slaves, Freedmen, and Indentured Laborers in Colonial Mauritius*. Cambridge: Cambridge University Press, 1999.

Al-Muhaqqiq al-Hilli, Ja'far ibn al-Hasan. *Droit Musulman. Recueil de lois concernant les Musulmans Schyites*. Trans. Amédée Querry. 2 vols. Paris: Imprimerie nationale, 1871.

Alpers, Edward A. *Ivory and Slaves in East Central Africa*. Berkeley: University of California Press, 1975.

———. *The Indian Ocean in World History*. Oxford: Oxford University Press, 2014.

———. "On Becoming a British Lake: Piracy, Slaving, and British Imperialism in the Indian Ocean during the First Half of the Nineteenth Century," In *Indian Ocean Slavery in the Age of Abolition*, edited by Harms, Freamon, and Blight, 45–58.

Alpers, Edward A., Gwyn Campbell, and Michael Salman, eds. *Slavery and Resistance in Africa and Asia*. London and New York: Routledge, 2005.

Al-Qasimi, Sultan Muhammad. *The Myth of Arab Piracy in the Gulf*. London: Croom Helm, 1986.

Amanat, Abbas. *Pivot of the Universe: Nasir al-Din Shah Qajar and the Iranian Monarchy, 1831–1896*. Berkeley: University of California Press, 1997.

———. *Resurrection and Renewal: The Making of the Babi Movement in Iran, 1844–1850*. Ithaca: Cornell University Press, 1989.

———. "Introduction: Iranian Identity Boundaries: A Historical Overview." In *Iran Facing Others: Identity Boundaries in a Historical Perspective*, edited by Amanat and Vejdani, 1–33.

Amanat, Abbas, and Farzin Vejdani, eds. *Iran Facing Others: Identity Boundaries in a Historical Perspective*. New York: Palgrave Macmillan, 2012.

Ameer Ali, Syed. *Personal Law of the Mahommedans, according to all the Schools, together with a Comparative Sketch of the Law of Inheritance among the Sunnis and the Shiahs*. London: W. H. Allen & Co., 1880.

Amid, Mohammad Javad. *Agriculture, Poverty and Reform in Iran*. Oxon: Routledge, 2011.

Amirahmadian, Bahram. "Evolution of Russo-Iranian Boundaries in the Caucasus." In *Boundary Politics and International Boundaries of Iran: With Afghanistan, Armenia, Azerbaijan Republic, Bahrain (the autonomous republic of Ganjah), Iraq, Kazakhstan, Kuwait,*

Oman, Pakistan, Qatar, Russia, Saudi Arabia, Turkey, Turkmenistan, and the United Arab Emirates, edited by Mojtahed-Zadeh, 51–64.

Arfa, Hassan. *Under Five Shahs*. New York: William Morrow & Co., 1965.

Arnold, Arthur. *Through Persia by Caravan*. New York: Harper & Brothers, 1877.

Ateş, Sabri. *Ottoman-Iranian Borderlands: Making a Boundary, 1843–1914*. New York: Cambridge University Press, 2013.

Atkin, Muriel. *Russia and Iran, 1780–1828*. Minneapolis: University of Minnesota Press, 1980.

Aubin, Eugène. *La Perse d'aujourd'hui*. Paris: Librairie Armand Colin, 1908.

Avery, Peter, Gavin Hambly, and Charles Melville, eds. *The Cambridge History of Iran*. 7 vols. Cambridge: Cambridge University Press, 1991.

Babaie, Sussan, Kathryn Babayan, Ina Baghdiantz-McCabe, and Massumeh Farhad. *Slaves of the Shah: New Elites of Safavid Iran*. London: I. B. Tauris, 2004.

Baddeley, John F. *The Russian Conquest of the Caucasus*. 1908. Repr., New York: Russell & Russell, 1969.

Bahá'u'lláh. *The Kitáb-i-Aqdás*. Pakistan: Bāhā'ī, 1997.

Bahá'u'lláh and 'Abdu'l-bahá. *Bahá'í World Faith*. Wilmette, IL: Bahá'í, 1956.

Bakhash, Shaul. *Iran, Monarchy, Bureaucracy, & Reform under the Qajars, 1858–1896*. London: Ithaca Press for the Middle East Centre, St. Antony's College, 1978.

Balfour-Paul, Glen. *The End of Empire in the Middle East: Britain's Relinquishment of Power in Her Last Three Arab Dependencies*. Cambridge: Cambridge University Press, 1991.

Bang, Anne K. "Cosmopolitanism Colonised? Three Cases From Zanzibar 1890–1920." In *Struggling with History: Islam and Cosmopolitanism in the Western Indian Ocean*, edited by Simpson and Kresse, 167–188.

Bashiriyeh, Hossein. *The State and Revolution in Iran: 1962–1982*. Oxon: Routledge, 2011.

Bassett, James. *Persia, the Land of the Imams: A Narrative of Travel and Residence, 1871–1885*. London: Blackie & Son, 1887.

Bayat, Mongol. *Iran's First Revolution: Shi'ism and the Constitutional Revolution of 1905–1909*. New York and Oxford: Oxford University Press, 1991.

Beachey, R. W. "The Arms Trade in East Africa in the Late Nineteenth Century." *Journal of African History* 3, no. 3 (1962): 451–467.

Beckles, Hilary McD. *Britain's Black Debt: Reparations for Caribbean Slavery and Native Genocide*. Kingston: University of the West Indies Press, 2012.

Belgrave, Charles. *The Pirate Coast*. London: G. Bell and Sons Ltd., 1966.

Benjamin, Samuel Greene Wheeler. *Persia and the Persians*. London: John Murray, 1887.

Bhacker, M. Reda. *Trade and Empire in Muscat and Zanzibar: The Roots of British Domination*. London: Routledge, 1994.

Bharier, Julian. *Economic Development in Iran, 1900–1970*. London: Oxford University Press, 1971.

———. "A Note on the Population of Iran, 1900–1966." *Population Studies* 22, no. 2 (July 1968): 273–279.

Binning, Robert B. M. *A Journal of Two Years' Travel in Persia, Ceylon, Etc.* 2 vols. London: Wm. H. Allen & Co., 1857.

Bird, Isabella L., *Journeys in Persia and Kurdistan*. 2 vols. London: John Murray, 1891.

Black, Jeremy. *Beyond the Military Revolution: War in the Seventeenth-Century World*. Basingstoke: Palgrave Macmillan, 2011.

Blackburn, Robin. *The Overthrow of Colonial Slavery, 1776–1848*. London: Verso, 1990.

Bondarevsky, G. "Turning the Persian Gulf into a British Lake: British Domination in the

Indian Ocean in the Nineteenth and Twentieth Century." In *The Indian Ocean Explorations in History, Commerce and Politics*, edited by Chandra, 317–325.

Bose, Sugata. *A Hundred Horizons: The Indian Ocean in the Age of Global Empire*. Cambridge, MA: Harvard University Press, 2006.

Bose, Sugata, and Ayesha Jalal. *Modern South Asia: History, Culture, Political Economy*. New York: Routledge, 2004.

Bosworth, Edmund, and Carole Hillenbrand, eds. *Qajar Iran: Political, Social and Cultural Change, 1800–1925*. Edinburgh: Edinburgh University Press, 1983.

Bournoutian, George A. *From Tabriz to St. Petersburg: Iran's Mission of Apology to Russia in 1829*. California: Mazda Publishers, 2014.

British and Foreign Anti-Slavery Reporter, London, January–February, 1898; March–May, 1903.

Brown, L. Carl. *The Tunisia of Ahmad Bey 1837–1855*. Princeton: Princeton University Press, 1974.

Browne, Edward Granville. *A Year amongst the Persians*. 1893. Repr., London: Adam and Charles Black, 1959.

Buckingham, J. S. *Travels in Assyria, Medina, and Persia*. 2 vols. London: Henry Colburn and Richard Bentley, 1830.

Burnaby, Frederick. *A Ride to Khiva: Travels and Adventures in Central Asia*. 1876. Repr., Oxford: Oxford University Press, 2005.

Burton, Richard F. *First Footsteps in East Africa*. London: J. M. Dent & Sons, 1910.

———. *Personal Narrative of a Pilgrimage to Al-Madinah & Meccah*. 2 vols. 1893. Repr., New York: Dover Publications, 1964.

Campbell, Gwyn. *An Economic History of Imperial Madagascar, 1750–1895: The Rise and Fall of an Island Empire*. Cambridge; New York: Cambridge University Press, 2005.

———. "Female Bondage and Agency in the Indian Ocean World." In *African Communities in Asia and the Mediterranean: Identities between Integration and Conflict*, edited by Toledano, 37–61.

Campbell, Gwyn, and Edward A. Alpers. "Slavery, Forced Labour and Resistance in Indian Ocean Africa and Asia." In *Slavery and Resistance in Africa and Asia*, edited by Alpers, Campbell, and Salman, 1–20.

Campbell, Gwyn, and Alessandro Stanziani, eds. *Bonded Labour and Debt in the Indian Ocean World*. London: Pickering and Chatto, 2013.

Capela, José. *O Tráfico de Escravos nos Portos de Moçambique 1733–1904*. Porto: Edições Afrontamento, 2002.

Chandra, Satish, ed. *The Indian Ocean: Explorations in History, Commerce and Politics*. New Delhi: Sage Publications, 1987.

Charlesworth, Hilary. "The Challenges of Human Rights Law for Religious Traditions." In *Religion and International Law*, edited by Janis and Evans, 401–416.

Carter, Marina, and Khal Torabully. *Coolitude: An Anthology of the Indian Labour Diaspora*. London: Anthem Press, 2002.

Chatterjee, Indrani, and Richard M. Eaton, eds. *Slavery in South Asian History*. Bloomington: Indiana University Press, 2006.

Chatterjee, Indrani. *Gender, Slavery and Law in Colonial India*. New Delhi: Oxford University Press, 2002.

Chaudhuri, K. N. *Trade and Civilization in the Indian Ocean: An Economic History from the Rise of Islam to 1750*. Cambridge: Cambridge University Press, 1985.

Chehabi, Houchang E. "Staging the Emperor's New Clothes: Dress Codes and Nation-Building under Reza Shah." *Iranian Studies* 26, no. 3/4 (1993): 209–229.

Chew, Emrys. *Arming the Periphery: The Arms Trade in the Indian Ocean during the Age of Global Empire*. Basingstoke: Palgrave Macmillan, 2012.

Clarence-Smith, William Gervase. *Islam and the Abolition of Slavery*. London: Hurst & Company, 2006.

Cooper, Frederick. *Plantation Slavery on the East Coast of Africa*. Portsmouth, NH: Heinemann, 1997.

———. "Islam and Cultural Hegemony: The Ideology of Slaveowners on the East African Coast." In *The Ideology of Slavery in Africa*, edited by Lovejoy, 271–307.

Crone, Patricia. *Roman, Provincial and Islamic Law*. Cambridge: Cambridge University Press, 1987.

Cunha, João Teles e. "The Portuguese Presence in the Persian Gulf." In *The Persian Gulf in History*, edited by Potter, 207–234.

Curtin, Philip D. *The Atlantic Slave Trade: A Census*. Madison: University of Wisconsin Press, 1969.

Curzon, George N. *Persia and the Persian Question*. 2 vols. 1892. Repr., New York: Barnes & Noble, 1966.

D'Allemagne, Henry-René. *Du Khorassan au pays des Backhtiaris: Trois mois de voyage en Perse*. 4 vols. Paris: Hachette, 1911.

Daniel, Elton L. *Society and Culture in Qajar Iran*. Costa Mesa, CA: Mazda Publishers, 2002.

Daniel, Elton L., and Ali Akbar Mahdi. *Culture and Customs of Iran*. Westport, CT: Greenwood Press, 2006.

De Groot, Joanna. *Religion, Culture and Politics in Iran: From the Qajars to Khomeini*. New York: I. B. Tauris, 2007.

De Monfried, Henri. *Pearls, Arms and Hashish: Pages from the Life of a Red Sea Navigator*, compiled by Ida Treat. London: Victor Gollancz, 1930.

De Rivoyre, Denis. *Obock, Mascate, Bouchire, Bassorah*. Paris: Imprimeurs, 1883.

De Silva jayasuriya, Shihan. "Identifying Africans in Asia: What's in a Name?" In *Uncovering the History of Africans in Asia*, edited by Jayasuriya and Angenot, 1–36.

De Silva Jayasuriya, Shihan, and Jean-Pierre Angenot, eds. *Uncovering the History of Africans in Asia*. Leiden: Brill, 2008.

Dieulafoy, Jane. *Une Amazone en Orient: Du Caucase à Ispahan, 1881–1882*. Paris: Phébus, 1989.

Durugönül, Esma. "Construction of Identity and Integration of African-Turks." In *African Communities in Asia and the Mediterranean: Identities between Integration and Conflict*, edited by Toledano, 285–295.

Doughty, Charles M. *Travels in Arabia Deserta*. 2 vols. 1888. Repr., London: Jonathan Cape and the Medici Society Limited, 1923.

Drescher, Seymour. *Capitalism and Antislavery: British Mobilization in Comparative Perspective*. London: Macmillan Press, 1986.

———. "Emperors of the World: British Abolitionism and Imperialism." In *Abolitionism and Imperialism in Britain, Africa, and the Atlantic*, edited by Peterson, 129–149.

Drouville, Gaspard. *Voyage en Perse, pendant les années 1812 et 1813*. 2 vols. St. Petersburg: Imprimé chez Pluchart, 1819.

Eastwick, Edward B. *Three Years' Residence in Persia*. 2 vols. London: Smith, Elder & Co., 1864.

El Hamel, Chouki. *Black Morocco: A History of Slavery, Race, and Islam*. New York: Cambridge University Press, 2013.

Eltis, David. "Assessing the Slave Trade." *Voyages: The Trans-Atlantic Slave Trade Database.* 2007. Accessed December 30, 2015, http://www.slavevoyages.org/assessment/estimates.

Enayat, Hadi. *Law, State, and Society in Modern Iran: Constitutionalism, Autocracy, and Legal Reform, 1906–1941*. New York: Palgrave Macmillan, 2013.

Ennaji, Mohammed. *Slavery, the State, and Islam*. Trans. Teresa Lavender Fagan. New York: Cambridge University Press, 2013.

Erdem, Y. Hakan. *Slavery in the Ottoman Empire and Its Demise, 1800–1909*. Oxford: St. Martin's Press, 1996.

Esmond, Martin B., and T. C. I. Ryan. "A Quantitative Assessment of the Arab Slave Trade of East Africa, 1770–1896." *Kenya Historical Review* 5, no. 1 (1977): 71–91.

Ettehadieh, Mansureh. "The Social Condition of Women in Qajar Society." In Daniel, *Society and Culture in Qajar Iran*, 69–97.

Fabietti, Ugo E. M. *Ethnography at the Frontier: Space, Memory and Society in Southern Balochistan*. New York: Peter Lang, 2011.

Fernyhough, Timothy. "Slavery and the Slave Trade in Southern Ethiopia in the 19th Century." *Slavery and Abolition* 9, no. 3 (1988): 103–130.

Ferrier, J. P. *Caravan Journeys and Wanderings in Persia, Afghanistan, Turkistan, and Beloochistan*. London: John Murray, Albemarle Street, 1857.

Feuvrier, Jean Baptiste. *Trois ans a la cour de Perse*. Paris: F. Juven, 1900.

Fisher, C. B. "The Feudal System in Persia." *Journal of Farm Economics* 13, no. 4 (October 1931): 621–629.

Fisher, Humphrey. *Slavery in the History of Muslim Black Africa*. London: Hurst, 2001.

Floor, Willem. *Agriculture in Qajar Iran*. Washington, DC: Mage Publishers, 2003.

———. "Change and Development in the Judicial System of Qajar, Iran (1800–1925)." In Bosworth and Hillenbrand, *Qajar Iran*, 113–147.

———. *A Fiscal History of Iran in the Safavid and Qajar Periods, 1500–1925*. New York: Bibliotheca Persica Press, 1998.

———. "Dutch Relations with the Persian Gulf." In *The Persian Gulf in History*, edited by Potter, 235–259.

Floyer, E. A. "Journal of a Route from Jask to Bampur." *Journal of the Royal Geographical Society* 47 (1877): 188–201.

Forbes-Leith, F. A. C. *Checkmate: Fighting Tradition in Central Persia*. New York: Robert M. McBride & Co., 1927.

Foster, Shirley. "Colonialism and Gender in the East: Representations of the Harem in the Writings of Women Travellers." *The Yearbook of English Studies* 34 (2004): 6–17.

Fraser, James Baillie. *Historical and Descriptive Account of Persia, from the Earliest Ages to the Present Time*. New York: Harper & Brothers, 1834.

———. *Narrative of a Journey into Khorasan, in the Years 1821 and 1822*. London: Longman, Hurst, Rees, Orme, Brown, and Green, 1825.

———. *A Winter's Journey from Constantinople to Tehran*. 2 vols. 1838. Repr., New York: Arno Press, 1973.

Francklin, William. *Observations Made on a Tour from Bengal to Persia: In the Years 1786–7*. London: T. Cadell, 1788.

Ganji, Mohammad Hassan. "The Historical Development of the Boundaries of Azerbaijan." In *The Boundaries of Modern Iran*, edited by McLaclan, 37–46.

————. "Stages in the Shaping of Iran's North-Western Boundaries." In *Boundary Politics and International Boundaries of Iran: With Afghanistan, Armenia, Azerbaijan Republic, Bahrain (the autonomous republic of Ganjah), Iraq, Kazakhstan, Kuwait, Oman, Pakistan, Qatar, Russia, Saudi Arabia, Turkey, Turkmenistan, and the United Arab Emirates*, edited by Mojtahed-Zadeh, 41–50.

Gershoni, Israel, Amy Singer, and Y. Hakan Erdem, eds. *Middle East Historiographies: Narrating the Twentieth Century*. Seattle: University of Washington Press, 2006.

Gilbert, Erik. "Oman and Zanzibar: The Historical Roots of a Global Community." In *Cross Currents and Community Networks: The History of the Indian Ocean World*, edited by Ray and Alpers, 163–178.

Glassman, Jonathon. *Feasts and Riot: Revelry, Rebellion, and Popular Consciousness on the Swahili Coast, 1856–1888*. Portsmouth, NH: Heinemann, 1995.

Goitein, Shlomo D. *Studies in Islamic History and Institutions*. Leiden: Brill, 2010.

Goldsmid, F. J. "Journey from Bandar Abbas to Mash-had by Sistan, with Some Account of the Last-Named Province." *Journal of the Royal Geographical Society of London* 43 (1873): 65–83.

Gordon, Matthew S. "The Turkish Military Elite of Samarra and the Third Century Land Tenure System." In *Slave Elites in the Middle East and Africa*, edited by Toru and Philips, 13–24.

Goswami, Chhaya. *The Call of the Sea: Kachchhi Traders in Muscat and Zanzibar, C. 1800–1880*. New Delhi: Orient Blackswan, 2011.

Green, Nile. *Sufism: A Global History*. Oxford: Wiley-Blackwell, 2012.

Greenwood, Anna, and Harshad Topiwala. *Indian Doctors in Kenya, 1895–1940: The Forgotten History*. New York: Palgrave Macmillan, 2015.

Gurney, J. D. "A Qajar Household and Its Estates." *Iranian Studies* 16, no. 3/4 (1983): 137–176.

Hairi, Abdul-Hadi. *Shī'ism and Constitutionalism in Iran*. Leiden: Brill, 1977.

Hallaq, Wael B. ed. *The Formation of the Classical Islamic World*. Aldershot: Ashgate Publishing, 2004.

Hambly, Gavin R. G. "The Pahlavī Autocracy: Muḥammad Riża Shāh, 1921–1941." In *The Cambridge History of Iran*, edited by Avery, Hambly, and Melville, 213–243.

Hamidullah, Muhammad. *Introduction to Islam*. Paris: Centre Culturel Islamique, 1957.

————. "Africans in Asian History." In *Global Dimensions of the African Diaspora*, edited by Harris, 325–337.

————, ed. *Global Dimensions of the African Diaspora*. 2nd ed. Washington, DC: Howard University Press, 1993.

Hamilton, Keith, and Patrick Salmon, eds. *Slavery, Diplomacy and Empire: Britain and the Suppression of the Slave Trade, 1807–1975*. Brighton: Sussex Academic Press, 2009.

Harms, Robert. "Introduction: Indian Ocean Slavery in the Age of Abolition." In *Indian Ocean Slavery in the Age of Abolition*, edited by Harms, Freamon, and Blight, 1–19.

Harms, Robert, Bernard K. Freamon, and David W. Blight, eds. *Indian Ocean Slavery in the Age of Abolition*. New Haven: Yale University Press, 2013.

Harris, Joseph E. ed. *Global Dimensions of the African Diaspora*. Washington, DC: Howard University Press, 1993.

————. "Return Movements to West and East Africa: A Comparative Approach." In *Global Dimensions of the African Diaspora*, edited by Harris, 51–64.

Heude, William. *A Voyage up the Persian Gulf and a Journey Overland from India to England in 1817*. London: Longman, Hurst, Rees, Orme, and Brown, 1819.

Hogendorn, Jan. "The Location of the 'Manufacture' of Eunuchs." In *Slave Elites in the Middle East and Africa*, edited by Toru and Philips, 13–24.

Hooper, Jane, and David Eltis. "The Indian Ocean in Transatlantic Slavery." *Slavery and Abolition* 34, no. 3 (2013): 353–375.

Hopper, Matthew S. *Slaves of One Master: Globalization and Slavery in Arabia in the Age of Empire*. New Haven: Yale University Press, 2015.

Huntington, Ellsworth. "The Depression of Sistan in Eastern Persia." *Bulletin of the American Geographical Society* 37, no. 5 (1905): 271–281.

Hunwick, John, and Eve Troutt Powell. *The African Diaspora in the Mediterranean Lands of Islam*. Princeton: Markus Wiener, 2002.

Hutton, James. *Central Asia: From the Aryan to the Cossack*. 1875. Repr., New Delhi: Manas Publications, 2005.

Issawi, Charles. *The Economic History of Iran, 1800–1914*. Chicago: University of Chicago Press, 1971.

———. *An Economic History of the Middle East and North Africa*. London: Routledge, 2006. First published by Columbia University Press, 1982.

———. *The Middle East Economy: Decline and Recovery*. Princeton: Markus Wiener Publishers, 1995.

Izady, M. R. "The Gulf's Ethnic Diversity: An Evolutionary History." In *Security in the Persian Gulf: Origins, Obstacles, and the Search for Consensus*, edited by Potter and Sick, 33–90.

Jahani, Carina, Agnes Korn, and Paul Titus, eds. *The Baloch and Others: Linguistic, Historical and Socio-Political Perspectives on Pluralism in Balochistan*. Wiesbaden: Reichert, 2008.

Janis, Mark W., and Carolyn Evans, eds. *Religion and International Law*. Boston: M. Nijhoff, 1999.

Jenson, John R., ed. *Journal and Letter Book of Nicholas Buckeridge, 1651–1654*. Minneapolis: University of Minnesota Press, 1973.

Johnston, J. H. "The Mohammedan Slave Trade." *Journal of Negro History* 13, no. 4 (October 1928): 478–491.

Jwaideh, Albertine, and J. W. Cox. "The Black Slaves of Turkish Arabia during the 19th Century." *Slavery and Abolition* 9, no. 3 (1988): 45–59.

Kashani-Sabet, Firoozeh. *Frontier Fictions: Shaping the Iranian Nation, 1804–1946*. Princeton: Princeton University Press, 1999.

Katouzian, Homa. *State and Society in Iran: The Eclipse of the Qajars and the Emergence of the Pahlavis*. London: I. B. Tauris, 2000.

Kazemzadeh, Firuz. *Russia and Britain in Persia, 1864–1914: A Study in Imperialism*. New Haven: Yale University Press, 1968.

Keddie, Nikki R. *An Islamic Response to Imperialism: Political and Religious Writings of Sayyid Jamal ad-Din "al-Afghani."* Berkeley: University of California Press, 1968.

———. *Qajar Iran and the Rise of Reza Khan, 1796–1925*. Costa Mesa, CA: Mazda Publishers, 1999.

———, ed. *Religion and Politics in Iran: Shi'ism from Quietism to Revolution*. New Haven: Yale University Press, 1983.

———. "The Roots of the 'Ulamā''s Power in Modern Iran." In *Scholars, Saints, and Sufis*, edited by Keddie, 216–229.

———, ed. *Scholars, Saints, and Sufis: Muslim Religious Institutions in the Middle East since 1500*. Berkeley: University of California Press, 1972.

Keddie, Nikki R., and Mehrdad Amanat. "Iran under the Later Qajars, 1848–1922." In *The Cambridge History of Iran*, edited by Avery, Hambly, and Melville, 174–212.

Keita, Maghan, ed. *Conceptualizing/Re-conceptualizing Africa: The Construction of African Historical Identity*. Leiden: Brill, 2002.

Kelly, J. B. *Britain and the Persian Gulf, 1795–1880*. Oxford: Clarendon Press, 1968.

Khadduri, Majid. *The Islamic Conception of Justice*. Baltimore: Johns Hopkins University Press, 1984.

Khamisi, Joe. *Dash before Dusk: A Slave Descendant's Journey in Freedom*. Nairobi: Kenway Publications, 2014.

Khazeni, Arash. *Tribes and Empire on the Margins of Nineteenth-Century Iran*. Seattle: University of Washington Press, 2009.

Kinneir, John Macdonald (1782–1830). *A Geographical Memoir of the Persian Empire*. 1813. Repr., London: Arno Press, 1973.

Klein, Herbert S., and Ben Vinson III, *African Slavery in Latin America and the Caribbean*. 2nd ed. Oxford: Oxford University Press, 2007.

Klein, Martin A., ed. *Slavery, Bondage, and Emancipation in Modern Africa and Asia*. Madison: University of Wisconsin Press, 1993.

Kresse, Kai. "The Uses of History: Rhetorics of Muslim Unity and Difference On the Kenyan Swahili Coast." In *Struggling with History: Islam and Cosmopolitanism in the Western Indian Ocean*, edited by Simpson and Kresse, 223–260.

Kurzman, Charles, ed. *Liberal Islam: A Source Book*. Oxford: Oxford University Press, 1998.

Laffin, John. *The Arabs as Master Slavers*. Englewood Cliffs, NJ: SBS, 1982.

Lambton, Ann. *Qajar Persia*. London: I. B. Tauris, 1987.

———. "Secret Societies and the Persian Revolution of 1905–1906." *St Antony's Papers* 4 (1958): 43–63.

———. *Landlord and Peasant in Persia*. London: Oxford University Press, 1953.

Landor, Henry Savage. *Across Coveted Lands*. 2 vols. New York: Charles Scribner's Sons, 1903.

Lang, David M. "Griboedov's Last Years in Persia." *American Slavic and East European Review* 7, no. 4 (December 1948): 317–339.

Law, Gwillim. *Administrative Subdivisions of Countries: A Comprehensive World Reference, 1900 through 1998*. Jefferson, North Carolina: McFarland & Company, 1999.

Law, Robin. "Slave-Raiders and Middlemen, Monopolists and Free-Traders: The Supply of Slaves for the Atlantic Trade in Dahomey c. 1715–1850." *Journal of African History* 30, no. 1 (1989): 45–68.

———. "Abolition and Imperialism: International Law and the British Suppression of the Atlantic Slave Trade." In *Abolitionism and Imperialism in Britain, Africa, and the Atlantic*, edited by Peterson, 150–174.

Lawyers Committee for Human Rights. *Islam and Justice*. New York: Lawyers Committee for Human Rights, 1997.

Lee, Anthony A. "Half the Household Was African: Recovering the Histories of Two Enslaved Africans in Iran, Haji Mubarak and Fezzeh Khanum." *UCLA Historical Journal* 26, no. 1 (2015): 17–38.

Le Strange, Guy. *Don Juan of Persia: A Shi'ah Catholic, 1590–1609*. New York: Harper & Brothers, 1926.

Lewis, I. M. "Zar in Context: The Past, the Present and Future of an African Healing Cult." In *Women's Medicine*, edited by Lewis, Al-Safi, and Hurreiz, 1–16.

Lewis, I. M., Ahmed Al-Safi, and Sayyid Hurreiz, eds. *Women's Medicine*. Edinburgh: Edinburgh University Press, 1991.

Lorimer, J. G. *Gazetteer of the Persian Gulf, Oman and Central Arabia*. 6 vols. Calcutta: Superintendent Government Printing, 1908–1915.

Lovejoy, Paul E. *Transformations in Slavery: A History of Slavery in Africa*. Cambridge: Cambridge University Press, 2012.

Lovejoy, Paul E., ed. *The Ideology of Slavery in Africa*. London: Sage, 1981.

Lovejoy, Paul E., and Jan S. Hogendorn. *Slow Death for Slavery*. 3rd ed. Cambridge: Cambridge University Press, 1993.

Malcolm, John. *Sketches of Persia*. 2 vols. London: John Murray, Albemarle Street, 1827.

MacKenzie, D. N. *A Concise Pahlavi Dictionary*. London: Oxford University Press, 1971.

Manning, Patrick. *Slavery and African Life: Occidental, Oriental, and African Slave Trades*. Cambridge: Cambridge University Press, 1995.

Marshman, John Clark. *The History of India*. 3 vols. London: Longmans, Green, Reader & Dyer, 1867.

Marvin, Charles. *Merv, the Queen of the World and the Scourge of the Man-Stealing Turcomans*. London: W. H. Allen & Co., 1881.

Massé, Henri. *Persian Beliefs and Customs*. New Haven: Human Relations Area Files, 1954.

Matthee, Rudolph P. *The Politics of Trade in Safavid Iran: Silk for Silver, 1600–1730*. Cambridge: Cambridge University Press, 1999.

Maurizi, Vincenzo. *History of Seyd Said, Sultan of Muscat*. 2nd ed. 1819. Repr., Cambridge: Oleander Press, 1984.

McBeth, B. S. *British Oil Policy 1919–1939*. London: Frank Cass, 1985.

McDow, Thomas F. "Deeds of Freed Slaves: Manumission and Economic and Social Mobility in Pre-Abolition Zanzibar." In *Indian Ocean Slavery in the Age of Abolition*, edited by Harms, Freamon, and Blight, 160–179.

McLachlan, Keith S., ed. *The Boundaries of Modern Iran*. New York: St. Martin's Press, 1994.

———. "Traditional Regions and National Frontiers of Iran: A General Overview." In *Boundary Politics and International Boundaries of Iran: With Afghanistan, Armenia, Azerbaijan Republic, Bahrain (the autonomous republic of Ganjah), Iraq, Kazakhstan, Kuwait, Oman, Pakistan, Qatar, Russia, Saudi Arabia, Turkey, Turkmenistan, and the United Arab Emirates*, edited by Mojtahed-Zadeh, 29–37.

McMahon, Elisabeth. *Slavery and Emancipation in Islamic East Africa: From Honor to Respectability*. New York: Cambridge University Press, 2013.

McNeill H., William. *Europe's Steppe Frontier, 1500–1800*. Chicago: University of Chicago Press, 1964.

Mekonnen, Yohannes K., ed. *Ethiopia: The Land, Its People, History and Culture*. Dar es Salaam: New Africa Press, 2013.

Miers, Suzanne. *Slavery in the Twentieth Century: The Evolution of a Global Problem*. Walnut Creek, CA: AltaMira Press, 2003.

———. "Slave Rebellion and Resistance in the Aden Protectorate in the Mid-Twentieth Century." In *Slavery and Resistance in Africa and Asia*, edited by Alpers, Campbell, and Salman, 99–108.

———. "The Anti-Slavery Game: Britain and the Suppression of Slavery in Africa and

Arabia, 1890–1975." In *Slavery, Diplomacy and Empire: Britain and the Suppression of the Slave Trade, 1807–1975*, edited by Hamilton and Salmon, 196–214.

Miers, Suzanne, and Richard Roberts, eds. *The End of Slavery in Africa*. Madison: University of Wisconsin Press, 1988.

Mignan, R. *Winter Journey through Russia, the Caucasian Alps, and Georgia*. 2 vols. London: Richard Bentley, 1839.

Mirzai, Behnaz A. "African Presence in Iran: Identity and Its Reconstruction in the 19th and 20th Centuries." *Revue française d'histoire d'outre-mer* 89, no. 336–337 (2002): 229–246.

———. "Qajar Haram: Imagination or Reality." In *Slavery, Islam and Diaspora*, edited by Mirzai, Montana, and Lovejoy, 77–89.

Mirzai, Behnaz A., Ismael Musah Montana, and Paul E. Lovejoy, eds. *Slavery, Islam and Diaspora*. Trenton, NJ: Africa World Press, 2009.

Mirzai, Behnaz A., ed. "The Baluch and Baluchistan." Special issue, *Journal of the Middle East and Africa* 4, no. 2 (2013).

———. "Identity Transformations of African Communities in Iran." In *The Persian Gulf in Modern Times: People, Ports and History*, edited by Potter, 351–376.

———. "The Persian Gulf and Britain: The Suppression of the African Slave Trade." In *Abolitions as a Global Experience*, edited by Suzuki, 113–129.

Mitter, Ulrike. "Unconditional Manumission of Slaves in Early Islamic Law: A Ḥadīth Analysis." In *The Formation of the Classical Islamic World*, edited by Hallaq, v. 27, 116–152.

Modarressi, Taghi. "The Zar Cult in South Iran." In *Trance and Possession States*, edited by Prince, 149–155.

Mojtahed-Zadeh, Pirouz. "The Eastern Boundaries of Iran." In *The Boundaries of Modern Iran*, edited by McLaclan, 128–139.

———. "Iran's Maritime Boundaries in the Persian Gulf: The Case of Abu Musa Island." In *The Boundaries of Modern Iran*, edited by McLaclan, 101–127.

———, ed. *Boundary Politics and International Boundaries of Iran: With Afghanistan, Armenia, Azerbaijan Republic, Bahrain (the autonomous republic of Ganjah), Iraq, Kazakhstan, Kuwait, Oman, Pakistan, Qatar, Russia, Saudi Arabia, Turkey, Turkmenistan, and the United Arab Emirates*. Boca Raton: Universal Publishers, 2006.

———. "The Concept of Boundary and Its Origin in the Ancient Persian Tradition." In *Boundary Politics and International Boundaries of Iran: With Afghanistan, Armenia, Azerbaijan Republic, Bahrain (the autonomous republic of Ganjah), Iraq, Kazakhstan, Kuwait, Oman, Pakistan, Qatar, Russia, Saudi Arabia, Turkey, Turkmenistan, and the United Arab Emirates*, edited by Mojtahed-Zadeh, 13–27.

———. *Small Players of the Great Game: The Settlement of Iran's Eastern Borderlands and the Creation of Afghanistan*. New York: Routledge, 2004.

Montana, Ismael M. *The Abolition of Slavery in Ottoman Tunisia*. Gainesville: University Press of Florida, 2013.

Mounsey, Augustus H. *A Journey through the Caucasus and the Interior of Persia*. London: Smith, Elder & Co., 1872.

Mulligan, William, and Maurice Bric, eds. *A Global History of Anti-Slavery Politics in the Nineteenth Century*. Basingstoke: Palgrave Macmillan, 2013.

Murav'yov, Nikolay. *Journey to Khiva through the Turkoman Country*. 1822. Repr., London: Oguz Press, 1977.

Myers, Garth. *African Cities: Alternative Visions of Urban Theory and Practice*. London: Zed Books, 2011.

Najmabadi, Afsaneh. *Land Reform and Social Change in Iran*. Salt Lake City: University of Utah Press, 1987.

———. *The Story of the Daughters of Quchan*. Syracuse: Syracuse University Press, 1998.

Nadjmabadi, Shahnaz Razieh. "The Arab Presence on the Iranian Coast of the Persian Gulf." In *The Persian Gulf in History*, edited by Potter, 130–145.

Nashat, Guity. *The Origins of Modern Reform in Iran, 1870–80*. Urbana: University of Illinois Press, 1982.

Natvig, Richard. "Oromos, Slaves, and the Zar Spirits: A Contribution to the History of the Zar Cult." *International Journal of African Historical Studies* 20, no. 4 (1987): 669–689.

Nicolini, Beatrice. *Makran, Oman and Zanzibar: Three-Terminal Cultural Corridor in the Western Indian Ocean (1799–1856)*. Trans. Penelope-Jane Watson. Leiden: Brill, 2004.

———. "The 19th Century Slave Trade in the Western Indian Ocean: The Role of the Baloch Mercenaries." In *The Baloch and Others: Linguistic, Historical and Socio-Political Perspectives on Pluralism in Balochistan*, edited by Jahani, Korn, and Titus, 327–344.

Niebuhr, M. (1733–1815). Travels through Arabia and Other Countries in the East. Trans. Robert Heron (1764–1807). 2 vols. Beirut: Librairie du Liban, 1968.

Nwulia, Moses D. E. *Britain and Slavery in East Africa*. Washington, DC: Three Continents Press, 1975.

Ogot, Bethwell, ed. *Hadith* 3. Nairobi: East African Publishing House, 1971.

Oliver, Edward E. *Across the Border: Or, Pathân and Biloch*. London: Chapman and Hall, 1890.

Onley, James. *The Arabian Frontier of the British Raj: Merchants, Rulers, and the British in the Nineteenth-Century Gulf*. Oxford: Oxford University Press, 2007.

Owen, Roger. *The Middle East in the World Economy 1800–1914*. 1981. Repr., London and New York: I. B. Tauris, 2005.

Öztürkmen, A., and E. B. Vitz, eds. *Medieval and Early Modern Performance in the Eastern Mediterranean*. Turnhout, Belgium: Brepols Publishers, 2014.

Pastner, Stephen, and Carroll McC. Pastner. "Agriculture, Kinship and Politics in Southern Baluchistan." *Man* 7 (March 1972): 128–136.

Peabody, Sue. "France's Two Emancipations in Comparative Context." In *Abolitions as a Global Experience*, edited by Suzuki, 25–49.

Pearson, M. N. *The Portuguese in India*. Cambridge: Cambridge University Press, 1987.

Pellat, Charles. *The Life and Works of Jāḥiẓ*. Trans. D. M. Hawke. London: Routledge & Kegan Paul, 1969.

Penzer, N. M., ed. *Sir John Chardin's Travels in Persia*. New York: AMS Press, 1927.

Peterson, J. E. "Britain and the Gulf: At the Periphery of Empire." In *The Persian Gulf in History*, edited by Potter, 277–293.

Peterson, Derek R., ed. *Abolitionism and Imperialism in Britain, Africa, and the Atlantic*. Athens: Ohio University Press, 2010.

Polak, Jakob Eduard. *Persien, das Land und seine Bewohner*. 2 vols. Leipzig: Brockhaus, 1865.

Potter, Lawrence G., ed. *The Persian Gulf in History*. New York: Palgrave Macmillan, 2009.

Potter, Lawrence, ed. *The Persian Gulf in Modern Times: People, Ports and History*. New York: Palgrave Macmillan, 2014.

Potter, Lawrence G., and Gary G. Sick, eds. *Security in the Persian Gulf: Origins, Obstacles, and the Search for Consensus*. New York: Palgrave Macmillan, 2003.

Prestholdt, Jeremy. "Portuguese Conceptual Categories and the "Other" Encounter on the

Swahili Coast." In *Conceptualizing/Re-Conceptualizing Africa: The Construction of African Historical Identity*, edited by Keita, 53–76.

Prestholdt, Jeremy. *Domesticating the World: African Consumerism and the Genealogies of Globalization*. Berkeley: University of California Press, 2008.

Prince, Raymond, ed. *Trance and Possession States*. Montreal: R. M. Bucke Memorial Society, 1966.

Ray, Himanshu Prabha, and Edward A. Alpers, eds. *Cross Currents and Community Networks: The History of the Indian Ocean World*. New Delhi: Oxford University Press, 2007.

Ricks, Thomas. "Slaves and Slave Trading in Shi'i Iran, AD 1500–1900." In *Conceptualizing/Re-conceptualizing Africa: The Construction of African Historical Identity*, edited by Keita, 77–88.

Risso, Patricia. *Oman and Muscat: An Early Modern History*. London: Croom Helm, 1986.

Robinson, Ronald, and John Gallagher. *Africa and the Victorians*. 2nd ed. London: Macmillan Press, 1981.

Schacht, Joseph. *An Introduction to Islamic Law*. Oxford: Clarendon Press, 1964.

Segal, Ronald. *Islam's Black Slaves: The Other Black Diaspora*. New York: Farrar, Straus and Giroux, 2001.

Sen, Amartya. *Development as Freedom*. New York: Alfred A. Knopf, 1999.

Sepsis, A. "De l'état administrative et politique de la Perse." *Revue de l'Orient* 4 (1844): 98–114.

———. "Quelque mots sur l'état religieux actuel de la Perse." *Revue de l'Orient* 3 (1844): 97–114.

Serrão, Joaquim Veríssimo. *Un voyageur Portugais en Perse au début du XVIIe siècle: Nicolau de Orta Rebelo*. Lisbon: Comité National Portugais, 1972.

Sheil, Lady Mary. *Glimpses of Life and Manners in Persia*. 1856. Repr., New York: Arno Press, 1973.

Shepherd, Gill. "The Comorians and the East African Slave Trade." In *Asian and African Systems of Slavery*, edited by Watson, 73–99.

Sheriff, Abdul. *Slaves, Spices and Ivory in Zanzibar: Integration of an East African Commercial Empire into the World Economy, 1770–1873*. Athens: Ohio University Press, 1987.

———. *Dhow Cultures of the Indian Ocean: Cosmopolitanism, Commerce and Islam*. New York: Columbia University Press, 2010.

———. "The Persian Gulf and the Swahili Coast: A History of Acculturation Over the Longue Durée." In *The Persian Gulf in History*, edited by Potter, 173–188.

———. "Social Mobility in Indian Ocean Slavery: The Strange Career of Sultan bin Aman." In *Indian Ocean Slavery in the Age of Abolition*, edited by Harms, Freamon, and Blight, 143–159.

———. "The Spatial Dichotomy of Swahili Towns: The Case of Zanzibar in the Nineteenth Century." *Azania* 36–37 (January 2001): 63–81.

Shōkō, Okazaki. *The Development of Large-Scale Farming in Iran*. Tokyo: Institute of Asian Economic Affairs, 1968.

Sikainga, Ahmad A. "Shari'a Courts and the Manumission of Female Slaves in the Sudan, 1898–1939." *International Journal of African Historical Studies* 28, no. 1 (1995): 1–23.

Simpson, Edward, and Kai Kresse, eds. *Struggling with History: Islam and Cosmopolitanism in the Western Indian Ocean*. New York: Columbia University Press, 2008.

Smith, Peter. *The Babi and Baha'i Religions: From Messianic Shi'ism to a World Religion*. Cambridge: Cambridge University Press, 1987.

Spinage, Clive Alfred. *African Ecology: Benchmarks and Historical Perspectives*. Berlin: Springer-Verlag, 2012.

Strausbaugh, John. *Black Like You: Blackface, Whiteface, Insult and Imitation in American Popular Culture*. New York: Jeremy P. Tarcher/Penguin, 2006.

Stebbins, H. Lyman. "British Imperialism, Regionalism, and Nationalism in Iran, 1890–1919." In *Iran Facing Others: Identity Boundaries in a Historical Perspective*, edited by Amanat and Vejdani, 151–167.

Sulivan, G. L. *Dhow Chasing in Zanzibar Waters*. 1873. Repr., London: Dawsons of Pall Mall, 1967.

Suzuki, Hideaki. "Baluchi Experiences under Slavery and the Slave Trade of the Gulf of Oman and the Persian Gulf, 1921–1950." In "The Baluch and Baluchistan," edited by Mirzai, 205–223.

———, ed. *Abolitions as a Global Experience*. Singapore: National University of Singapore, 2016.

Sykes, Percy Molesworth (1867–1945). "The Geography of Southern Persia as Affecting Its History." *Scottish Geographical Magazine* 18, no. 12 (December 1902): 617–626.

———. *A History of Persia*. 3rd ed. 2 vols. 1915. Repr., London: Macmillan & Co., 1963.

———. "Ten Thousand Miles in Persia." *Scottish Geographical Magazine* 18, no. 12 (1902): 626–631.

———. *Ten Thousand Miles in Persia or Eight Years in Iran*. London: John Murray, Albemarle Street, 1902.

Tabari, Azar. "The Role of the Clergy in Modern Iranian Politics." In Keddie, *Religion and Politics in Iran*, 47–72.

Tai, Hung-Chao. *Land Reform and Politics: A Comparative Analysis*. Berkeley: University of California Press, 1974.

Tavakoli-Targhi, Mohamad. *Refashioning Iran: Orientalism, Occidentalism and Historiography*. Basingstoke: Palgrave Macmillan, 2001.

Temu, Arnold J. "The Role of the Bombay Africans on the Mombasa Coast, 1874–1904." In *Hadith* 3, edited by Bethwell Ogot, 53–81.

Thomson, Madia J. A. *The Demise of Slavery in Southwestern Morocco, 1860–2000: Economic Modernization and the Transformation of Social Hierarchy*. Lewiston: Edwin Mellen Press, 2010.

Toledano, Ehud R. "Ottoman Concepts of Slavery in the Period of Reform, 1830s–1880s." In *Slavery, Bondage, and Emancipation in Modern Africa and Asia*, edited by Klein, 37–63.

———. *The Ottoman Slave Trade and Its Suppression, 1840–1890*. Princeton: Princeton University Press, 1982.

———. "The Imperial Eunuchs of Istanbul: From Africa to the Heart of Islam." *Middle Eastern Studies* 20, no.3 (July 1984): 379–390.

———. *Slavery and Abolition in the Ottoman Middle East*. Seattle: University of Washington Press, 1998.

———. "Enslavement and Abolition in Muslim Societies." Review of *Islam and the Abolition of Slavery*, by William Gervase Clarence-Smith. *Journal of African History* 48 (2007): 481–485.

———. *As If Silent and Absent: Bonds of Enslavement in the Islamic Middle East*. New Haven: Yale University Press, 2007.

———. "Introduction." In *African Communities in Asia and the Mediterranean: Identities between Integration and Conflict*, edited by Toledano, 3–20.

———. "Abolition and Anti-Slavery in the Ottoman Empire: A Case to Answer." In *A Global History of Anti-Slavery Politics in the Nineteenth Century*, edited by Mulligan and Bric, 117–136.

———. "The Fusion of *Zar-Bori* and Sufi *Zikr* as Performance: Enslaved Africans in the Ottoman Empire." In *Medieval and Early Modern Performance in the Eastern Mediterranean*, edited by Öztürkmen, Vitz, 216–240.

———, ed. *African Communities in Asia and the Mediterranean: Identities between Integration and Conflict*. Trenton: Africa World Press, 2012.

Toru, Miura, and John Edward Philips, eds. *Slave Elites in the Middle East and Africa*. London and New York: Kegan Paul International, 2000.

Trimingham, Spencer. *The Sufi Orders in Islam*. Oxford: Clarendon, 1971.

Troutt Powell, Eve M. "Will That Subaltern Ever Speak? Finding African Slaves in the Historiography of the Middle East." In *Middle East Historiographies: Narrating the Twentieth Century*, edited by Gershoni, Singer, and Erdem, 242–261.

Taylor, Bayard. *Central Asia Travels in Cashmere, Little Tibet and Central Asia*. New York: Charles Scribner's Sons, 1889.

United Nations. *Land Reform Defects in Agrarian Structure as Obstacles to Economic Development*. New York: United Nations, Department of Economic Affairs, 1951.

Vambéry, Arminius. *Arminius Vambéry: His Life and Adventures*. London: T. Fisher Unwin, 1889.

Vernet, Thomas. "Slave Trade and Slavery on the Swahili Coast, 1500–1750." In *Slavery, Islam and Diaspora*, edited by Mirzai, Montana, and Lovejoy, 37–76.

Vosoughi, Mohammad Bagher. "The Kings of Hormuz: From the Beginning until the Arrival of the Portuguese." In *The Persian Gulf in History*, edited by Potter, 89–104.

Walker, Timothy. "Slaves or Soldiers? African Conscripts in Portuguese India, 1857–1860." In *Slavery in South Asian History*, edited by Chatterjee and Eaton, 234–261.

Walz, Terence, and Kenneth M. Cuno. "The Study of Slavery in Nineteenth-Century Egypt, Sudan, and the Ottoman Mediterranean." In *Race and Slavery in the Middle East: Histories of Trans-Saharan Africans in Nineteenth-Century Egypt, Sudan, and the Ottoman Mediterranean*, edited by Walz and Cuno, 1–15.

———, eds. *Race and Slavery in the Middle East: Histories of Trans-Saharan Africans in Nineteenth-Century Egypt, Sudan, and the Ottoman Mediterranean*. Cairo: American University in Cairo Press, 2010.

Waring, Edward Scott. *A Tour to Sheeraz by the Route of Kazroon and Feerozabad*. 1807. Repr., New York: Arno Press, 1973.

Warriner, Doreen. *Land Reform and Development in the Middle East: A Study of Egypt, Syria, and Iraq*. 2nd ed. London: Oxford University Press, 1962.

Watson, James L. ed. *Asian and African Systems of Slavery*. Berkeley: University of California Press, 1980.

Wellsted, J. R. *Travels to the City of the Caliphs, along the Shores of the Persian Gulf*. 2 vols. London: Henry Colburn, 1840.

Wilber, Donald N. *Riza Shah Pahlavi: The Resurrection and Reconstruction of Iran*. New York: Exposition Press, 1975.

Williams, Eric. *Capitalism and Slavery*. Chapel Hill: University of North Carolina Press, 1944.

Willis, John Ralph, ed. *Slaves and Slavery in Muslim Africa*. 2 vols. London: Frank Cass, 1985.

Wills, C. J. *In the Land of the Lion and Sun, or Modern Persia*. London: Ward, Lock, & Co., 1891.

———. *Persia as It Is*. London: Sampson Low, Marston, Searle, & Rivington, 1886.

Wilson, Arnold T. "Notes on a Journey from Bandar Abbas to Shiraz via Lar, in February and March, 1907." *Geographical Journal* 31 (February 1908): 152–169.

———. *Persia*. New York: Charles Scribner's Sons, 1933.

———. *The Persian Gulf*. 1928. Repr., London: George Allen & Unwin, 1959.

Wilson, Rodney. *Economic Development in the Middle East*. London: Routledge, 2013.

Wright, Denis. *The English amongst the Persians during the Qajar Period, 1787–1921*. London: Heinemann, 1977.

———. *The English amongst the Persians: Imperial Lives in the Nineteenth Century*. London: I. B. Tauris, 1977.

Zarqání, Mírzá Maḥmúd. *Maḥmúd's Diary: The Diary of Mírzá Maḥmúd-i-Zarqání chronicling Ábdu'l-Bahá's Journey to America*. Trans. Mohi Sobhani. Oxford: George Ronald, 1998.

Zdanowski, Jerzy. *Slavery and Manumission: British Policy in the Red Sea and the Persian Gulf in the First half of the 20th Century*. Reading: Ithaca Press, 2013.

Zilfi, Madeline C. *Women and Slavery in the Late Ottoman Empire: The Design of Difference*. New York: Cambridge University Press, 2010.

UNPUBLISHED DISSERTATION

Brown, Walter. "Pre-colonial History of Bagamoyo: Aspects of the Growth of an East African Coastal Town." PhD diss., Boston University, 1971.

MEDIA

Mirzai, Behnaz A. *Afro-Iranian Lives*. Toronto: AfroIranianfilm, 2007, DVD.

———. *The African-Baluchi Trance Dance*. Toronto: AfroIranianfilm, 2012, DVD.